The Tudor nobility

Edited by G. W. BERNARD

The Tudor
nobility

MANCHESTER UNIVERSITY PRESS

MANCHESTER AND NEW YORK

Distributed exclusively in the USA and Canada by St. Martin's Press

Published by MANCHESTER UNIVERSITY PRESS
Oxford Road, Manchester M13 9PL, UK
and Room 400, 175 Fifth Avenue, New York, NY 10010, USA

Distributed exclusively in the USA and Canada
by ST MARTIN'S PRESS, INC., 175 Fifth Avenue, New York, NY 10010, USA

British Library Cataloguing-in-Publication Data
A catalogue record for this book is available from the British Library

Library of Congress Cataloging-in-Publication Data
The Tudor nobility / edited by G. W. Bernard.
    p.   cm.
    Includes index.
    ISBN 0–7190–3625–9
    1. Great Britain—History—Tudors, 1485–1603—Biography.   2. Great
Britain—Politics and government—1485–1603.   3. Nobility—Great Britain—
History—16th century.   4. Nobility—Great Britain--
Biography.   I. Bernard, G. W.
DA317.T84   1992
942.05'092'2—dc20   91–373369

ISBN 0 7190 3625–9 *hardback*

Typeset by J&L Composition Ltd, Filey, North Yorkshire
Printed in Great Britain by Billing and Sons, Worcester

Contents

Contributors

SIMON ADAMS is Senior Lecturer in History
in the University of Strathclyde

G. W. BERNARD is Senior Lecturer in History
in the University of Southampton

S. J. GUNN is Fellow and Tutor in Modern History
at Merton College, Oxford

R. W. HOYLE is British Academy Postdoctoral Fellow
at Magdalen College, Oxford

STEPHEN E. KERSHAW is in the Cabinet Office;
previously he was a Lecturer
at Wadham College, Oxford

T. B. PUGH was Reader in History
in the University of Southampton

G. WALKER is Lecturer in English
in the University of Leicester

Preface

This collection of essays reflects the common conviction of the contributors that the nobility of Tudor England deserve closer attention than they have generally received from historians. But we are neither a party nor a school, and where we agree most is in our shared determination to question conventional assumptions and to scrutinise critically the often difficult and tantalisingly incomplete sources available for the study of the nobility. Attentive readers may well note differences in emphasis and even disagreements over individual details between us. But we shall think this enterprise well justified if by showing the importance of the nobility in Tudor England, it stimulates others to continue the search.

G. W. BERNARD
December 1991

The Tudor nobility in perspective

Can one write about the Tudor nobility as a whole? At any time between 1485 and 1603, the English nobility – the parliamentary peerage – consisted of a number of men (in the early Tudor period around fifty) of different ages, experience and ability, defying easy generalisation. So a vital approach to the study of the nobility must lie in the painstaking pursuit of individual nobles and families, deriving as much as one can from incomplete and frustratingly dry sources. The essays in this volume on the Percys, earls of Northumberland, Henry Bourchier, second earl of Essex, Thomas Seymour, Lord Seymour of Sudeley, the Dudley faction, and George Talbot, sixth earl of Shrewsbury, offer such studies. The English nobility, as S. J. Gunn (Ch. 3, this volume) points out, was varied. There were regional magnates such as the Talbots, earls of Shrewsbury, the Percys, earls of Northumberland, the Howards, dukes of Norfolk, the Stanleys, earls of Derby. There were new men such as Seymour or Charles Brandon, duke of Suffolk, who rose from obscurity essentially through royal favour or a royal marriage; and rising men like Thomas, first Lord Wharton, whose ascent was an acceleration of their already considerable role as loyal and talented local servants of the crown. There were also much less talented and much less ambitious country peers such as Henry Bourchier, second earl of Essex, who flourished briefly at court in their adolescence but who later resided principally on their estates and consolidated a comfortable position of local dominance.[1] Monographic studies of such various individuals and families can contribute to a sounder understanding of the nobility as a whole.

Another approach to the study of the Tudor nobility is that adopted by Helen Miller in her *Henry VIII and the English Nobility*.[2] One can ask a series of carefully-defined questions about noblemen. Who was created, restored or promoted? Who lost his nobility through treason or attainder?

How often did nobles attend court, and how many became knights of the garter? How often did nobles attend parliaments and sit on the king's council? Which nobles served in war and against rebellion? What crown offices did nobles get? What crown lands/ex-monastic lands did nobles receive as gifts or in part exchange? Such an approach risks turning into antiquarian league tables of meetings attended, grants received, and so on, and it makes the distinction between parliamentary peer and non-noble into a very rigid boundary, but within its limits it is obviously informative.

Should one stop there, with studies in detail of individual families and of specific activities? Should one raise questions about the nobility as a group? 'Class' explanations in history are becoming distinctly unfashionable, surviving largely in the history of art (in exhibition catalogues) and of music. Interpretations based on the 'rise' or the 'fall' of classes seem very tired and have little force as explanations. Detailed studies undermine them. If the English nobility was not a monolithic block, it makes it hard to argue (for example) for a tradition of baronial protest. A recent attempt to invoke a 'common baronial culture' in early Stuart England fails to explain away the fact that noblemen took opposite sides in the English civil war of the 1640s, let alone the different fractions within each side. It therefore makes little sense to treat their political quarrels as the product of any 'baronial' or 'chivalric' rhetoric or imagery.[3] But since broad ideas, whether explicitly recognised or not, can influence the interpretation of details, and since without them studies of noble families can disintegrate into myriad particularities, it remains important to generalise. This introduction will raise some larger questions and, in attempting to suggest answers, will not hesitate to search for clues in countries other than England and in periods other than the sixteenth century. It will not seek to recapitulate old controversies, but will concentrate on significant recent discussions.

The most tenaciously-held general view of the nobility in the early modern period deserves closer scrutiny. Its most eloquent elaboration in recent years has been in the essays of Mervyn James.[4] James puts forward a grand theme of a fundamental shift in culture from honour, lineage and locality to obedience, civil society and the nation – that is, from values associated with noble power in a decentralised society to those associated with royal power in a centralised state. In this scheme the sixteenth century is a period of transition.[5] James's work cannot easily be summarised: it is richly suggestive and allusive, full of details directly linked to broad ideas. His sources are the familiar political sources – state papers, ambassadors' letters and some family archives, particularly those of the Percys, earls of Northumberland – together with a striking use of literature – poems, plays, histories, philosophical works, educational treatises, theological and liturgical works – and architecture, art and ceremonies, not least funerals. All are used for the light they shed on social and political attitudes, and related to what men said and did in particular political circumstances. He explores the use of language as closely as he does literary, philosophical and religious influences. He combines this interest in concepts and attitudes with a Namierite approach to participants in rebellions, uncovering family and personal connections of a highly specific kind. But he does not always pursue such laudable methods with sufficient rigour. His sources are neither comprehensively presented nor meticulously questioned: they are often deployed for rhetorical effect, with little indication of how typical or of how reliable they are. Moreover, James rarely pays attention to the arguments, especially contrary arguments, offered by other historians, rarely explaining why he finds different views unpersuasive.

Is James right to claim there was so vast a cultural shift? Does he tend, for example, to misread writers on honour and on attitudes to nobility? The sixteenth-century emphasis on virtue as a source of true nobility was not novel (as James half-admits, but without grasping the implications for his broader claims): virtue was not newly given preference over lineage. In the thought of sixteenth-century writers such as Sir Thomas Elyot, lineage and magnificence remained important. If Elyot castigated nobles for not behaving as virtuously as they ought, that tended to imply that noblemen ought to behave better than other men, and that they were somehow intrinsically or potentially superior to other men. Once the idea of a hierarchy was in this way retained as inherently good (as James concedes), that crucially qualified writers' emphasis on virtue. Moreover, writers did not replace military skills by classical learning as the source of true nobility: their emphasis on classical learning was rather a matter of fashion in which noblemen were following the lead of scholars by the early seventeenth century. The Reformation introduced ideological divisions, but in assessing the nobility, the transformation from crusading Christian knight to godly magistrate does not (if one is considering the power of the nobility) seem fundamental. Continuities seem more significant than novelties.[6]

In detail there are difficulties in James's own arguments. Honour is supposedly declining, yet duelling was increasing in the late sixteenth century, and honour and violence are strongly present in Elizabethan literature, notably in Sir Philip Sidney's *Arcadia*. James presents the heightened role of heralds as the crown nationalising – that is, monopolising and controlling – the system of honour: yet he then notes the pressures from below, from would-be gentry seeking authentication of their newly-claimed social status.[7] Nor does the behaviour of noble traitors on the scaffold shift from one of honour-defiance to one of obedient acceptance of God's providence: for example, Thomas Seymour in 1549 did not accept his end, nor, on James's evidence, did the seventh earl of Northumberland, executed in 1572.[8]

Above all, James exaggerates the power, social and local, of the nobility in the early sixteenth century and especially in periods before the sixteenth century, and minimises it in the later sixteenth century and beyond. In arguing that there was a fundamental shift in the role of the nobility in this period, James does not stand alone. Indeed, that has been a common theme since the mid seventeenth century. Algernon Sidney, a younger son of Robert, second earl of Leicester and Dorothy, sister of the tenth earl of Northumberland, and a great-nephew of the poet Sidney, was one of the earliest to do so, in works of historical and political reflection that he wrote while in exile from the England of Charles II. Sidney's notions demand attention here since they have recently been taken up by modern historians as a valid picture. In the past, great baronial families, gallant and heroic, powerful and warlike, had, he claimed, kept would-be tyrannical kings in check, only to destroy themselves in the Wars of the Roses and then to be tamed and seduced by the luxurious and lascivious courts of the Tudor and Stuart monarchs. No doubt Sidney saw himself as a revival of those vigorous medieval noblemen who had curbed royal power. No doubt Sidney's view of the past offered him an explanation, a consolation and a remedy for his personal discontents. But as history, it should not be taken at face value. Sidney's own political eclipse should not be mistaken for the decline of a social class. As with James's argument, much of Sidney's case rests heavily on a somewhat romantic exaggeration of the power of the medieval nobility, especially that of the Percys, earls of Northumberland.[9]

Yet James never demonstrates the existence of the golden age of the unqualified submission of tenants to their lords, of the north knowing no prince but a Percy; he relies too much on Elizabethan myth-makers such as George Clarkson;[10] he makes very few detailed references at all to the fourteenth and fifteenth centuries: and he has not answered the powerful arguments of M. Weiss and M. A. Hicks questioning the power of the Percys, earls of Northumberland in the mid and late fifteenth century, arguments which are here developed for the sixth earl of Northumberland by R. W. Hoyle (Ch. 4, this volume).[11] Despite some qualifications, James presents the fifth earl of Northumberland as 'the type of the "over-mighty" subject',[12] yet his own argument is that the fifth earl succeeded in his main aim, securing for his family the post of warden of the east marches, only after his death in 1527, when his son the sixth earl was appointed. James sees the fifth earl as forcing that decision on Henry VIII and Wolsey by showing that only the Percys could control the borderer Sir William Lisle. But there is no evidence that the Percys encouraged Lisle's violence. Lisle's quarrel with the Heron family, its occasion, was sincere and typical, not staged; Lisle was in increasing difficulties before he submitted; the crown's hand was not forced (Henry and Wolsey waited till the fifth earl died before appointing his son); and the sixth earl was unable to prevent Lisle's execution.[13] As Hoyle shows in his chapter in this volume, James misreads the sixth's earl's bequest of his patrimony to the king: far from disinheriting his brothers as a contingency in case rebellion was unsuccessful and thus showing his concern for his family and lineage, he did it rather to thwart them (and, possibly, his estranged wife Mary Talbot).[14]

James's model, moreover, sees changes in tenurial arrangement as affecting lord–servant relationships, leading to a shift from feudalities to friendships. Yet that obscures the point that at all times the relationship between a lord and his servants, tenants and friends depended on personalities and circumstances, irrespective of the precise type of tenure, which might indeed sometimes be irrelevant, for example when the men a lord hoped to raise were his neighbours rather than his tenants. Studies by R. W. Hoyle have emphasised the need for caution in discovering untypically harsh estate policies, and suggest that there are no easy generalisations to be made about tenure and the quality of service.[15]

James's underlying claim is that nobles (and their followers) naturally came together to resist kings, ministers and their policies: he then proves his claim for a fundamental shift by showing that the sixteenth century is not like this. He writes of 'the traditional objective of the dissident aristocracy, to assist the claims of the respublica, the realm or common weal, against an unworthy king and his councillors', but sees the sixteenth century as characterised by a loss of nerve on the part of noblemen, by the decline of the system of honour and by the growth of a counter system of obedience.[16] Such an antithesis only works, however, by taking the most heated moments of political conflict in the thirteenth and fourteenth centuries as typical. James is then embarrassed by the attitudes of northern noblemen during the Pilgrimage of Grace. He criticises them for holding aloof and behaving uncertainly. In so doing he is somewhat forcing the evidence for the earls of Northumberland, Westmorland and Lord Dacre.[17] He rightly notes the loyalty to Henry VIII of the earls of Shrewsbury and Cumberland.[18] But it is worrying for his argument that it is such nobles of ancient lineage who display so vigorously the supposedly newer attitude of obedience to the crown; and it is troubling for any argument for a shift in attitudes from honour/rebellion to obedience/ loyalty that (on James's own evidence) one finds such various attitudes at that moment among the northern nobility. James then sees Robert Devereux, second earl of Essex's revolt as the last honour revolt, but, as a consequence of that interpretation, has trouble with aristocratic opposition in the 1620s and in 1640–2: he has to claim, for example, that in the style and content of his attacks on the royalists, the parliamentarian peer, Robert Greville, second Lord Brooke, struck 'an archaic tone full of romancing bombast'.[19]

Arguments for a shift in power from the nobility to the crown tend to be elusive. When did that power supposedly decline? Some speak of the decline in the overall power of great magnates by 1485. Some think that the territorial influence and military power of the aristocracy declined under Henry VII. Others think it was not until the later sixteenth century that the local power of the nobility dwindled. Such a lack of consensus among historians might suggest that a more nuanced approach, in which the power of the nobility is seen as fluctuating, may offer a more plausible interpretation. It is very tempting to read apparent changes over a short period, for example, a single reign, as evidence for larger and more long-term trends, but that can easily prove very misleading.

Another long-held belief about the nobility in sixteenth-century England was that it suffered financial decline. Elaborated in grand theories of the 'crisis of the aristocracy' (according to which noblemen's incomes fell as the expenditure rose) or the 'rise of the gentry' (according to which the gentry acquired wealth and status at the expense of the nobility), such arguments read somewhat flatly now. A recent contribution, a study of the finances of the Radcliffes, earls of Sussex in the later sixteenth century, concludes that some noblemen, at least, were successful in meeting the challenge of inflation by raising their landed rents, and questions the notion of crisis, as did an earlier survey of the Stanleys, earls of Derby.[20] It is no longer possible to argue that the dissolution of the monasteries and subsequent redistribution of church lands adversely affected the nobility. Noblemen, like virtually all landowners, benefited from the opportunity to increase their estates, especially consolidating their existing spheres of influence. The brute facts of demography had long meant a constantly shuffling pattern of landholding: it did not need the dissolution of the monasteries to create an active land market. 'Few historians nowadays', it has been aptly remarked, 'would quarrel with an explanation of "the rise of the gentry" which stresses that it was mostly a phenomenon whereby men who already held land were further enriched by the monastic spoils and high agricultural profits.' As rents and the volume of agricultural production rose in the later sixteenth and early seventeenth centuries, it may well be that land that earlier could have supported one gentleman could now support more, and it is clear that there were more gentlemen by 1640 than there had been by 1540 – but not at the expense of the nobility.[21] And if one looks at the fortunes of the nobility over a much longer span, it becomes difficult to see the late sixteenth century as exceptional or as a turning point: 'the "crisis of the aristocracy", if it existed at all, now appears as little more than a hiccup in the long term fortunes of the greatest landowners.' What strikes the historian of social structure in early sixteenth century England is that 'individually most of the nobility were men of great wealth', while historians studying the nobility in the later seventeenth and eighteenth centuries emphasise great families' remarkable powers not only of survival, but even of recuperation, and stress their great wealth, to which countless grand country houses still bear vivid testimony. It is hard not to see the aristocratic world portrayed in *An Open Elite* as a refutation of the argument of *The Crisis of the Aristocracy*.[22]

It is perhaps worth considering recent discussions of the fortunes of nobilities or other countries. Whether the French nobility went through a period of financial crisis in the later sixteenth century has been much debated. Noblemen certainly complained about their ruined condition. But studies of particular regions have cast doubt on such grievances, and show rather that on the whole noble revenues rose. Seigneurial rents may not have risen very fast, but often they were paid in kind, and in any case they were only part of a nobleman's income. Sales of land reflected accidental factors such as bad luck, incompetence or the absence of a direct heir, rather than any general structural factors: when lands were sold off, the purchasers were often other noblemen. The wars of religion did not ruin the nobility as a class: some were indeed impoverished, but others prospered. If the greatest families shouldered the greatest burdens and incurred the greatest debts, so too did they show remarkable powers of recuperation. An interesting test case is that of the family of Nevers, especially Louis de Gonzague, duc de Nevers, who was apparently profligate, entertained expensively, gambled, provided large dowries for his daughters, lent to the crown and served in the wars of religion. Yet if the debts of the Nevers family were two-and-a-half times their annual income, that seems well within the bounds of tolerance. And if in 1593 a third of their income was swallowed in servicing their debts, that does not seem obviously crippling for what was after all a period of renewed civil war.

Moreover, family income from all sources was nearly four times higher in 1612 than in 1551, significant even allowing for inflation. A study of Constable Anne de Montmorency, faithful servant of Henry II, demonstrates how much 'stealth and steady application, complemented by the work of loyal and efficient stewards' could achieve in consolidating a noble patrimony. The 'financial crisis' remains unproven.[23]

Keith Brown has argued that the Scottish nobility experienced a 'financial crisis' in the decades around 1600. But it is not easy to grasp just when these difficulties were most acute. On his account, by the 1570s half the Scots peerage were visibly suffering; in the early seventeenth century their problems were alleviated by better harvests, increased rents and crown patronage, but by the late 1620s and 1630s reductions in crown patronage, bad harvests, and high and regular taxation had once more weakened their economic position. That created the background for noble revolt in 1637. But Brown's evidence is insufficiently strong to bear the weight of such an interpretation. He cites reports by Englishmen in 1577 and 1583, but these offer a much more mixed view than Brown suggests: some Scottish nobles were very rich, others not. Brown's claim for noble indebtedness rests on figures from testaments, but these do not clearly bring out any continuing problem. The trends they show do suggest a worsening between 1590 and 1609, but they do not suggest the severe difficulties that Brown claims for the 1630s. Brown cites a number of instances of indebted noblemen, but without showing that their difficulties were overpowering or typical. Some noblemen were lending as well as borrowing. Evidence of rents is meagre, but Brown cites one family whose rents rose dramatically in this period. The 'financial crisis of the Scottish aristocracy' is not yet solidly established.[24] And thus neither French nor Scottish experiences can be invoked as part of a European trend and then used to reinforce claims about England.

Nor does that European phenomenon termed the 'military revolution' greatly assist the case for a transformation of the nature of the English nobility. Were there such sweeping changes in the art of war that the role of the nobility was diminished? In the very long run this was undoubtedly true, but it must be emphasised that it was a very long run indeed, and it is questionable whether changes in military technology significantly affected the role of the English nobility in the sixteenth century. At first glance the invention and development of gunpower in the later middle ages should have eroded the role of knights on horseback. Heavy cavalry should have been reduced to ineffectiveness by firepower. Armies stronger in artillery and in well-trained infantry should in theory have made short work of heavy cavalry. Scientifically-designed fortifications should have changed the nature of war. But in practice these developments were delayed. The development of armour in the later fourteenth and fifteenth centuries – from mail to plate, offering better protection – redressed the balance somewhat. Without heavy cavalry, fifteenth-century armies were unable to achieve a decisive victory by pursuing an enemy defeated in the field. It was never easy to move artillery, and crippling logistical problems often made it less effective than it should have been. The period 1450–1530 saw an exceptional number of pitched battles, most notably Marignano (1515) and Pavia (1525), in which cavalry played a vital part. After the 1520s the development of new pistol tactics and more effective handguns radically altered the nature of mounted combat as the weight of armour required for adequate protection rendered the knight less effective. But the consequences of this were not immediate, since much of the fighting of the mid and later sixteenth century consisted of siege and counter-siege. Moreover, cavalrymen developed new styles of combat – fighting in groups, fighting at greater speed, riding lighter horses – new styles which were fostered by changes in the practice of tournaments, such as running at the ring, quintain and head, each designed to offer appropriate training.[25]

The English experience fits uneasily, if at all, into the broad pattern of a military revolution. With the exception of the Scottish marches, England and Wales saw little large-scale fighting in the sixteenth century, since there were no civil wars, no protracted disputed successions and no successful invasions. That early-seventeenth-century inventories list out-dated weapons and armour is evidence, not of the military decline of the nobility, but rather of that long period of domestic peace. In such circumstances changes in military technology thus made no more than a brief impact: only Henry VIII's coastal forts (and then in an idiosyncratic way) and the Marian fortifications at Berwick are clear examples. And when violent conflict did again occur in the civil wars of the 1640s, its nature was more like that of the middle ages. The fighting has been characterised as 'a bitter and dirty war ... between the various opposing garrisons, with each local commander striving to destroy his enemy's resources' by raids and skirmishes while preserving his own. Such a war left plenty of scope for local landowners to play a significant role.[26]

Much depended on the way in which soldiers were raised. In England, armies continued to be raised and led by noblemen and leading gentry. In the first half of the sixteenth century, nobles raised their servants, tenants and friends under contract from the crown; in the second half they raised the county militia as lords lieutenants. It is often claimed that this was a striking change. 'Military power instead of being distributed round a number of barons and knights was concentrated (and diffused) in the hands of the militia.'[27] But the difference was more apparent than real. Noblemen were still ultimately responsible for raising and leading military forces. Lord lieutenants were indeed appointed by the crown, but monarchs did not have a great deal of choice in any individual county. Indeed, it makes more sense to see the development of the lord lieutenancy as a formalisation of the existing regional powers and responsibilities of the nobility. A standing army with professional officers would have been a very different matter, but such an arrangement did not exist in Tudor England.

Nor was the nobility weakened, as is sometimes claimed, because it was losing control over lesser men. The rising of the northern earls of 1569 is often cited as an example of the inability of the nobility to raise their tenants. A full study has shown, however, that the seventh earl of Northumberland raised few men for the very simple reason that he made little effort to do so.[28] But even if it were true that the northern nobility failed to raise their forces, that would be less novel than it has sometimes seemed. When Edward IV landed in Yorkshire in 1471, the fourth earl of Northumberland failed to rally the county. Percy served the king truly but (according to the official history of Edward IV's restoration), 'many gentlemen, and other, whiche would have be araysed by him, woulde not so fully and extremly have determyned them selfe in the kyng's right and qwarell as th'erle wolde have done hymselfe'. Northumberland was able to restrain opposition to Edward IV in Yorkshire but was unable to overcome unwillingness and offer more positive support. Later that year Richard Nevill, earl of Warwick, vainly appealed desperately to Henry Vernon of Haddon to support him: 'Henry I pray you ffayle not now as ever I may do ffor yow', he wrote in his own hand. In that emergency, which decided the fate of the Houses of Lancaster and York, Vernon was also asked for help by Edward IV and George duke of Clarence: he did not stir for them either. When in 1450 Henry VI wanted to send certain lords against the rebellious Kentishmen, 'thair men that sholde haue gon with thayme ansuerde to thair lordis and saide, that thay wolde not fite ayens thaym that labourid forto amende and refourme the comune profit; and whanne the lordis herde this, they lefte thair purpoz.' In 1403 Henry Percy (Hotspur) overestimated his territorial influence and the power of his family's military resources: in 1405 the earl of Northumberland failed to carry all his Yorkshire retainers with him.[29] Such instances warn against the danger of exaggerating the extent of the medieval dominance of nobles over lesser men and going on to prove a Tudor decline by contrasting medieval exaggeration with Tudor realities.

Moreover, in judging noble power, it is important to grasp that a county was not necessarily dominated by a single magnate. Influence in Essex, for example, as S. J. Gunn shows, was shared between the earl of Essex, the earl of Oxford and the Radcliffes, Lords Fitzwalter, later earls of Sussex.[30] Magnates were never all-powerful. Even John of Gaunt, one of the greatest of English magnates, was unable on several occasions to impose his will on his own affinity or to protect the interests of his own retainers against those of independent local gentry.[31] Such lesser men could appeal to the central law courts, to parliament, to a leading minister or the king himself. It is of course essential to strike a proper balance. Some recent writers run the risk of exaggerating the limits to noble power. It would be wrong to go as far as to claim that 'where effective political power is concerned noble lords had become by the mid fifteenth century no more than socially prestigious puppets, whose strings were worked by knights, esquires and gentlemen'.[32] Noblemen remained important, influential and powerful: a nobleman 'inherited rank and great possessions to do with what he could. They gave him vast opportunities had he the wits to use them.'[33] His powers of leadership mattered: a weak man would not realise that potential, while a confident and skilful adult nobleman could exercise considerable, but not exclusive, influence.

Were kings trying to destroy or to curb the nobility? Did kings have 'absolutist' intentions? Much writing still assumes that they were and did. There is some early modern warrant for such beliefs. Algernon Sidney characterised Henry VII's rule in such terms.

> His own meanness inclined him to hate the nobility; and thinking it to be as easy for them to take the crown from him, as to give it to him, he industriously applied himself to glean up the remainders of the house of York, from whence a competitor might arise, and by all means to crush those who were most able to oppose him. This exceedingly weakened the nobility, who held the balance between him and the commons, and was a great step towards the dissolution of our antient government.[34]

Royal propaganda might sometimes use such terms, for example in the reign of Louis XIV. Modern historians remain influenced (if somewhat confused) by such notions.

> It was for Henry VII and his successors at best to subdue, at worst to preside over, aristocratic faction, while positively deploying the existing private

resources of the peerage, along channels commensurate with wider royal interests. In other words 'overmighty subjects' . . . were essential to the running of the country. Both Henry VIII and Cardinal Wolsey appreciated this conventional wisdom: between them they tamed the aristocracy in order to ride upon its back.[35]

It might be sensible to distinguish between royal policy towards the nobility in general, on the one hand, and towards princes of the blood royal, *les grands*, on the other. The latter could appear or present themselves as aspirants to the crown. They would by definition by untypical. How much of a threat they were would obviously depend on circumstances. At many times – such as the sixteenth century – there would simply be no adult princes of the blood. In other reigns kings could work happily together with such relatives. Edward IV's use of his brother, Richard, duke of Gloucester, in the North from the early 1470s, as a manifestation of royal authority, not as an independent and over-mighty subject, is telling here.[36] But on other occasions such men could hold destabilising ambitions, for example if, like John of Gaunt, they sought to marry into foreign ruling dynasties and then to press acquired territorial claims, behaving more like a duke of Brittany than a conventional English magnate, asserting a European, not just an English, role.[37] So prudent governments trod warily here. Richelieu claimed he had set out the '*rebaisser l'orgeuil des grands*'. But the nuance should be noted. It was their pride and their ambition that Richelieu sought to hold in check, not their power as such, and it might be added in passing, it was the pride of the *grands*, not that of the nobility as a whole, that Richelieu wished to constrain.[38] But it would be wrong to see princes of the blood royal as an inevitable or constant threat, or rulers as devoting their energies to the destruction of potential dynastic rivals. The Condés co-operated with Louis XIII and Richelieu. The king's kinsman, Henri de Bourbon, third prince de Condé (d. 1646), was allowed to buy much ex-Montmorency land, and Louis XIII offered him Montmorency's house at Chantilly, greatly increasing his landed interests near Paris, in circumstances which would have allowed the crown to deny Condé his right altogether. Condé was *gouverneur* of Berry and the Bourbonnais before 1626 and was appointed *governeur* of Burgundy in 1631. During the war years of the mid-1630s he held many military offices. His son and heir, Louis, duc of Enghein, afterwards the fourth prince and famous as 'le grand Condé', married Richelieu's niece in 1641, the culmination of plans dating back to 1632. Condé undoubtedly had a sense of his high rank and royal ancestry – after he made a solemn entry into Dijon in September 1632 he prayed at the tombs of the Valois, dukes of Burgundy, extinct in 1477 – but clearly his life was devoted to royal service.[39]

For England, M. L. Bush has perceptively noted how what at first sight seems like a policy against the royal race in Henry VIII's reign was in fact nothing of the kind.[40] It is worth looking at one apparent example in greater detail. It has sometimes been suggested that Henry VIII destroyed members of the Pole and Courtenay families in the late 1530s in this sort of spirit. But that does not withstand scrutiny. If Henry had wished to liquidate them, it is hard to see why he should have waited until 1538. Such a view, moreover, ignores the considerable favour and friendship that Henry showed to Henry Courtenay, the king's first cousin, one of his closest companions in the 1520s, and promoted by him from the rank of earl of Devon to that of marquess of Exeter in 1525. What had changed by the late 1530s was the stark fact of the break with Rome. Reginald Pole had gone into exile and from 1536 took an increasingly violent stand against Henry. In 1536 he completed his diatribe *De Unitate* which denounced Henry as a tyrant.[41] In 1537 he was sent as papal legate to France and to the Low Countries in the hope of persuading Francis I and Charles V to take joint action against the schismatic king of England. Not surprisingly Henry was angry and, at times, frightened. He tried to have Pole assassinated. Pole's family in England, headed by his mother, the last surviving Plantagenet, Margaret, countess of Salisbury (Clarence's daughter), did very little to the king's displeasure. The marquess of Exeter raised troops loyally against the Pilgrims of Grace in 1536. But in the summer of 1538 the government discovered from the testimony of his servant Hugh Holland that Sir Geoffrey Pole had had some contacts with his brother Reginald, warning him of the danger of assassination, and offering sympathy. Interrogated ruthlessly, Geoffrey in effect turned king's evidence, and revealed criticisms that his elder brother, Lord Montagu, and the marquess of Exeter had made of government policy. Montagu had expressed sympathy for the Pilgrims of Grace and denounced both the treason laws and the new bishops that he saw as heretics. Exeter complained of the knaves ruling about the king and hoped to give them a buffet one day. None of that amounted to a conspiracy, much less rebellion, but in the emergency of late 1538 it is not surprising that Henry took it very seriously and set in motion a series of trials and legal procedures that led to executions and imprisonments. But this episode emphatically does not show that Henry wished to destroy the nobility.[42]

Although not of the blood royal, the Percys, earls of Northumberland are often regarded as overmighty subjects whom the Tudors pursued. It has already been suggested that the Percys were not that overmighty: now it is necessary to ask whether the crown sought to reduce their power. If, of course, they were by no means as powerful as has sometimes been supposed, then there would have been correspondingly less need to reduce their power. Peter Gwyn has suggested that there was something of an atmosphere between the Tudors and the fifth earl of Northumberland: neither Henry VII nor Henry VIII were willing to entrust him with the wardenship of the east and middle marches. But that is a far cry from wishing to destroy the earl, let alone destroy the nobility. Their judgement was simply that the fifth earl was not the man most suited for that office. But he was not ostracised; he was entrusted with some lesser tasks, and his local power was not undermined.[43] Henry VIII had no hesitation in trusting the sixth earl – appointed warden in 1527, active in the defence of the borders in 1532–3, a knight of the garter in 1532, and *de facto* president of the northern council in 1532 – as R. W. Hoyle's chapter in this volume shows. Nor did the crown exploit the earl's financial difficulties. Its intention was rather to protect the earl from his creditors (see the restriction on sales of land in 1532 and 1535). No courtiers profited from the earl's problems: the beneficiaries of his profligacy were his own chosen favourites such as Sir Thomas Arundel and Sir Reynold Carnaby. In 1536 the earl named the king his heir, in the following year (the year of his death) he exchanged his lands for a royal pension, but this was not the culmination of any destructive royal policy. It is highly likely that Henry VIII would have granted the family lands to the earl's half-brother, Sir Thomas, on the earl's death, had Sir Thomas not meanwhile been executed for treason for his alleged part in the Pilgrimage of Grace.[44]

What Simon Adams (Ch. 6, this volume) shows is that rulers were cautious in their attitudes towards families which had been involved in treason. Elizabeth was slow in restoring the Dudleys. It was not till December 1561 that Ambrose was, on successive days, created Lord Lisle and then earl of Warwick, and it was not till September 1564 that Robert was created earl of Leicester. Robert did not receive grants of land till 1561 and 1563. By 1567 it was clear that the family was re-established. What had mattered was Robert's abilities and Elizabeth's likings: the crown clearly wished to make use of noble affinities, connections and talents.[45]

That the government could and would intervene to restrain the oppressive behaviour of individual noblemen is shown by Stephen Kershaw (Ch. 7, this volume). George Talbot, sixth earl of Shrewsbury, provoked his Glossopdale tenants into appealing to the council against their lord's threatened exactions, and the council supported the tenants, not the earl. Kershaw's chapter shows that the royal council was prepared to intervene in relations between a noble and his tenants; that tenants dared to appeal over the head of their lord to the council; that the council was concerned with order, social harmony, and conventions of landholding, and it was prepared to bend noblemen to its will. But that was in no way an attempt to undermine the nobility, or to impoverish or humiliate a nobleman. Nor should this episode be seen in terms of a conflict between crown and nobility, since Shrewsbury's aggression was unusual. Shrewsbury had brought his troubles upon himself, in part as a result of 'the awkward relations which Earl George seemed unable to avoid provoking in his business dealings'. The council made it as easy as possible for Shrewsbury to retreat. Interestingly, Earl George did succeed in defeating the privilege granted to the projector William Humfrey for a water-powered lead furnace, and did so by exploiting his friendship with Lord Burghley, thus showing that there was no constant ill-feeling towards him on the part of the government.[46] But the Tudor governments did believe in a sort of moral economy of landlordship. The state was prepared to interfere in enclosures against the economic interests of landlords, as Wolsey's inquiry in 1517 vividly shows. More generally, a recent study suggests, 'the temporing of strict law with ... humanity appears to have been typical of early modern judicial practice'. Lord Buckhurst warned Gilbert, seventh earl of Shrewsbury in 1592, that 'whan in the contry you dwell in you will nedes enter into a war with your inferiors there, we think it both justis, equity and wisedome to take care that the weaker part be not put downe by the mightier'.[47]

But such intervention should not be taken as evidence for the notion that the crown was recovering ground that had been lost in the later middle ages. Henry VIII (or his ministers Wolsey or Cromwell), Henry VII, and Edward IV have each been seen as instigators of such reassertion of monarchical authority. Obviously crown power will look greater after the ending of any minority or period of civil war. But such a view must be treated cautiously. It makes debatable assumptions that the power of a supposedly unruly nobility had increased in the fifteenth century. The Tudors neither held nor articulated any new theory of kingship. They did not seek to become 'absolute' rulers, whatever meaning is given to that term, although they undoubtedly did strive, like all capable rulers, to increase their power, or, more simply, to get their own way. Claims that kings had a carefully-defined centralising plan, at the expense of the nobility, need to rest on more precise evidence than mere assumption. The reigns of Edward I, Edward III and Henry V, moreover, show clearly that whatever the condition of England in the later middle ages, and however powerful the nobility may have been, given determination, competence, resources, charm and luck, strong kingship was entirely possible.

It may be instructive to look back at earlier rulers who have been accused of absolutist aspirations and anti-noble intentions. Henry III has been seen as challenging the position of the magnates both in theory and in practice. According to M. T. Clanchy, he developed an absolutist theory with threatening implications for the local power of the nobility, and after 1232 ruled with officials and foreign officials at court, excluding the nobility as a class from the council.[48] Such arguments have been devastatingly attacked by David Carpenter, who has denied that Henry III held a theory of royal absolutism. Henry did not think that he was above the law, nor did his judges and lawyers; nor was he accused of seizing lands and goods. When, occasionally, he did contravene the laws, he did not do so inspired by theory. He did not attack the liberties of noblemen in general. He was tolerant about noble debts to the crown. He did not exclude the English nobility from court. What happened in 1258 was that one group of courtiers, composed of English magnates, but also including Simon de Montfort and the queen's Savoyard kinsmen, turned on another group headed by the king's half-brothers, the Lusignans. It was a dispute within the royal court. Henry was insufficiently politically skilled to maintain, at least within the circumstances of 1258, a harmonious circle at court: he failed to secure the acceptance of his Lusignan half-brothers, who had come to England after 1247. In years of financial difficulty, his efforts to build up a large group of royal clients proved imprudent. But his underlying purpose was to maintain peace and tranquillity in England, and his dearest interests were his pilgrimages, alms-giving and building works.[49]

Did Richard II seek to become an absolute ruler dispensing with the nobility? Here one must distinguish carefully. Richard clearly disliked (and feared) certain noblemen, the former Lords Appellant, and eventually destroyed them and seized their inheritances. In 1397 he had his uncle, Thomas of Woodstock, duke of Gloucester, murdered; Richard, earl of Arundel, executed; and Thomas Beauchamp, earl of Warwick, imprisoned, dispossessed and banished. After John of Gaunt's death early in 1399, he excluded Henry Bolingbroke from his inheritance, the greatest in the realm – a flagrantly unjust act. He was personally vindictive, recklessly seeking revenge for the pressures that had been put upon him in 1388. He was secretive and broke his word. He was volatile. He clearly did not regard property rights as unchallengeable. He was clearly innovating. In 1398 he bullied the Commons in parliament into granting him the wool subsidy for life. A recent judgement, that 'it seems unlikely that these injustices, which formed the normal small change of English medieval kingship, were unduly resented, or were so unpopular as seriously to undermine Richard's government', is too kind. But what characterises Richard's rule is the lengths to which we went to pursue personal enemies, and his determination to win and to increase his freedom of action. In the political circumstances in which he grew up, that is hardly surprising, and it does not amount to a clearly-thought-out plan of absolutism. His conception of royal power did not differ markedly from that of Edward I or Henry V. His actions were born of weakness, or of a sense of insecurity, as his efforts to build up a personal bodyguard, and a contingent of archers based in Cheshire, show. Yet it would be wrong to regard him as anti-baronial. His regime depended on the support of a strong court party among the higher nobility. He created five new dukes and promoted other noblemen: however irritating that may have been to those noblemen not favoured, it shows that his policy was not directed against the noble order as such. What he wanted was a loyal nobility, composed of loyal servants such as the Hollands, dukes of Exeter.[50]

In Ch. 1 of this volume, T. B. Pugh denies the claim that Henry VII deliberately threatened and oppressed the English nobility as a class by unjust exactions, particularly by a terrifying system of bonds and recognizances (i.e. suspended penalties). Bonds and recognizances were not in themselves new, and had indeed been harshly used on at least one occasion under Edward IV. There were few cases of bonds between 1485 and 1502. The purpose of the increased number of bonds and recognizances between 1502 and 1509 was often fiscal (to augment royal revenues and so to pay off the rulers of the Low Countries for not supporting the Yorkist pretender Edmund de la Pole) and dynastic, especially over wardship and marriage. Many nobles willingly did business involving bonds and recognizances over wardships and marriages, notably with the king's minister Edmund Dudley. Between 1502 and 1509 only twenty-seven out of forty adult nobles were involved in any form of bonds and recognizances, and only sixteen out of forty were involved as principals rather than as sureties. Dudley's petition, drawn up after the king's death and listing those whom he judged had been harshly treated by the king, names only a handful of noblemen. Henry VIII's subsequent remissions are not necessarily evidence of the injustice of his father. Henry VII's ministers may well have worsened terms and conditions, but most bonds and recognizances were taken for lawful purposes, quite justly: Yorkist sympathies, excessive retaining, or insanity. The supposed *causes célèbres* were not typical, but the product of exceptional circumstances: Henry VII's actions were not unjustified. The treatment of Thomas, second marquess of Dorset was not harsh but an understandable precaution; the treatment of the Suffolk heir Edmund de la Pole was unjust – but his later brother's behaviour made it inevitable; the punishment of George Nevill, Lord Abergavenny was disproportionate, but he had been retaining and his Yorkist sympathies during the rebellion 1497 were damagingly revealed in 1506; and Richard Grey, third earl of Kent, brought his own troubles on himself by his profligacy. Mr Pugh does, however, accept that some magnates were treated with excessive severity, were grievously wronged, or were brought to a state of dependence on Henry's goodwill by the use of bonds and recognizances, notably the fifth earl of Northumberland and the Stanleys; while Henry VII acted harshly and arbitrarily over lands or titles in his dealings with the Berkeleys, Edward Courtenay, earl of Devon, Edward Stafford, third duke of Buckingham and the queen's younger sisters.

Mr Pugh's chapter raises the question whether it was necessary for the crown to curb the nobility. He stresses the strength of the crown *vis-à-vis* the nobility; notes the paucity of new creations; and argues that by 1509 the peerage, depleted in numbers, was incapable of resisting or opposing the royal will, and that there was no risk of an aristocratic league against the crown. None of the ten major families of the higher nobility was strong enough to launch a rebellion against Tudor rule. Even the most eminent had come to recognise that masterful exercise of royal authority required them to accept a reduced role. As Mr Pugh recognises, however, the crown did remain considerably dependent on the co-operation and support of the nobility, qualifying such trends. At Bosworth both Richard III and Henry Tudor prospered or fell according to the loyalty or treachery of the nobility: it was the lack of enthusiastic noble support (especially from the fourth earl of Northumberland and the Stanleys) that cost Richard his crown. Henry VII needed to conciliate the nobility after Bosworth, much as Henry VIII found it politic to buy noble support after his accession by sacrificing Empson and Dudley.[51]

Did the Tudors try to control retaining? Should we agree with Professor J. M. W. Bean that 'it was only in the reign of Henry VII that the crown dealt effectively with the need to maintain a balance between the maintenance of the military resources of the kingdom and the dangers inherent in uncontrolled retaining'?[52] Once again, such a view depends on assumptions about the degree of control that nobles had over their retainers and on the extent of noble retaining. If noblemen were not as much in control and did not wield such extensive powers as was once thought, than the need for crown attacks on retaining was that much less. Certainly there seems to have been an attempt at discipline, under Henry VII and under Henry VIII and Wolsey, but it would be wrong to treat that as an attack on the nobility as such or to see it as unprecedented.

Did the early Tudors attempt to exploit any financial weaknesses among the nobility? Did they use noble debts as a political weapon? This has been suggested, for example, in the case of the sixth earl of Northumberland, but, as R. W. Hoyle's chapter shows, the crown rather did what it could to protect Percy patrimony against the earl's creditors, placing restrictions on sales of land in 1532 and 1535. Much the same appears to be the case for Richard Grey, third earl of Kent and John de Vere, the short-lived fourteenth earl of Oxford. If (possibly) royal servants were not squeamish about trying to gain a share of the spoils of a fecklessly improvident nobleman in difficulties as Earl Richard was, no courtiers seem to have profited from Northumberland's or Oxford's difficulties.[53]

The crown took a close interest in the marriages of the nobility, but this was hardly a novel concern. Wolsey attempted to direct the marriages of the children of the third duke of Buckingham, the fourth earl of Shrewsbury and the fifth earl of Northumberland in the 1510s, but it would be wrong to read into such attempts any anti-noble prejudice or any attempt to curb the nobility.[54] Some family alliances were considered more suitable than others, and rulers naturally attempted to foster those and deter others. Henry VII and Henry VIII had been very suspicious of anyone seeking to marry into the royal family, or so Lord Russell reminded Lord Seymour when warning him against marrying Princess Elizabeth: Edward VI, when he came of age, 'maye perhaps take occasion therof to haue you thereafter in great suspecte, and as often as he shall see yow to thincke, that you gape and wishe for his deathe'.[55]

Was the royal court, and in particular its alleged development under Henry VIII, designed to reduce the power of the nobility? Was it true that

the concentration of absolute power in a single person conferred a huge advantage on those who had easy access to that person. High politics came to be dominated by events in the monarch's antechamber (or indeed bedchamber) on the one hand and by cliques and factions on the other, every member of the court gravitating around those with direct access to the king, exchanging personal services along the line of access.[56]

Were noblemen excluded, becoming mere ornaments of the court if present, or reduced to impotent provincial obscurity if absent? Was it true that 'by the end of the sixteenth century, partly as a result of the increasing royal use of patronage, the authority of great aristocratic families over the local gentry was coming to depend less upon territorial power than upon their influence at court'?[57]

The king's household was obviously important. As early as the years after the Norman Conquest, if not before, the household was the 'mainspring of government' and the centre of display, while household knights played an important part in war.[58] As early as the twelfth century, writers satirised the hell of the court.[59] A rare surviving fifteenth-century remark showing that contemporaries took a close interest in shifts of influence at the centre has prompted the suggestion that the sudden abundance of sources such as ambassadors' letters in the early sixteenth century has led 'some Tudor historians to exaggerate the novelty of the court-centred politics of Henry VIII's reign'.[60] It is unlikely, then, that the Tudor court was as significantly different as some have maintained.

Moreover, from the point of view of the nobility, the importance of the court varied. It was evidently crucial for courtier magnates – men on the make who rose through royal favour. In a minority, or period of weak government, access to the king might be unusually significant. Thomas Seymour clearly thought so. Yet his failure suggests that a well-entrenched regional base was more important. The unsuccessful makers of Lady Jane Grey's coup in 1553 were largely courtier- and administrator-magnates: they were defeated by the provincial nobles and gentry whom Mary rallied to her cause. Robert Devereux, second earl of Essex, succeeded for a while in building a nationwide following held together by little more than his influence over royal patronage, but once that influence was removed by the queen, he found he had no solid resources of his own to mount a credible rebellion.[61]

Whether the court affected the interests of established noblemen in more normal times is doubtful. Even at the court of Louis XIV, 'the king was certainly the principal source of favours and patronage, but personal attendance upon him or upon his ministers was not the only way of claiming a share in his beneficence'. Most great nobles, especially provincial governors, did not lose influence because they were not daily at court. 'An aspirant for patronage could usually find someone to champion his cause at court without having to leave his province.'[62]

Claims that this was not so, or no longer so, in the late-sixteenth-century England have been made by several historians, but they all cite as proof the same dispute, between Gilbert, seventh earl of Shrewsbury, and the

Stanhope family.[63] A single instance is hardly sufficient to sustain grand conclusions about the decline of noble power. Nor did Shrewsbury fail to get all he wanted just because he lacked influence at court. It is true that in November 1592 he was told by Lord Buckhurst, one of the councillors to whom he had appealed for help in his struggle with Sir Thomas Stanhope (whose brothers John and Michael were prominent courtiers) that 'the continuall presens of thes two brethren in court, with the nere place that they have with her Majestie, and that which is above all the rest, the especial favor which hir Highnes doth beare unto them, will alwaies prevaile with so great advantage against you'.[64] But that often-quoted passage needs to be read more carefully and placed in context. Shrewsbury had recently been at court himself and seen the queen: soon she would pass on her continuing affection to him.[65] It may well be that Stanhope's brothers spoke against the earl to the queen, but not to the complete exclusion of the earl's case. Shrewsbury evidently had friends at court who would defend his interests and offer him advice. What barred him from success in his dispute was the outrageous nature of his demands and actions. Buckhurst, in saying that the Stanhopes were favoured by the queen and thus by the council, warned that it would therefore be hard for Shrewsbury to win against them in council, vitally adding, 'except your caus be marvelous plain and just'.[66] Shrewsbury's problem was that his demands were not obviously just. Nor did his methods help. The queen was especially annoyed that Shrewsbury's men had intimidated fishermen and merchants into signing a petition against the weir that Sir Thomas Stanhope had built across the Trent some fifteen years earlier.[67] Thus, Shrewsbury failed to secure a conciliar decision ordering the destruction of the weir. Yet his local power was hardly humiliatingly ruined as a result. He was able to manipulate the parliamentary elections in Nottinghamshire in January 1593, defeating the Stanhopes.[68] And after his men resorted to force in April and May, destroying the weir, he was rather leniently treated: his men were fined in star chamber, but he himself was not punished for the offence.[69] Earl Gilbert was an aggressive and truculent man, too ready to stand on his dignity.[70] His experiences make for an exciting story but they do not support the claim that power had moved in any new way from the provinces to court. As Lord Howard of Effingham told Shrewsbury, 'in all times and in all princes' reigns they who have had their kin and friends near unto the prince hath always found favour of the prince for them':[71] but that did not mean that the earl's local power was no longer considerable, as the Stanhopes were all too aware.

Since continuous residence at court was not essential for an established magnate, nobles spent most of their time in their 'countries'. It is striking how many nobles were on their estates when the Pilgrimage of Grace broke out in October 1536.[72] Most noblemen did not have any continuous desire to take part in day-to-day conciliar government or to hold offices with daily executive responsibilities. When nobles (and others) criticised the court, that should not be read as evidence of the political importance of the court. Such critics may well have been attacking not so much the cost of the household or the nature of the court as, much more generally, the policies and methods of the king and his advisers, especially if the government was in difficulties. When such urgent and important matters arose, noblemen were properly concerned and they did get involved, but they were not, as a group, overwhelmed by the desire to take part in high politics for its own sake.[73]

That said (and it does much to explain the ascendancy of a Wolsey or a Cromwell), a few noblemen did combine regional pre-eminence with a career as active counsellors or diplomats. Many of these, for example men such as Daubeney, Willoughby de Broke and Somerset under Henry VII, were first-generation peers and special friends of the monarch of the day.[74] But it is misleading to see such noblemen as 'a new style of service aristocracy' and part of 'a major realignment of relations between king and nobility'. Such nobles were indeed creations and close servants of the crown, and they were often too busy at court or in central administration to become immediately involved in the government of the localities. But they usually sought to turn such possibly ephemeral royal favour into a lasting landed inheritance for their families – and they were often assisted in such an aim by the crown's continuing needs for reliable servants in the localities. It is misleading to suggest, however, that the Russells, for example, were advanced 'with the firm understanding that they were to be the crown's agents, never an independent territorial power': the massive grants of former monastic land that Russell received in the late 1530s were made in perpetuity and were regionally concentrated in the South-West.[75]

Such new creations cast doubt on the tenaciously-held belief that the Tudors sought to forge an alliance with the gentry and work with the gentry against the nobility. 'The crown,' it has been suggested, 'was now more able to use the lesser nobility and gentry (often those with court connections) as instruments for direct royal influence within the shire.'[76] A subtler rendering notes 'the tendency of late medieval government, accelerating under the Tudors, to centralise the distribution of royal patronage at the expanding court and to increase direct contact between crown and gentry'.[77] The use of justices of the peace in the localities is often seen as a feature of such a shift. That interpretation assumes that gentry were inherently more sensitive to royal wishes than noblemen, which was not necessarily the case. It is interesting, however, to set such views of the power of Tudor governments against views of historians of twelfth- and thirteenth-century England. Many of them see the decline of the judicial eyre and the declining role and status of the sheriff and their replacement by unpaid local men as a sign of royal weakness in contrast to the earlier assertion of royal and judicial authority in the later twelfth and thirteenth centuries. They see it as an abdication of responsibility to local landed interests, great and small, and as a diminution of royal power. Edward III's excellent relationship with the landed classes in the mid fourteenth century is on this view seen as a surrender of crucial elements of power (and even as a factor that led in the mid fifteenth century to the Wars of the Roses). The triumph of the JPs 'represents the surrender, however slow and reluctant, of the significant degree of judicial initiative and control long claimed by the crown'. Yet the late medieval crown did not abandon the localities to the gentry: royal supervision remained, with the continuing role of royal judges at the assizes. Moreover such a view rests on the assumption of a conflict of interests between crown and landed classes and on a view of local government as a constant battle. If, however, royal government and local government are seen as complementary rather than antagonistic, then it is by no means self-evident that relying on local men to rule the localities is necessarily a weakening of royal authority. It can rather be seen as 'self-government at the king's command'. Moreover, such views take too hopeful a view of the efficiency of royal judges in the thirteenth and fourteenth centuries: not only were they in practice overworked, and their effective jurisdiction confined to felony, but they could be partial and corrupt, and their role in raising royal revenues weakened their moral authority. Whatever the relative merits of royal judges and local gentry, however, what is striking is that important contact between crown and gentry was no novelty of the sixteenth century but was already well established. Governments had long needed to rule with the co-operation and the support of the landed classes as a whole.[78]

This leads to a consideration of local disorder in late medieval England. Was local society so violent, and was that violence so clearly the result of noble fractiousness, as to require and justify royal control of the power of the nobility? Was 'one of the greatest threats to the peace of the realm ... the day-to-day conduct of the knightly classes whose tendency to violent self-help was often proudly proclaimed and recognised as a right, rather than condemned as a crime'?[79] Was a royal policy against the nobility necessary? This is a large and difficult subject. It is likely that there was nothing like as much disorder as has long been thought, and that, whatever its level, it was not increasing. Indictments reflect institutional developments as much, if not more, than actual offences. What prompted the phenomenal growth of litigiousness in the later middle ages was the diffusion of property rights amongst an increasingly wide class of landowners, accentuated by the complexity of the land law, the confusion of tenures and the spread of trusts and uses. It is probable that there was more local disorder when central government was weak or contested. The later years of Edward II's reign, the early years of Edward III's reign, the reign of Henry IV and the 1450s appear to stand out. That is when the most notorious instances of local upper-class violence may be found. It is in the 1450s that disputes between rivals for lands and influence in the localities have been seen as alienating some magnates and gentry from the central government – because the Lancastrian regime was partial and ineffective in its attempts to settle local disputes. Henry VI 'was incapable of that personal assertion of royal power so necessary to the restraint of local conflict'. But all may not be what it seems. Allegations that an act had been committed with violence in breach of the king's peace – *vi et armis et contra pacem* – were essential if a matter was to fall within the sphere of jurisdiction of the royal court, so such allegations could be legal fictions. They cannot be counted up at face value. Similarly, complaints against magnates made by the Commons in late-fourteenth-century parliaments have been seen, not as proof of the deterioration of public order under the unrestrained magnate grip on local society, but as self-interested efforts by gentry (who were by no means innocent victims) to seize a moral advantage. At first glance a system in which many were indicted but few were convicted suggests that things were not working well. But that is to accept too literal an interpretation. Men used the law as one way among others of resolving their disputes. Force was a last, not a first, resort. It is unlikely therefore that the Tudors faced any increasing or novel problems. What was required was firm and impartial government at the centre, and a willingness to discipline any excesses.[80]

If monarchs did not need and did not seek to attack the nobility, did nobles in turn try to oppose monarchs? In what circumstances were noblemen to be found in opposition or rebellion? Were they influenced by a tradition of opposition? Were they exponents of aristocratic constitutionalism? Were they putting forward an ideology of aristocratic conciliarism? Much of the discussion above has already cast doubt on whether noblemen would have needed to behave in such ways (since they were not being attacked) or could have behaved in such ways (since they were not as all-powerful as may have been supposed). But nonetheless a model of aristocratic protest remains influential. Underlying M. E. James's work, as we have seen, is the assumption that nobles (and their followers) naturally came together to resist kings, ministers and their policies: 'the traditional objective of the dissident aristocracy, was to assist the claims of the res publica or common weal, against an unworthy king and his councillors'. That is how James characterises the reigns of Edward II and Richard II. In such arguments James anticipated the later presentations by David Starkey and John Guy of the aristocrats as exponents of a coherent conciliar ideology. James then goes on to criticise the nobles for their loss of nerve, pointing to the decline of the system of honour in favour of one of obedience as demonstrated by the allegedly pusillanimous behaviour of sixteenth-century nobles compared with that of their predecessors.[81] Some more recent writers, on the other hand, have claimed that early modern nobles did behave like their predecessors, speaking of 'the tradition of aristocratic protest which . . . had opposed the rise of the Renaissance and Baroque monarchies'.[82] T. F. Mayer has argued that Thomas Starkey wrote his *Dialogue between Pole and Lupset* as a manifesto of aristocratic conciliarism.[83] J. S. A. Adamson has offered a view of the English civil war of the 1640s that stresses the revolt of the noble earl of Essex and the interest of the leading parliamentary peers in medieval baronial rebellions.[84] Such interpretations of noble revolts can be either sympathetic, seeing nobles as defending some concept of the public good, or unsympathetic, seeing nobles as acting in their own narrow self-interest against a disinterested and paternal monarchy.

Such views overlook noblemen's distaste for instability and civil wars. It is difficult to see why landowners, whose income was primarily derived from rents on land devoted to agriculture, should have gained from disorder. They surely had an immense interest in the maintenance of the status quo. As T. B. Pugh shows in Ch. 1, nobles did not enjoy fighting civil wars or becoming involved in disputed successions. The majority held aloof in 1469–71 and in 1483–5. Only a few nobles joined Henry VII or Lambert Simnel in 1487. By contrast, noblemen and gentry gave overwhelming support to Henry VII against a small-scale popular rebellion in Yorkshire in 1489. Later, very few noblemen were interested in Perkin Warbeck's ambitions in the 1490s. Only James Tuchet, Lord Audley attempted to exploit the Cornish peasants' revolt against taxation in 1497. In 1525 noblemen did not join the resistance to the Amicable Grant but helped to secure acquiescence in it, to deal with those who refused to grant and, in some cases, to deal with insurrection against it. The role of the nobility in the Pilgrimage of Grace of 1536 has, it is true, been disputed. Some have seen Lord Hussey, Lord Darcy and the younger brothers of the earl of Northumberland as prominently involved, but recent studies, and especially R. W. Hoyle's chapter in this volume, question such interpretations. Hussey was frightened and fled before the rebels. Darcy may well have seen himself as loyal. The earl of Northumberland played a very limited part in the Pilgrimage. He did go to the meetings at York on 28 November and 9 December, but he did not participate in the rebels' conferences, and he defended the king and Thomas Cromwell in front of Sir Thomas Percy. As for Sir Thomas and Sir Ingram Percy, they were the prisoners of a movement not of their own making. Sir Ingram used the raising as a cover for his personal quarrel with Sir Reynold Carnaby, one of the earl's closest favourites, hoping that the general pardon the rebels sought might cover his misdemeanours. Neither of these two younger Percy brothers was at York or Pontefract. There was no special connection between the Percys and Robert Aske.[85]

When noblemen did get caught up in conspiracies and rebellions, often the whole business seems bumbling. Algernon Sidney may have had a vision of recreating what he saw as the stand of powerful medieval nobles against tyranny, but his crass behaviour during his exile in the 1660s and 1670s and his ill-judged return to England simply point to the gap between ideal and reality.[86] The revolt of the northern earls in 1569 was a hurried, ill-prepared and defensive affair.[87] Sir William Stanley in the mid-1490s acted without the support of his family, local servants or friends.[88] The Southampton plot of 1415 similarly seems a foredoomed fiasco.[89] Such noble involvement in rebellion and conspiracy as there was seems largely provoked by some personal injustice.[90] Sir William Stanley thought himself hard done by because he was not granted a peerage.[91] Richard, earl of Cambridge, plotted in 1415 because Henry V had disappointed his legitimate hopes of a landed endowment. Edmund Mortimer, earl of March, dabbled in Cambridge's treason because Henry had imposed on him an excessive fine of 10,000 marks. Henry, Lord Scrope, disappointed because he had been reappointed Lord Treasurer, became entangled in Cambridge's schemes, though his offence was probably no more than the concealment of treason. Henry Bolingbroke rebelled after Richard II had broken his word and seized the lands of the duchy of Lancaster.[92] Simon de Montfort held deeply bitter personal grievances against Henry III.[93]

Did nobles hold a theory of resistance? That seems unlikely. Magna

Carta is now seen, not as a struggle over opposing principles, but as a clash of interpretations of shared principles, just as the English civil war is seen not as a conflict between two rival theories of government, but as over different views of what an agreed belief in the divine right of kings and in the rule of law meant for the conduct of royal government.[94] The opposition to Henry III is not seen as particularly baronial or constitutional. If, as was suggested above, Henry III had no theory-driven, absolutist, anti-noble intentions, then it is hardly likely that noblemen should have needed to elaborate constitutional theories against him. Noble action against Henry III was not 'a baronial movement of reform', but rather a plot hatched by the enemies of the Lusignans, the Poitevin half-brothers of the king, at court. It is true that some magnates were at the forefront of this protest. It is also true that one of the ways in which they tried to secure control of central government was to appoint a justiciar and a chancellor. But it would be wrong to overlook the extent to which magnate opponents of Henry III in 1258 were also reflecting the grievances and demands of a wider political society. What appalled men was the farcical Sicilian expedition, the increasing role of the Lusignans and their monopoly of patronage, and the behaviour of Henry III himself. That the king succeeded in forming a party of his own, including barons, further calls into question a simplistic constitutional interpretation of the reign.[95] Did those nobles who opposed Richard II hold a theory of resistance? Here Richard II's behaviour after 1397 – the banishment of Henry of Bolingbroke and Thomas Mowbray, duke of Norfolk, and the seizure of the duchy of Lancaster – would amply seem to explain their reaction.[96] Similarly, the prominence of noblemen among the critics of Charles I in 1640–2 is striking and has prompted descriptions of the politics of these years culminating in the outbreak of civil war as a 'baronial revolt'.[97] But this may not amount to 'a tradition of aristocratic protest'. The flaw in the medieval and early modern system of monarchical government was the possible accession of an inadequate ruler. At such times of unusually incompetent, corrupt, partial, militarily unsuccessful or weak government, some nobles – and, importantly, lesser men – would understandably, if reluctantly, and often in self-defence, criticise the king's government and seek changes. Such criticisms, from nobles and non-nobles,[98] might include requests for nobles to hold specific offices or to dominate the royal council: and such claims might be justified by analogy with the past. But that does not amount to 'a continuous tradition of aristocratic protest', however much some of the participants tried to invent one; such claims were rather rough-and-ready expedients by which men facing appalling political difficulties attempted to resolve them, drawing not on any ideology but on a much vaguer sense of right and wrong, and using theory (if at all) to justify after the event actions that had been instinctive and immediate reactions to perceived abuses.

T. F. Mayer has argued that Thomas Starkey's *Dialogue between Pole and Lupset* was a 'reform programme to be taken seriously as a plan to rehabilitate the high nobility and to restore it to its proper place at the head of the English commonwealth'.[99] Such an interpretation takes as fact the highly questionable assumption that the power of the nobility had declined in the early Tudor period. Neither of the debaters in the *Dialogue* says any such thing: rather, noblemen are seen as having too much of the wrong kind of power – too many servants, too many opportunities for waste. 'Pole' criticises noblemen for their ignorance, idleness, extravagance and barbarous habit of living in the country rather than in cities, which greatly undermines Mayer's attempt to present the *Dialogue* as a manifesto for the nobility. When 'Pole' offers a plan for the creation of a standing council to meet when parliament is not in session, he puts a few of the greatest and most ancient lords on it, and suggests that its head should be a nobleman holding the revived office of constable; but he also includes bishops, lawyers and citizens of London, so putting the noble members in a minority and making the *Dialogue* far less of a scheme of 'aristocratic constitutionalism' than Mayer would claim. More particularly, Mayer argues that the *Dialogue* was written by Starkey as a call to his patron, Reginald Pole, to assume the leadership of a group of aristocratic reformers.[100] Yet there is no tangible evidence for this. In the *Dialogue*, 'Lupset' urges 'Pole' to take an interest in public affairs, but he has little difficulty in persuading 'Pole' to do just that for most of the *Dialogue*. 'Pole' behaves as a free-ranging counsellor offering criticism and advice on all manner of contemporary problems, not as a leader of the nobility, for which role Reginald Pole, as a younger son, was not an obvious choice. Mayer then offers a distressingly circular argument in which the supposed aristocratic conciliarism of the *Dialogue* and of a single document written by Thomas Tempest for the Pilgrims of Grace in 1536 is used to support, and is in turn supported by, stray evidence of noble discontent over the break with Rome in the early 1530s and by Pole's later actions which deeply provoked Henry VIII.[101] Mayer's argument demands that the *Dialogue* be taken as critical of the king. Yet 'Pole' repeatedly insists that he is in no way criticising Henry, but simply drawing attention in a general way to the fundamental flaws in a system of hereditary monarchy. 'Pole' rejects papal supremacy, deplores appeals to Rome, and denounced the payment of annates to Rome. That the real Pole did not, but instead came so vigorously to defend the papacy, must cast doubt on Mayer's association of 'Pole' with Pole. 'Pole' is more obviously a reflection of Starkey's own views: Starkey, unlike Pole, went on in the mid-1530s to defend the break with Rome and the royal supremacy, and to urge a *via media* in religion directed by the king. The *Dialogue* had much less to do with particular political issues than Mayer believes. Much of it reads as a moral treatise deploring moral failings – idleness, selfishness, gluttony – and their economic and social consequences. But in so far as the *Dialogue* is a political text, it is best seen as a theoretical exercise exploring how Italian and classical forms of government might be applied to deal with English ills, an exercise that its authority may have hoped would win him recognition and patronage, not least from the king or from leading ministers.

The real Pole did, of course, oppose Henry VIII. But his opposition was not based on an aristocrat's resentment of a ruler whose dynasty had deprived his family of an august position in the realm, but quite simply on the merits of Henry's case and actions. Pole was horrified by the break with Rome. He tried to avoid making his opposition open, but in 1536 he sent Henry VIII *De Unitate* which made it plain. Even so, *De Unitate* was never published. In 1537 Pole appealed to Pope Paul III, to Francis I and to Charles V, and was prepared to make use of popular insurrection, but he never tried to foment any rising of nobles, nor did he appeal to the nobility as such. Mayer makes a great deal of Pole's connections, beginning with his family and friends, and including anyone who at any time in the 1530s had expressed the slightest dissent from royal policy, but none of this convinces that Pole could have led a noble rebellion in England in the late 1530s.[102]

The nobility were not a unified class, but a disparate group of men. That observation, with which this introduction begins, in itself makes it difficult to sustain the concept of a rebellious nobility. J. O. Prestwich has writen of Geoffrey de Mandeville, the archetypal rebellious baron, that 'he thought first in terms of his family, of what his grandfather had been and of what he and his heirs might be, rather than in terms of any such supposed ideology as "Geoffrey and his class". What he sought was to restore and advance the fortunes of his family in the service of the crown.'[103] If, however, a nobleman took the interests of his family seriously, this does not mean that family alliances played a significant part in creating political groupings that enabled nobles to pursue their ends. What looks like good evidence of this is often an illusion of the evidence. J. R. Lander has shown in his studies of the fifteenth-century Berkeleys and Nevilles how blood relationships and marital connections did not create strong bonds of mutual interest or political support: disputes over inheritances and territorial influence were as likely to produce bitterly hostile feelings.[104]

Noblemen were not as a rule resentful of royal ministers. It is not fair to say that 'new men in government were always resented by baronial families, however short their own pedigrees were' or to describe the Tudor nobility as 'the group most strenuously opposed to ministerial power'.[105] Such opposition was exceptional, and the product of unusual misgovernment, not intrinsic. It has often been claimed that the English nobility disliked Wolsey and struggled with ultimate success to bring him down.[106] Such arguments have been comprehensively disproved by Peter Gwyn. The third duke of Norfolk was much involved in government in the 1520s: serving in Ireland in 1520 and on the Scottish borders in 1523 and 1524; involved in making decisions at the highest level; vigorously pursuing the Amicable Grant in 1525, and watching over the risk of social unrest in 1528. Charles Brandon, duke of Suffolk, very much the creation of the king, remained close to Henry between 1527 and 1529 and obeyed with enthusiasm the king's every command. He did not openly commit himself either for or against Wolsey. He did not lead a hostile aristocracy against Wolsey, motivated by anticlericalism: the supposed evidence for that rests solely on an excessively free translation of a remark by Chapuys, the imperial ambassador. Suffolk was sent by Henry to sound out Francis I whether Wolsey was obstructing the divorce: had he been hostile to Wolsey, Suffolk had plenty of opportunity to have intrigued and invented charges against Wolsey. Suffolk's speech at the legatine court was not a personal attack on Wolsey, but a considered royal statement against papal delays.[107] The poetry of John Skelton is often cited as evidence of noble attitudes towards politics in general and towards Wolsey in particular. But G. Walker (Ch. 2, this volume) suggests that Skelton's treatment of the nobility was determined more by his overall satirical intentions than by any detailed knowledge of what noblemen wanted, or by any deep conviction of how noblemen should behave.[108]

Castles have often been cited as illustrative of the relationship between crown and nobility and in particular as evidence for the power or the decline of the nobility. Castles have been seen as 'feudal', 'baronial', as independent fortresses from which nobles pursued their private feuds: kings and their advisers have been seen as planning to take over and destroy such baronial castles. The words of Anglo-Saxon chronicle on the reign of Stephen – 'for every man built him castles and held them against the king: and they filled the land with these castles' – have been taken as typical.[109]

Castles have then been seen as declining in the later middle ages from their supposed feudal impregnability: the dwindling defensibility of the castle thus parallels the alleged decline in the fortunes of the nobility. Such views are somewhat misleading.

Medieval castles were never just about defence. Even twelfth-century castlebuilding was 'a complex and fascinating mixture' of defence on the one hand and display, assertion of social standing, domestic comfort, on the other, the whole tempered by what could be afforded. The military significance of medieval castles was complex.[110] No castle was ever utterly impregnable. Castles were often important just as much as treasuries, safe stores of military materials, or as rallying points than they were as defences. They denied an opponent control of a region. Indeed, in the early Norman period they were used to enable a few men to dominate a subject population from a strongpoint, and tied down forces in time-consuming seiges, though much depends on whether castles controlled a naturally strategic site, of which there are relatively few in southern England. They could shelter garrisons who could make brief sorties to harry an enemy.[111]

Thus medieval castles were not primarily symbolic, however much some of the decorative features of late medieval castles strike us as exercises in nostalgia. It is a distortion to claim that 'above all else, their builder sought to evoke in some manner the moeurs of chivalry, the life-style of the great, and the legends of the past'. Bodiam Castle, built after 1384, was not just 'an old soldier's dream house'.[112] It might not have withstood a long siege, but it could certainly hold out against a lightning strike. Its entrance is remarkably strong, with a formidable gatehouse, gunports and machicolations – as terrible, in the opinion of D. J. C. King, as anything in Edward I's Welsh castles.[113] Nor are fifteenth-century castles show castles, caricatures, or merely theatrical. The invention and development of gunpowder did not quickly make castles obsolete. It was not always easy for the defender to use his own cannon: wall-walks might be too narrow, roofs could not easily support guns. Ultimately an artillery train was more potent than a moated stronghold. But offensive ordnance was not always effective or safe, and it was difficult to transport. Artillery was often used in sieges in fifteenth-century France, but this did not prevent considerable castlebuilding there. Late medieval castles were defensible. Northern castles in the late fourteenth century were strong and intimidating: examples include Bolton, Chillingham, Lumley, Wressle and Sheriff Hutton. 'Castles could integrate defensive artillery and resist siege-guns.' Gunports could be introduced. If Bodiam, Cooling, Scotney, Wingfield, Shirburn and Maxstoke were not built to withstand a royal siege, nevertheless they would at least require an opponent to drain the moat, and they could withstand attacks from raiders or rebels. The portcullis groove, the arrow slits, the moats and especially the curtain wall of Wingfield show that it was not ornamental in purpose. The new works at Warwick Castle were not just for show. The gunports at Caister must be taken seriously. Kirby Muxloe shows considerable provision for gunnery, with gunports, and it has a drawbridge with a portcullis. After a careful discussion of Tattershall Castle, Pevsner concluded that 'the keep must be regarded as built for defence'. Its machicolations are interrupted by the large angle turrets, but that does not mean that their only purpose was display. Raglan is manifestly a defensible castle, with moats, strong angle-towers, mural towers, gun loops (some of which, whatever doubts there may be about others, could certainly have accommodated guns) and a gatehouse.[114]

Castles did play some part in the Wars of the Roses. There are signs that some efforts were made in the 1450s to strengthen royal castles: Kenilworth, for example, was prepared as a principal royal base in 1460. No sieges played a decisive part in these wars, but the control of major castles was an issue. There was something of a siege of the Tower of London by the Yorkists in 1460, cut short by the Yorkists' decisive victory at Northampton. There was widespread manning of fortifications in 1461: Pembroke Castle was besieged for six months. Harlech held out against Edward IV until 1468. Attempts to hold castles were factors in the renewed fighting in 1469–71. Caister was defended in 1469 against an irresistibly superior force: the commander did not explain his surrender by weakness, even though the castle was badly damaged by bombardment. The earl of Oxford was to hold St Michael's Mount from Michaelmas 1473 to February 1474. Edward IV and Richard III spent on fortifications: Edward especially at Nottingham between 1476 and 1480, Richard at Warwick and at York after his usurpation. Edward's close servant, William Herbert, earl of Pembroke, completed the substantial castle at Raglan, and William, Lord Hastings, built Kirby Muxloe and the keep at Ashby de la Zouche.[115] It has been suggested that the avoidance of sieges owes something to contemporary styles of fighting, in particular to a preference for hand-to-hand fighting on foot, and settling issues in short sharp fights.[116] But castles still remained important in that style of warfare; they offered breathing spaces, comparative safe places in which to wait for allies or to negotiate. Defence was not wholly absent even from Elizabethan builders' concerns. 'Thei say my lord of Lecester hathe many worke men at Kyllinworthe [Kenilworth] to make his howse stronge, and dothe furnishe it with armour, munition and all necessaries for defence.'[117] In the civil wars of the 1640s many castles were used as strongpoints, suggesting a degree of defensibility or at least utility: that so many inland castles were slighted after the wars were over is a commentary on contemporary perceptions of their continuing potential.[118] Moreover, it should not be forgotten that castles were as much deterrents as defences.[119]

The mere possession of large numbers of castles did not in itself make a king powerful. Castles had to be equipped and maintained. No king could control more than a handful himself. That meant that castles had to be entrusted to deputies. For this reason it is highly questionable whether 'a castle in the hands of the crown was safer than one in the hands of an over-mighty subject':[120] it is likely that a nobleman would be as least as loyal a constable as any royal servant or professional soldier, especially in a domestic political crisis.[121] Moreover, 'the distinction of ownership was one that scarcely mattered if baron and king operated in harmony'.[122] There is no evidence that rulers normally saw castles as a threat to their authority. R. W. Kaeuper argued that 'the existence of private fortifications, which could act as bases for feuding, disorder and brigandage, was clearly not closely controlled by the royal licences granted by the king in England.' Some licences were granted after the fact of building. 'The most telling fact is the absence of licence requests denied.' 'Regulation which misses many castles, licenses others only after they are built, and never says no, cannot be considered a model of stern efficiency.'[123] In fact, licences were refused three times between 1260 and 1270. But this may be to mistake the aims of licences. They were not intended to control castle-building. The granting of licences to crenellate in medieval England was not a special and reluctant royal concession. It was a courtesy, not an obligation. Great magnates did not seek licences. 'A licence was sought most usually by lesser men in order to exhance their own social status.' The descriptions concentrated not on the defensive features such as the height or thickness of walls, but on the most visible and symbolic features such as battlements. It is notable that while rulers did legislate to control retaining, there was no equivalent legislation against the building or ownership of castles.[125] It is most unlikely that Henry VIII feared the third duke of Buckingham's power as demonstrated in Thornbury Castle, a very conventional manor house for its date. The charges against Buckingham mention no such thing.[126] It has been suggested that there was a dangerous imbalance in the mid fifteenth century between royal and private fortifications, that the midlands and north were 'studded with private fortresses built and maintained by the over-mighty subjects into whose quarrels the crown was soon to be drawn'.[127] It is, however, very hard to see that any such imbalance ever weakened royal authority during the wars. The Tudor monarchs acquired many castles after nobles who were involved in rebellion forfeited them: but many were then granted out to royal servants, and there was no deliberate policy of confiscation. Henry VIII sometimes asked noblemen to give him their houses – but these were almost always because they were agreeable and conveniently-situated residences, which Henry hoped to use, not because he saw them as any kind of threat.[128] Some kings did destroy castles, especially after periods of civil strife. Stephen destroyed castles in the last year of his life and Henry II followed him. Henri IV of France destroyed a number of castles and forts after 1593; Richelieu destroyed over a hundred in the South after the Huguenot rebellions in the 1620s.[129] Sixteenth-century English monarchs and their advisers were perhaps more likely to lament the accelerating decay of English castles. Leland visited some 500–600 castles: of 258 that he described in detail, 91 were in normal use, 30 partially derelict, and 137 ruinous.[130]

It would be possible to accept much of the argument so far – to accept that kings were not trying to crush nobles, and that nobles were not incessantly trying to overthrow kings, but (and arguably it would be a large 'but') to go on to ask whether the whole culture of honour was not a 'zero-sum game' in which one man's gain was inevitably another man's loss and inherently biased towards instability. To raise that possibility is to undermine the particular claim that informal mechanisms such as arbitration or feud could work to promote stability and the larger claim that there was a community of interest between crown and nobility. Such an interpretation has been essayed most forcefully by Keith Brown in his study of feuds in late-sixteenth century Scotland, and on the face of it, he makes a strong case. For this reason it deserves extended and careful attention as a test case, the conclusions from which might have important implications for other countries and other periods. Brown sees Scottish feuding as violent, as intensifying in the mid and late sixteenth century – not just as an aberration in a royal minority but having its origins in the enormous power of lords. The darker side of lordship was the countenancing of offenders, the maintenance of private armies, the perversion of justice and the close links with the rural underworld. Universal carrying of weapons made every confrontation a potential manslaughter. 'Competition and conflict flowed naturally from the structure and mentality of the kindreds.' The society of the male elite was extremely tense. Honour 'propelled men into feuds and intensified existing ones because it was imperative that honour, and hence power, be defended, and it ensured that feud be prosecuted *without restraint* [my italics] because it was a code of behaviour which recognised none'; revenge in Scottish society was itself honourable. Blood feuds were private revenge with little sign of strict rules of conduct, and much indiscriminate vengeance and mystical bloodletting. Men who found themselves in a feud were prepared to use violence. 'Feuding was an essentially violent means of resolving disputes', an ideology which made private violence not only obligatory, but reasonable. 'Every issue, however small, was a measure of a man's honour. The freedom to choose an alternative to violence was not always there.' 'Defensive relationships were themselves responsible for sustaining the violence by making offensive actions worthwhile, by making it more likely that violence could be sustained over a longer time, by dragging more people into it.' Feud was eternal, peace a temporary calm, lasting only as long as it took to find a new issue over which to quarrel as the problems of living together threw men into repeated competition and conflict. Landownership led to conflict over such issues as fishing rights, seating in church, offices on ex-monastic lands. 'The basic violence of the bloodfeud' reflected a 'mistaken concept of honour and loyalty'. It sounds an impressive case.[131]

Yet there is another side to Brown's study. He accepts that 'a great deal of lordship had nothing at all to do with violence', but was about good counsel and household service. He says that most tensions in local society were peacefully resolved. Arbitration was difficult, but many settlements were reached. Lordship was a highly effective means of persuading men that they should make peace. The fear of incurring a bloodfeud was itself an inhibition of violence. When force was used, 'the violence was neither anarchic *nor without restraints* [my italics]'. 'Even the most excessive violence of the feud . . . was not simply bloodletting for its own sake.' Feuds were conducted within fairly tight guidelines; anarchy was avoided: 'all forms of conflict have rules built into them, and it was this evolved common sense and self-interest which contained the violence of this feud within limits which were largely acceptable to both sides.' It was 'a violence contained within social rules', not anarchy, and not the product of a self-interested, lawless nobility. 'On the question of violence it is puzzling to imagine that the nobility had any vested interest in anarchy and bloodshed.' In assessing the hostile language in which feuds were described, due allowance must be made for propaganda. 'There was no reason to suppose that the crown could have offered a better means of restoring (*sic*: sc. 'bringing'?) peace to local communities.' 'In its rough violence, the feud was often able to provide a form of just deserts – the law could embitter.' 'A feuding society did not have to be as violent as this one clearly was': the fifteenth century had seen feuds, but less private violence. Noblemen co-operated with the crown in reducing levels of violence in the late sixteenth and early seventeenth centuries: 'the level of local peace secured before 1609 suggests that ... the hereditary courts and the leaders of local society did a far better job in co-operating with the crown in establishing peace than crown propaganda had led one to believe.'[132]

Examined in detail, the disputes that Brown discusses seem to be the product (at a general level) of royal minorities, religious divisions and military defeat, and (at a local level) of men acting, as so often, largely in self-defence – not in pursuit of honour. Self-defence includes fears of a deterioration of one's local position at a time when ex-monastic lands and offices are being distributed, as at Kilwinning Abbey. Servants, rather than nobles, took the initiative in the feud between Glamis and Crawford in 1578. The crown, far from standing above the fray, inspired some spectacular feuds itself, for example those between Hume and Bothwell, or between Huntley and Moray in the late 1580s/1590s. Above all, the weakness of royal authority seems crucial.[133] Here there is a parallel with the 1450s in England, a time of both inadequate kingship and important local feuds – between Neville and Percy, Bonville and Devon – which Henry VI did little to check. Such periods should not, however, be taken as characteristic. If this Scottish case, which at first seems to bear out the argument from honour, in the end fails to clinch it, then that argument is weakened elsewhere.

But what of the wider claim that notions of honour, ideals of chivalry, in themselves fostered a climate of violence? Did a society based on privileges, many of them honorific and symbolic such as heraldic devices and arms, or highly visible such as the location of pews or family tombs in churches, inevitably spawn violent quarrels? Did 'l'orgueil familial et le maintien de la reputation aupres du voisinage exigaient de considerer comme insupportable la moindre atteinte a l'honneur'? How far did noblemen feel the temptation to do something extraordinary to force the admiration of their contemporaries and of posterity? 'It is the violence of the powerful and privileged classes which so sharply differentiates the medieval from the modern problem of order,' writes Kaeuper: such a noble code of violence 'glorified proud sword strokes in defence of honour and buttressed a sense of the knightly right to decisive, independent action'. Was it the case that 'a manor that was lost had to be recovered because a lineage's reputation depended on it'? Were 'men trained in the school of chivalry more likely to settle their differences by violent means'? More specifically, were noble/gentry feuds a primary determinant of the Wars of the Roses?[134]

While there is obviously some truth in such characterisations, especially in individual cases, it is unconvincing as a view of the nobility in general. Nor does it satisfactorily explain the fall of the House of Lancaster. A recent study of aristocratic lawlessness shows clearly how 'disputes between rivals for land and influence had a significant potential for alienating individual magnates and gentry from the Lancastrian regime'. But that was largely because Henry VI was unable to show the qualities of character that the holding in check of rivalries among his leading subjects required: in particular, the king's weakness allowed those dominant at court to bend the law to their own ends. As a result, local quarrels were intensified rather than restrained: 'the paralysis of central government . . . allowed these disputes to escalate' and gave those dissatisfied with their treatment an incentive to support the Yorkists.[135] More usually kings could exploit honour to their own advantage. 'A king who could bring his nobility into a companionship of honour and renown in war, as did Edward I, Edward III and Henry V, laid a foundation of political support which was not easily shaken.'[136] Honour was a force making for royalism in the 1640s: 'the strength and fighting spirit of his [Charles I's] supporters may well have owed more to the concepts of honour and loyalty' than to the force or validity of the various arguments deployed on the king's behalf from 1641.[137] Honour, and true chivalry, was service to the prince. 'Service was personal and honourable.' Honour and chivalry are broad concepts that do not invariably lead to violence. 'Historians of chivalry have been attracted to the type of behaviour appropriate to the younger man – the knight errantry and the individualism – and have in consequence tended to neglect the more prudential behaviour of the knight with responsibilities.' 'Good knights were expected to behave differently at different stages of their chivalry.' A case can be made that chivalry channelled youthful violence into proper military service.[138] Honour was open to different interpretations and did not therefore inevitably lead to violence. This emerges from a recent attempt to reinterpret the dispute between Somerset and York in the 1450s in the light of considerations of honour. York saw Somerset's behaviour in Normandy in the late 1440s, especially his controversial surrender of Rouen, for which he held responsibility, as dishonourable, as a treasonable premature surrender of the city. But Henry VI refused to accept York's demand that Somerset be dismissed and put on trial, and maintained him in high favour. Henry's sense of 'honour' was evidently very different from York's. And if the king had been more politically skilful, and retained his sanity, he might by arbitration or by firmness have contained the incipient feud between Somerset and York. It is possible, of course, that York's anger was not so much the result of his sense of honour, as of his very real material losses in Normandy, but allowing that honour was a significant factor, the difference between his and the king's attitudes shows that honour was not, in its practical application, a rigid prescription.[139] An honourable settlement of a dispute was as likely as a fight over honour. Chivalry has also acquired a bad name because it was so often an ideal, an aspiration: any society can be made to look tawdry if its ideals are compared with the messy reality. Chivalry could be dismissed as a sham, 'a tinsel covering disguising the ugliness of war and political strife and permitting the nobility to glamourise the misdeeds on which, all too often, gentlemen as well as mercenaries maintained their estate'. But that would be to deny the legacy of ideals such as service, courtliness, generosity, loyalty, prowess, boldness, and the influence of rules of conduct on such dangerously rowdy sports as high medieval tournaments. It implicitly supposes that some better, more peaceful order was easily attainable: it is as arguable that, however dangerous chivalric behaviour could be in the wrong circumstances, nevertheless it was chivalric ideals that fostered a more peaceable society. The late medieval fusion of chivalry with civic humanism, with its emphasis on personal honour and public service, exemplified in Castiglione's *Courtier*, powerfully reinforced the beneficent side of chivalry.[140]

Reviewing a collection of essays on the Scottish nobility, Robin Frame welcomed the promise of a further volume, and added: 'by the time its results appear, Scottish historians should no longer need to parade as a novelty or as a badge of professional rectitude, the idea that crown and nobility were not natural enemies'.[141] But how far should one go in the opposite direction? Rees Davies wondered, reviewing the same volume, 'whether the revisionist card has not been overplayed. Barons and nobles may not be the irresponsible trouble-makers of earlier historiography, but they were not altruistic defenders of monarchy and of the "community of the realm", at least at all times, either.'[142] In a rich sociological essay, Patricia Cronne, outlining the attitude of rulers, expressed scepticism that kings for their part governed in the interest of all. In practice, she argued, kings strove to satisfy their private needs and treated public revenues as private income.[143] These reservations are important. But it is worth noting Cronne's concession that 'repressive government is more time-consuming, difficult and expensive than social collaboration' and Davies's perceptive suggestion that 'the chemistry of a political community depended both on aristocratic restraint and on royal sensitivity'.[144] To argue for a community of interest and values between kings and noblemen, to suggest that royal sensitivity and aristocratic restraint were not uncommon, is not to take a Panglossian view of late medieval and early modern political society, nor to assert a complete and constant identity of interest. It is rather to suggest that both the probing of tenaciously-held assumptions about the inevitability of conflict on the one hand, and detailed studies of noblemen on the other, reveal just such a community. Since it was so obviously in their interests to maintain the political order and social harmony on which their privileged position stood, it should not be surprising that kings and nobles are best seen, when characterised in general terms, as natural and trusted partners in government.[145]

NOTES

I should wish to thank Dr S. J. Payling, Mr P. J. Gwyn, Mr C. S. L. Davies, Mr H. James, Mr T. B. Pugh, Mrs S. J. Loach and Dr K. M. Sharpe for their comments.

Note: Place of publication is London unless otherwise stated.

1   See below, pp. 134–79.
2   Oxford, 1986.
3   J. S. A. Adamson, 'The baronial context of the English Civil War', *Transactions of the Royal Historical Society*, 5th series, xl (1990), pp. 93–120, and cf. his 'The political culture of chivalry in Caroline England', paper read at the History Faculty Centre, Oxford, 12 October 1989. Adamson uses the term 'baronial' to describe so many different things that it loses any explanatory force. In his paper it can mean: (i) all the parliamentary peers in the 1640s (making the point that noblemen led armies on both the parliamentarian and the royalist sides: 'the aristocratic leadership in the civil war' (art. cit., pp. 94, 101)); (ii) the royalist peers; (iii) the parliamentary peers, especially Essex, Warwick, Northumberland, Mandeville, Pembroke, Brooke, Saye, who put forward 'a revived, baronial view of the nobility's role as counterpoise to the arbitrary powers of the king' and stood behind the Nineteen Propositions (art. cit., pp. 95, 98, 101); (iv) the earl of Essex: especially seen as an overmighty subject who led and personified a rebellion against the king and behaved in a quasi-regal style (art. cit., pp. 94, 100, 105–6, 108–9); (v) political action by noblemen who seek to hold particular offices of state, especially revived ancient offices such as constable or steward (art. cit., pp. 96, 99, 100) or to sit on or to control the king's council (art. cit., pp. 97, 105); (vi) a description of particular codes of fighting – especially challenges to personal combat (art. cit., pp. 102–4); (vii) an interest in medieval (or 'gothic') political disputes or manifestos from the reigns of Henry III to Richard III or even Henry VIII (art. cit., pp. 93, 95, 97); (viii) those noblemen who reacted against the ambitions of the earl of Essex from the autumn of 1643, especially Saye and Northumberland, and intrigued against him (art. cit., pp. 94, 109–10). For further criticism see M. A. Kishlansky, 'Saye What?', *Historical Journal*, xxxiii (1990), pp. 917–37. Cf. remarks of N. Hampson, *Times Literary Supplement*, 15 June 1990, p. 637.
4   M. James, *Society, Politics and Culture: Studies in Early Modern England* (Cambridge, 1986), which includes essays published since 1965.
5   For a critique of similar views of the French nobility see P. Contamine, 'L'état et les

aristocraties', in P. Contamine, ed., *L'état et les aristocraties: XIIe–XVII siècle. France, Angleterre, Écosse* (Paris, 1989), pp. 14–22.

6   Cf. A. Murray, *Reason and Society in the Middle Ages* (Oxford, 1978), pp. 328–9 and G. W. Bernard, *The Power of the Earl Tudor Nobility: A Study of the Fourth and Fifth Earls of Shrewsbury* (Brighton, 1985), pp. 188–9.

7   James, *Society, Politics and Culture*, p. 381.

8   *Ibid.*, p. 373.

9   J. Robertson, ed., *The Works of Algernon Sydney* (1772), pp. 205, 213, 425–6; B. Worden, 'The commonwealth kidney of Algernon Sidney', *Journal of British Studies*, xxiv (1985), pp. 1–40; J. Scott, *Algernon Sidney and the English Republic 1623–1677* (Cambridge, 1988), pp. 40, 43–7, 48–9, 224. Worden has been much influenced by Sidney: 'over the previous century the Tudors had overcome fundamental opposition in their rule and built a durable system of government. The great baronial families which had fought the Wars of the Roses in the later fifteenth century had been tamed or extinguished, and their military followings abolished. By the end of the sixteenth century a high proportion of noble families owed their eminence not to independent bases of power in the regions where their estates lay, but to the favour of the crown, whose policies they implemented in the localities and at whose court they competed for further rewards.' 'By the time of James I's accession the regional rebellions of 1536–69 belonged to the past.' Seventeenth-century republicans believed – Worden continues, without adding any qualifications – that 'in the Middle Ages ... kings had been kept in order, and their subjects protected from them, by powerful, frugal barons. Now in the "new monarchies" of the renaissance, kings had been made into demi-gods, indecently flattered by obsequious nobles in luxurious and lascivious courts and absurdly idealised in masques and pageants.' (B. Worden, 'Introduction', in B. Worden, ed., *The Stuart Age* (1986), pp. 7–8). Worden further argued for the 'final taming' of the nobility under the Tudors in 'Shakespeare's politics', paper read at the History Faculty Library, Oxford, 22 April 1991.

10   James, *Society, Politics and Culture*, pp. 278–92.

11   M. Weiss, 'A power in the north? The Percies in the fifteenth century', *Historical Journal*, xix (1976), pp. 501–9; M. A. Hicks, 'Dynastic change and northern society: the carer of the fourth earl of Northumberland, 1470–89', *Northern History*, xiv (1978), pp. 78–107. J. A. Tuck, 'The emergence of a northern nobility', *Northern History*, xxii (1986), p. 17 exaggerates the power of the Percys. For earlier brief but salutary scepticism see M. L. Bush, 'The problem of the far north: a study of the crisis of 1537 and its consequences', *Northern History*, vi (1971), pp. 40 n. 1, 41–2.

12   James, *Society, Politics and Culture*, p. 65.

13   *Ibid.*, pp. 56–62; P. Gwyn, *The King's Cardinal: The Rise and Fall of Thomas Wolsey* (1990), pp. 229–34.

14   See below, pp. 191–2, 195–7, 199–200, 202–3.

15   R. W. Hoyle: 'The first earl of Cumberland: a reputation reassessed', *Northern History*, xxii (1986), pp. 63–94: 'An ancient and laudable custom: the definition and development of tenant-right in north-western England in the sixteenth century', *Past and Present*, cxvi (1987), pp. 24–55.

16   James, *Society, Politics and Culture*, pp. 351, 354–6.

17   *Ibid.*, pp. 353–4.

18   *Ibid.*, pp. 114, 161, 174–5, 251–5.

19   *Ibid.*, p. 406.

20   S. Doran, 'The finances of an Elizabethan nobleman and royal servant: a case study of Thomas Radcliffe, 3rd earl of Sussex', *Bulletin of the Institute of Historical Research*, lxi (1988), pp. 286–300; B. Coward, 'A "crisis of the aristocracy" in the sixteenth and early seventeenth centuries? The case of the Stanleys, earls of Derby, 1504–1642', *Northern History*, xviii (1982), pp. 54–77. For past discussion see especially L. Stone, *The Crisis of the Aristocracy 1558–1642* (Oxford, 1965) and reviews by J. P. Cooper, *Times Literary Supplement*, 7 April 1966, pp. 285–7, and D. C. Coleman, *History*, li (1966), pp. 165–78 esp. pp. 171–6.

21 J. Kew, 'The disposal of crown lands and the Devon land market, 1536–58', *Agricultural History Review*, xviii (1970), pp. 93–105; T. H. Swales, 'The redistribution of the monastic lands in Norfolk at the dissolution', *Norfolk Archaeology*, xxxiv (1970), pp. 14–44; C. W. Brooks, *English Historical Review*, ci (1988), p. 178; P. J. Bowden, 'Agricultural prices, farm profits and rents', in J. Thirsk, ed., *Agrarian History of England and Wales, Vol, iv., 1500–1640* (Cambridge, 1967), pp. 593–695, esp. pp. 674–95; C. S. L. Davies, 'Landed society: the upper classes', unpublished paper.

22 Brooks, *English Historical Review*, ci (1988), p. 178; J. C. K. Cornwall, *Wealth and Society in Early Sixteenth Century England* (1988), pp. 143–4; H. J. Habakkuk, 'The rise and fall of English landed families, 1600–1800', *Transactions of the Royal Historical Society*, 5th series, xxviii (1979), p. 206; J. V. Beckett, *The Aristocracy in England 1660–1914* (Oxford, 1986); L. & J. F. C. Stone, *An Open Elite? England 1540–1880* (Oxford, 1984).

23 A. Jouanna, *Le devoir de révolte: la noblesse française et la gestion de l'état moderne, 1559–1661* (Paris, 1989), pp. 92–8; A. Jouanna, 'Des "gros et gras" aux "gens d'honneur"', in G. Chaussinand-Nogaret, ed., *Histoire des élites en France du XVIᵉ au XXᵉ siècle: L'honneur, le mérite, l'argent* (Paris, 1991), pp. 83–4; D. Crouzet, 'Recherches sur la crise de l'aristocratie en France au XVIème siècle: les dettes de la maison de Nevers', *Histoire, economie et société* (1982), pp. 7–50 (but his arguments are not compelling); M. Wolfe, 'Piety and political allegiance: the duc of Nevers and the protestant Henry IV, 1589–93', *French History*, ii (1988), pp. 1–21; J. R. Major, 'Noble income, inflation and the wars of religion in France', *American Historical Review*, lxxxvi (1981), pp. 21–48; M. Greengrass, 'Property and politics in sixteenth-century France: the landed fortune of Constable Anne de Montmorency', *French History*, ii (1988), pp. 371–98.

24 K. Brown: 'Aristocratic finances and the origins of the Scottish Revolution', *English Historical Review*, civ (1989), pp. 46–87; 'Noble indebtedness in Scotland between the Reformation and the Revolution', *Historical Research*, lxii (1989), pp. 260–75.

25 G. Parker, *The Military Revolution: Military Innovations and the Rise of the West 1500–1800* (Cambridge, 1988), pp. 1–2, 7, 10–11, 24, 26–9, 41–5, 57–8, 69, 147; I. Roy, 'England turned Germany? The aftermath of the Civil War in its European context, *Transactions of the Royal Historical Society*, 5th series, xxviii (1978), p. 134; H. Watanabe-O'Kelly, 'Tournaments and their relevance for warfare in the early modern period', *European Studies Quarterly*, xx (1990), pp. 451–63; S. J. Gunn, 'Tournaments and early Tudor chivalry', *History Today* (June 1991), pp. 15–21.

26 M. G. A. Vale, *War and Chivalry: Warfare and Aristocratic Culture in England, France and Burgundy at the End of the Middle Ages* (1981), pp. 104–5, 126, 130, 172, 174; cf. S. Anglo, *Times Literary Supplement*, 25 September 1981, p. 1103.

27 C. Russell, 'The Scottish party in English parliaments 1640–1642, or the myth of the English revolution' (1991), inaugural lecture, King's College, London, 29 January 1991, p. 6.

28 James, *Society, Politics and Culture*, pp. 293–6; S. E. Taylor, 'The crown and the north of England, 1559–70: a study of the rebellion of the northern earls, 1569–70, and its causes', University of Manchester Ph. D. thesis (1981), pp. 186, 211–12, 252–3, 261.

29 S. Walker, 'Autorité des magnats et pouvoir de la gentry en Angleterre à la fin du moyen âge', in Contamine, *L'état, les aristocraties*, pp. 189–211; *Historical Manuscripts Commission, xxiv, Rutland i*, pp. 3–4; J. Bruce, ed., *History of the Arrivall of Edward IV in England, Camden Society*, i (1838), p. 6; J. S. Davies, ed., *An English Chronicle, Camden Society*, lxiv (1856), p. 65; cf. C. Ross, *Edward IV* (1975), p. 154; A. J. Pollard, *North-Eastern England During the Wars of the Roses: Lay Society, War and Politics 1450–1500* (Oxford, 1990), pp. 308–13; T. B. Pugh, *Henry V and the Southampton Plot* (Gloucester, 1988), pp. 14, 20–1. Further instances may include the reluctance of the gentry of Brecon to support the duke of Buckingham in October 1483 (T. B. Pugh, *The Marcher Lordships* (Cardiff, 1963), pp. 240–1; C. Rawcliffe, *The Staffords, Lords Stafford and Dukes of Buckingham 1394–1521* (Cambridge, 1968), p. 34; R. Horrox, *Richard III: A Study in Service* (Cambridge, 1989), pp. 162–4) and the report that instead of joining Richard Nevill, earl of Warwick, in 1470, men 'left their gathering and sat still' for fear of facing defeat at the king's hands (J. G. Nichols, ed., 'The chronicle of the rebellion in Lincolnshire, 1470', *Camden Miscellany i, Camden Society*, old series, xxxix (1847), pp. 5, 12; Pollard, *North-Eastern England*, pp. 307–8; but cf. P. Holland, 'the Lincolnshire rebellion of March 1470', *English Historical Review*, ciii (1988), p. 865 n. 2, who suggests that there was insufficient time for mobilisation).

30   See below, pp. 152–8.

31   Walker, 'Autorité des magnats', p. 91; S. Walker, *The Lancastrian Affinity 1361–1399* (Oxford, 1990), pp. 139–41, 160–2, 166, 221, 232–4, 250, 260–1.

32   C. F. Richmond, '1485 and all that, or what was going on at the Battle of Bosworth?', in P. W. Hammond, ed., *Richard III: Loyalty, Lordship and Law* (1986), p. 197 n. 59.

33   K. B. McFarlane, *England in the Fifteenth Century* (1981), p. 20.

34   Robertson, *Works of Algernon Sydney*, p. 213.

35   J. A. Guy, 'The Tudor age (1485–1603)', in K. O, Morgan, ed., *The Oxford Illustrated History of Britain* (Oxford, 1984), p. 234.

36   R. Horrox, *Richard III: A Study of Service* (Cambridge, 1988), pp. 39–43, 45, 47, 61–2, 65–6, 70–2 for a forceful if controversial argument: cf. M. A. Hicks, 'The last days of Elizabeth, countess of Oxford', *English Historical Review*, ciii (1988), pp. 76–95 for a less agreeable view of Richard. Although Pollard (*North-Eastern England*) can write of Gloucester's 'awesome power' (p. 338), he stresses Richard's dependence on the continuing favour of his brother and emphasises the effectiveness of his regional political leadership (p. 316): Richard's power enhanced his brother's authority (p. 338 n. 67). Pollard does not think it was inevitable or predictable that Richard would seize the crown (pp. 316, 338 n. 67)

37   A. Goodman, 'John of Gaunt', in W. M. Ormrod, ed., *England in the Fourteenth Century* (Woodbridge, 1986), pp. 86–7.

38   A. Jouanna, *Le devoir de révolte: la noblesse française et la gestion de l'état moderne, 1559–1661* (Paris, 1989), p. 111; R. Mettam, *Power and Faction in Louis XIV's France* (Oxford, 1988), p. 21.

39   C. Jouhaud, 'Politique de princes: les Condé (1630–1652)', in Contamine, *L'état et les aristocraties*, pp. 335–55.

40   M. Bush, 'The Tudors and the royal race', *History*, lv (1970), pp. 37–48.

41   *Letters and Papers, Foreign and Domestic, of the Reign of Henry VIII* (1862–1932) (hereinafter *LP*), X, 420, 426, 441, 600, 619, 974–5, 1093; XI, 72.

42   *LP*, XII, i, 1032; XIII, ii, 695, 797, 986 (10, 11). C. Höllger suggests that Henry, incensed by *De Unitate*, took revenge against members of Reginald Pole's family. (C. Höllger, 'Reginald Pole and the legations of 1537 and 1539: diplomatic and polemical responses to the break with Rome', University of Oxford D.Phil. thesis, 1989, pp. 84–6, 93–4, 103–4, 122.) But the limited contacts that they had with him, together with some loose talk, may have been enough to ruin them.

43   Gwyn, *The King's Cardinal*, pp. 220–5.

44   See below, pp. 180–211.

45   See below, p. 241–65.

46   See below, pp. 266–95; D. Kiernan, 'The Derbyshire lead mining industry in the sixteenth century', *Derbyshire Record Society*, xiv (1989), p. 111.

47   R. W. Hoyle, 'Tenure and the land market in early modern England: or a late contribution to the Brenner debate', *Economic History Review*, 2nd ser., xliii (1990), pp. 3–6; Gwyn, *The King's Cardinal*, pp. 412–35; J. J. Scarisbrick, 'Cardinal Wolsey and the Common Weal', in E. W. Ives, R. J. Knecht and J. J. Scarisbrick, eds., *Wealth and Power in Tudor England* (1978), pp. 45–67; *Historical Manuscripts Commission, Bath, v, Talbot, Dudley and Devereux Papers, 1553–1659* (1980), p. 111. Cf. 'the king's favour did not license arbitrary or harsh local government, but magistrates so guilty lost reputation not least because they were believed to abjure the king's honour': K. M. Sharpe, *Politics and Ideas in Early Stuart England* (1989), p. 305.

48 M. T. Clanchy: 'Did Henry III have a policy?', *History*, lv (1968), pp. 203–16; *England and its Rulers 1066–1272* (1983), pp. 214–15, 239–40, 263–4, 268, 270–3, 276.

49 D. A. Carpenter: 'King, magnates and society: the personal rule of Henry III, 1234–1258', *Speculum*, lx (1985), pp. 39–70; 'What happened in 1258?', in J. Gillingham and J. C. Holt, eds., *War and Government in the Middle Ages: Essays in Honour of J. O, Prestwich* (Woodbridge, 1984), pp. 106–19; cf. H. Ridgeway, 'King Henry III and the "aliens", 1236–72', in P. R. Coss and S. D. Lloyd, eds., *Thirteenth Century England*, ii (1988), pp. 81–92.

50 Most of this is documented by C. M. Barron: 'The tyranny of Richard II', *Bulletin of the Institute of Historical Research*, xli (1968), pp. 1–18; 'The art of kingship: Richard II, 1377–99', *History Today*, xxxv (June 1985), pp. 33–5; 'The deposition of Richard II', in J. Taylor and W. Childs, eds., *Politics and Crisis in Fourteenth-Century England* (Gloucester, 1990), pp. 132–6 (the last takes a noticeably more favourable view: the quotation in the text is from p. 136); cf. Pugh, *Southampton Plot*, p. 1; C. Given-Wilson, *The English Nobility in the Late Middle Ages* (1987), pp. 169–70; J. L. Gillespie, 'Richard II's Cheshire archers', *Transactions of the Historic Society of Lancashire and Cheshire*, cxxv (1974), pp. 1–40, esp. 1–2, 13, 32.

51 See below, pp. 49–110.

52 J. M. W. Bean, *From Lord to Patron: Lordship in Late Medieval England* (Manchester, 1989), p. 225.

53 See below, pp. 192–5; Gwyn, *King's Cardinal*, pp. 172–3; G. W. Bernard, 'The fortunes of the Greys, earls of Kent, in the early sixteenth century', *Historical Journal*, xxv (1982), pp. 671–85.

54 Bernard, *Power of the Early Tudor Nobility*, pp. 11–29.

55 Public Record Office, SP10/6/16.

56 P. Cronne, *Pre-Industrial Societies* (Oxford, 1989), p. 60.

57 J. R. Dias, 'Politics and administration in Nottinghamshire and Derbyshire, 1590–1640', University of Oxford D.Phil. thesis, 1973, p. 174.

58 J. O. Prestwich, 'The place of the royal household in English history, 1066–1307', *Medieval History*, i (ii) (1991), pp. 37–52; 'The military household of the Norman kings', *English Historical Review*, xcvi (1981), pp. 1, 33–4. Cf. for the reign of Richard II, C. Given-Wilson, *The Royal Household and the King's Affinity: Service, Politics and Finance in England, 1360–1413* (1986).

59 L. Harf-Lanener, 'L'enfer de la cour: la cour de Henri II Plantagenet et la Mesnie Hellequin', in Contamine, *L'état et les aristocraties*, esp. p. 27; cf. F. Autrand, 'De l'enfer au purgatoire', *ibid.*, pp. 51–78.

60 Horrox, *Richard III*, p. 251.

61 Gunn, *Charles Brandon*, p. 226.

62 Mettam, *Power and Faction*, p. 22.

63 Dias, 'Politics and administration', pp. 174, 263, 292–8; W. T. MacCaffrey, 'Talbot and Stanhope: an episode in Elizabethan politics', *Bulletin of the Institute of Historical Research*, xxxiii (1960), pp. 73–85, esp. 85; K. M. Sharpe, 'Crown, parliament and locality: government and communication in early Stuart England', *English Historical Review*, ci (1986), p. 332 (reprinted in Sharpe, *Politics and Ideas*, p. 84); C. Haigh, *Elizabeth I* (1988), pp. 88–9.

64 *HMC, Bath, v*, p. 110.

65 *Ibid.*, pp. 103, 115.

66 *Ibid.*, p. 110.

67 *Ibid.*, pp. 105, 108.

68 J. E. Neale, *The Elizabethan House of Commons* (rev. ed., 1963), pp. 59–63.

69 Dias, 'Politics and administration', ch. vi; MacCaffrey, 'Talbot and Stanhope'.

70 G. R. Batho, 'Gilbert Talbot, seventh earl of Shrewsbury (1553–1616): the "great and glorious earl"?', *Derbyshire Archaeological Journal*, xciii (1973), p. 26.

71 *HMC, Bath, v*, p. 111.

72 I owe this point to Mr H. James.

73 K. B. McFarlane, *The Nobility of Later Medieval England* (Oxford, 1973), p. 120; Given-Wilson, *The English Nobility in the Late Middle Ages*, p. 177. Cf. R. G. Davies, *English Historical Review*, civ (1989), p. 464.

74 See below, pp. 134, 136.

75 M. L. Robertson, 'Profit and purpose in the development of Thomas Cromwell's landed estates', *Journal of British Studies*, xxix (1990), pp. 317–46 at 317–19. Robertson seems to misunderstand the implications of the very considerable landholdings that Cromwell was amassing. His was a long-term investment for his family; that he did not at once join the ranks of the local governing elites in those counties where he acquired land is not because 'he felt no need to join their ranks' (p. 346) but because of his immense duties as Henry VIII's chief minister.

76 G. L. Harriss, 'Introduction', in K. B. McFarlane, *England in the fifteenth century* (1981), p. xxvi.

77 Gunn, *Charles Brandon*, p. 226; J. Guy, *Tudor England* (Oxford, 1988), pp. 63–4.

78 R. W. Kaeuper, *War, Justice and Public Order: England and France in the Later Middle Ages* (Oxford, 1988), pp. 132, 153, 155, 176–8, 181, 282; P. R. Coss, 'Bastard feudalism revised', *Past and Present*, cxxv (1989), esp. pp. 41–2, 47, 50–1, 54–5, 61; A. J. Pollard, *The Wars of the Roses* (1988), pp. 49–50, 53; but contrast with E. Powell, *Kingship, Law and Society: Criminal Justice in the Reign of Henry V* (Oxford, 1989), pp. 10–11, 14–20, 111, 113; J. B. Gillingham, 'Crisis or continuity? The structure of royal authority in England, 1369–1422', in R. Schneider, ed., *Das Spätmitteralterliche Königtum in Europaischen Vergleich* (1987), pp. 64–5, 77–8; J. R. Maddicott, 'Edward I and the lessons of baronial reform: local government, 1258–80', *Thirteenth Century England*, i (1986), p. 29; W. M. Ormrod, *The Reign of Edward III: Crown and Political Society in England 1327–1377* (1990), pp. 157–60.

79 Kaeuper, *War, Justice and Public Order*, p. 185.

80 Harriss, 'Introduction', pp. xx–xxi; Powell, *Kingship, law and society*, pp. 48–9, 97 and *passim*; N. Saul, 'Conflict and consensus in English landed society', in J. Taylor and W. Childs, eds., *Politics and Crisis in Fourteenth-Century England* (Gloucester, 1990), pp. 38–58, esp. pp. 41–2, 45; S. J. Payling, 'The Ampthill dispute: a study in aristocratic lawlessness and the breakdown of Lancastrian government', *English Historical Review*, civ (1989), p. 881; Walker, 'Autorité des magnats', pp. 200–2; Walker, *Lancastrian Affinity*, pp. 4–5; M. H. Keen, *English Society in the Later Middle Ages 1348–1500* (1990), ch. viii, esp. pp. 191, 197, 199–203, 205–6, 214 (a touch too pessimistic in places).

81 James, *Society, Politics and Culture*, pp. 351, 354–6; D. R. Starkey: 'Privy secrets: Henry VIII and the Lords of the Council', *History Today*, xxxvii (August 1987), pp. 23–31; 'Reform in theory and practice, 1450–1540', and 'Winners or losers? The aristocracy, ideology and the establishment of the Tudor privy council', papers read at the Institute of Historical Research, 5 March 1984 and 8 December 1986; J. A. Guy, 'The king's council and political participation', in J. A. Guy and A. Fox, eds., *Reassessing the Henrician Age* (Oxford, 1986), pp. 121–47.

82 B. Worden, *London Review of Books*, 24 November 1988, p. 5.

83 See below, pp. 28–9.

84 Adamson, 'The baronial context', pp. 94, 100–2, 105–6, 108–9 (Essex); 93, 95, 97 (medieval).

85 On 1469–71, 1483–5, see above pp. 10, 41–2, below, pp. 49–51 (but the deficiency of sources for 1469–71 may lead to an underestimation of the involvement of noblemen: I owe this suggestion to Mr C. S. L. Davies); M. Bennett, 'Henry VII and the northern rising of 1489', *English Historical Review*, cf (1990), pp. 34–59, esp. 48; I. Arthurson, 'The rising of 1497: a revolt of the peasantry', in J. Rosenthal and C. Richmond, eds., *People, Politics and Community in the Later Middle Ages* (Gloucester, 1987), p. 11; G. W. Bernard, *War, Taxation and Rebellion in Early Tudor England: Henry VIII, Wolsey and the Amicable Grant of 1525* (Brighton, 1986), esp. pp. 76–95, 136–8; James, *Society, Politics and Culture*, pp. 115,

168–75, 353–4; R. B. Smith, *Land and Politics in the England of Henry VIII: The West Riding of Yorkshire, 1530–1546* (Oxford, 1970), ch. v; C. S. L. Davies, 'Popular religion and the Pilgrimage of Grace', in A. J. Fletcher and J. Stevenson, eds., *Order and Disorder in Early Modern England 1500–1750* (Cambridge, 1985), pp. 58–91; S. J. Gunn, 'Peers, commons and gentry in the Lincolnshire Revolt of 1536', *Past and Present*, cxxiii (1989), pp. 52–79. Cf. the pertinent comments on the minority of Henry III by H. Ridgeway, *English Historical Review*, cvi (1991), p. 668: 'the relative speed with which the baronage returned to accustomed habits of obedience and conservatism'; 'given the extraordinary recent political situation and the fact that the king was a minor it is surprising to note everywhere their reluctance to rebel again after 1217, and the scant support that any such rebellions aroused ... given a reasonably acceptable and (above all) stable regime at court, they seem to have been quite easily manipulated or even circumvented by the government of the day.'

86 Scott, *Algernon Sidney*, pp. 43–7, 146–8, 175, 183–4, 224; Worden, 'Algernon Sidney', esp. p. 17.

87 Taylor, 'The crown and the north of England', pp. 191, 284.

88 M. K. Jones, 'Sir William Stanley of Holt: politics and family allegiance in the late fifteenth century', *Welsh History Review*, xiv (1988), pp. 20–1.

89 Pugh, *Southampton Plot*.

90 Harriss, 'Introduction', pp. xxiii–xxiv.

91 Jones, 'Stanley', pp. 20–1.

92 Pugh, *Southampton Plot*, p. xiv.

93 Cf. J. R. Maddicott, *English Historical Review*, civ (1989), p. 1014.

94 J. C. Holt, *Magna Carta* (Cambridge, 1965); C. Russell, *The Causes of the English Civil War* (Oxford, 1990), pp. 131–53.

95 Carpenter, 'King, magnates and society'; Ridgeway, 'King Henry III and the "Aliens"', pp. 79, 90, 98–9. If it was possible for Edward I to adopt in 1274 the reforms proposed by the 'barons' in 1258–60, if Edward could thus 'steal the whigs' clothes', that does rather suggest what the 'barons' wanted was effective royal government: Maddicott, 'Edward I and the lessons of baronial reform', pp. 10–11, 28. It is only fair to point out that Carpenter has recently adopted a more 'whiggish' approach, emphasising the rapid acceptance of Magna Carta as the foundation of political activity and stressing the role of wider assemblies, especially Great Councils: D. A. Carpenter, *The Minority of Henry III* (1990).

96 Barron, 'The art of kingship', pp. 32–3, 35. Cf. J. Hughes, *Pastors and Visionaries: Religion and Secular Life in Late Medieval Yorkshire* (Woodbridge, 1988), pp. 23, 25.

97 Adamson, 'The baronial context'; H. R. Trevor-Roper, 'The continuity of the English Revolution', *Transactions of the Royal Historical Society*, 6th series, i (1991), pp. 121–35. Russell seems to endorse an aristocratic *constitutionalism*, writing of 'the whole conciliar tradition of English constitutionalism', illustrating it from the reigns of Henry III, Edward II and Richard II, and stressing the desire of some noblemen to secure appointment to specified offices and to the council. But elsewhere Russell plays down that supposed tradition and links those demands rather to the wishes of the Scots and to the example furnished by the quasi-conciliar role of the General Assembly of the Kirk. And in denying that there was any *parliamentary* constitutionalism, Russell seems to undermine his case for an aristocratic conciliar tradition. In arguing that such constitutional theories as were bruited in 1640–2 were *ad hoc*, makeshift, ramshackle, and designed for the immediate purpose of clipping the king's wings, Russell inadvertently casts doubt on *any* constitutional interpretation of the politics of 1640–2: 'aristocratic conciliarism' is as vulnerable as parliamentary constitutionalism to such criticisms (Russell, *Causes of the English Civil War*, pp. 28, 34, 133, 159–60, 188).

98 On the role of the Commons in the 1380s in seeking to influence the composition and powers of the council and the choice of chancellor, treasurers and officers of the royal household, see W. M. Ormrod, 'The peasants' revolt and the government of England', *Journal of British Studies*, xxx (1990), pp. 28–9.

99   T. F. Mayer, *Thomas Starkey and the Commonwealth: Humanist Politics and Religion in the Reign of Henry VIII* (Cambridge, 1989), p. 107, and pp. 32, 69, 71, 103, 132–4, 137, 154–7, 166–8; 'Faction and ideology: Thomas Starkey's dialogue', *Historical Journal*, xxviii (1985), pp. 17–18; K. M. Burton, ed., *A Dialogue between Reginald Pole and Thomas Lupset by Thomas Starkey* (1948), pp. 79–80, 123–4, 148, 161 (still the most accessible edition).

100   Mayer, *Starkey and the Commonwealth*, pp. 4–5, 8, 90, 104; 'Faction and ideology', p. 2.

101   Mayer, *Starkey and the Commonwealth*, pp. 6, 90, 103–4; 'Thomas Starkey: an unknown conciliarist at the court of Henry VIII', *Journal of the History of Ideas*, xlix (1988), p. 226.

102   Mayer, *Starkey and the Commonwealth*, pp. 4–5; 'A diet for Henry VIII: the failure of Reginald Pole's 1537 legation', *Journal of British Studies*, xxvi (1987) pp. 305–31; Hollger, 'Reginald Pole', pp. 7–11.

103   J. O. Prestwich, 'The treason of Geoffrey de Mandeville', *English Historical Review*, ciii (1988), p. 309.

104   J. R. Lander, 'Family, "Friends" and Politics in fifteenth-century England', in R. A. Griffiths and J. Sherborne, eds., *Kings and Nobles in the Later Middle Ages* (Gloucester, 1986), pp. 27–40. For scepticism about blood-relationships in forming baronial parties in an earlier period see J. C. Holt, 'Feudal society and the family in early medieval England: III, Patronage and Politics', *Transactions of the Royal Historical Society*, 5th series, xxxiv (1984), pp. 1–26.

105   Clanchy, *England and its rulers*, pp. 214–5. Was it not conventional for fallen ministers to be charged with having disdained the nobility of the realm, as Thomas Cromwell was? (*LP*, XV, 498 (60)).

106   E. g. Starkey, 'Privy secrets and Henry VIII', pp. 23–31; D. R. Starkey, 'Court, council and nobility in Tudor England', in R. G. Asch and A. M. Birke, eds., *Princes, Patronage and the Nobility: The Court at the Beginning of the Modern Age* (Oxford, 1991), pp. 176, 189; Miller, *Henry VIII and the English Nobility*, p. 79.

107   Gwyn, *King's Cardinal*, pp. 565–72, 582; Gunn, *Charles Brandon*, pp. 103, 106, 109–10.

108   See below, pp. 111–33.

109   Cited by Kaeuper, *War, Justice and Public Order*, p. 220.

110   Cf. P. Dixon, *English Historical Review*, c (1985), pp. 372–3; A. Macquarrie, *English Historical Review*, ciii (1988), pp. 105–6; D. J. C. King, *The Castle in England and Wales* (1988), p. 2.

111   R. Eales, 'Castles and politics in England, 1215–1224', *Thirteenth Century England*, ii (1986), pp. 26, 41; R. R. Davies, 'Kings, lords and liberties in the March of Wales, 1066–1272', *Transactions of the Royal Historical Society*, 5th series, xxviii (1978), pp. 47–8; King, *Castles*, pp. 10–11.

112   Pace C. Coulson, 'Structural symbolism in medieval castle architecture', *Journal of the British Archaeological Association*, cxxxii (1979), pp. 79–90.

113   D. J. Turner, 'Bodiam, Sussex: true castle or old soldier's dream house', in W. M. Ormrod, ed., *England in the Fourteenth Century* (Woodbridge, 1986), pp. 267–77; Coulson, 'Structural symbolism', p. 76; D. A. Hinton, *Archaeology, Economy and Society: England from the Fifth to the Fifteenth Century* (1990), p. 188; King, *Castles*, p. 150.

114   M. W. Thompson, *The Decline of the Castle* (Cambridge, 1988), pp. 79, 38–42, 4, 1, 99; King, *Castles*, pp. 150–1, 156, 162–3; M. G. A. Vale, *War and Chivalry*, p. 143; J. R. Kenyon, *Medieval Archaeology*, xxiii (1989), p. 263; Hinton, *Archaeology, Economy and Society*, pp. 209–10; N. Pevsner, J. Harris and N. Antram, *The Buildings of England: Lincolnshire* (2nd ed., 1989), p. 749; A. Emery, 'Ralph, Lord Cromwell's Manor at Wingfield (1439–c. 1450): its construction, design and influence', *Archaeological Journal*, cxlii (1985), pp. 276–339 (for comments about Tattershall, pp. 314, 321; and for scepticism about the defensive potential of South Wingfield, Derbyshire); J. R. Kenyon, 'The gunloops

at Raglan Castle, Gwent', in J. R. Kenyon and R. Avent, eds., *Castles in Wales and the Marches* (Cardiff, 1987), pp. 161–72.

115 A. Goodman, *The Wars of the Roses* (1981), pp. 183–6, 188–9, 191; King, *Castles*, p. 162; A. Emery, 'The development of Raglan and keeps in late medieval England', *Archaeological Journal*, cxxxii (1975), pp. 151–86.

116 Thompson, *Decline of the Castle*, pp. 33, 35; Goodman, *Wars of the Roses*, p. 183.

117 E. Lodge, ed., *Illustrations of British History* (3 vols., 1791), ii. 49.

118 Thompson, *Decline of the Castle*, pp. 139, 141–2, 154.

119 Cf. S. J. Gunn and P. G. Lindley, 'Charles Brandon's Westhorpe: an early Tudor courtyard house in Suffolk', *Archaeological Journal*, cxiv (1988), p. 278.

120 Kaeuper, *War, Justice and Public Order*, p. 217.

121 Eales, 'Castles and politics', pp. 28–9.

122 Hinton, *Archaeology, Economy and Society*, p. 115.

123 Kaeuper, *War, Justice and Public Order*, p. 211.

124 King, *Castles*, p. 23.

125 Coulson, 'Structural symbolism', pp. 72 n. 1, 78–9, 84; Thompson, *Decline of the Castle*; pp. 18–19, 111; Kaeuper, *War, Justice and Public Order*, pp. 214, 219, notes Coulson's evidence but fails to grasp how it must undermine his own argument.

126 As claimed by e.g. Hinton, *Archaeology, Economy and Society*, p. 210; J. R. Kenyon, 'Early artillery fortifications in England and Wales: a preliminary survey and reappraisal', *Archaeological Journal*, cxxxviii (1981), p. 228. But cf. A. D. K. Hawkyard, 'Thornbury Castle', *Transactions of the Bristol and Gloucestershire Archaeological Society*, xc (1977), pp. 51–8.

127 R. A. Brown and H. M. Colvin, 'The king's castles', in H. M. Colvin, ed., *The History of the King's Works, vol. I, The Middle Ages* (1963), p. 240.

128 H. M. Colvin and J. Summerson, 'The royal castles', in H. M. Colvin, ed., *The History of the King's Works, vol. III (part I) 1485–1660* (1975), p. 226, who read too much deliberate policy into the evidence they present; Miller, *Henry VIII and the English Nobility*, pp. 217–20, 227–30.

129 King, *Castles*, p. 23; Thompson, *Decline of the Castle*, pp. 4, 13; Parker, *Military Revolution*, p. 42.

130 Thompson, *Decline of the Castle*, p. 109.

131 K. M. Brown, *Bloodfeud in Scotland, 1573–1625: Violence, Justice and Politics in an Early Modern Society* (Edinburgh, 1986), pp. 7, 19, 22, 17, 24, 26, 28, 30, 33, 58, 65–71, 267, 190. Cf. 'Gentlemen and thugs in seventeenth century Britain', *History Today* (October 1990), pp. 27–32.

132 *Ibid.*, pp. 18–19, 22, 52, 48, 22, 43, 98, 101, 133, 234, 192, 57, 272, 267, 266, 216, 234, 258. Cf. C. V. Phythian-Adams, 'Rituals of personal confrontation in late medieval England', *Bulletin of the John Rylands Library*, lxxiii (1991), pp. 65–90.

133 *Ibid.*, chs. 4 and 6; pp. 124–5, 91, 127–9, 157, 165, 172.

134 M. Jones, 'L'aristocratie bretonne au XVe siècle', in Contamine, ed., *L'état et les aristocraties*, pp. 133; Kaeuper, *War, Justice and Public Order*, pp. 188, 195; Pollard, *Wars of the Roses*, p. 57; Payling, 'Ampthill dispute', pp. 881–2, 907.

135 Payling, 'Ampthill dispute'. Pollard, *North-Eastern England*, emphasises (sometimes against the main thrust of his argument) that the Percys and the Nevills were not long-standing enemies before 1450 and that as late as 1453 there was no dispute between them. Even in 1454 reconciliation was not impossible. What was crucial was the failure of Henry VI to arbitrate between and to discipline those disputing the complex landed transactions arising from a marriage. That makes it difficult to accept Pollard's assertion that the Nevills of Middleham were 'over-mighty subjects'. At most the Percys – or Egremont – perceived them as threatening, and feared a reduction of Percy influence, but that hardly makes the Nevills 'over-mighty' on a national scale. It would have made little difference if the crown had had more lands directly under its control in the north-east. Moreover, the swings and roundabouts of the mid and late 1450s make it hard to write of a 'Nevill

ascendancy' then: the Nevills had to fight for the supremacy that they from time to time enjoyed. (Pollard, *North-Eastern England*, pp. 245–6, 248, 253, 255–7, 262, 273–8, 413.)

136   Harriss, 'Introduction', p. xxiv; cf. W. M. Ormrod, 'Edward III and the recovery of royal authority in England, 1340–60', *History*, lxxii (1987), pp. 6, 9; *Reign of Edward III*, pp. 18–19, 44–5; Gunn, 'Tournaments and early Tudor chivalry'.

137   G. E. Aylmer, 'Collective mentalities in mid seventeenth century England: II, Royalist attitudes', *Transactions of the Royal Historical Society*, 5th series, xxxvii (1987), p. 30.

138   J. Gillingham, 'War and Chivalry in the *History of William the Marshal*', *Thirteenth Century England*, ii (1988), pp. 3 n. 3, 12–13.

139   M. K. Jones, 'Somerset, York and the Wars of the Roses', *English Historical Review*, civ (1989), pp. 306–7.

140   M. Keen, *Chivalry* (1984), pp. 232, 236, 250, 6–15, 21, 29–31, 225–7, 229; M. Vale, *War and Chivalry: Warfare and Aristocratic Culture in England, France and Burgundy at the End of the Middle Ages* (1981), pp. 1, 6, 24, 39–51, 87, 167–8, 170, 174; pp. 33–61 do not give an impression of political rivalry.

141   R. Frame, review of K. J. Stringer, ed., *Essays on the nobility of Scotland* (Edinburgh, 1985), *History*, lxxi (1986), p. 504.

142   R. R. Davies, *Welsh History Review*, xiii (1987), p. 368.

143   Cronne, *Pre-industrial societies*, pp. 58, 66.

144   *Ibid.*, p. 182; Davies, *Welsh History Review*, xiii (1987), p. 368.

145   Cf. Jouanna, *Le devoir de révolte*, p. 39; Given-Wilson, *English Nobility*, p. 136; Pugh, *Southampton Plot*, p. xii.

Henry VII and the English nobility

The battle of Bosworth, fought on 22 August 1485, was not one of the greatest conflicts that took place during the Wars of the Roses. The fighting, which apparently began early in the day, lasted for only about two hours, and the outcome of this short contest between two armies whose strength was probably evenly matched was soon decided by treachery and treason. Henry Percy, fourth earl of Northumberland, who had brought to the field the largest contingent on the king's side (perhaps 3,000 men) wisely took care to remain inactive. Lord Stanley's followers (in all probability just as numerous as the Percy squadron), who were commanded in his absence by his more venturesome younger brother, Sir William, ended the rule of the Yorkist dynasty by at last intervening in the fray on behalf of Henry Tudor.[1] Although thirty-eight English peers were summoned to parliament in 1484, only five of them felt sufficiently committed to King Richard's cause to join him and fight at Bosworth. John Howard, duke of Norfolk and Walter Devereux, Lord Ferrers of Chartley (both elderly men) were the most notable casualties among Richard III's staunch partisans. Norfolk's heir, Thomas Howard, earl of Surrey, Francis, Lord Lovel (one of the king's few personal friends) and the young John, Lord Zouche of Harringworth were able to make their escape in the rout after the battle, and all three of them were inevitably attainted in Henry VII's first parliament, held late in 1485.[2] Despite the great redistribution of patronage that he had carried out, it is remarkable how little loyalty Richard III could inspire or compel among the magnates, knights and gentry more than two years after his usurpation. By holding aloof from the struggle for the crown (as they had already done so effectively in 1470–1), the majority of the English nobility demonstrated in August 1485 that once again they had the power to settle the fate of the House of York, and that political decision soon proved final and irreversible.

When Henry VII became king of England, he was well known to only a few of the English peers. His boyhood acquaintance with them had become remote during his prolonged French exile, which lasted for fourteen years after he fled to Brittany in 1471. When he was resident in the Herbert household at Raglan between 1462 and 1469, as the ward and prospective son-in-law of William (d. 1469), Lord Herbert (and afterwards briefly earl of Pembroke), he was brought up with his guardian's heir, William (d. 1490), afterwards earl of Huntingdon, and Henry Percy (d. 1489), who became fourth earl of Northumberland and married Maud Herbert, Henry Tudor's intended bride. Young Henry Tudor's contacts with William Berkeley (1426–92), earl of Nottingham were probably a consequence of his early connections with the Herberts of Raglan.[3] In 1485 the new king's most pressing political need was to win the confidence and trust of the English magnates, who numbered no more than fifty-five families. During the decisive battle that gained him the kingdom, the Tudor pretender was attended by only one English noble, his fellow exile, John de Vere (1443–1513), earl of Oxford, who promptly became one of the principal profiteers who were enriched by this latest change of dynasty.[4] There is no contemporary record that Jasper Tudor, earl of Pembroke, fought at Bosworth, and in view of the presence of a hostile Yorkist garrison at Harlech, held by that staunch Ricardian, Sir Roger Kynaston of Hordley, co. Salop, he may have decided as a precaution to remain in Wales in order to safeguard his nephew's line of retreat, in case their hazardous enterprise should end in failure and defeat.[5]

The founding of the Tudor dynasty was the consequence of a shrewd and well-timed French intervention in English affairs, and the credit for triumphant success of the Bosworth campaign must be chiefly ascribed to the military skill of Philibert de Chandée, the captain of Henry VII's mercenary troops, who was created earl of Bath as his reward for his invaluable services on 6 January 1486. The fiasco of Buckingham's rebellion in October 1483 had demonstrated that the age of the over-mighty subject was already past. Although Henry Stafford (c. 1456–83), second duke of Buckingham, was more of a kingmaker in 1483 than Richard Nevill (1428–71), earl of Warwick had ever been, his decision to desert Richard III within a few months of his accession and replace him by the exiled Henry Tudor was a fatal error of judgement. There was scant support among the English nobility in the autumn of 1483 for Buckingham's bid to use the Tudor pretender in order to overthrow King Richard. Without massive French assistance, which provided him with a well-equipped army of some 4,000 troops, a fleet under the capable command of the Vice-Admiral Coulon and a loan of 40,000 *livres tournois* to meet his expenses, Henry Tudor could not have embarked on his great adventure and invaded England in August 1485.[6] Richard III under-estimated the ample resources that Charles VIII's government had so astutely put at his rival's disposal, and his mismanagement of the Bosworth campaign did much to give Henry Tudor his easy and unexpected victory. By contrast, Philibert de Chandée conducted his *blitzkreig* in August 1485 with Napoleonic efficiency, and within a fortnight he accomplished his mission in England. King Richard was the victim of his own miscalcula-tions and his inability to recall the strategic lessons of the battle of Tewkesbury, fought on 4 May 1471, in which, as one of Edward IV's principal lieutenants, he had played a prominent part. After their unopposed landing in Milford Haven on 7 August, the well-disciplined invading army advanced on its carefully-chosen route through Wales with great speed and took Richard III by surprise. By 17 August, Henry Tudor's troops, now strongly reinforced by his Welsh allies and some of his English adherents, were at Shrewsbury, having covered a distance of about 150 miles in only ten days, and that was a remarkable feat.[7] When his last battle was fought at Bosworth five days later, King Richard was not adequately prepared, as he had been unable in so sort a time to muster sufficiently strong support from his friends and well-wishers north of the Trent. Robert Morton, esquire, of Bawtry, co. York, who in his will, made on 20 August, affirmed that he was going forth 'to maintain our most excellent king Richard III against the rebellion raised against him in this land',[8] had, fortunately for himself, left his journey too late and so he avoided disaster. How far his political opinions may have been shared by other members of the Yorkshire gentry we cannot tell, but when the first serious challenge to Tudor rule occurred during Lambert Simnel's rebellion in the summer of 1487, most erstwhile Ricardians had already rapidly become reconciled to the new regime and, with sound common sense, they did not stir. Apart from Richard III's nephew (and prospective heir-apparent), John de la Pole, earl of Lincoln, and Francis, Lord Lovel (who had gone into hiding after Bosworth), the only malcontent peers disposed to aid the imposter Lambert Simnel's pretensions, when he was posing as the captive Edward Plantagenet, earl of Warwick, were two Yorkshire barons, John (d. 1498), Lord Scrope of Bolton, and his distant kinsman, the impoverished Thomas (1459–93), Lord Scrope of Masham. Bosworth was (as Dr B. P. Wolffe observed) 'the victory of the loyal Yorkists',[9] and regardless of the obvious defects in Henry VII's claim to the crown by hereditary right, the English nobility as a class had no difficulty in 1485 in accepting another change of dynasty.

Foreign intervention in English affairs had on three occasions (in 1470, 1471 and 1485) within less than twenty years brought about the replacement of one king by another, and the ease with which Richard III's downfall had been accomplished was bound to encourage before long an attempt to reverse the verdict of Bosworth. Margaret of York (1446–1503), dowager–duchess of Burgundy, was Edward IV's youngest sister and Henry VII's most dangerous foe abroad. As Charles the Bold's widow, she had ample resources to finance the force of some 2,000 German and Swiss mercenaries, led by their experienced captain, Martin Schwarz, who landed in Ireland on 5 May 1487, in a bid to make the bogus 'King Edward', alias Lambert Simnel (who was crowned in Dublin on 24 May) king of England. When Schwarz and his army landed near Furness, co. Lancashire, on 4 June, his troops had been reinforced by a horde of some 6,000 ill-equipped Irish levies, but when the last battle of the Wars of the Roses was fought on 16 June 1487 at Stoke-by-Newark (East Stoke), co. Notts., the invaders found themselves heavily outnumbered by Henry VII's loyal supporters. This incursion had been instigated by John de la Pole, earl of Lincoln, who was killed during the fighting, and the irreconcilable Francis, Lord Lovel (once again fortunate enough to survive defeat and make his escape, this time to Scotland).[10] The assistance from former Ricardians that Lincoln had led Schwarz to expect was not forthcoming, and before the two armies met at Stoke, the brave German commander realised that he had been deceived. He discovered too late that he had no hope of reenacting the role that Philibert de Chandée had played during the Bosworth campaign, and regardless of the odds against him, he faced defeat and annihilation with great courage.

There was no prospect that Stoke would become another Bosworth, and this little-known battle did not go on for three hours (as Francis, Lord Bacon, in *The History of the Reign of King Henry the Seventh* (1622), so wrongly believed), with the issue in doubt until the last. Because Henry VII's army was so much stronger than the alien troops recruited by his enemies, Schwarz and the earl of Lincoln resolved to concentrate all their forces in a single massive squadron, instead of dispersing their men in three battalions as was customary and by that time traditional in late medieval warfare. Schwarz's strategy was successfully countered by the earl of Oxford's sound decision to reinforce the vanguard of the king's army, which was under his command, with two flanking wings. Because of their overwhelming superiority in archers, Stoke proved a swift and easy victory for Henry VII's followers, and as the royal army was advancing in column, with plenty of strength held in reserve, only the vanguard was engaged in routing the rebels and their German hirelings. It was not necessary or possible (in view of the limited scope of the battle-front) for two of the three squadrons of the king's supporters to take part in the mêlée, and that consideration has given rise to the unfounded and misleading conjecture (first put forward by H. A. L. Fisher in 1906) that the majority of Henry VII's men at Stoke were too timid or disloyal to fight on his behalf. During this short campaign the king was attended by the earls of Oxford and Shrewsbury, Edward Grey, Viscount Lisle and six barons, amongst whom his step-brother, George (d. 1503), Lord Strange (the earl of Derby's eldest son and heir) brought the largest single contingent, a striking display of the military resources that the Stanley family could now employ.[11]

There was no major rebellion in England during the decade following the battle of Stoke. The local rising in Yorkshire, which led to the murder of Henry Percy, fourth earl of Northumberland, on 28 April 1489, was easily suppressed, and, in that short-lived crisis, Henry VII had the active support of the majority of the English peers. Chiefly because of the emergence of another pretender, Perkin Warbeck, who proved far more dangerous and resourceful than the boy Lambert Simnel, the atmosphere of political insecurity still persisted throughout those relatively peaceful years. Warbeck, a native of Tournai, was induced by Yorkist conspirators when he was in Ireland in 1491 to assume the role of Richard, duke of York, Edward IV's younger son, who had in 1483 been put to death in the Tower, together with his elder brother, Edward V. After the fiasco of his attempt to land in Kent (with a force of Flemish mercenaries) on 3 July 1495, Warbeck eventually found refuge at the Scottish court, and James IV married this audacious fraud to his kinswoman, Lady Catherine Gordon.[12] Despite the measure of international recognition and encouragement that Warbeck was able to procure (especially from Maximilian of Habsburg, who ruled the Netherlands during the minority of his son, Philip, the future king of Castile), the English nobility showed scant interest in his claims. In 1495, the earl of Derby's younger brother, Sir William Stanley, who had indiscreetly been prepared to consider the possibility that Warbeck might indeed be a son of King Edward IV, was executed for treason, but only one peer, John Radcliffe, Lord FitzWalter, was among the small group of notables who became involved in this affair. Although Radcliffe had been made steward of the king's household in October 1485, little is known of his previous career, and it is not easy to see what he had done to merit his appointment to high office at court. By 1495 he undoubtedly had a grievance against Henry VII, because a few years earlier he had been worsted in a dispute with William Doget, and his wife, Jane, concerning Curson's manor in co. Norfolk. When the case was heard at a meeting of the king's council in the Star Chamber, the Dogets won because of royal intervention in their favour. Unlike Edward IV, who chose to side with the stronger of the two parties when the Pastons were at odds with the last Mowbray duke of Norfolk, Henry VII preferred to dispense impartial justice, and it is noteworthy that he personally summed up the issues raised in this lawsuit. Lord FitzWalter's treason cost him his life only because he attempted, without success, to escape from his imprisonment at Guines, near Calais, in 1496.[13]

1497 was a year of acute and dangerous political upheaval, and once these perils had subsided, this interlude could be seen as a major turning point in the establishment of the Tudor dynasty. After Henry VII's government had put down the two west country risings that occurred within the space of six months, his throne was never again in jeopardy. The Cornish revolt, which broke out suddenly in May 1497, was provoked by an exceptionally burdensome levy of direct taxation; two grants (amounting to four fifteenths and tenths) had been made in the king's sixth parliament, held chiefly for fiscal reasons, which had been summoned for a short session early in that year. These taxes were likely to yield about £135,000, a sum greater than the oppressive poll tax of 1381 had been expected to produce. Furthermore, as the traditional exemptions of £6,000 in respect of each fifteenth and tenth were omitted in the second grant made by the Commons, the charge imposed on the inhabitants of the less prosperous parts of the realm was bound to be severe. No resistance was expected, and this uprising was remarkable because Cornwall, one of the poorest counties in England, had never rebelled against royal authority before. In failing to foresee that trouble was likely, the king and his ministers had evidently already forgotten the disturbances in Yorkshire that led in April 1489 to the death of Henry Percy, fourth earl of Northumberland; on that occasion, a formidable local riot had been caused by the collection of direct taxation in a region unaccustomed to contributing overmuch to relieve the crown's financial necessities. This eruption of popular discontent in a shire as remote as Cornwall found Henry VII wholly unprepared, and at first he was at a serious disadvantage because most of the troops that should have been at his disposal were already engaged in preparations for the forthcoming Scottish campaign. Until the army of 8,000 men commanded by Giles, Lord Daubeney had been recalled from northern England where they had been despatched to assist the king's lieutenant, Thomas Howard, earl of Surrey, the king (who was in Oxfordshire in mid-June) was unable to resist the advance of the rebels, and consequently they marched unopposed across southern England from Cornwall to Kent.[14]

The defeat of the insurgents at Blackheath on 17 June led to the collapse of this spontaneous and short-lived rising, and the king's victory was not followed by harsh reprisals. Although Kent was the most rebellious county in fifteenth-century England, in 1497 the Kentishmen prudently decided to remain loyal to the king (as they had done two generations earlier when Richard Plantagenet, duke of York, made his first, and sadly ill-judged, attempt to overthrow Henry VI's government in the spring of 1452). Kent was quiet during this last crisis towards the close of the fifteenth century, largely because both the chief magnates in the county, George Nevill (d. 1535), Lord Abergavenny and John Brooke (d. 1512), Lord Cobham, did not waver in their allegiance to the king. The gentry, the dominant class in Kentish society, followed their lead and showed no readiness to identify themselves with a lower-class rebel movement.[15] Only one member of the English peerage, James Tuchet (1463–97), Lord Audley, ignored the risks that treason involved and joined the Cornish insurgents; he became their chief captain when their host reached Wells. His defection has been attributed to a private grievance, a quarrel with John, Lord Cheyne, but financial difficulties may have been a more compelling motive for Audley's decision to align himself with a taxpayers' revolt; he was one of the poorer English barons, less wealthy than some of the richer gentry.[16] In what proved to be the last battle that he ever had to fight, Henry VII was heavily dependent on the support of that veteran of the dynastic civil wars, John de Vere, earl of Oxford, and his retainers, and he owed much to the reckless valour of the chamberlain of the royal household, Giles, Lord Daubeney (who was at one stage captured by the rebels during the engagement at Blackheath) and his indispensable followers. Despite the grave dangers presented by the progress of the Cornishmen as they stubbornly made their way towards London, the king did not think it necessary in this crisis to issue commissions of array. He was confident of the loyalty of the Londoners and he was able to weather this storm, relying on the military strength of the royal household and that of his own retainers and feed-men in the shires. Before the débâcle at Blackheath, some of the rebels, dismayed by the power of the king's army, sought to buy a royal pardon by betraying their own leaders, Lord Audley, Michael Joseph the blacksmith, and the lawyer, Thomas Flammock. Although a few peers, including George Grey (d. 1503), earl of Kent, his half-brother, Henry Bourchier (d. 1540), earl of Essex, the young Henry Percy (1478–1527), earl of Northumberland, and probably Lords Abergavenny and Cobham, came to the king's aid, Henry VII was able to surmount this sudden challenge to his government without help from most of the English nobility,[17] and, fortified by his success, he encountered no further resistance to his policies during the rest of his reign.

Throughout his career, Henry VII was a lucky man and it was one of his greatest strokes of good fortune that the handsome and plausible imposter, Perkin Warbeck (who had left Scotland and returned to Ireland in a bid to gain support), did not arrive in Cornwall until 7 September, and by that time he had already missed his only chance of putting himself at the head of a major popular revolt in any part of England. The failure on 17–18 September of the rebels' attack on Exeter, which was strongly defended in the king's name by the only great magnate in the west country, the trustworthy Edward Courtenay, earl of Devon, and his son and heir, Sir William, soon caused Warbeck to lose heart, and his surrender, soon after his flight to take sanctuary at Beaulieu Abbey, co. Hants., completed the final stage of the Tudor triumph over the king's enemies in England.[18] Warbeck was not the last pretender to trouble Henry VII. Ralph Wilsford, the son of a London cordwainer, who was foolhardy enough to seek to repeat Lambert Simnel's venture and impersonate the last of the male Plantagenets, the imprisoned Edward, earl of Warwick, was soon apprehended and executed on 12 February 1499.[19] After 1497, Tudor government did not have to withstand a widespread popular insurrection again for nearly forty years; in 1525, timely concessions pacified the resistance aroused by the Amicable Grant. The Pilgrimage of Grace late in 1536 was the next challenge to royal authority resulting from discontent among the lower classes, and throughout that period there was never any danger of an aristocratic conspiracy or revolt. During the last twelve years of his reign, Henry VII was able to govern England as he wished. His growing international prestige was enhanced by the successful conclusion of the lengthy negotiations for a Spanish marriage alliance. In August 1497 Arthur, prince of Wales, was betrothed to Catherine of Aragon, whose political assets included her descent from John of Gaunt (d. 1399), duke of Lancaster. From 1497 onwards, foreign envoys began to comment on Henry VII's accumulated wealth, and his reputation for great affluence did much to strengthen confidence abroad in the growing stability of his newly-founded regime.[20]

The insecurity of the Tudor dynasty in the early years of Henry VII's reign has frequently been exaggerated and his victory at Bosworth has often been reckoned as a fortuitous event, merely the chance and unpredictable outcome of the shallowness and fickleness of aristocratic loyalties in the age of Lancaster and York. In G. R. Elton's view, 'if Henry VII had depended for his success on physical force he would not have lasted many years', and furthermore he finds that 'it is not easy to say in what his strength lay'.[21] During his later years, the first Tudor king was more fully in control of England than any of his predecessors since the Norman conquest, and the greater effectiveness of royal authority that was now firmly exercised was most manifest in the crown's dealings with the English nobility. For S. T. Bindoff, the principal task that faced 'the most uniformly successful of English kings' was deflating the swollen pretensions of an insubordinate and over-mighty aristocracy, and his problem was 'how to suppress the magnates' abuse of their power while preserving the power itself'. By the opening decade of the sixteenth century, that aim had apparently been achieved, and Professor J. R. Lander has depicted the parliamentary peerage of early Tudor England as politically impotent, after having been reduced to a state of nervous subjection to the royal will.[22] As Henry VII's reign still awaits its historian, it is far from clear how this remarkable transformation in the relationship between the monarchy and the nobility had been brought about within the space of less than twenty-four years.

II

Tudor rule provided a welcome and prolonged period of political stability for the English aristocracy between the overthrow of Richard III and the trial and execution in 1521 on charges of high treason of the richest and most powerful magnate of that age, Edward Stafford, duke of Buckingham, who had royal ancestry. After the sentences imposed on the vanquished in the parliament of 1485, only four peers suffered the penalties of attainder during Henry VII's reign. John de la Pole, earl of Lincoln, who was killed at the battle of Stoke, was the most prominent of the Yorkist malcontents involved in Lambert Simnel's rebellion in 1487; John Radcliffe, Lord FitzWalter was attainted over a year before he was beheaded for treason in 1496; and one of the leaders of the Cornish rebels, James, Lord Audley, was executed in 1497. There were no more attainders of members of the English peerage between 1497 and 1523, apart from that in 1504 of the former earl of Suffolk, Edmund de la Pole (d. 1513), who had fled abroad for a second time in 1501. Four of the five attainders enacted in 1485 of lords who had fought for Richard III at Bosworth were reversed only four years later in 1489.[23] Although these facts are well known and are not in dispute, Professor Lander has argued that for the English nobility 'matters changed considerably for the worse under Henry VII'. His views are largely based on an analysis of the bonds and recognizances that were used in an unprecedented fashion, especially between 1502 and 1509, to bind most members of the English nobility with financial obligations towards the crown. These recognizances (i.e., bonds, subject to a condition, with a monetary penalty attached, in case of non-observance) have come to be regarded as comprising an essential part of Henry VII's system of government. K. B. McFarlane even considered that the 'point had almost been reached where it could be said that Henry VII governed by recognizance'.[24]

In his essay on 'Bonds, coercion and fear: Henry VII and the peerage' (published in 1971 and reprinted without revision in 1976), Professor J. R. Lander vividly depicted the king's suspicions in his later years as being expressed in his oppression of the English magnates by means of a 'terrifying system of suspended penalties'. According to Lander's calculations, as a consequence of these recognizances the majority of the English peers (at least 75 per cent of them) were 'legally and financially in the king's power and at his mercy' at some time during Henry VII's reign. These conclusions have been accepted by Professor S. B. Chrimes in his *Henry VII* (1972), a laborious 'study of the impact of Henry Tudor upon the government of England', and C. S. L. Davies in *Peace, Print and Protestantism 1450–1558* (1976) found Henry VII's treatment of the English magnates in his last years as 'uncomfortably reminiscent of the reign of King John'.[25]

Until far more is known of the relations between the early Tudor kings and the English baronage, the political history of that period is likely to remain insufficiently investigated and inadequately understood. Lately Henry VII's personal reputation as a ruler who aimed to do justice has been adversely affected, and his government of England, particularly in its last phase, has come to be seen as unduly arbitrary and oppressive. These views have now become firmly established as a result of a cursory and superficial enquiry into his dealings with some English noble families and other members of the propertied classes. The publication in 1955 and 1963 of the final volumes of the *Calendar of Close Rolls*, which covered Henry VII's reign, at last made available in print summaries of most of the recognizances given by members of the English nobility to the crown between 1485 and 1509. Although the calendaring of documents in the second of those two volumes is regarded as generally of a high standard, the quality of the work in the first volume left much to be desired; furthermore, important details in these recognizances were omitted and therefore reference to the series of

Chancery Close Rolls in some instances is unavoidable.[26] Recognizances made between Henry VII and his subjects can be grouped into three main categories. First, some (but not very many e were concerned with securing a better maintenance of public order, and bonds were given as a guarantee of keeping the peace, being of good conduct and, on occasion, appearing in person before the king and his council on specified dates. Secondly, royal officials, and especially the constables of the king's castles, were bound, often under elaborate conditions, to be of good conduct during their period of office, and they were made liable to serious financial penalties in case of default of duty. Thirdly, and these recognizances were probably the most numerous category, the king was concerned to ensure the full satisfaction of fiscal claims arising from the crown's prerogative rights of the wardship and marriage of minors who held tenancies-in-chief, and also the payment of rent due from leases of lands belonging to the king or in his custody. A distinction must be drawn between the recognizances given by peers (and also lesser persons) on their own behalf, in respect of their own conduct, and similar bonds that were often given as sureties in respect of obligations incurred by others as a result of recognizances made with the king. Those who entered into such onerous commitments on behalf of their relatives, friends or business associates presumably did so of their own volition, having appraised the measure of financial risk that was probably involved, and there is no evidence to suggest that they were acting in response to royal influence or pressure put upon them.

Since the reign of Henry V, it had become a regular part of the practice of English government for the king to take recognizances for great sums of money, in an attempt to curb outbreaks of aristocratic lawlessness; in November 1413 ten peers (including the earls of Arundel, March and Nottingham) were required to give bonds totalling in all 80,000 marks, which were liable to forfeiture if they committed a breach of the peace.[27] During the Yorkist period there was a further development in this well-established system of financial penalties; an obligation to appear before the king and council on a fixed day became a feature of some recognizances, and on occasion persons who defaulted were liable to forfeit huge sums that they could not possibly have paid. Until the use of such punitive sanctions by Edward IV and Richard III has been more thoroughly investigated, we cannot be sure how far Henry VII was following precedents set by the Yorkist kings, but it is clear that, after the recovery of his throne in 1471, at times Edward IV took rigorous measures to repress the worst disorders that were prevalent in the Welsh marches. The outbreak of a quarrel between the young William Herbert (1455–90), earl of Pembroke and his turbulent kinsmen, the Vaughan family of Tretower, in the lordship of Brecon, led the king early in 1479 to prohibit the earl and his more vigorous younger brother, Sir Walter Herbert, from crossing the River Severn or residing in any part of Wales for the duration of a whole year, under pain of forfeiting £1,000 each. Their three mainpernors, namely their mother, Anne, dowager-countess of Pembroke, her brother, Walter Devereux (d. 1485), Lord Ferrers of Chartley, and Ralph Hothom, esquire, of Leconfield, co. York, on 21 March 1479 were all made subject to a similar penalty if the earl or Sir Walter disobeyed this ban imposed by royal authority. The second Herbert earl had few estates in England at that time, and in 1479 he found himself banished by the king from all his Welsh castles and lordships, including Chepstow, Gower, Pembroke and Raglan, which constituted the basis of his power as a great magnate. Although he had married Mary Wydevill, one of the six sisters of Queen Elizabeth, Pembroke had fallen out of royal favour, and the restrictions to which he was subjected by Edward IV were as humiliating as any terms ever imposed by Henry VII on members of the English nobility. The dispute with the Vaughans of Tretower was probably one of the reasons why a few months later, in July 1479, the Herbert heir was deprived of the earldom of Pembroke and meagrely compensated for his losses by his creation as earl of Huntingdon, with a grant of a dozen manors in the west of England.[28] When Henry VII ruled England, no magnate family was largely dispossessed by a forced exchange of lands as the Herberts of Raglan had been as a consequence of a change of royal policy during Edward IV's later years.

For most of his reign, it cannot be said that Henry VII made a great deal of use of recognizances in order to bring English magnates into a state of subjection and dependence on the crown through the threat of financial penalties. Before the death of Arthur, prince of Wales on 2 April 1502, only six peers had been obliged to give the king recognizances concerning their own conduct in the sixteen years that had elapsed since Henry Tudor's triumph at Bosworth. The reasons for the taking of these bonds from four lords – William (d. 1507), Viscount Beaumont, Ralph Nevill (d. 1499), third earl of Westmorland, Thomas Grey (d. 1501), marquis of Dorset, and Edward Courtenay (d. 1509), earl of Devon – can clearly be established and require little explanation.[29] Lord Beaumont, who had to give the king a bond for £10,000 on 8 December, 1485, had become insane by April 1487, and because of his insanity his inheritance was subsequently taken into the king's hands. His estates, which had been forfeited during Edward IV's reign, had recently been restored to him by virtue of legislation in Henry VII's first parliament, but it was unlikely that he would prove capable of managing his own affairs. This recognizance, payable at Christmas 1485, was taken as a guarantee of Lord Beaumont's good conduct, and as this bond was promptly cancelled, such rigorous measures to put him under restraint were presumably considered to be unnecessary.[30]

In view of his close association with Richard III, Ralph Nevill (d. 1499), earl of Westmorland could hardly have expected to survive the change of dynasty in 1485 with little material loss. Inevitably he was deprived of the valuable lands, rents and annuities that he had been granted by King Richard, and on 5 December 1485 he was made to surrender to Henry VII the custody and marriage of his heir, Ralph (d. 1498), Lord Nevill. Three bonds for a sum totalling in all 1,000 marks, and made payable between Christmas 1485 and Michaelmas 1487, were probably taken as sureties that this transaction would be carried out.[31] Although Earl Ralph was deprived of a valuable asset (as he could have raised a considerable sum of money by arranging a suitable marriage for his only son and heir), it can hardly be maintained that he was treated harshly. His loyalty to Richard III necessitated some reinsurance concerning his political conduct early in the new reign, and these safeguards seem to have served their purpose, as the earl of Westmorland kept out of trouble and wisely avoided participation in Lambert Simnel's rebellion in 1487.

These two magnates, William, Lord Beaumont and the third Nevill earl of Westmorland, needed, for very different reasons, to be put under restraint soon after Henry VII became king; in both cases, the action that he took was justified and they can hardly be regarded as victims of royal oppression. There appear to be no grounds for criticism of the king's dealings with Edward Courtenay, earl of Devon, who was obliged on 14 March 1494 (together with his associates and sureties, Robert, Lord Willoughby de Broke and Piers Edgecombe) to give a bond for 1,000 marks as a guarantee that he would not retain men unlawfully in the counties of Devon and Cornwall. Subsequently, when the earl of Devon contravened statute law in that respect, he could be fined (as he was in 1506) without the necessity of a prosecution for his offences.[32] Perhaps his offence in giving livery illegally to three men (all named Wode) before 27 October 1497 may explain why John (d. 1499), Lord Grey of Wilton, together with two knights, namely the earl of Devon's heir, Sir William Courtenay and Sir John Mortimer of Great Kyre, co. Worcester, gave Henry VII a bond for £300; this was a guarantee that they would pay the king a sum of £232 11s 6½d, in five instalments, by the feast of All Saints, 1500 (and those payments were duly made).[33] The reasons for the transactions that took place in 1500 between Henry VII and Edward Sutton, Lord Dudley cannot be ascertained; on 20 July, Lord Dudley and three other men gave the king recognizances for sums totalling £1,000, and the condition attached was that they should pay the king £733 6s 8d, in seven instalments by All Saints Day, 1503.[34] Perhaps, as on two subsequent occasions in 1502 and 1504, Lord Dudley was trafficking with the king for the purchase of a wardship belonging to the crown. Only one of the six peers required, on their own behalf, to give Henry VII recognizances in the fifteen years between 1485 and 1500, namely Thomas Grey, marquis of Dorset, can be regarded as having been treated with undue severity.

Henry VII's treatment of his queen's surviving half-brother, Thomas Grey (d. 1501), marquis of Dorset, has been strongly censured by Mr Lander, but the relevant facts concerning those much misunderstood transactions in 1492 have been oddly misrepresented and need to be clarified.[35] Dorset was the elder of Queen Elizabeth Wydevill's two sons by her first marriage with Sir John Grey (d. 1461) of Groby, co. Leicester, and as King Edward IV's stepson he had enjoyed an increasingly powerful and privileged position among the Yorkist nobility down to 1483. By his vacillating conduct during Richard III's reign, Thomas Grey had demonstrated that (like his mother, who exerted strong influence over him) he was inconstant and unreliable. According to Polydore Vergil, when the marquis of Dorset was in exile in France in 1485, he decided to abandon Henry Tudor's cause, and he attempted to defect so that he could join Richard III. It was necessary for the French government to ensure that he was arrested in order to prevent him from returning to England and betraying Henry Tudor's plans, and during the Bosworth campaign he was left in pawn at the French court as a security for the repayment of the money loaned to the earl of Richmond by Charles VIII. After the change of dynasty in 1485, Dorset had no prospect of recovering valuable patronage granted to him by Edward IV (especially the wardship and marriage of the child heiress, Anne, duchess of Exeter, and that of the luckless Edward Plantagenet (1475–99), earl of Warwick, who spent the rest of his short life as a state prisoner). What had been lost as a consequence of the usurpation of Richard III could not be regained once Henry VII was king of England, and Dorset's reduced place and influence in English politics gave him grounds for discontent with the new regime. As a precaution he was imprisoned in the Tower at the time of Lambert Simnel's rebellion in 1487 and, in view of his dubious political record, the measures that the king subsequently took to put him under restraint five years later were neither unreasonable nor unjustified.

Shortly before Henry VII's French expedition in 1492 (the first occasion during his reign when the king went abroad), there were apparently grounds for suspecting Dorset's loyalty, but substantive proof of treasonable activities (as distinct from 'informacion, reporte and supuyses') was still lacking. By an indenture made on 4 June, the marquis was obliged, in return for a royal pardon for unspecified offences, to convey most of his own lands (and those of his wife, Cecily, the Bonville and Harington heiress) to a group of twelve feoffees, who were to hold them to the use of Dorset and his marchioness, and for the performance of their last wills. If, after the making of this contract, Dorset were to commit treason or be guilty of misprision (i.e., concealment) of treason, his feoffees would henceforth hold those lands to the king's use. There is no reason to assume (as Mr Lander did) that Dorset was deprived of control of his estates for several years and left virtually landless, without an adequate income; as he was taking part in the forthcoming French campaign, provision was made for the sale of part of his lands, should that become necessary in the event of his capture, in order to pay the cost of his ransom. If Dorset did not henceforth commit treason (or conceal treason of which others were guilty), the enfeoffment of his (and his wife's) lands made at the king's direction in 1492 was to be null and void. These arrangements, together with other conditions laid down in the indenture, were to be confirmed in the next parliament, and that was done in 1495.[36] Dorset was, in effect, put under a suspended sentence in 1492, but if he behaved himself in future and committed no further indiscretions, his great landed inheritance was not at risk.

This contract imposed on Dorset in 1492 did involve him in considerable financial loss in one respect. He was required to surrender to the king the wardship and marriage of his elder son and heir, Thomas Grey (1477–1530), with the proviso that he would be obliged to pay Henry VII the sum of £1,000 if the boy was returned to him still unmarried before he reached the age of nineteen. The second marquis of Dorset, who succeeded his father in 1501, was apparently still unmarried when the king died on 21 April 1509, so that penalty was probably incurred. For every default in the terms of this indenture made on 4 June 1492, Dorset was bound to pay the king a fine of £1,000 and he was also obliged to find sureties willing to give recognizances totalling £10,000 as a guarantee of his good conduct. He had already met that requirement almost in full on 22 May, when fifty-five mainpernors (including the bishops of Ely, Lincoln and Worcester and four peers) entered into obligations on his behalf.[37] They could do so quite safely, because Dorset had learnt his lesson and he gave the king no further reason to doubt his loyalty. The restrictions imposed on him by the indenture of 1492, which proved effective as a deterrent, may have been removed some years before his death on 30 September 1501, perhaps as early as 1496. Because of the long survival of his widow, Cecily Bonville (1460–1530), who held the greater part of the family estates as her own inheritance (the Bonville and Harington baronies), Dorset's heir, Thomas, did not have the resources necessary to maintain his status and he was not summoned to parliament as a marquis until 1511. Although in titular rank he belonged to the small group of the English higher nobility, his landed income was that of a lesser baron, Lord Ferrers of Groby. Like his father, he incurred Henry VII's suspicions and he did not get off so lightly; in the later years of the reign, he was imprisoned, first in the Tower of London and afterwards at Calais.[38] Dorset was the only marquis in England, and that title had virtually lapsed for some years before the accession of Henry VIII in 1509.

Unlike Edward IV (and Henry VIII) Henry VII was no ruthless head-chopper; he was well aware that his aim of restoring political stability in England was unlikely to be achieved if there were frequent treason trials and executions. As his faithful servant, Sir Hugh Conway, discovered to his cost early in the new reign, the first Tudor king was wary of informers, and at his court (so different in that respect from Edward IV's) delation was not encouraged.[39] As a near kinsman of Queen Elizabeth of York, the marquis of Dorset was treated leniently. By contrast, the de la Pole heir, Edmund (c. 1471–1513), earl of Suffolk, who had not yet committed treason, was made to pay a high price for restitution of his inheritance, which the king chose to regard as being at his disposal as a consequence of the rebellion and attainder of Suffolk's elder brother, John de la Pole, earl of Lincoln. The second duke of Suffolk, John (1442–91) had settled a large part of his estates on his eldest son and heir, John, and his wife, Margaret Arundel, and those lands were consequently forfeited to the crown after Lincoln's death as a rebel in the battle of Stoke on 16 June 1487. Edmund de la Pole was still a minor when his father, John, duke of Suffolk, died, and by an indenture made with the king on 26 February 1493, he had to agree to pay £5,000, in yearly instalments of £200, in order to secure possession of the greater part of his late father's lands. Sixteen de la Pole manors were appropriated and put in the hands of feoffees in accordance with the terms of this agreement to ensure that these payments were duly made to the king, and moreover these instalments were to be doubled to the sum of £400 a year after the death of his mother, Elizabeth, dowager-duchess of Suffolk. Probably several de la Pole manors that had not belonged to the late earl of Lincoln were unjustly retained by the king in 1493, and, as the Suffolk heir no longer had the estates and income appropriate to support the status of duke, he was demoted to the rank of earl, a title which his ancestors had held since Richard II had bestowed it on Michael de la Pole in 1385.[40]

Although he was the victim of royal injustice in 1493, the last de la Pole earl of Suffolk merits little sympathy; violent and lawless, he was unfit to exercise power and responsibility. In 1499 he fled to Calais and afterwards found refuge in Flanders, but was soon persuaded by the king's agents to return to England. It was one of Henry VII's worst failures that Suffolk was able to escape abroad again in the summer of 1501, this time together with his brother, Richard, and he became a pawn of the Habsburgs until he was handed over to the king of England as a result of his treaty with the Archduke Philip in February 1506.[41] Suffolk's nuisance value as a Yorkist pretender was enhanced after the judicial murder of Edward Plantagenet, earl of Warwick in 1499, and his intrigues while he was at liberty on the continent added to the king's anxieties and increased political tensions in England. Control of the exiled earl of Suffolk enabled the Emperor Maximilian I and his heir, the Archduke Philip, to extract huge sums of money from Henry VII in the guise of 'loans'; in 1505, the English king is said to have advanced to Philip, now styled king of Castile, no less than £138,000. The Habsburgs are reckoned to have obtained at least £260,000 from the first Tudor monarch in the later years of his reign.[42] The young Henry VIII would have inherited a much greater fortune in 1509 if Suffolk had been more vigilantly watched and kept safely in England. For the sake of dynastic security, Henry VII had to finance heavy demands on his revenues in the early years of the sixteenth century, and it is in the light of this situation that his reliance on bonds and recognizances as part of his governmental system in the latter half of his reign should be reconsidered.

III

The death of Henry VII's eldest son and heir, Arthur, prince of Wales, on 2 April 1502, at the age of fifteen, was followed within a year by that of the king's consort, Queen Elizabeth of York. The queen survived the birth of her last child, Catherine, by only nine days, dying on 11 February 1503, her thirty-seventh birthday. Only three of the eight children of Henry VII and Elizabeth of York lived long enough to become adults; after the king's eldest daughter, Margaret (1489–1541), married James IV of Scotland on

8 August 1503, the Tudor dynasty was represented in England only by the prematurely ageing and ailing Henry VII, his second son, the future Henry VIII (who was only ten years old when he became heir to the throne) and the younger of the king's two surviving daughters, Mary (1496–1533), destined at an early age for a royal marriage abroad.[43] During the later years of Henry VII's reign there was the unavoidable prospect that the king's death would be followed by a royal minority, and as early as 1499 his illness when he was staying at Wanstead manor, co. Essex had led to seditious speculation among the officers of the Calais garrison concerning the possible succession to the throne by a rival claimant of full age, regardless of the rights of the young prince of Wales.[44] By March 1507 the king's declining health made him decide to make his will (presumably his first, which has not survived), but, despite another crisis in March 1508, he lived longer than contemporaries expected. For some months before his death on 21 April 1509, Henry VII appears to have been completely incapacitated, and it is remarkable that he did not make his last will until 31 March, when he had only three weeks to live. In view of the uncertainties of this situation, it is not surprising that in the early years of the sixteenth century, Tudor rule had (as Margaret M. Condon has observed) an air of impermanence.[45]

The extensive use of recognizances by Henry VII in his dealings with many of his wealthier subjects, including most of the English peerage, was a characteristic feature of his rule only in the course of the last seven years of his reign, between 1502 and 1509. There were forty English peers of full age during that period, and at various times as many as two-thirds of them were required to give Henry VII recognizances, either on their own behalf or as sureties for other persons. The number of peers who gave the king recognizances as principals was sixteen (and thirteen of them were also bound by other recognizances in their role as sureties). Eleven other peers were also made liable to financial penalties by their recognizances given to the king as sureties.[46] The belief that the English nobility as a class was threatened and oppressed by unjust royal exactions during the first decade of the sixteenth century has been established by uncritical acceptance of Mr Lander's conclusions. This opinion is based on a cursory examination of the numerous recognizances taken by Henry VII in his dealings with the majority of the lords temporal during a short period of years that seemed likely to terminate in a royal minority if the king were to die before his surviving son, Henry, was old enough to rule.

Most of these recognizances taken by Henry VII were made (as Mr Lander has conceded) for just and lawful purposes (including the preservation of public order) and it seems likely that in general the king's aims were primarily fiscal rather than political. His chief concern in these matters, especially in his later years, was to ensure that he received full satisfaction of the lucrative fiscal claims that arose from his systematic reassertion of the crown's feudal rights of marriage and wardship, which already before 1509 were being made to yield over £6,000 p.a.[47] His growing avarice prompted the increasing use of bonds and recognizances to augment royal revenues, but those peers who chose to do business with Henry VII and buy marriages and wardships in the king's gift did so willingly, at their own risk and probably to their own advantage, as his transactions with the hard and unscrupulous Edward Sutton (d. 1532), Lord Dudley, illustrate so well. Between 1500 and 1509, Lord Dudley, on his own behalf, gave the king nine recognizances (and only one peer, William Blount (1478–1534), Lord Mountjoy, was obliged to give a greater number; his recognizances totalled a record number of twenty-three).[48] As we have seen, the purpose of seven recognizances (all relating to the same matter) taken of Lord Dudley and his three associates on 20 July 1500 cannot be ascertained; both the other two of these bonds were probably necessitated, in 1504, by the purchase, as an investment, of a valuable marriage and possession of a wardship that promised to yield a good return. Firstly, on 29 November 1494, Dudley obtained a royal grant of the wardship and marriage of a minor, John Grey (*c.* 1485–1504), Lord Powis, who was afterwards married to Margaret Sutton, one of Dudley's seven daughters. When his young son-in-law died on 15 April 1504 at the age of nineteen, Lord Dudley's chief concern was to perpetuate his interest in the lordship of Powys (one moiety of which was part of his own family inheritance) by gaining the wardship and marriage of the heir, his infant grandson, Edward Grey (*c.* 1503–51), who was to prove the last of the marcher lords of Powys.[49] Secondly, Lord Dudley was undoubtedly successful in that endeavour (although no new royal grant of the Grey of Powys lands made in 1504 has been traced), because he remained in occupation of his young grandson's Welsh inheritance until he surrendered the wardship (and the heir's marriage) about eight years before Edward Grey came of age in 1525. The recognizance for £800 which Dudley gave to the king on 26 November 1504 as a guarantee that he would make payment of £600 on 1 November 1505 probably relates to his bargain with Henry VII concerning this marriage and wardship. Another recognizance, this time for a sum of 1,000 marks, given to the king on 4 December 1504, bound Dudley to continue to pay £100 p.a. for his custody of the Grey moiety of the lordship of Powys, which had been in his hands since 1494. As those Welsh lands were valued at £181 12s 2d, when Edward Grey's prolonged minority at last came to an end in 1525, it is clear that Lord Dudley had made a considerable margin of profit out of his tenure of that part of the Grey of Powys estates, especially if he kept his widowed daughter, Margaret (d.c. 1525), Lady Grey, out of her common law dower share of one-third of that moiety, as she and her second husband, Robert Sutton, later alleged. This episode does not suggest that Lord Dudley was financially exploited by the king in respect of their business dealings, but he undoubtedly had grievances against Henry VII's government. His indictment for felony before the justices in Staffordshire in 1503 led to his trial for that offence before Thomas Howard, earl of Surrey, in his capacity as steward of England. Although Dudley was probably acquitted by his peers, at Easter, 1505, Piers Newton was instructed by the Council Learned in the Law to obtain further details of the indictments for unlawful retaining made against Lord Dudley and others. His kinship with his cousin, the king's trusted councillor, Edmund Dudley, did not protect him against injustice in the form of a royal claim in 1506 to part of his estates worth £120 a year. That misfortune cost him a payment of £1,000, made to secure the discharge of the king's title to those lands. No recognizances were enrolled on the Chancery Close Roll concerning this obscure episode, which is known only because it was recalled three years later by Edmund Dudley, then a prisoner in the Tower of London, shortly after he was sentenced to death as a traitor in 1509.[50]

While Edward Sutton, Lord Dudley's lucrative purchase of the custody of a half-share of the Welsh marcher lordship of Powys, which gave him a conveniently long lease of a valuable estate, shows the profits that an influential English peer could obtain as a consequence of Henry VII's rigorous exercise of the crown's feudal rights, the misfortunes that overtook Thomas (1467–1525), Lord Dacre of Gilsland, and his mother, Lady Mabel (d. 1508) demonstrate the heavy penalties that were that were incurred in the later years of the reign, by contravening the king's prerogative where the marriage or custody of minors in royal wardship was concerned. Lady Mabel was accused of 'ravishing' a young esquire, Richard Huddleston (1481–1502), who had inherited lands in co. Cumberland and was therefore subsequently claimed by the crown (probably some years after his early death) as a royal ward. The nature of this offence, which was not a moral lapse, must be made clear; the lad had not been raped by the elderly Dacre dowager. Instead Lady Mabel had married the short-lived Huddleston heir (who was a grandson of Richard Nevill (1428–71), earl of Warwick, 'the kingmaker') to her daughter,

Elizabeth, thereby depriving the king of the cash that could have been raised by the sale of his marriage. Her punishment was imprisonment in Lancaster castle, where she spent nine months in jail, until Lord Dacre (and his mother) undertook by four recognizances made on 21 September 1507 to pay a fine of 1,000 marks, and 600 marks of that sum had been duly exacted before Henry VII's death. This fine was greatly in excess of the market value of young Huddleston's marriage. In his petition to the young Henry VIII, Lord Dacre alleged that the death of his sister, Elizabeth Huddleston, which occurred in Lancaster castle, had been occasioned by the distress resulting from her mother's imprisonment there.[51]

The severity of Henry VII's reaction to what, at first sight, appears to have been no more than a minor infringement of the crown's right of prerogative wardship in Richard Huddleston's case becomes more understandable if we recall that Thomas, Lord Dacre himself had acquired a wife (and eventually the lands of the Greystock barony) by abducting and marrying, probably in 1488, Elizabeth (1472–1516) the granddaughter and eventually sole heiress of Ralph (1414–87), Lord Greystock. He was fortunate to get away with that exploit and to avoid any fine or penalty imposed by the king; when she married Lord Dacre, Elizabeth Greystock was no longer a royal ward, because Henry VII had granted her marriage to John de Vere, earl of Oxford, who appears in his turn to have sold it to Henry, Lord Clifford. When, after Henry VII's death, Dacre petitioned Henry VIII for redress of his grievances, he listed in all five recognizances involving large sums of money that he had, at various times, been compelled to give to the late king. He alleged that four of them had been fraudulently forfeited and converted into debts owing to the crown, which had come to amount to 6,450 marks. Although Dacre was (in company with the imprisoned traitor, Edmund de la Pole, earl of Suffolk and Thomas Grey, marquis of Dorset, also in jail) one of the few peers excluded by name from the general pardon granted by Henry VIII on 30 April 1509 only nine days after his accession, some at least of these debts were later pardoned by the new king. In deciding to remit to Dacre and other peers (including Dorset and Northumberland) penalties arising from the recognizances still held by the crown, Henry VIII was probably more moved by the pressing political need to conciliate the English nobility as a class than by a genuine conviction that his late father had often been guilty of a denial of justice in his treatment of individual peers. The heaviest of the fines with which Dacre was burdened in 1509 had been incurred, so he maintained, as a result of a fraud perpetrated by the malign influence of Empson and Dudley. He had, on 20 July 1506, been obliged to give the king a recognizance of £2,000, with no condition attached; Henry VII's purpose was apparently not to require payment of this sum, but to use it as a suspended penalty, presumably as a guarantee of Dacre's good conduct. Although Empson and Dudley later turned this bond into a debt owing to the crown, contrary to the late king's intentions (so Dacre alleged), Henry VIII showed himself in no hurry to cancel this obligation, which was left outstanding until 1516.[52]

By use of recognizances which could involve the forfeiture and payment to the king of huge sums of money, Henry VII did undoubtedly seek to bring some magnates into a state of dependence and submission to his will and he was successful in that aim. Four instances of such recognizances taken from peers have been considered at length by J. R. Lander, who regarded them as typical of Henry VII's hard dealings with the English peerage throughout his reign, but these contracts – made respectively with Thomas Grey (d. 1501), marquis of Dorset, George Nevill (1469–1535), Lord Abergavenny, Richard Grey (d. 1524), earl of Kent and Henry Percy (1478–1527), fifth earl of Northumberland – all resulted from exceptional circumstances, and the king's actions were not unjustified. His difficulties in his relations with Queen Elizabeth's half-brother, the marquis of Dorset, have already been re-examined, and the circumstances that led in 1507 to the prosecution of George Nevill, Lord Abergavenny on charges of illegal retaining are already well known. Early in 1507 he was indicted at Maidstone, co. Kent, and accused of having broken statute law by having 'excited, requested, solicited and retained' no fewer than 471 men, all below the rank of esquire, in a period of thirty months following 10 June 1504 down to 9 December 1506. When he was brought to trial in the court of King's Bench in Michaelmas term of that year, Abergavenny could not deny his offences and he thought it best to plead guilty; as the penalty for such unlawful retaining was a fine of 100 shillings per month for every one of the men involved, his accumulated fines were reckoned in all to total £70,550. Such a sum was far greater than the capital value of the whole of his English estates (and he was, of course, never in possession of the Welsh marcher lordship of Abergavenny, to which his family had vainly laid claim since 1435), and he was now at the king's mercy. By an indenture made on Christmas Eve 1507, Henry VII was graciously pleased to commute this gigantic burden of unpayable debt (which had meanwhile increased inexplicably to £100,000 'or thereabouts') for a fine of £5,000, payable in ten years. Already on 5 November Abergavenny had been compelled to find twenty-six mainpernors willing to give recognizances amounting to £3,233 6s 8d on his behalf. Furthermore, two recognizances had been exacted from him on 23 December; the first of these, for £5,000, was a guarantee that he would be true to his allegiance (and find other sureties, if the king thought it necessary), while the second, for 5,000 marks this time, imposed a condition that Lord Abergavenny was not to enter the counties of Kent, Surrey, Sussex or Hampshire at any time for the rest of his life without the king's licence. As the best part of his estates lay in those shires, and moreover he was normally resident at Birling, or Chatham, co. Kent, during the last years of Henry VII's reign George Nevill was excluded from that region of south-east England where his territorial influence could be most effectively exercised.[53] These penalties seem disproportionate to his offences, but he had brought his punishment upon himself.

Although other peers (notably Edward, duke of Buckingham and the earls of Derby, Essex, Northumberland, Oxford and Shrewsbury, besides one peeress, the king's mother, Lady Margaret Beaufort, countess of Richmond and Derby) were indicted in 1504 for illegal retaining,[54] George, Lord Abergavenny is the only nobleman known to have been put on trial in Henry VII's reign for an offence that was common and widespread. His local dominance in Kent was a threat to public order and he had begun to cause the king concern several years before 1507. A Royal proclamation issued in March 1502 which prohibited all retaining in Kent and Sussex was probably intended to limit the activities of Lord Abergavenny's retinue, and in 1503 he may have been fined for retaining contrary to law. His arrest and imprisonment in the Tower in 1506 seems to have been prompted by graver considerations. An indictment made by a grand jury in Kent in June 1506 had found that, during the Cornish rebellion in 1497, Lord Abergavenny had treasonably incited Edmund de la Pole, earl of Suffolk to desert the king's troops and join the rebels. This incident was alleged to have occurred on 13 June, when the rebel force, led by Lord Audley, had reached Wallingford, co. Berks., and Abergavenny was with Suffolk at his manor house at Ewelme, co. Oxon, only a few miles away. Although this indictment was returned into the court of King's Bench, that appears to have been the end of the matter. Perhaps the evidence was insufficient to enable Abergavenny to be put on trial for treason, and the king chose other means of making him politically innocuous. It is significant that Henry VII did not take effective action to repress illicit retaining by an unruly magnate until he became fully aware of the closeness of Abergavenny's former intimacy with the last de la Pole earl of Suffolk (who was by that time in safekeeping in the Tower of London) and moreover the king had grounds for suspecting him of disloyalty during the gravest crisis of the reign in 1497. Although in Edmund Dudley's opinion (expressed two years later), 'the Lord Abergeny had a very sore end, for any prooffe that was against him to my knowledge', he eventually got off lightly, having probably paid no more than £1,000 of the £5,000 due before the king died and Henry VIII was soon induced to cancel Abergavenny's recognizances and the residue of his debts owed to the crown.[55]

Unlike George Nevill, Lord Abergavenny, the feckless and improvident Richard Grey (d. 1524), earl of Kent could never be regarded as a threat to the stability of the Tudor regime. Because his abilities were so mediocre he carried no weight in English politics, and his sole achievement during the twenty years of his futile career as earl of Kent was the dissolution and ruin of one of the richest magnate estates in England. As his father, George (d. 1503) is said to have predicted, Richard Grey proved to be a wastrel, but the tradition that the burden of his gambling debts made him sell and squander his lands is not derived from any contemporary source; this cautionary tale first made its appearance in Sir William Dugdale's *Baronage* (1675–6). The accumulation of English manors spread over eight counties, together with the Welsh marcher lordship of Ruthin (the most extensive domain in North Wales still in private hands) inherited by Earl Richard in 1503 were probably worth £1,500 p.a., and at that date his debts (and those of his late father) could doubtless have been paid off within a few years by good management. His livery fine (perhaps a half of his annual income) when he was granted seisin of the Grey of Ruthin lands of his earldom by the crown was assessed at £750, and he was also charged 400 marks for royal licence to enter upon the properties that descended to him as heir to his mother, Anne Wydevill (d. 1489), an aunt of Henry VII's queen. The financial morass in which Richard, earl of Kent soon became engulfed was largely a consequence of his own folly. His abduction of the heiress Elizabeth Trussell, who was left in the custody of his stepmother, Catherine Herbert (d. 1504), dowager-countess of Kent (probably as the intended bride of Richard's half-brother, Sir Henry Grey) was seen as a transgression of the king's feudal rights, and the fine of 2,500 marks imposed by Henry VII was not excessive in view of the gravity of his offence. As security for the payment in instalments of his debts to the king, which were now reckoned to amount to a total of £1,683 6s 8d, Kent was required on 25 July 1506 to give a recognizance for 4,000 marks. As part of this bargain, his fine for the 'ravishment' of Elizabeth Trussell was reduced to only 1,000 marks, and moreover he undertook (ostensibly of his own volition) to settle lands worth £100 a year to the use of himself and his heirs male, with remainder, in the event of failure of heirs, to the king and his heirs. His troubles began when he defaulted on this undertaking to pay his debts to the crown, at an agreed rate of 400 marks a year, and so forfeited his recognizance of 4,000 marks, which accordingly augmented his indebtedness beyond his capacity to repay.[56]

As Earl Richard was disposing of valuable manors at low prices in order to satisfy the demands of his private creditors, Henry VII could hardly be expected to overlook this tempting opportunity of acquiring a substantial part of the Grey of Ruthin inheritance on similar advantageous terms. The settlement imposed by the king in an indenture made on 6 May 1507 involved the sale to the crown of the reversion of the marcher lordship of Ruthin (valued at £216 p.a., and already in the hands of the king's trustees), and also the appropriation of the profits of five Grey manors in the Midlands, in order to pay off Earl Richard's outstanding debts, which were found to be £1,800, at a rate of £300 a year during the course of the next six years. Already at this stage it was forseeable that before long Richard, earl of Kent would seek to alienate his Welsh inheritance, as well as the residue of his English possessions. As the marcher lordship of Ruthin in the early sixteenth century was an enclave, surrounded on all sides by territories ruled by the crown, as marcher lord, or by the prince of Wales, Henry VII would have been neglectful of his responsibilities if he had allowed Earl Richard's Welsh dominion to be taken over by speculators in the land market. For the benefit of its inhabitants (and their neighbours), it was desirable that the lordship of Ruthin should be acquired by the crown and brought more effectively under the control of the Council in the Marches.

Some years after the accession of Henry VIII (probably in 1518), when he was still vainly endeavouring to recover his valuable Welsh marcher lordship (now lost to his family for ever as a consequence of his own incompetence), Richard, earl of Kent petitioned Cardinal Wolsey concerning 'the discharge of the consciens' of Henry VII in that matter. Even after his losses in 1507, Earl Richard found it expedient to speak well of the king and to attribute to him benevolent intentions. Despite his judicious protestations, he cannot possibly have regarded these transactions in 1507 as fair or just, and, in view of his debts and problems, there was the risk that his resentment against Henry VII might lead him into bad company and mischief. These considerations probably explain the drastic measures taken by the king on 19 August 1507 to put Kent under restraint, and Richard Grey might well have complained that he was being treated as if he were a child or a madman. He was required to give a recognizance for £10,000 as a guarantee that he would observe stringent and unprecedented conditions. For the rest of Henry VII's reign (and later), he was deprived of control of his own estates and even of the management of his own household, and moreover he was bound to be in daily attendance upon the king, being allowed only eight days leave in each quarter, when he was permitted to depart without royal licence. These restrictions which, *inter alia*, prevented him from selling, leasing or making any other grant relating to his lands without the king's written consent, have been seen as an attempt on Henry VII's part to prevent the destruction of his patrimony in order to preserve the legitimate rights of his heirs. More probably the main purpose of this recognizance was to ensure that in future Earl Richard sold what was left of his lands only to the king, or to his greedy and self-interested councillors, Edmund Dudley and Sir Richard Empson, whose appetite had already been whetted by easily acquiring some of his property. Early in his reign, Henry VIII cancelled this recognizance for £10,000 and so Richard, earl of Kent was left once more free to resume his reckless alienations. When he died in 1524 there was little left of the family estates for his disappointed and irrascible half-brother, Sir Henry Grey (d. 1562) to inherit, and consequently he did not succeed to the earldom.[57] The irresponsibility of a spendthrift nobleman, and not the tenor of royal policy, caused the earldom of Kent to lapse for nearly a half-century before its revival by Elizabeth I in 1571.

No English magnates did more in 1485 to determine the fate of Richard III and bring the Yorkist dynasty to an end than the astute Henry Percy, fourth earl of Northumberland, and the time-serving Thomas, Lord Stanley (soon to become earl of Derby), who was ably supported in his changes of front by his younger brother, Sir William, already a substantial landowner in his own right. The politic inactivity of Northumberland at Bosworth had conveniently left the way clear for the Stanley squadron, commanded by Sir William because of Lord Stanley's enforced absence from the battlefield, to act decisively on behalf of Henry Tudor.[58] When Henry VII paid his first visit to Yorkshire in April 1486, he found himself largely dependent on the protection afforded by the Percy earl's enormous retinue (probably the largest private army in England in the aftermath of Bosworth), which included no fewer than thirty-three knights drawn from the most prominent gentry families in Yorkshire, besides many esquires and yeomen. The untimely accident of the fourth earl's murder, which occurred in a sudden local rising at Cocklodge, near Thirsk, on 28 April 1489, marked the end of an era in north-country politics and the beginning of the decline in the fortunes of the Percy family.[59] Henry Percy (*c.* 1449–89) was undoubtedly the shrewdest politician that his line ever produced, and his skilful exploitation of a series of dynastic changes had enabled him to regain almost all the English possessions ever held by his ancestor, the first earl of Northumberland, in Henry IV's reign. His early death, when he was probably only forty years old, was followed by the long minority of his heir, and that put all the estates belonging to the earldom of Northumberland at the crown's disposal for the next nine years. The Percy family was never again so dominant north of the Trent as it had been for a brief interlude during the early years of Henry VII's reign.

Besides the Northumberland earldom, the fifth earl, Henry Algernon Percy (1478–1527), who was given special livery of his estates on 14 May 1498 at the age of twenty, also inherited the Poynings barony, which made him one of the chief landowners in Kent and Surrey. While he was still a royal ward he had supported the king in the battle at Blackheath on 17 June 1497, and his promotion to the Order of the Garter at an early age was a sign of royal favour. He lacked his father's caution and prudence, and the development of the Council of the North during his minority had ensured that he would play a less prominent governmental role in northern England. His quarrel with Archbishop Thomas Savage of York required royal intervention late in 1504; both parties had to appear before the king's council at Westminster and give recognizances of £2,000 each as a security for keeping the peace.[60] His punishment for usurping the king's right of prerogative wardship by abducting Elizabeth, daughter and heiress-presumptive of the wealthy Yorkshire knight, Sir John Hastings (d. 1504) of Fenwick, was more salutary; in 1505 he was fined £10,000. Payment of the whole of that huge sum was suspended during the king's pleasure, but meanwhile Northumberland (and four sureties) were required, under pain of forfeiting 6,000 marks, to render annual instalments of 500 marks at Candlemas (2 February) until 3,000 marks had been paid. As the child Elizabeth Hastings (who cannot have been more than eight years old) had died while in the earl's custody (and the king had thereby been deprived of a valuable wardship, as the next heir, her uncle, Sir George Hastings (d. 1511) was of full age), a fine of £2,000 cannot, in these circumstances, be regarded as excessive.[61] According to the testimony of Edmund Dudley, when it was given five years later, Henry VII had intended to be content with that amount, but subsequently Northumberland was made to pay £3,000. His alleged offences included unlawful retaining, for which he was indicted (with several other peers) at the quarter sessions held at York in 1504, and other retainders may help to explain why the arrangements for the payment of his fine were later revised. In November 1507 he had to enter into another recognizance for the payment of £5,000, and he was obliged to put many of his Yorkshire manors into the hands of feoffees, who were to hold them to the king's use until this debt had been paid by half-yearly instalments of 500 marks. These debts and recognizances were eventually cancelled by Henry VIII on 21 March 1510, but by then the hard terms imposed by his father had served their purpose.[62] Before Henry VII died, the most powerful of the surviving English earls had been drastically humiliated and reduced to a state of financial dependence on the crown.

Henry Tudor owed as much to the support of the Stanley family in 1485 as Edward IV had done to that of the Nevills in 1461, and no magnate family derived more profit from the Wars of the Roses and from the founding of the Tudor dynasty than the new king's stepfather, Thomas Stanley, earl of Derby and his kinsmen. The hegemony of the Stanley family in north-west England was not much affected by the trial and execution of Sir William in 1495 on charges of treason. Thomas Stanley (d. 1504), earl of Derby added to his lands throughout his long career, and his grandson and heir, the second Earl Thomas (d. 1521) inherited the Strange barony on the death of his mother, Jane (d. 1514), a cousin of Henry VIII.[63] He was less capable than his grandfather, but more intelligent than his eldest son and successor, the third Stanley earl, Edward (1509–72), who was described in 1538 as 'the greatest of power and land' but contemptuously dismissed as no more than 'a child in wisdom and half a fool'.[64] The second Stanley earl of Derby was a loyal (if mediocre) servant of the Tudor state. Unlike the fifth Percy earl, he ravished no royal ward; his misfortunes came about because Henry VII (in Edmund Dudley's opinion) 'was much sett (i.e. resolved) to have many persons in his danger at his pleasure'.[65] The indiscretions of one of the first earl of Derby's younger sons, James Stanley (d. 1515), newly promoted in 1506 to the bishopric of Ely, gave the king the opportunity that he wanted to diminish the wealth and power of a great magnate who threatened to become overmighty. Bishop Stanley (who was the king's step-brother) was fined at the Lancaster assizes the incredible sum of £245,680 for illicit retaining in 1506, and on 16 July his nephew, the young earl of Derby, was made to assume responsibility, by a series of recognizances given to the king, for payment of £1,833 13s 4d of that fine in eleven annual instalments. Consequently he soon became enmeshed in the web of the crown's financial transactions, and unless Bishop Stanley as his nephew's agent had been acting on the earl's behalf when he was retaining contrary to statute law, there was no justification for the penalties that Derby now incurred. His debts to the crown were promptly increased to a total of £6,000 by another eighteen recognizances given to the king in November 1506, and it was laid down that this amount (probably double Derby's landed income) was to be paid in instalments by Easter 1516. Like Edward Stafford, duke of Buckingham, the second Stanley earl of Derby might well have complained of the 'great and importunate charges' that Henry VII had inflicted on him. Probably only £1,000 had been paid before the king's death on 21 April 1509, but as Edmund Dudley recalled, 'the Earle of darbie was often tymes hardly intreated and to sore'. Although Henry VIII was belatedly induced to pardon 2,100 marks of this huge debt when at last a settlement was reached with Cardinal Wolsey in 1517, the residue was left outstanding and Earl Thomas Stanley II remained in debt to the crown for the rest of his life as a consequence of Henry VII's punitive actions that appear to have been unfairly directed against him.[66]

When Edward IV died prematurely at the age of forty on 9 April 1483, the royal council was dominated and divided by quarrelling noble factions, and the minority of the young Edward V threatened the realm with the prospect of renewed political instability. There is good reason to believe that by codicils added to his will on his deathbed, King Edward committed the personal custody of his twelve-year-old elder son and heir, Edward, to the boy's maternal uncle, Antony Wydevill, Earl Rivers and his two half-brothers, Thomas Grey, marquis of Dorset and Sir Richard Grey. Those 'wise dispositions' (as the anonymous continuator of the Crowland Chronicle regarded them in retrospect when he was writing three years later in April 1486) made by Edward IV were promptly revoked and set aside by the late king's councillors meeting shortly after his death. Their fatal decision gave Richard, duke of Gloucester some justification for his *coup d'état* when he seized control of the person of the young Edward V at Stony Stratford, co. Bucks., on 30 April, as the first step towards his usurpation of the throne.[67] The political situation in England when Henry VII died in 1509 was a striking contrast with the legacy of Yorkist rule in 1483. The first Tudor king had no need to make testamentary provisions concerning the custody of his heir, Henry, prince of Wales, or the government of his dominions after his death. At the close of Henry VII's long and remarkably successful reign, his kingdom was governed by loyal and united royal councillors who owed their careers to the Tudor dynasty, and their aim was to carry out the wishes of their deceased master. By 1509, Henry VIII at the age of seventeen was legally old enough to rule, and two days after his accession he ordered the arrest of Sir Richard Empson and Edmund Dudley, the highly unpopular agents of the late king's policies. Nothing was more likely to conciliate those whom Henry VII had

grievously wronged. Apart from the mysterious episode of the imprisonment in the Tower of Edward, duke of Buckingham's younger brother,
Lord Henry Stafford (*c.* 1479–1523), soon released (and politically
rehabilitated in the new king's first parliament by his creation as earl of
Wiltshire, on 28 January 1510), no other emergency measures were
deemed necessary in that situation. Perhaps Lord Henry, who was arrested
on the day of Henry VIII's accession on suspicion of treason but
subsequently found to be innocent, had unwisely become associated with a
scheme (attributed to the earl of Northumberland's servants) to make the
duke of Buckingham lord protector of England.[68] The English peerage in
1509, weakened and depleted in numbers, was incapable of resisting or
opposing the king's will, and even in the reaction that inevitably followed
Henry VII's long-awaited death, there was no risk of the formation of an
aristocratic league against the crown. It is indisputable that Henry VIII's
position in 1509 was as strong and unchallengeable as that of the mature
and well-trained Henry V on his accession in 1413. Perhaps Henry VII in
the last phase of his reign opted for too many safeguards against ill fortune,
but he has never been given the credit that he deserves for the wise and
judicious precautions taken to ensure the peaceful accession of the young
and inexperienced Henry VIII.

IV

When Henry VII's first parliament met on 7 November 1485, only thirty-
four peers (two dukes, ten earls, two viscounts and twenty barons) had
received writs of summons from the new king, although the English
nobility at that date (including six minors who were still under the age of
twenty-one) numbered in all fifty-five lords temporal. At the accession of
Henry VIII in 1509, there were no more than forty-one noblemen in
England (as Thomas Grey (1477–1530), second marquis of Dorset,
whose right to inherit that rank was apparently in doubt, was being held in
prison at Calais). At that date, Edward Stafford (1478–1521), duke of
Buckingham was the only English duke; there were no more than ten earls
and thirty barons, three of whom (Daubeney, Ferrers and Grey of Powis)
were minors in royal wardship.[69] The high rate of natural extinction in the
male line was the main reason for this remarkable reduction in the size of
the parliamentary peerage which had taken place in less than a quarter of a
century, but Henry VII (in striking contrast to Edward IV's practice) had
chosen to create few new titles, and furthermore his promotions of existing
peers to the ranks of the higher nobility were even less frequent.[70] Those

who received the highest peerage honours from the first Tudor king did not (with only one exception – the first Stanley earl of Derby) leave heirs or descendants to perpetuate their dignities.[71] The dukedom of Bedford conferred on the king's uncle, Jasper Tudor on 27 October 1485 was extinguished by his death just over ten years later on 21 December 1495. The marquisate of Berkeley, which came into existence early in 1489 as a consequence of an unscrupulous bargain made between Henry VII and the elderly, thrice-married and childless William, earl of Nottingham, proved ephemeral because it lapsed when he died on 14 February 1492.[72] Two earldoms were created as a reward for services rendered during the Bosworth campaign: the king's stepfather, Thomas (*c.* 1435–1504), Lord Stanley, became earl of Derby on the day when Jasper Tudor received his dukedom, and on 6 January 1486 Philibert de Chandée, the captain of the French mercenaries who had contributed so much to Henry Tudor's victory over Richard III, was created earl of Bath. Probably he had already left England and nothing further is known of his career; as he was given no endowment in cash or land to maintain his comital status, his enoblement was an expression of gratitude that cost Henry VII nothing.[73] During a period of thirty years between 1483 and 1513, only one English baron was promoted to the rank of viscount; Lady Margaret Beaufort's half-brother, John (1448–99), Lord Welles attained that dignity early in the new reign because Henry VII had so few relatives and Welles was the king's uncle of the half-blood. His marriage, which took place late in 1487, with Edward IV's second daughter, Cecily (d. 1507) produced no surviving issue, and he died childless. Between September, 1485 and November 1488, six new barons were summoned to parliament; they included, as Lord Rochford, the great Irish magnate Thomas Butler (*c.* 1424–1515), earl of Ormond, who had no son. Two of these titles (Cheyne and FitzWalter) were already extinct before the end of the first Tudor reign. Several of these baronies (Darcy, FitzWalter and Willoughby de Broke) can be regarded as a revival of honours that had lapsed. Although the barony created in 1486 for Giles Daubeney was an hereditary dignity, that was a special mark of royal favour, and it is doubtful if Henry VII intended that all these seven barons would in due course be succeeded in their dignities by their heirs male. Thomas Darcy (d. 1537), captain of the king's guard, was styled Lord Darcy in Henry VII's later years, but he did not receive a summons to parliament as a peer before Henry VIII's accession.[74] By 1507, Sir William Conyers may have become Lord Conyers; he was summoned to parliament as a baron for the first time in October 1509.[75] Apart from the possible enoblement of Thomas Darcy and Sir William Conyers, and the belated recognition, probably in 1504, of the king's second cousin, Sir Charles Somerset (c. 1460–1526) as Lord Herbert (eleven years after his marriage with the Herbert heiress, Elizabeth),[76] Henry VII preferred after his early years not to augment the dwindling body of lords temporal. In Edward IV's last parliament early in 1483, the majority of the forty-four peers who had been summoned to attend owed their titles to the reigning king;[77] by contrast, Henry VII did not seek to create a new Tudor nobility.

In early Tudor England, the parliamentary peerage, which had mustered sixty-four lords before the onset of civil war in 1455, was reduced in size and became once more no more numerous than the small and exclusive group of lords temporal that had existed during the reigns of Henry IV and Henry V.[78] Those magnate families unlucky enough to forfeit their estates as a consequence of remaining loyal to Henry VI for too long were, for the most part, successful in 1485 in recovering what they had lost after the usurpation of Edward IV in 1461. William (d. 1507), Lord Beaumont was a rare exception to that reversal of fortunes because he was prevented by his insanity from reuniting the whole of his dispersed family heritage.[79] Remarkably few baronial families were extinguished in the male line or permanently dispossessed directly as a result of the dynastic civil wars between the Houses of Lancaster and York; the most notable casualties were the Beaufort dukes of Somerset, the main line of the Courtenay earls of Devon, and the last holder of the Hungerford and Moleyns baronies, but it is difficult to identify many other noble houses that were, in fact, terminated by political strife.[80] Even the Bonvilles of Shute (co. Devon), a recently-enobled family, survived in the male line in a cadet branch down to 1495; although three generations of male Bonvilles were eliminated by battle and execution in the course of the upheavals of 1460–1, the bulk of their estates passed to Thomas Grey, marquis of Dorset, after his second marriage with the heiress, Cecily Bonville (1460–1530).[81] Robert, Lord Hungerford (executed in 1464) was succeeded by his daughter, Mary (d. 1533), who married the Hastings heir, Edward (d. 1506), but part of the family estates was eventually recovered by the Hungerford heir male, Sir Walter (d. 1516). Throughout the later middle ages, natural extinction caused by the failure of heirs was by far the most potent force at work in regularly thinning the ranks of the peerage, and that social trend continued unabated well into the Tudor age.[82] Between 1485 and 1509, three viscounties (Beaumont, Lisle and Welles) and four baronies (Beauchamp of Powick, Cheyne, Dinham and St Amand) disappeared permanently for lack of heirs, and in the case of only one of those dignities (the Lisle viscounty) was there an heiress; in 1513 her proposed marriage with

Charles Brandon (afterwards duke of Suffolk) made possible the revival of that title.[83] Two baronies (Audley and FitzWalter) ceased to exist during that period as a consequence of attainder and execution; the Strange barony after 1504 was held by the second Stanley earl of Derby, and the Burgh barony lapsed between 1496 and 1528 because Thomas, Lord Burgh's heir, Edward, was a lunatic.[84] The rapid decrease in the number of lords temporal in the upper house in parliament was not significantly arrested by the few hereditary titles that Henry VII chose to create.

The decline in the military power and territorial influence of the aristocracy that occurred under Henry VII's rule is most clearly reflected in the drastic reduction in the size of the higher nobility, which in 1485 numbered twenty peers, but only ten of those historic titles still survived when Henry VIII's coronation took place on 24 June 1509.[85] Only one dukedom (Bedford was a recent revival) and three earldoms (Huntingdon, Rivers and Wiltshire, all created or revived by Edward IV) lapsed during that period as a consequence of the familiar process of natural extinction. Royal intervention was more effective than the failure of male heirs in diminishing the group of great magnate families; the second Herbert earl left a younger brother, Sir Walter (d. 1507), who had a good claim to the earldom of Huntingdon and much of the family's estates, which Henry VII preferred not to recognise.[86] Political miscalculations, the judicial murder of Edward Plantagenet, the last male representative of that royal line, in 1499, and Henry VII's greedy acquisition of the great Berkeley heritage together combined to bring about the elimination of the duchy of Suffolk, the temporary disappearance of the marquisate of Dorset, and the loss of another four earldoms (Devon, Lincoln, Nottingham and Warwick).[87] The hegemony traditionally exercised in the provinces by the greatest magnate houses in late medieval England depended mainly on long-established and uninterrupted possession of their vast inherited estates, which gave them close ties with the local gentry sometimes extending over several generations. Only two of the most powerful families in the land (represented by that veteran survivor, William (1417–87), earl of Arundel, who for most of his long career wisely kept clear of political involvement, and the dim-witted Ralph Nevill (*c.* 1404–84), second earl of Westmorland,[88] even more long-lived but inactive for very different personal reasons) were lucky enough to survive in peaceful occupation of their lands, unscathed by all the disasters and upheavals that afflicted their social class in the years between the first battle of St Albans in 1455 and what K. B. McFarlane described as 'the final terminus at Stoke' in 1487.[89]

None of the small group of ten great magnates (one duke and nine earls) who constituted the higher nobility in 1509 was strong enough to launch a rebellion against Tudor rule, even if any of them had been minded to do so. Even the most eminent members of the aristocracy had come to recognise that the masterful exercise of royal authority required them to accept a reduced role in English politics, and besides his use of bonds and recognizances, Henry VII had taken ruthless measures to bring some of them, notably the restored Courtenay earl of Devon and the last Stafford duke of Buckingham, into a state of dependence on the king's goodwill. As a reward for his services to Henry Tudor, both during his French exile and at the battle of Bosworth, Sir Edward Courtenay of Boconnoc, co. Cornwall, had been created earl of Devon on 26 October 1485, and he was soon able to recover all the lands formerly held by his kinsmen, the main line of the Courtenay family; their house had been extinguished, on the final defeat of the Lancastrian cause, by the death of John, earl of Devon, at the battle of Tewkesbury fought on 4 May 1471. Because of his own inherited Cornish estates, Earl Edward was richer and better endowed with landed wealth in Devon and Cornwall than his ancestors and predecessors, the Courtenay earls who had dominated the west country for over a century between 1335 and 1461.[90] His prospects of rebuilding his family's fortunes and re-establishing its former deeply-rooted ascendancy in that region were marred by the troubles that overtook his heir, Sir William (*c.* 1475–1511), perhaps largely as a consequence of royal suspicions aroused by his ambitious marriage with Katherine (1479–1527), one of the younger daughters of Edward IV, which was arranged in 1495. The arrest and imprisonment of Sir William Courtenay on charges of treason was one of the precautions considered necessary in 1503, shortly after the death of his sister-in-law, Queen Elizabeth of York, and in the following year he was attainted in Henry VII's last parliament. It was a rare stroke of good fortune for the unlucky Courtenay family that Edward, earl of Devon managed to outlive Henry VII, but after his death, which took place on 28 May 1509, the lands belonging to his earldom were once again forfeited to the crown for the third time since 1461.[91]

Although Henry VII never had grounds for doubting the loyalty of his young kinsman, Edward, duke of Buckingham, he showed himself avaricious, unjust and unscrupulous in his dealings with the Stafford heir. Some of the accusations and complaints made by Buckingham to the late king's executors shortly after Henry VII's death appear to have been well-founded. When, at the age of twenty, Edward Stafford was allowed to have seisin of his inheritance in 1498 a year before the ending of his long minority, he was charged a livery fine of £2,000, which may have amounted to one half-year's income from all his lands in England and Wales. In order to increase his heavy burden of indebtedness to the crown, he was also made responsible for the payment of the punitive fine of £2,000 incurred by his mother, Katherine Wydevill (1457–97), because she had married her third husband, Sir Richard Wingfield, without royal licence. As the Buckingham dowager had left her son, Duke Edward, none of her goods, and he had inherited so little property as her heir, there could be scant justification for the king's action in making him wholly responsible for the settlement of her large debts.[92] By demanding payment of substantial arrears of uncollectable revenues due from Buckingham's Welsh marcher lordships, which had been allowed to accumulate while his lands were in royal wardship, and by imposing other exactions, Henry VII was able to inflict on the young duke debts due to the crown totalling over £6,000 (perhaps more than a year-and-a-half's income from the Stafford estates), which Buckingham was never able to pay off in full.[93] Duke Edward was not as wealthy as his great-grandfather, Humphrey Stafford (1402–60), first duke of Buckingham, whose landed income in 1447–8 was reckoned to be worth more than £5,000 p.a. in clear value.[94] Although the Stafford estates in the hands of Edward, duke of Buckingham were managed with harshness as well as efficiency, his lands could not be made to produce all the money that his lavish expenditure required, and, in order to satisfy his creditors, shortly before his execution in 1521 he was reluctantly compelled to sell some manors that had been held by the House of Stafford for more than two centuries. Although he maintained a great household, employing at times over 200 servants, and chose to build a palatial new castle (never completed) at Thornbury, co. Gloucester, the last Stafford duke of Buckingham was no overmighty subject, because he did not have the military strength or the retinue of retainers in his pay that previous holders of that title had possessed in fifteenth-century England. The dilapidated state of the Stafford inheritance, chiefly brought about by the harm wrought during two prolonged minorities, is registered by the revealing survey of the state of the duke's Welsh marcher lordships, made by his council on their circuit of his lands in 1500.[95] The early Tudor kings, whose annual revenues were more than twenty times as great as the income of the greatest nobleman in England, had nothing to fear from the resentment aroused by the grievances, however keenly felt, of the discontented Edward Stafford, duke of Buckingham.

From the start of his reign, Henry VII was the greatest royal landowner in England since the Norman Conquest, and apart from the extensive estates that were soon bestowed on his mother, Lady Margaret Beaufort, and his uncle, Jasper, duke of Bedford, the first Tudor king did not alienate much of the vast possessions which he had acquired by winning the crown. Lady Margaret Beaufort accumulated manors and lordships in various English shires valued at £3,394 p.a., but as the king was her only son and heir, the rich appanage created for her (fit to support the household of a queen dowager, as she lived in great state) was bound in due course to revert to the young Henry VIII, as it did after her death, which occurred on 29 June 1509.[96] Royal grants soon made Jasper Tudor the greatest of the Welsh marcher lords; besides recovering his earldom of Pembroke, he gained the lordships of Builth, Caldicot, Cilgerran, Glamorgan and Morgannwg, Haverfordwest, Llanstephan and Magor. When, shortly after his accession, he made the newly-created duke of Bedford the most powerful member of the English nobility, Henry VII was not only lavishly rewarding the invaluable services that his uncle, Jasper, had rendered to him during the early years; it was also a prudent recognition of the political necessity of strengthening extending Tudor influence in South Wales, which was imperative during the first decade of the new reign. When Duke Jasper married Katherine Wydevill (1457–97), dowager-duchess of Buckingham (a widow with four children) in the autumn of 1485, his wife was still young enough to make it likely that she would provide him with an heir. Fortunately for the new dynasty, their marriage was childless and consequently it did not establish a line of Tudor dukes of Bedford, too richly endowed with lands in southern England and the Welsh marches. Shortly before his death on 21 December 1495, an act of parliament settled the reversion of all Bedford's enormous estates on his great-nephew, the king's second son, Henry, duke of York (and immediately afterwards this enactment took effect, even to the exclusion of the common law dower rights of Duke Jasper's widow, Katherine).[97] Once Prince Henry had become heir to the throne on the death of his elder brother, Arthur, prince of Wales, on 2 April 1502, all of the duke of Bedford's lands reverted to the crown.

Besides the duchy of Lancaster (to which he had no claim by hereditary right, because he was not a descendant of John of Gaunt's first wife, Blanche (d. 1368) of Lancaster), Henry VII also had possession after 1495 of the whole of the estates of the duchy of York and the Mortimer earldom of March, an asset largely denied to the Yorkist kings. The long survival of Duke Richard Plantagenet's widow, Cecily Nevill (1415–95) cost the crown much-needed revenues totalling in the course of thirty-four years some £100,000, because her huge jointure of lands and rents worth 5,000 marks a year, conveyed to her in 1461, had been wholly assigned on the

York and Mortimer lands in England.[98] As a consequence of the over-generous provision made for their mother, Edward IV and Richard III never enjoyed the advantage of holding the bulk of the York inheritance; instead they were left only the late duke's Welsh marcher lordships, which in the latter half of the fifteenth century were increasingly a declining fiscal asset, and the residue of his English manors, some of whose profits had to be used to pay Duke Richard's legacy of enormous debts.[99] Throughout his reign, Henry VII retained in his own hands the York–Mortimer heritage, which enabled him to endow his queen (without much depleting the crown lands), regardless of the legal rights of her three surviving younger sisters, Cecily (d. 1507), Anne (d. 1511) and Katherine (d. 1527), who were therefore disinherited. It was not in Henry VII's interest to investigate the fate of Edward V and his younger brother, Richard (1473–83), duke of York; legal proof that they were dead would have enabled their sisters to claim that the landed possessions belonging to the duchy of York should have been partitioned into four equal shares.[100] Before the onset of civil war in 1455, there had been six English dukes, namely Buckingham, Exeter, Norfolk, Somerset, Suffolk and York. After the flight abroad in 1501 of Edmund de la Pole, earl (and former duke) of Suffolk, the Stafford lands held by Edward, duke of Buckingham were the only ducal estates still left in private hands. Apart from a portion of the former Mowbray inheritance in East Anglia recovered by Thomas Howard (1443–1524), who in 1489 had been restored to the earldom of Surrey,[101] almost all the endowments of the duchies of Exeter, Norfolk, Somerset, Suffolk and York had become the property of the crown. Henry VII's land revenues were further augmented by all the Beauchamp, Despenser, Nevill and Montagu estates that had once belonged to Richard Nevill (1428–71), earl of Warwick, 'the Kingmaker'. His widow, Anne Beauchamp (1426–93), who had already been totally disinherited by an act of parliament in 1474, was obliged on 13 December 1487 to make the king her heir after her lands had been nominally restored to her. The purpose of this transaction was to extinguish the claims of her grandson, the ill-fated Edward Plantagenet, earl of Warwick , who was after 1478 successively a royal ward and a state prisoner until his execution in 1499 on trumped-up charges of treason.[102] Like Edward IV, the founder of the Tudor dynasty had few scruples about disinheriting lawful heirs, and his gigantic acquisitions whetted his appetite for more unjust takeovers of aristocratic landed property. His dealings with William Berkeley, earl of Nottingham (soon to become the first and last marquis of Berkeley) in 1487 deprived the earl's brother and heir, Maurice (1436–1506) of his legitimate expectations of succeeding to one of the oldest and richest baronies in England.[103] The contract made in 1491 that would have enabled Henry VII to buy (at a bargain price of £1,000) the castle and lordship of Codnor, co. Derby (the *caput* of that barony) and other lands, in accordance with the last will of the childless and impoverished Henry (1435–96), Lord Grey, failed to take effect. This transaction, made for the benefit of the king's second son, Henry, was nullified because the last Lord Grey of Codnor's three sisters were ultimately successful in upholding their legal rights.[104] While the disinherited Berkeley heir, Maurice, was persistent enough to recover by his own efforts some fifty manors belonging to his family estates that should not have been alienated to the crown,[105] Henry VII was (as we have already seen) more fortunate in his dealings with the feckless Richard Grey (d. 1524), earl of Kent, who was willing to deprive his young half-brother, Sir Henry Grey (*c.* 1490–1562) of his hopes of succeeding to that great magnate inheritance, which was among the finest in the realm. After he had obtained possession of several of the earl of Kent's English lordships and manors, including the best of them, Ampthill, co. Bedford, the purchase of the marcher lordship of Ruthin, held by the Grey family since 1282 (when it was created by Edward I a few months before he completed the conquest of the principality of Wales) was the king's last major acquisition in the aristocratic land market.[106]

Although the amount of wealth amassed by Henry VII has until recently often been exaggerated, the extent of his success in dealing with the English crown's financial problems remains indisputable. In a period of less than a quarter of a century he probably doubled his royal revenues with little recourse to direct taxation, and that transitory achievement was never repeated by any subsequent ruler in England as long as the age of personal monarchy lasted. The sources of income at his disposal were never as great or as readily available as those enjoyed by Edward III, Richard II and the early Lancastrian kings.[107] The loss of most of the fiscal records of the king's chamber makes it impossible to estimate accurately the crown's receipts from all sources in any one year, but after 1504 they seem to have averaged annually some £113,000 (including the king's pension of about £5,000 p.a., paid by Louis XII of France). Land revenues from all sources, both permanent and temporary, are reckoned to have yielded £40,000 p.a., of the cash handled by the treasurer of the king's chamber during those years,[108] and it is clear that the duchy of Lancaster estates made the largest single contribution to that total. Towards the end of Henry VII's reign, the English manors and lordships belonging to the duchy of Lancaster were probably more productive than they had been in the early decades in the fifteenth century, although a high standard of efficiency had been maintained by the officials of Henry IV and Henry V. Between 1505 and 1507 the cash receipts from the duchy lands supplied the considerable sum of £20,538 3s 11d to the king's coffers (and it is noteworthy that only £1,080 13s 6½d of that total came from the duchy's Welsh marcher lordships). The gross income of the duchy of Lancaster in those years averaged over £14,000 p.a., but annual expenditure on fees, wages, annuities and other charges amounted to over £4,000.[109] There is evidence that in the Midlands the duchy estates were being over-exploited by the king's officials at that time. Although Henry VII appears to have maintained close personal supervision of the affairs of the duchy, the initiative in this temporarily successful bid to rackrent that part of his lands may well have come from Sir Richard Empson acting in his capacity as chancellor of the duchy, rather than from the king himself, and, as events proved, it could not be continued for long.[110]

When Henry VII became king of England, he was well aware that the political advantages of possession of the duchy of Lancaster could be at least as great as the fiscal value of those estates, and he soon set out to rebuild the power-base that had been the mainstay of the Lancastrian dynasty in its most successful years before the untimely death of Henry V in 1422. Life annuities granted by Henry VII in the first year or so of his reign to 104 men (including fifteen knights and thirteen esquires) were charged on the county palatine of Lancaster and the lordship of Tutbury, co. Stafford, at a cost of £1,033 6s 8d a year.[111] Perhaps his chief motive was to reinforce the crown's territorial influence in those regions in order to avoid excessive dependence on the loyalty of the Stanley family, which had greatly strengthened its local power and authority as a consequence of the latest change of dynasty. It did not prove necessary for Henry VII to burden the duchy of Lancaster estates with excessive charges in the form of annuities paid to retainers, as Henry IV had been obliged to do throughout his reign. Nearly all of the annuities given by Henry VII to sixteen members of the Cheshire gentry (and a few Welshmen) which were payable out of the revenues of the lordship of Denbigh (in its best days by far the most lucrative part of the earldom of March) were granted during the first eighteen months of his reign.[112] Retaining by grants of local offices in the king's gift, which could provide the fortunate recipients with substantial income from valuable fees, proved to be the most effective way of extending and maintaining the king's retinue in early Tudor England. In every English shire, the Tudor kings had at their disposal a greater fund of royal patronage than their predecessors in the later middle ages had ever possessed. Because of the vast accumulation of estates now added to the crown lands, they could reward (or ensure) service by grants of the offices of steward, receiver and surveyor of lordships, constables and porters of castles, and foresters, rangers, parkers and warreners of forests, woods, parks and warrens. These officers, which some of the most powerful members of the English nobility had for so long used to uphold their traditional ascendancy in the provinces, became an effective means of asserting royal authority. Those of Henry VII's local offices who failed in their duty to rally to his support and render military service in time of need forfeited the offices they had had of his gift.[113] The highly successful career of Sir Ralph Egerton (d. 1528), whose annuities and fees held in respect of offices granted to him by the king were worth over £300 p.a., shows how rewarding loyalty to the Tudor dynasty could be; at Ridley, he had by royal grant what John Leland regarded as 'the fairest gentleman's house of al Chestreshire'.[114] Skilful and efficient deployment of such patronage after 1485 made the king's affinity far stronger than that of any member of the English nobility. After 1497, despite Henry VII's growing unpopularity in his last years, there was no risk or prospect of an aristocratic rebellion and he was free to govern his kingdom as he willed.

While Edmund Dudley lay in prison in the Tower of London, awaiting execution after his show trial and condemnation on charges of constructive treason on 18 July 1509, he felt morally bound to address to Henry VII's executors a petition, in which he listed many acts of injustice and oppression committed by the late king. According to Dudley's testimony (and his influence in Henry VII's counsels in the last phase of the reign made him well qualified to judge), over a hundred persons, all of whom he named, had suffered wrongs at the king's hands that needed to be redressed. This was an urgent matter of religious duty, lest the salvation of the deceased monarch's soul should be imperilled and his ascent to heaven be impeded, because he had failed to do right and justice to many of his subjects.[115] It is significant that only three earls (the second Stanley earl of Derby, the fifth earl of Northumberland and Thomas Howard, earl of Surrey), four barons (Abergavenny, Clifford, the late Lord Daubeney and Edward Sutton, Lord Dudley) and one baroness in her own right (Jane, Lady Strange, whose husband, George Stanley (d. 1503), had been the late earl of Derby's heir) appear among the names of the aristocratic persons catalogued in this list, which (apart from the omission of Edward, duke of Buckingham's grievances) appears to be comprehensive as far as the English nobility were concerned. Dudley's aim was also to prevent further wrongs from being done by the levying of outstanding debts owed to the crown; he believed that Northumberland, who had already paid £3,000, had been mulcted of £1,000 more than Henry VII had at first intended to exact, and that fines still owed by others had been unjustly imposed. Perhaps influenced by Dudley's representations, Henry VIII was moved to cancel the sums that Henry Percy, earl of Northumberland, George Nevill, Lord Abergavenny and the executors of Giles (d. 1508), Lord Daubeney were under obligation to pay, and eventually, in May 1517, he reduced the debts owed by Thomas Stanley (d. 1521), earl of Derby, by £1,400, but in respect of these grievances he was not prepared to do more.[116] The petition of Edmund Dudley does much to modify the impression created by J. R. Lander that the English nobility as a class suffered grave hardships and misfortunes as a consequence of royal tyranny during Henry VII's reign. In some instances Dudley took a too unfavourable view of the late king's financial dealings with great magnates who could well afford to pay what was demanded. When Thomas Howard, earl of Surrey was charged £1,000 for royal licence to inherit the dower lands of Elizabeth (d. 1506), duchess of Norfolk, he was sure to get his money back soon because he was acquiring estates worth some £600 a year and so doubling his possessions in East Anglia.[117] If Henry VII was guilty of rapacity (and in some cases that conclusion seems indisputable), his lengthy will, made on 31 March 1509, shows little sign of remorse, and he relied chiefly on his investment in the purchase of 10,000 masses to guarantee his own eternal salvation.[118]

The reaction against Henry VII's methods of government after his death on 21 April 1509 cost far more than the lives of his most unpopular agents, Edmund Dudley and Sir Richard Empson. To appease discontent it was not enough for Henry VIII, on the advice of his councillors , to cancel during the early years of his reign at least 175 recognizances taken by his father, including fifty-one that had been unjustly extorted, 'contrary to law, reason and good conscience'.[119] Only two of those fifty-one recognizances concerned peers (Lords Daubeney and Mountjoy). When Henry VIII became king of England at the age of seventeen, he needed to buy support and goodwill and to win the confidence of some of the English magnates whom the late king had perhaps treated with excessive severity. Between April 1510 and Michaelmas 1515, lands, rents and farms alienated (some temporarily, some permanently) by Henry VIII, together with the cost of the fees, wages and annuities that he had granted, reduced the king's annual income by £19,257.[120] The most deserving of these recipients of royal largesse was the widowed Lady Margaret Pole, sister of the last male Plantagenet, the hapless Edward, earl of Warwick, who had been put to death in 1499. As some recompense for the wrongs that her family had suffered, Lady Margaret (d. 1541) was restored to part of the great possessions formerly held by her father, George, duke of Clarence (executed in 1478) and his wife, Isabel Nevill (d. 1476), the elder daughter of Warwick 'the Kingmaker'; she was granted the lands of the earldom of Salisbury, valued at £1,285 a year.[121] Undoubtedly the most fortunate of the peers who benefited from the young king's liberality was George Nevill (d. 1535), Lord Abergavenny, who was not only released from the enormous penalties imposed on him in 1507 for unlawful retaining, but was also granted the Welsh marcher lordship of Abergavenny, to which his family had a longstanding claim but no valid title at law.[122] As a consequence of the numerous royal grants made by Henry VIII in the first six years of his reign, the crown's annual land revenues in 1515 were worth only about £25,500 (out of which provision for Queen Catherine was costing a further £4,000 a year), as compared with receipts of at least £40,000 in 1509.[123] The relative affluence that the English crown had achieved in Henry VII's later years, when the king's lands had been worth as much in annual income as the proceeds of the customs duties, had proved only a transient phenomenon.

When he concluded his laborious study of Henry VII's reign, Dr S. B. Chrimes had difficulty in assessing the significance of the political and governmental record of the ablest of the Tudor monarchs. With characteristic lack of enthusiasm, he reiterated the familiar textbook verdict that Henry VII was 'no great innovator'; instead his historical role was seen as that of 'a stabilizer, for lack of whom the ships of state are apt to founder'.[124] The first Tudor king cannot be dismissed as a piece of ballast, and his success in founding a dynasty that ruled England for longer than the Houses of Lancaster and York had managed to do was not attained merely by making existing governmental institutions work more efficiently. The trends that characterised Tudor rule before 1509 tend to challenge that opinion. Knowledge of English government finance in that period remains sadly incomplete, but Henry VII probably amassed a greater hoard of treasure than any previous English ruler, without much recourse to direct taxation (and that achievement was never repeated).[125] In dealing with unlawful retaining, the court set up by statute in 1487 (and still in existence in 1529) may well have served a useful purpose.[126] Henry VII's policy of seeking to make all substantial property owners tenants-in-chief of the crown (and so liable to the hazards of prerogative wardship) was a rewarding new fiscal development with important and lasting political consequences; he anticipated much of the business of the Court of Wards and Liveries, established in 1540.[127] 'The king's Council learned in the Law' (in existence by 1500) was in effect a new revenue court, one of whose chief functions was to enforce payment of debts claimed by the crown, and the office of surveyor of the king's prerogative (created in 1508) was designed to intensify lucrative exploitation of royal feudal rights and financial interests.[128] The more unpopular features of Henry VII's government did not survive his death; if ever there was a 'New Monarchy' in England, it began and ended with Henry VII.

NOTES

Note: Place of publication is London unless otherwise stated.

1   There is no satisfactory account of the Bosworth campaign; W. H. Hutton, *The Battle of Bosworth Field* (1788), was reprinted (second edition, 1813) in 1974. S. B. Chrimes, *Henry VII* (1972) relied mainly on *Three Books of Polydore Vergil's English History* (ed. H. Ellis, Camden Society, vol. XXIX, 1844) for his narrative and recent works (especially M. J. Bennett, *The Battle of Bosworth* (1985) and R. A. Griffiths and R. S. Thomas, *The Making of the Tudor Dynasty* (1985)) have contributed little towards a better understanding of the causes of the final overthrow of the House of York.

2   *Calendar of Close Rolls* (hereinafter CCR), *1476–85*, 340–1; *Rotuli Parliamentorum*, 6 vols., 1767–77 (hereinafter *RP*), VI, 275–8; J. C. Wedgwood, ed.: *History of Parliament: Biographies of the Members of the Commons House 1439–1509* (1936); *Register of the Ministers of the Members of Both Houses 1439–1509* (1938), 481–5, 496.

3   G. E. Cokayne, *The Complete Peerage* (ed. V. Gibbs *et al.*, 13 vols., 1910–59, hereinafter cited as *CP*), II, 133–5; *ibid.*, IX, 717–8. For Lady Margaret Beaufort's visits to her son, Henry, at Raglan Castle, in Gwent, see M. A. Hicks, 'The career of Henry Percy, fourth earl of Northumberland, with special reference to his retinue' (unpublished Southampton University MA thesis, 1971), p. 8. For William (d. 1469), earl of Pembroke's wish to marry his daughter, Maud, to Henry Tudor, see N. H. Nicolas, *Testamenta Vetusta* (2 vols., 1826), I, 305. William Berkeley, earl of Nottingham testified on 16 January 1486 that he had known Henry Tudor 'well for twenty years and more'; for the depositions made by eight witnesses on Henry VII's behalf in support of his petition for a papal dispensation to enable him to marry Elizabeth of York, see *Calendar of Papal Registers relating to Great Britain and Ireland* (hereinafter cited as *Cal. Pap. Reg.*), XIV, *1484–92* (1960), 17–21.

4   See Appendix II. For lands and offices gained by John de Vere (1443–1513), earl of Oxford, during Henry VII's reign, see n. 101.

5   R. S. Thomas, 'The political career, estates and "connection" of Jasper Tudor, earl of Pembroke and duke of Bedford (d. 1495)' (unpublished University of Wales Ph.D. thesis, 1971, henceforth cited as Thomas, 'Jasper Tudor'). For a biographical note on Sir Roger Kynaston (d. 1492), of Myddle and Knockin, co. Salop, see J. B. Blakeway, *The Sheriffs of Shropshire* (Shrewsbury, 1831), pp. 73–4; he was appointed constable of Harlech Castle, with a garrison of twenty men under his command, and made sheriff and escheator of the county of Merioneth for life by Richard III (*British Library Harleian Manuscript 433*, ed. R. Horrox and P. W. Hammond (4 vols., 1979–83), I, 104, 139, 155). For the recovery of Harlech Castle by Richard Pole, esquire, early in 1486, see Public Record Office (hereinafter PRO) DL 29/636/10,342 (account of William Griffith, chamberlain of North Wales, 1485–6), m. 7.

6   A. V. Antonovics, 'Henry VII, King of England, "By the Grace of Charles VIII of France"', *Kings and Nobles in the Later Middle Ages* (ed. R. A. Griffiths and J. W. Sherborne, Gloucester, 1986), pp. 169–84) is sceptical about the scale of French military help to Henry Tudor in August 1485. According to G-M de Fontanieu, *Histoire du règne de Charles VIII*

(unpublished manuscript, BN 10, 450, 13759–60), t.i, p. 68, Anne of Beaujeu provided the Tudor pretender with '4,000 hommes de troupes d'élite'; I am obliged to the Bibliothèque Nationale for providing me with a microfilm of the relevant part of this ms. For the role of Vice-Admiral Coulon as commander of the French fleet that transported Henry Tudor's troops, see A. Spont, 'La marine française sous le règne de Charles VIII', *Revue des questions historiques*, LV (1894), pp. 387–454, esp. p. 394.

7   W. Tom Williams, 'Henry of Richmond's Itinerary to Bosworth', *Y Cymmrodor*, XXIX (1919), 33–4; W. Rees, *An Historical Atlas of Wales* (Cardiff, 1951), plate 54; R. A. Griffiths and R. S. Thomas, *The Making of the Tudor Dynasty* (Gloucester, 1985), pp. 146–50.

8   J. Hunter, *South Yorkshire: The History and Topography of the Deanery of Doncaster* (1828), I, 75. Robert Morton (d. 1396), of Bawtry, co. Notts., whose descendant and namesake was a loyal Ricardian in 1485, was steward of the Yorkshire lands of Edmund of Langley, duke of York (*Calendar of Patent Rolls, 1381–5* (1898) (hereinafter *CPR, 1381–5*), p. 320), but his loyalty rested chiefly with John of Gaunt (1340–99), duke of Lancaster. His son and heir, Robert Morton (d. 1424) was in the service of Edward, duke of York, but later generations of the Mortons of Bawtry, co. Notts., were not retainers of the House of York. (T. B. Pugh, 'The lands and servants of Edmund of Langley (1342–1402), duke of York, and Edward, duke of York (c. 1373–1415)', unpublished University of Oxford B.Litt. thesis (1948), pp. 156–74).

9   *English Historical Review* (hereinafter *EHR*), XCI (1976), 373; 'it was the loyal Yorkists who triumphed at Bosworth'. For Lambert Simnel's rebellion, see M. J. Bennett, *Lambert Simnel and The Battle of Stoke* (Gloucester, 1987); other recent publications on this subject include D. E. Roberts, *The Battle of Stoke Field* (Newark and District Council, 1987).

10   The rebels at the battle of Stoke mustered about 8,000 men (*RP*, VI, 397; *Chroniques de Jean Molinet* (ed. G. Doutrepont and O. Jodogne, 3 vols., Brussels, 1935–7, I, 564). According to the *Book of Howth* (*Calendar of Carew MSS.*, ed. J. S. Brewer and W. Bullen, vol. V (*Rolls Series*, hereinafter *RS*), 1871), p. 189), 4,000 Irishmen were killed at Stoke. There is no reliable contemporary estimate of the size of the king's army, which was probably at least 12,000 strong. *The Great Chronicle of London* (ed. A. H. Thomas and I. D. Thornley, 1938, henceforth cited as *Gt. Chron. Lond.*) states (p. 241) that Henry VII's troops outnumbered those of his opponents by 20,000 men, but that figure seems unlikely and excessive. For Francis, Lord Lovel's escape to Scotland, see Sheilah O'Connor, 'Francis Lovel and the rebels of Furness Fells', *The Ricardian*, VII (1987), 366–70.

11   F. Bacon, *History of the Reign of King Henry VII* (ed. J. Rawson Lumby, Cambridge, 1902), pp. 36–7; H. A. L. Fisher, *History of England (1485–1547)*, second edition (1928), pp. 17–18, based his account of the battle of Stoke on Bacon's work, and M. J. Bennett, *op. cit.*, is inadequate. For the narrative written by a herald who was with Henry VII's army in this campaign, see J. Leland, *De rebus Brittanicis collectanea* (ed. T. Hearne, 1774, henceforth cited as Leland, *Collectanea*), IV, 209–15; Jean Molinet (*op. cit.*, I, 564) makes clear that the superiority of the king's army in archers soon proved decisive; he states that Schwarz's German mercenaries were 'filled with arrows like hedgehogs'.

12   M. J. Bennett, 'Henry VII and the northern rising of 1489', *EHR*, CV (1990), 34–59; J. Gairdner, 'The story of Perkin Warbeck', *History of the Life and Reign of Richard the Third* (Cambridge, 1898), pp. 263–335.

13   Gladys Temperley, *Henry VII* (1914), pp. 122–4; W. A. J. Archbold, 'Sir William Stanley and Perkin Warbeck', *EHR*, XIV (1899), 529–34. For Sir William Stanley's wealth, see *Chronicles of London* (ed. C. L. Kingsford, Oxford, 1905, henceforth cited as Kingsford, *Chron. Lond.*), pp. 204–5. For John Radcliffe (d. 1496), Lord FitzWalter, see *CP*, V, 486–7; *RP*, VI, 504; *Select Cases in the Council of Henry VII* (ed. G. C. Bayne and W. H. Dunham, *Selden Society*, vol. 75 (1956), pp. 23, 25 and J. A. Guy, *The Cardinal's Court* (1977), pp. 16–17, 148. For Edward IV's dealings with the Paston family and their dispute with John Mowbray (1444–76), duke of Norfolk, see *The Paston Letters* (ed. J. Gairdner, 6 vols., 1904), I, 246, 294–5; V, 30–3, 239–40, and *Paston Letters and Papers of the Fifteenth Century* (ed. N. Davis, Oxford, 1971–6), Part I, pp. 543–5, 595–6.

14 G. Temperley, *op.cit.*, pp. 145–9; I. Arthurson, 'The rising of 1497', *People, Politics and Community in the Later Middle Ages* (ed. J. Rosenthal and C. Richmond, Gloucester, 1987), pp. 1–18 and I. Arthurson, 'The king's voyage in Scotland: the war that never was', *England in the Fifteenth Century* (ed. D. Williams, Leicester, 1987), pp. 1–18. For the career and fate of Henry Percy (1449–89), earl of Northumberland, see M. E. James, 'The murder of Cocklodge, 28 April, 1489', *Durham University Journal*, LVII (1964), 80–7; M. Weiss, 'A power in the north? The Percies in the fifteenth century', *Historical Journal*, 19 (1976), 501–9; M. A. Hicks, 'Dynastic change and northern society: the career of the fourth earl of Northumberland, 1470–89', *Northern History*, XIV (1978), 78–107, and M. A. Hicks, 'The Yorkshire rebellion of 1489 reconsidered', *ibid.*, XXII (1986), 39–62.

15 For rebellions in Kent during the fifteenth century and Richard, duke of York's insurrection in 1452, see R. L. Storey, *The End of the House of Lancaster* (1966), pp. 61–8, 93–104. There were major uprisings in Kent in 1450, 1460, 1471 and 1483; see R. A. Griffiths *The Reign of King Henry VI* (1981), pp. 610–55, 859–61; C. F. Richmond, 'Fauconberg's Kentish rising of May, 1471', *EHR*, IXXXV (1970), 673–92 and Agnes E. Conway, 'The Maidstone sector of Buckingham's rebellion, October 18th, 1483', *Archaeologia Cantiana*, XXXVII (1925), 97–119. For George Nevill (d. 1535), Lord Abergavenny and John Brooke (d. 1512), Lord Cobham, see *CP*, I, 31–3; *ibid.*, III, 346–7. For the social structure of fifteenth-century Kent, see *Inquisitions and assessments relating to feudal aids, 1284–1431* (6 vols., 1899–1920), VI, 465–77, and *Archaeologia Cantiana*, XI (1899), 394–7; B. Cope, 'List of the gentry of Kent in the time of Henry VII', *ibid.*, XL (1928), 89–104.

16 *CP*, I, 342. The suggestion made by *Gt. Chron. Lond.*, p. 278 and W. Busch, *England under the Tudors* (translated by Alice M. Todd, 1895), p. 346 that James, Lord Audley had a private quarrel with John, Lord Cheyne appears to be unfounded; see *Deputy Keeper's Reports*, XXXVII, App. II, p. 723, cited by Busch as evidence for this surmise. James (d. 1459), Lord Audley was one of the few barons whose taxable income in England in 1436 was assessed at less than £400; he declared that he had no more than £200 p.a., and the dower lands held by his mother, Elizabeth, Lady Audley, were valued at £100 p. a. (*EHR*, XLIX (1934), 618).

17 G. Temperley, *op. cit.*, pp. 149–51; *Gt. Chron. Lond.*, pp. 276–8; *The Anglica Historica of Polydore Vergil, 1485–1537* (ed. D. Hay, *Camden Series*, LXXIV, 1950, henceforth cited as *Polydore Vergil*), pp. 95–7.

18 *Polydore Vergil*, pp. 104–11; *Hall's Chronicle* (ed. H. Ellis, 1809), p. 484; Busch, *op. cit.*, pp. 116–17; G. Temperley, *op. cit.*, pp. 155–8; L. C. Attreed, 'A new source for Perkin Warbeck's invasion of 1497', *Medieval Studies*, 48 (1986), 514–22.

19 Kingsford, *Chron. Lond.*, pp. 225, 331; *Hall's Chronicle* (ed. H. Ellis, 1809), p. 490.

20 F. C. Dietz, *English Government Finance, 1485–1558* (Illinois, 1921), p. 79. By his second wife, Constanza of Castile (d. 1394), John of Gaunt had a daughter, Katalina, who married Henry III (d. 1406), king of Castile; Catherine of Aragon was a granddaughter of Henry III's son and heir, John II (d. 1454), king of Castile.

21 G. R. Elton, *England under the Tudors* (1955), p. 42.

22 S. T. Bindoff, *Tudor England* (1950), pp. 53, 66. For J. R. Lander's opinions, see below, n. 24.

23 *RP*, VI, 275–8, 397–400, 504, 544–8; for the restoration of Thomas Howard, earl of Surrey, and John, Lord Zouche to forfeited dignities and the partial restitution of their lands, see *ibid.*, VI, 410–11, 424, 426–8, 448–50, 478–9, 484–7.

24 *EHR*, LXXXI (1966), 154; J. R. Lander, 'Bonds, coercion and fear: Henry VII and the peerage', *Florilegium Historiale: Essays presented to Wallace K. Ferguson* (ed. J. G. Rowe and W. H. Stockdale, Toronto, 1971), pp. 328–67, esp. p. 339. This essay (henceforth referred to as Lander, *Ferguson Essays*) was subsequently reprinted in J. R. Lander, Crown and Nobility 1450–1509 (1976), pp. 267–300 (henceforth cited as Lander, *Crown and Nobility*); see also J. R. Lander, 'Attainder and forfeiture 1453–1509', *Historical Journal*, IV (1961), 120–51 (reprinted in *Crown and Nobility* pp. 127–58).

25 Lander, *Ferguson Essays*, pp. 335, 339, 347, 351; Lander, *Crown and Nobility*, pp. 276, 281, 292, 297; S. B. Chrimes, *Henry VII* (1972), pp. 214–15; C. S. L. Davies, *Peace, Print and Protestantism 1450–1558* (1976), p. 114.

26 See K. B. McFarlane, in *EHR*, LXXIV (1959), 114–15, and *ibid.*, LXXXI (1966), 153–4.

27 *CCR, 1413–9*, 97–9.

28 Patricia M. Barnes (ed.), 'The Chancery *corpus cum causa* file, 10–11 Edward IV', *Medieval Legal Records Edited in Memory of C. A. F. Meekings* (ed. R. F. Hunnisett and J. B. Post, 1978), pp. 429–76, esp., pp. 438–41, 445; *CP*, XI, 402–3; *RP*, VI, 202–4; *Glamorgan County History*, vol. III (ed. T. B. Pugh, Cardiff, 1971), pp. 261–2, 625, n. 264. For Gurney's lands, see B. P. Wolffe, *The Royal Demesne in English History* (1971), esp. pp. 182, 188, 296.

29 *CCR, 1485–1500*, Nos. 52 (Beaumont), 82 (Westmorland), 612 (Dorset), 753 (Devon), 1056 (Grey of Wilton), 1222 (Dudley). This calculation does not include bonds given to Henry VII by two peers in connection with the settlement of private disputes; namely, No. 227 (Richard (d. 1503), Lord Beauchamp of Powick), and No. 407 (Edward (d. 1506), Lord Hastings), or a bond for £300 (No. 412) taken by the king on 14 February 1489 from Edward (d. 1492), Viscount Lisle (and two others), on behalf of Sir William Berkeley, of Weoley, co. Worcs., who had suffered the penalties of attainder and forfeiture in 1485 as a supporter of Richard III. Three bonds (Nos. 974, 1008–9) given to Henry VII between 18 December 1496 and 16 March 1497 by Sir Edward Burgh (d. 1528) have likewise not been included in this reckoning; although Burgh was the son and heir of Thomas (d. 1496), Lord Burgh (*CP*, II, 422–3) he was never summoned to parliament and cannot be regarded as a member of the peerage. After 8 December 1499, the failure of Chancery officials to enrol recognizances in cases of treason, or misprision of treason, was a punishable offence, and that enactment (*CCR*, 1485–1500, No. 1199) may partly explain the great increase in the number of recognizances henceforth enrolled during Henry VII's reign. Some bonds and recognizances taken by the king from nobles before 1499 were not enrolled on the Chancery Close Rolls; notably the bonds for £3,000 each given by both John, Lord Scrope of Bolton and Thomas, Lord Scrope of Masham on their release from jail after Lambert Simnel's rebellion in 1487 (*CPR, 1485–1500*, pp. 190, 199, 216, 238, 264, 273).

30 *CCR, 1485–1500*, No. 52; *CP*, II, 62–4.

31 *CCR, 1485–1500*, No. 82; for Richard III's grants to Ralph (d. 1499), earl of Westmorland, see *CPR, 1476–85*, pp. 427–8 and *British Library Harleian Manuscript 433* (ed. Rosemary Horrox and P. W. Hammond, 4 vols., 1979–83), I, 169.

32 *CCR, 1485–1500*, No. 753; it should be noted that this entry is calendared inaccurately (see PRO C.54/354, m.13d.; I am indebted to Dr S. J. Payling for this information and for the references in n. 33 and n. 34 to the Chancery Close Rolls); *Select Cases in the Council of Henry VII* (ed. C. G. Bayne and W. H. Dunham, *Selden Society*, vol. 75 (for 1956, published 1958, henceforth cited as Bayne and Dunham, *Select Cases*), p. cxxxv.

33 *CCR, 1485–1500*, No. 1056 (PRO C54/358, m.12d.).

34 *Ibid.*, No. 1222 (PRO C54/360, m.25d.).

35 J. R. Lander, *op. cit.*, pp. 342–4. For Thomas Grey (d. 1501), marquis of Dorset, see *CP*, IV, 418–19; C. L. Kingsford, in *Dictionary of National Biography*, XXIII, 201–2; *Three Books of Polydore Vergil's English History* (ed. H. Ellis, *Camden Society*, XXIX, 1844), pp. 200, 203, 210, 214; C. D. Ross, *Richard III* (1981), *passim*.

36 *CCR, 1485–1500*, No. 612; see Appendix I, pp. 101–5; *RP*, VI, 472–3.

37 *CCR, 1485–1500*, No. 618.

38 *CP*, IV, 419–20; Busch, *op. cit.*, p. 172; H. Miller, *Henry VIII and the English Nobility* (1986), pp. 7–8. Dorset and Sir William Courtenay were removed from the Tower of London and taken to Calais on 28 October 1508; see The *Chronicle of Calais in the Reigns of Henry VII and Henry VIII* (ed. J. G. Nichols, *Camden Society*, XXV, 1846), p. 6.

39 *Letters and Papers . . . of the Reigns of Richard III and Henry VII* (ed. J. Gairdner, 2

vols., R. S., 1861, 1863, henceforth cited as Gairdner, *LP. Richard III and Henry VII*), I, 234–5. For the part played by informers in bringing about the downfall of George (1449–78), duke of Clarence, see *The Crowland Chronicle Continuations 1459–1486* (ed. N. Pronay and J. Cox, 1986, henceforth cited as *Crowland Chronicle*), pp. 144–5.

    40   *CP*, XII, pt. I, 438–53; *RP*, VI, 474–8.

    41   According to *Hall's Chronicle*, p. 495, Edmund de la Pole, earl of Suffolk committed a murder and was pardoned by Henry VII, after he had been indicted in the Court of King's Bench. This crime was probably committed in 1498, when he was charged with felonies and murders in co. Middlesex (H. A. Napier, *Historical Notices of Swyncombe and Ewelme* (Oxford, 1858), pp. 171–2). *Polydore Vergil* (p. 123) states that Suffolk fled abroad partly because he was heavily in debt. For Suffolk's character and his career after his escape from England (and that of his younger brother, Richard de la Pole, d. 1525), see Napier, *op. cit.*, pp. 173–97; Gairdner, *LP. Richard III and Henry VII*, I, xxxvi–lvii; Busch, *op. cit.*, pp. 165–98; Alison Hanham, 'Edmund de la Pole, defector', *Renaissance Studies* (ed. D. S. Chambers and J. E. Law, Oxford, 1988), 240–50.

    42   Busch, *op cit.*, p. 186, n. 2 did not believe that Henry VII could have loaned the Archduke Philip a total of £138,000 in 1505; in his opinion, an error had occurred in BL.Add.MS.7099 (Craven Ord's transcripts from the king's Book of Payments, 1491–1505, printed in part in S. Bentley, *Excerpta Historia* (1831), pp. 87–133). The payment of £138,000, as loans made to the Archduke Philip in 1505, is recorded in an account book of payments made between 1502 and 1505 by John Heron, treasurer of the king's chamber, acquired by the British Library in 1978 (BL.Add.MS.59, 899, fos. 85, 101). Dietz, *op. cit.*, p. 85 reckoned that the Archduke Philip and his son, Charles (the future Emperor Charles V) had borrowed at least £260,000 from the king of England by 1509; this estimate was based on totals extracted from two of John Heron's Books of Payments (BL.Add.MS.21, 480, 1 October 1499–1 October 1505, and PRO E.36/214, 1 October 1505–1 October 1509). B. P. Wolffe, *op. cit.*, p. 224 recognised that these 'loans' provided by Henry VII (without prospect of repayment) indicated the cash price that the first Tudor king 'was able and willing to pay in his efforts to make the continent unsafe for pretenders'.

    43   *Handbook of British Chronology* (ed. E. B. Fryde *et al.*, 3rd edition, 1986), pp. 42, 60; *Gt. Chron. Lond.*, p. 321; F. Sandford, *Genealogical History of the Kings and Queens of England, 1066–1707* (1707), pp. 475–8.

    44   Gairdner, *LP. Richard III and Henry VII*, I, 231–40.

    45   *The Will of King Henry the Seventh* (ed. T. Astle, 1775); M. R. Horowitz, 'Richard Empson, Minister of Henry VII', *Bulletin of the Institute of Historical Research* (hereinafter *BIHR*), LV (1982), 35–49, esp., 43; Margaret M. Condon, 'Ruling elites in the Reign of Henry VII', *Patronage, Pedigree and Power in Later Medieval England* (ed. C. D. Ross, Gloucester, 1979), pp. 109–42, esp. p. 134.

    46   Lander, *Ferguson Essays*, pp. 339, 360, n. 80; Lander, *Crown and Nobility*, p. 282, n. 80.

    47   Lander, *Ferguson Essays*, p. 352; Lander, *Crown and Nobility*, p. 298; Dietz, *op. cit.* p. 31, n. 27.

    48   Lander, *Ferguson Essays*, p. 347; Lander, *Crown and Nobility*, p. 292.

    49   *CPR, 1494–1509*, p. 11; *CP*, VI, 141–3; W. R. B. Robinson, 'Edward Grey, Lord Powis; the last medieval lord of Powys', *The Montgomeryshire Collections*, vol. 67 (1979), pp. 117–58, esp. pp. 119–20.

    50   *CCR, 1500–1509*, Nos. 408, 415; Edward, Lord Dudley appears to have surrendered his custody of his grandson's moiety of the lordship of Powys in 1517; see W. R. B. Robinson, *op. cit.*, 121–2; *CPR, 1494–1509*, p. 360; L. W. Vernon Harcourt, *His Grace the Steward and Trial of Peers* (1907), pp. 435, 467–8; Dietz, *op. cit.*, p. 43; C. J. Harrison, 'The petition of Edmund Dudley', *EHR*, LXXXVII (1972), 82–99, esp. pp. 88, 93, n. 25.

    51   *CP*, IV, 20–1; *LP. Henry VIII*, I, pt. I, No. 131 (PRO SP 1/1/712); *CCR, 1500–1509*, Nos. 818, 955 (xxvi); H. S. Cowper, 'Millom Castle and the Hudlestons', *Transactions of the Cumberland and Westmorland Antiquarian and Archaeological Society*,

XXIV (1924), 181–234, esp. 207, 211; C. R. Hudleston, 'Sir John Hudleston, Constable of Sudeley', *Transactions of the Bristol and Gloucestershire Archaeological Society* (henceforth cited as *TBGAS*), XLVIII (1926), 117–32, esp. p. 118; for lands in co. Cumberland inherited by Richard Hudleston (d. 1502) and held in chief of the king, see *Calendars of Inquisitions Post Mortem, Henry VII*, III, Nos. 66, 213, 724.

52   *CP*, VI, 199–201; 'A narrative written by Lord William Howard' (in 1605) (*Selections from the Household Books of Lord William Howard of Naworth Castle*, ed. G. Ornsby, *Surtees Society*, vol. 68 (1878), p. 391); *CCR, 1500–1509* No. 543; *LP. Henry VIII*, I, pt. I, No. 11 (10) (Lord Dacre of the North excluded from the king's general pardon, 30 April 1509), and No. 131 (PRO SP 1/1/712); *ibid.*, No. 309 (list of debts owed to Henry VII, not pardoned but respited by Henry VIII in 1509).

53   *CP*, I, 27–9, 31–3; Bayne and Dunham, *Select Cases*, pp. xxx, cxxi; *CCR, 1500–1509*, No. 825 (i)–(iv).

54   A. Cameron, 'The giving of livery and retaining in Henry VII's reign', *Renaissance and Modern Studies*, XVIII (1974), 17–35, esp. 26–7.

55   Bayne and Dunham, *Select Cases*, p. xxx; A. Cameron, *op. cit.*, pp. 31–4; W. H. Dunham, *Lord Hastings' Indentured Retainers, 1461–1483: The Lawfulness of Livery and Retaining under the Yorkists and the Tudors* (*Transactions of the Connecticut Academy of Arts and Sciences*, vol. 39 (1955), 1–175, reprinted by Archon Books, USA, 1970), pp. 103–5; Harrison, 'Edmund Dudley', pp. 88, 91–2, n. 14.

56   *CP*, VII, 167–8; W. Dugdale, *The Baronage of England* (2 vols., 165–6, hereinafter Dugdale, *Baronage*), I, 718, citing *Catalogue of Nobility, by R.B.*; *CCR, 1500–1509*, Nos. 482, 553.

57   *Ibid.*, Nos. 765, 797, 955 (xxi), 956; *Descriptive Catalogue of Ancient Deeds*, V (1906) (hereinafter cited as *Ancient Deeds*), A13484 (indenture made between Henry VII and Richard Grey, earl of Kent, 28 November 1508, concerning the sale of the residue of his lands to the king, together with the annuity of £40 p.a. that Kent was receiving from the lordship of Ruthin, sold to Henry VII in May 1507). For the income derived from the marcher lordship of Ruthin, see R. I. Jack, 'The Lords Grey of Ruthin, 1325–1490: a study of the lesser baronage' (University of London unpublished PhD. thesis, 1961). For Earl Richard's petition to Cardinal Wolsey (probably in 1518), his sales of land during Henry VIII's reign and a favourable view of Henry VII's dealings with the Grey family, see G. W. Bernard, 'The fortunes of the Greys, earls of Kent, in the early sixteenth century', *Historical Journal*, 25 (1982), 671–85, esp. 677–9. According to J. R. Lander (*Ferguson Essays*, pp. 352, 367, n. 176; *Crown and Nobility*, p. 299, n. 176), Henry VIII during the first year of his reign cancelled bonds and recognizances affecting Kent (and nine other peers), but at least one of the recognizances given to Henry VII by Earl Richard remained in force; no evidence is cited in support of this statement. The cancellation of the recognizance for £10,000 taken by the king on 19 August 1507 has not been traced, but as Kent resumed the alienation of his lands shortly after Henry VII's death, the restraints imposed upon him had evidently been relaxed.

58   Michael K. Jones, 'Sir William Stanley of Holt: politics and family allegiance in the late fifteenth century', *Welsh History Review*, vol. 14 (1988), 1–22, and Michael K. Jones, 'Richard III and the Stanleys', *Richard III and the North* (ed. Rosemary Horrox: University of Hull, 1986), PP. 27–50. According to Thomas, earl of Derby's deposition made on 16 January 1486, he had known his stepson, Henry VII, well since 24 August 1485. Apparently they met for the first time two days after Bosworth (*Cal. Pap. Reg.*, XIV, 17); if that statement was correct, Lord Stanley was not present at the battle of Bosworth.

59   *Plumpton Correspondence* (ed. T. Stapleton, Camden Society, 1839, henceforth cited as *Plumpton Correspondence*), p. 53; Leland, *Collectanea*, IV, 186; M. A. Hicks, *Northern History*, XIV (1978), 99. For Henry VII's first visit to York (21–8 April, 1486), see 'Historical illustrations of the reign of Henry VII derived from the municipal archives of York', *Gentleman's Magazine*, XXXV (1851), 477–85; the earl of Northumberland, with his retinue, joined the king between Doncaster and Pontefract, in preparation for his entry into

York. G. Temperley, *op. cit.*, p. 54, n. 1 was mistaken in believing that 'A plot to seize the king just escaped success'; there was no such conspiracy at York.

60 *CP*, XI, 719–20; *ibid.*, X, 464, 665; Bayne and Dunham, *Select Cases*, pp. xliii, lxxvi, xcvii, cxlix–cl, 41–1, 44; R. Reid, *The King's Council in the North* (1921, reprinted 1975), pp. 73–86.

61 *CP*, VI, 362–3, 366–7 (Pedigree of the Hastings Family); as Sir John Hastings' first wife, Margaret Midelton, died on 31 August 1495, Elizabeth, his daughter by his second wife, Katherine Aske (d. *c.* 1507), cannot have been born before 1496, and it has been assumed that she predeceased her father, who has been described (*CP*, VI, 362) as dying without surviving issue. Sir John died on 12 July 1504, and an inquisition *post mortem* taken on 20 April 1505 found that his heir was his brother, George (*c.* 1474–1511). Probably Elizabeth Hastings died between 12 July 1504 and 20 April 1505. The Hastings family estates, which included Fenwick Hall and other lands in Yorkshire, as well as four manors in Norfolk, were held in chief of the king, as belonging to the duchy of Lancaster. Perhaps Sir John's father, Sir Hugh (d. 1488) was a kinsman of Henry Percy (d. 1489), earl of Northumberland; in 1486, he was described in York city records as the earl's 'cousin' (Reid, *op. cit.*, p. 74; *The Parliamentary Representation of the County of York 1258–1832* (ed. A. Gooder, *Yorkshire Archaeological Society Record Series*, vol. XCI), vol. I (1935), 207–8). Sir Hugh's great-great-grandfather, Sir Edward Hastings (d. 1438) was the unsuccessful claimant in a celebrated (and expensive) lawsuit against Reynold (d. 1440), Lord Grey of Ruthin, for the right to bear the undifferenced arms of the Hastings family, as heir to John Hastings (d. 1389), earl of Pembroke (*CP*, VI, 358–60). For the death of Elizabeth Hastings while she was in the earl of Northumberland's custody, see G. R. Elton, in the *Times Literary Supplement*, 27 February 1981, p. 230 (review of M. Van Cleave Alexander, *The First of the Tudors: A Study of Henry VII and his Reign* (1980)). For Henry VII's dealings with the fifth Percy earl, see *CCR, 1500–1509*, No. 821 (i); W. C. Richardson, *Tudor Chamber Administration 1485–1547* (Louisiana State University Press, 1952), p. 150; J. M. W. Bean, *The Estates of the Percy Family 1416–1537* (Oxford, 1958), pp. 142–3; Lander, *Ferguson Essays*, pp. 341–2, 361; Lander, *Crown Nobility*, pp. 285–6.

62 Harrison, 'Edmund Dudley', pp. 87, 91, n. 13; A. Cameron, *op. cit.*, p. 26; Bean, *op. cit.*, p. 143; *LP, Henry VIII*, I, Pt. I, No. 414 (58) (Northumberland's pardon, 21 March 1510).

63 *CP*, IV, 208–9; *ibid.*, XII, Pt. I, 396–7; Jane, Lady Strange's mother, Jacquetta, was the elder sister of Queen Elizabeth Wydevill (Dugdale, *Baronage*, I, 666). For the growing power of the Stanley family during Henry VII's reign, see J. M. Williams, 'The Stanley family of Lathom and Knowsley *c.* 1450–1504: a political study' (unpublished Manchester University MA thesis, 1979), pp. 89–91, 93–5, 99–100, 141–45, 179–82, 199–200, 212, 306.

64 *LP, Henry VIII*, XII, Pt. II, No. 732; Dr. G. W. Bernard considers that these comments on the capabilities of members of the English nobility in 1538 (made by a former servant of Thomas Cromwell, Anthony Budgegood, who had defected to the papal service) are probably generally unreliable.

65 Harrison, 'Edmund Dudley', p. 86.

66 Bayne and Dunham, *Select Cases*, p. cxxi, n. 1; *CCR, 1500–1509*, Nos. 635, 658; B. Coward, *The Stanleys: Lords Stanley and Earls of Derby 1385–1672* (Manchester, 1983), pp. 147–8, 159; Harrison, 'Edmund Dudley', pp. 88, 93, n. 26. For Edward, duke of Buckingham's complaints against Henry VII, see n. 92.

67 *Crowland Chronicle*, pp. 152–7; *Usurpation of Richard III* (ed. C. A. J. Armstrong, Oxford, 2nd ed., 1969) contains (pp. 58–61, 68–79) a less accurate and reliable account of these events by Dominic Mancini.

68 For the arrest and imprisonment of Edmund Dudley and Sir Richard Empson, see *Gt. Chron. Lond.*, pp. 336–7 and Ellis, *Hall's Chronicle*, p. 505. For Henry Stafford (d. 1523), earl of Wiltshire, see *CP*, XII, Pt. II, 738–9; Ellis, *Hall's Chronicle*, pp. 505, 512; in a letter written after 10 August 1509 to Richard Fox, bishop of Winchester and keeper of the privy seal, Thomas (d. 1537), Lord Darcy reported rumours of a plan to make Edward, duke

of Buckingham lord protector of England (*Letters of Richard Fox 1486–1527*, ed. P. S. and H. M. Allen (Oxford, 1929), pp. 43–4).

69   For a list of members of the English peerage during Henry VII's reign, see Appendix II, pp. 105–10. Writs of summons enrolled on the Chancery Close Roll (C 54/346, m.3d.), and dated 15 September 1485 were issued to two dukes (Bedford and Suffolk), nine earls and twenty other peers; at that date Jasper Tudor was earl of Pembroke (he did not become duke of Bedford until 27 October) and likewise Thomas, Lord Stanley was not yet earl of Derby. How many peers attended Henry VII's first parliament, which met for two sessions between 7 November 1485 and 4 March 1486 cannot be ascertained, but it is known that some lords not summoned were present. See Wedgwood, *Hist. Parl. Reg.*, pp. 501–4; and W. Dugdale, *A perfect copy of all summons of the nobility to the great councils and parliaments of the realm* (1685, repr., 1794), pp. 476–7 omits the names of Lords FitzHugh and Ogle in the list of peers summoned in 1485; for the English peerage in 1509, see H. Miller, *Henry VIII and the English Nobility* (1986), pp. 7–8; *LP, Henry VIII*, I, Pt. I, Nos. 205; Thomas Grey (d. 1530), marquis of Dorset was still imprisoned at Calais on 10 July 1509 (*ibid.*, No. 104).

70   K. B. McFarlane, *The Nobility of Later Medieval England* (Oxford, 1973, henceforth cited as McFarlane, *Nobility*), pp. 172–6; for English peerages created by Edward IV (1461–83), see T. B. Pugh, 'The magnates, knights and gentry', *Fifteenth-Century England 1399–1509* (ed. S. B. Chrimes *et al.*, Manchester, 1972, hereinafter cited as Chrimes (ed.), *Fifteenth-Century England*), pp. 116–17.

71   For Thomas Stanley (d. 1504), earl of Derby (and his descendants), and other peers mentioned below, see *CP, passim*.

72   *CP*, II, 133–5; J. Smythe, *The Berkeley Manuscripts: The Lives of the Berkeleys* (ed. J. Maclean, 3 vols., Gloucester, 1883–5), II, 127–30.

73   *CP*, II, 15–16; probably Philibert de Chandée (of whose career little is known) came from the county of Bresse (A. V. Antonovics, 'Henry VII, king of England, "By the Grace of Charles VIII of France"', Griffiths and Sherborne (ed.), *Kings and Nobles*, pp. 169–84, esp. pp. 176, 183, n. 60). His employment in the service of the French crown may have been a consequence of Louis XI's second marriage with Charlotte of Savoy (d. 1483).

74   *CP*, IV, 73–4, n.(d); *Plumpton Correspondence*, pp. 187–8; *Ancient Deeds*, V, A 12116; Leland, *Collectanea*, IV, 304. S. B. Chrimes, *Henry VII* (1972), p. 139 wrongly states that Thomas Darcy was summoned to Henry VII's first parliament.

75   *CP*, III, 404, n.(a) states that Sir William Conyers was styled Lord Conyers by 1506–7, but no evidence is cited.

76   *CP*, VI, 440; Sir Charles Somerset married Elizabeth Herbert on 2 June 1492, in the king's presence (S. Bentley, *Excerpta Historica* (1831), p. 90). The Herbert heiress had probably been obliged to accept this match as a consequence of her dispute with her uncle, Sir Walter (see n. 86). Somerset was styled Lord Herbert at least as early as 21 February 1504 (*CPR, 1494–1509*, p. 348), but there is no record that he was summoned to Henry VII's last parliament (25 January–30 March 1504).

77   Wedgwood, *Hist. Parl. Reg.*, pp. 452–7; Chrimes (ed.), *Fifteenth-Century England*, pp. 116–17.

78   Wedgwood, *Hist. Parl. Reg.*, pp. 189–95; only five earls and thirty-three barons were summoned to Henry IV's last parliament, which met on 3 February 1413 (*CCR, 1409–13*, p. 406).

79   *CP*, II, 62–3; a large part of the Beaumont estates forfeited in 1461, and subsequently granted by Edward IV to William (d. 1483), Lord Hastings, remained after 1485 in the hands of his heir, Edward (d. 1506), Lord Hastings (*ibid.*, VII, 374–5).

80   T. L. Kington Oliphant, 'Was the Old English aristocracy destroyed by the Wars of the Roses?', *Trans. Royal Hist. Soc.*, 1st ser., I (1872), 351–6; see also McFarlane, *Nobility*, pp. 148–9.

81   *CP*, II, 218–19; *ibid.*, IV, 418–19; W. D. Cooper, 'The Bonvilles of Halnaker', *Sussex Archaeological Collections*, XV (1863), 57–66; McFarlane, *Nobility*, p. 149 reckoned

the Bonvilles among 'five noble houses whose disappearance ... can legitimately be ascribed to the effects of civil war and royal vengeance' between 1450 and 1500.

82 H. Miller, *Henry VIII and the English Nobility* (Oxford, 1986), pp. 38–40.

83 The Lisle heiress, Elizabeth (1505–19), was betrothed (but never married) to Charles Brandon (c.1484–1545), who was consequently created Viscount Lisle on 15 May 1513; despite his subsequent marriage in 1514 with Henry VIII's younger sister Mary (c.1496–1533), the French queen-dowager, and his creation as duke of Suffolk on 1 February 1514, Brandon retained the Lisle title until 20 April 1523 (*CP*, VIII, 62 3).

84 *CP*, II, 422–3.

85 See Appendix II, pp. 105–10.

86 *CP*, X, 402; Edward IV's charter, dated 4 July 1479, creating William Herbert (d. 1490) earl of Huntingdon, with remainder to the heirs of the body of his father, William Herbert (d. 1469), earl of Pembroke, was confirmed by Richard II, on 27 May 1484, and again by Henry VII, on 17 May 1488, with (on the latter occasion) right of succession apparently reserved to the heirs male of Earl William Herbert I (d. 1469); see *Report ... touching the Dignity of a Peer*, vol. V (1829), 417–18 (henceforth cited as *RDP*), and *Cal. Charter Rolls*, VI, 250; *CPR, 1476–85*, p. 431 and *ibid., 1485–94*, p. 237. For the partition of the Herbert estates between William, earl of Huntingdon's daughter, Elizabeth (who was briefly (in 1491) styled countess of Huntingdon; *CCR, 1485–1500*, No. 617), see W. R. B. Robinson, 'The Earls of Worcester and their estates, 1526–1642' (unpublished Oxford B.Litt. thesis, 1958), pp. 4–8.

87 See Appendix II, pp. 105–10.

88 *CP*, XII, Pt. II, 549–50; *William Worcestre, Itineraries* (ed. J. H. Harvey, Oxford, 1969), p. 345.

89 K. B. McFarlane, *England in the Fifteenth Century* (ed. G. L. Harris, 1981), p. 240 (reprint of British Academy Raleigh Lecture (1964), published in *Proceedings of the British Academy.*, vol. L (1964), 87–119).

90 M. R. Westcott, 'The estates of the earls of Devon, 1485–1538' (unpublished University of Exeter MA thesis, 1958), pp. 31–4, 38, 140–44, 180, 294–6.

91 *CP*, IV, 329–330; *RP*, VI, 544. After Sir William Courtenay's attainder had been reversed in Henry VIII's first parliament, he was created earl of Devon on 10 May 1511, but he died on 9 June, before his investiture could take place.

92 For Edward, duke of Buckingham's complaints against Henry VII (made to the late king's executors), see T. B. Pugh (ed.), *The Marcher Lordships of South Wales, 1415–1536* (Cardiff, 1963, hereinafter cited as Pugh, *Marcher Lordships*), p. 242, and C. Rawcliffe, 'Henry VII and Edward, duke of Buckingham: the repression of an "Over-mighty Subject"', *BIHR*, LVIII (1980), 114–18. Katherine Wydevill (d. 1497), dowager-duchess of Buckingham, was one of the sisters and coheiresses of Richard Wydevill (d. 1491), Earl Rivers (*CP*, II, 390; *ibid.*, XI, 24–5).

93 Barbara J. Harris, *Edward Stafford, Third Duke of Buckingham*, 1478–1521 (Stanford University Press, 1986, hereinafter cited as Harris, *Buckingham*), pp. 42–3, 165.

94 Pugh, *Marcher Lordships*, pp. 176–7; in 1447–8, the clear value (i.e., the net income that Humphrey, duke of Buckingham should have received) of the Stafford estates in England and Wales was over £5,000, but it is unlikely that cash receipts paid to Duke Humphrey in that year amounted to over £3,700.

95 For the survey of the Stafford estates in England and Wales in 1500, and Duke Edward's conflicts with his tenants in the lordship of Brecon, see Pugh, *Marcher Lordships*, pp. 239–75; McFarlane, *Nobility*, p. 211; Harris, *Buckingham*, p. 134. For differing views concerning the efficiency of Edward, duke of Buckingham's management of the Stafford estates, see C. Rawcliffe's review of Harris, *Buckingham*, in the *Huntington Library Quarterly*, vol. L (1987), pp. 85–8. For Duke Edward's household, see K. Mertes, *The English Noble Household* (Oxford, 1988), pp. 1, 43, 129, 135, 188, and A. D. K. Hawkyard, 'Thornbury Castle', *TBGAS*, XC (1977), 51–8.

96 Lady Margaret Beaufort's estates were valued in 1509 at £3,394 p. a. (Michael K.

Jones, 'Henry VII, Lady Margaret Beaufort and the Orléans Ransom', Griffiths and Sherborne (eds.), *Kings and Nobles*, pp. 254–73, esp., p. 273, n. 99, citing the muniments of St John's College, Cambridge, D 102/7); for Lady Margaret Beaufort's household, see Michael K. Jones, 'Collyweston – an Early Tudor Palace', *England in the Fifteenth Century* (ed. D. Williams, Leicester, 1987), pp. 129–41.

97   *Glamorgan County History*, vol. III (ed. T. B. Pugh, Cardiff, 1971), pp. 556–8, 680; *RP*, VI, 470–1; *Statutes of the Realm*, II, 602–3.

98   *CP*, XII, Pt. II, 908–9; *CPR, 1461–67*, pp. 131–2.

99   *Ibid.*, p. 107. Although Richard (d. 1460), duke of York left a valid will (*ibid.*, *1467–77*, p. 261), his executors refused to act and intestacy resulted because his goods were inadequate to pay his debts. The administration of the late duke's estate was committed by Thomas Bourchier, archbishop of Canterbury, to Thomas Colt, esquire, one of Edward IV's councillors (Lander, *Crown and Nobility*, pp. 314, 317, n. 41), on 15 December 1461 (*Registrum Thome Bourgchier*, ed. F. R. H. Du Boulay, 2 vols., Oxford, 1957, I, 200); Duke Richard's debts were never paid in full.

100   For Queen Elizabeth of York's jointure, see *RP*, VI, 462–5; and for the marriages of her sisters, Katherine (d. 1527), Anne (d. 1511) and Cecily (d. 1507), see *CP*, IV, 330; *ibid.*, IX, 619; XII, Pt. II, 449–50. In 1511, Henry VIII reached a settlement with his surviving aunts, Anne, wife of Thomas (d. 1554), Lord Howard (afterwards duke of Norfolk), and Katherine, wife of Sir William Courtenay (d. 1511), which enabled the king to retain the whole of the York-Mortimer inheritance (*LP, Henry VIII*, I, Pt, Nos. 520, 546 (27), 749 (23); *Calendar of Ancient Deeds*, IV, A. 7551, V, A. 13, 566.

101   R. Virgoe, 'The Recovery of the Howards in East Anglia, 1485–1529', *Wealth and Power in Tudor England; Essays Presented to S. T. Bindoff* (ed. E. W. Ives *et al.*, 1978), pp. 1–20, esp. 12–16. Dr. Virgoe comments (p. 9) on the unrivalled agglomeration of lands and offices in East Anglia held after 1485 by John de Vere (1443–1513), earl of Oxford.

102   *CP*, XII, Pt. II, 393–7; *RP*, VI, 391–2; *CPR, 1485–94*, p. 298; *Materials for a History of the Reign of Henry VII* (ed. W. Campbell, R. S., 2 vols., 1873), henceforth cited as *Materials* (ed. Campbell), II, 211–12.

103   J. Smythe, *op. cit.*, II, 127–30 (see n. 72).

104   *CP*, VI, 130–3; *CCR, 1500–1509*, Nos. 160, 377 (XV) 379, 782; *Ancient Deeds*, V, No. A13484; Henry VII made a profit of £400 when he surrendered his interest in the castle and manor of Codnor, co. Derby, and four manors in co. Notts., in 1507, in return for payment of £1,400 (*CPR, 1494–1509*, pp. 583–4).

105   J. Smythe, *op. cit.*, II, 155–72.

106   For Henry VII's acquisitions of lands belonging to Richard Grey (d. 1524), earl of Kent, see n. 57.

107   J. H. Ramsay, *A History of the Revenues of the Kings of England 1066–1399* (2 vols., Oxford, 1925) provides unreliable estimates of the crown's annual income during that period. For recent work on English government finance during the later middle ages, see G. L. Harris, *King, Parliament and Public Finance in Medieval England to 1369.* (Oxford, 1975), and G. L. Harris (ed.), *Henry V: The Practice of Kingship* (Oxford, 1985), pp. 155–79.

108   B. P. Wolffe, *The Royal Demesne in English History* (1971, HEREINAFTER CITED AS WOLFFE, *Royal Demesne*), pp. 195–225; 'Henry VII's Land Revenues and Chamber Finance', reprinted from *EHR*, LXXIX (1964), 225–54, esp. pp. 216–17, 219.

109   R. Somerville, *History of the Duchy of Lancaster*, vol. I *1265–1603* (1953), pp. 274–5 gives a misleading impression of the duchy of Lancaster's revenues during Henry VII's later years; see PRO DL 29/23/14 (1505–6) and DL 29/23/16 (1506–7) for cash receipts from the duchy lands between 1505 and 1507.

110   I. S. W. Blanchard, *The Duchy of Lancaster's Estates in Derbyshire 1485–1540* (*Derbyshire Archaeological Society Record Series*, vol. III (for 1967), 1971), pp. 12–13, and see *Midland History*, III (1975), 59–63 for a review of Dr Blanchard's book by E. W. Ives; Somerville, *op. cit.*, I, 264–5.

111   *Materials* (ed. Campbell, II, 30, 35–7.

112 PRO S.C.6. Henry VIII/4990 (account of the receiver of the lordship of Denbigh, 1509–10).

113 For the political significance of royal patronage (and offices in the gift of great magnates), see J. Fortescue, *The Governance of England* (ed. C. Plummer, Oxford, 1885), pp. 150–3, 326–7; *The Household of Edward IV: The Black Book and the Ordinance of 1478* (ed. A. R. Myers, Manchester, 1959), pp. 85, 98. For the forfeiture of office granted by Henry VII to some of the king's servants, see *CPR, 1494–1509*, pp. 113–14, 120–1. In accordance with an Act of 1495, those of the king's officers and retainers who failed to attend him in time of war forfeited their offices, fees and annuities (*Statutes of the Realm*, II, 582 (II Henry VII, c.18)).

114 E. W. Ives, 'Sir Ralph Egerton of Ridley', *John Rylands Library Bulletin*, 52 (1969–70), 346–74; for Ridley, co. Chester, see *Leland's Itinerary in England and Wales* (ed. L. Toulmin Smith, 5 vols., repr. 1964), IV, 3; *ibid.*, V, 28.

115 Harrison, 'Edmund Dudley', p. 84.

116 For debts owed to the king by Giles (d. 1508), Lord Daubeney and his executors, see *ibid.*, pp. 88, 93, n. 27; *LP, Henry VIII*, I, Pt. I, No. 749 (24). For payments due from Thomas Stanley (d. 1521), earl of Derby, Henry Percy (d. 1527), earl of Northumberland and George Nevill (d. 1535), Lord Abergavenny, see nn. 53, 61–2, 66.

117 Harrison, 'Edmund Dudley', pp. 89, 96, n. 51; Virgoe, *op. cit.*, p. 16 (see n. 101).

118 For Henry VII's last will, see n. 45; it included detailed provisions for the redress by the king's executors of wrongs that he had committed (J. P. Cooper, 'Henry VII's last years reconsidered', *Historical Journal*, II (1959), 103–29, esp., 112–14).

119 *LP, Henry VIII*, I, Pt. I, No. 448.

120 PRO S.C. 11/837; see abstract in B. P. Wolffe, *The Crown Lands 1461–1536* (1970, henceforth cited as Wolffe, *Crown Lands*), pp. 181–2.

121 PRO S.C. 11/837, m.5.

122 *LP. Henry VIII*, I, Pt. I, 1123 (36) (grant dated 18 December 1512).

123 PRO S.C. 11/837; Wolffe, *Crown Lands*, p. 85; Wolffe, *Royal Demesne*, 225.

124 S. B. Chrimes, *op. cit.*, pp. 319, 322.

125 Wolffe, *Royal Demesne*, pp. 223–4.

126 Bayne and Dunham, *Select Cases*, li–liv, lxi, lxiv.

127 *Prerogativa Regis* (ed. S. E. Thorne; New Haven, USA, 1949), v–li; H. E. Bell, *The Court of Wards and Liveries* (Cambridge, 1953), pp. 2–3.

128 R. Somerville, 'Henry VII's "Council Learned in the Law"', *EHR*, LIV (1939), 427–42; W. C. Richardson, 'The surveyor of the king's prerogative', *EHR*, LVI (1941), 52–75.

APPENDIX I

The indenture made between Henry VII and Thomas Grey (d. 1501), Marquis of Dorset

[PRO, C 54/352, m. 14d.]

EDITORIAL METHOD

i   Standard abbreviations have been extended (e.g., a has been replaced by and, or et), without indicating that this has been done.

ii   Roman numerals have been used in place of arabic numerals. Numerals have been replaced, where appropriate, by words; wherever it occurs, ii has been substituted for ij, and £1,000 has been used instead of *Mᵉ li*.

iii   Punctuation has been added as required and the use of capital letters has been modernised throughout the text.

iv   Spelling has been retained unaltered, with two exceptions: (i) use of the letters u and v has been modernised, and (ii) in words beginning with ff, either a capital letter or the lower case has been used, in accordance with modern practice.

v   Use of apostrophes: where it has not been possible to extend, because the right ending is uncertain, an apostrophe has been used.

vi   Use of brackets: words and numerals introduced by the editor are enclosed in square brackets, and words interlined in the text are contained in obtuse-angled parentheses.

This indenture made the 4ᵗʰ day of June, the 7ᵗʰ yere of the reign of our sovereign, the Kyng Henry the viiᵗʰ, bitwixt our seid sovereign lord on the on[e] partie and Thomas, marquis [of] Dorsett on that other partie, witnesseth that wher afore this tyme informacion, reporte and supuyses[1] hath ben had and shewed to our seid sovereign lord that the seid marques shuld be of unfittyng demeanyg toward His Highnes and for that His Grace hath not be content. Nevertheless uppon trust the seid marques shall be here after lovyng and trewe and hath and shall fynde suertee so to be, in the manour and fourme as her after is expressed, our seid sovereign lord nowe is content to accept the seid marques to his grace and favour and to graunte to hym his lettres of pardon in right large maner and fourme.

[1] And for that it is agreed be twixt our seid sovereign lord and the seid marques in the manour and fourme folowyng, that is to sey that the seid marques, at his own costis, except the fynes, seales and suche other duties as to His Grace belongeth in such cases, shall make or cause to be made a sufficient and lawfull estate in fee simple unto John, the archebusshop of Canterburie,[2] Thomas, th'archebusshop of York, John, busshop of Ely, Richard, busshop of Bathe and of Wellis, John, erle of Oxford, Thomas, erle of Arundell, George, erle of Shrewsbury, Thomas, erle of Derby, William Curteneye, knyght, Raynold Bray, knyght, Thomas Lovell, knyght, and Thomas Greynfeld, esquier, aswell of all the castelles, honuris, maners, londis, rentis, services and possessions, wher of he is sole in his own right, or in the right of Cecill' his wiff or iontly witheny other, seased to his use, or whereof eny other person or persones be seased to his use or unto the use of Cecill' his wiff, or either of theym, in Ingland, by recoveree or other wise, as by our seid sovereign lord and his councell shalbe advysed, the maners of Multon[3] and Flete[4] with th'

appurtenaunces and all other landis and tenementis in the countie of Lincoln, the maners of Lutterworth and Broughton Asteley[5] in the countie of Leicestre, with ther appurtenaunces, and all other his londis, rentis and services in his possession or eny other to his use in the countie of Kent and all other londis and tenementis in the possession of the seid marques or any other to his use in the cities of London and Coventre and a pastur called 'Lesethorp'[6] in the countie of Leicestre and the reversions of the maners of Stobhying[7] and Fairested[8] in the countie of Essex, with ther appurtenaunces, always except and forprised, to th'ententes that the seid persones shall stand and be seased ther of <to> the use of the seid marques and Cecill' his wiff and to ther heires, accordyng to ther inheritaunce of and in the same, and to perfourme the last will of the seid marques in his own landis and tenementis and the last will of the seid Cecill' in her inheritaunce, if the seid marques offendit not the kyng or his heires of his body comyng in the fourme folouyng;

[2] That is to sey, if the seid marques fromhensfourth committe or doo any treason ayenst the person of our seid sovereign lorde or his seid heires or committe or doo mesprision touching or concernyng the destruccion or iuperdie of the kyngis roiall person or his heires of his body comyng, contrarie to the dutie of his allegeaunce, or conceille any treason to be commytted compassed or imagined to the iuberdie of his <seid> most roiall person, or his seid heirs, and disclose and show it not to the kyng or his seid heirs, by writyng or otherwise, assone and in as convenient season as he goodly may, and the same or any of theym be herafter sufficiently and lawfully proved and demed and the same marques therof convicted, accordyng to the lawe of this land, that then the seid John, archebisshop of Canterbury, Thomas, archebisshop of Yorke, John, bysshop of Ely, Rychard, bysshop of Bathe and of Wellys, John, erle of Oxford, Thomas, erle of Arundell, George, erle of Shrewesbury, Thomas, erle of Derby, William Courteney, knyght, Reynold Bray, knyght, Thomas Lovell, knyght, and Thomas Graynfeld, ther heires and assignes shall stand and be seased of and in the same maners, londis and oder the premisses, except before except, to th'use of oure seid sovereign lord and of his heires.

[3] And it is aggreed, any entent or graunt to the kyng or his heires afore rehersed notwithstandyng, it shalbe lefull to the seid marques, if he fortune to be taken prisoner beyond the see in the kynge's service afore any offence in fourme aforesaid by hym commytted or don, to sell or do with asmoche and asmany and suche of the seid maners, londis and tenementis as the seid marques shall name and assigne, only as shall serve for his redempcion and delyverans in that behalf.

[4] Also, it is aggreed that, in the next parlyament herafter to be holden, the seid marques shall assent and labour that it shalbe ordeyned and enacted that the seid estates and recoverees and th'ententes teruppon declared, as afore is rehersed, if the seid marques then be on lyf, shalbe by auctoritie of the same ratified and confermed.

[5] And also that, in the same parliament, the same marques shall labour and assent that it shall be enacted that all other maners, londis, tenementis and reversions to the said marques and Cecill' his wif ioyntly or severally belongyng, whereof they be seased or any other to ther use or to th'use of eny of them, in the

countie of Lancastre or ells wher in Ingland, wherof suche astates or recoveres shall then fortune not to be made, that lyke estates and suerties shall be made in fee simple to the seid persones then lyvyng, accordyng to th'ententes aforerehersed of the maners, londis and tenementis, and other the premisses afore not except nor forprised; and, by the same auctoritie in the same parliament, it is agred that it shall be enacted that, if the seid marques offend not in any of the premisses duryng his liff, that immediatly aftre his decesse the seid recoverees, estates and suertees of the seid maners, londis, tenementis and reverciones and other the premisses and th'ententes ther upon declared, as is afore seid, shalbe utterly voide and of non effect and that the same maners, londis and other the premisses wherof the seid estatis, recoverees, suretees and actes shalbe had fromthensfourth stand and be in the same condicion of inheritaunce as they shuld have be if the seid estatis, recoveres, suertees and actis had not be had nor made, savyng only for the perfourmge of the last willis of the seid marques and Cecill' and erther of theym in the manour and fourme afore seid, if the seid marques offend not, as is aforesaid.

[6] Also it is agreed betwixt our seid sovereygn and the seid marques that whansoever the persons to whom the seid estate shalbe made die in the lif of the seid marques to the nombre of six, that then the seid six persons overlyvng shall enfeff twenty other persons by our seid sovereign lord or by his seid heires and the same marques to be named of all the said castelles, honuris, maners, londis and other the premisses in fee to th'ententes afore rehersed.

[7]Also the seid marques graunteth and by thes presentes gevith to our seid sovereign lord the mariage and custodie of Thomas, his son and heire aparant, and graunteth to finde hym at his charge in the kynge's service. And that whansoever aftre the space of two yeris next aftre the date of thes presentes, if it shall please the kynge's grace to delyvere the seid Thomas, his son and heire, the same sonne then beyng unmaried and uncontracted and under the age of nineteen yeris, to the seid marques then beyng in lyff, that then the seid marques byndith, graunteth and promiseth to pay or cause to be paied to our seid sovereign lorde a £1,000 of laufull money of Inglond within the tyme of three yeris next after the same delyvere, that is to say in every of the same three yeris 500 marc', in full accomplysshment of the paiement of the said £1,000.

[8] And wher the seid marques hath promised to our seid sovereign lord[e] to cause dyverse persones to be bounden in severall recogniysaunces to His Grace in the some of ten towsant pounde for the more suertie of his trewe allegeaunce to be continued to His most noble Grace, the seid marques by thes presentes graunteth that, after notice made to hym by the kynge's writyng under any of his seales directed to hym, that any of the suertees be ded and that notice beyng trewe, the seid marques shall, within three monethes after that notice so made, cause som other sufficient person or persones to be bounden to our said sovereign lorde in a recognysans or severall recognysaunces in such somme or sommes of money, with suche condicion as the persone or persones suerte or suerties beyng ded was bounden, in so that our seid sovereign lord or his heirs, after the same recognysaunce or recognysaunces newly to be taken, do discharge the heres,

executours, admynystratours and successours of the suertie or suertees so beyng ded, at the chargis and costes of our seid sovereign lord or his heires.

[9] To the whiche covenauntes fore rehersed, and every of theym, of the partie of the seid marques to be perfourmed, the seid marques graunteth to pay to our seid sovereign lord, for every defalt, a £1,000, and, to the covenauntes, appoynte-mentes, intentes and promyses afore hersed of the behalf of our seid sovereyng lord and his heires to be perfourmed, our seid sovereign lord, for hym and for his heires, in the wordys of a kynge promytteth to obs[erve] and kepe theym and every of theym.

[10] In witnesse whereof, our seid sovereign lord to the one partie of this indentures with the seid marques remanynyng hath caused his greate seale to be put unto, and, to the other partie of the same indenturis with our sovereign lord remanynyng, the seid marques hath putte his seale of armes, the day and yere above seid.

[11] Memorandum quod predictus marchio venit coram domino rege in cancellaria sua apud Westmonaster[ium] nono die Julii anno presenti et recognovit se indenturam predictam et omnia in eadem contenta in forma predicta.

NOTES TO APPENDIX I

1 *supposes*; i.e., suppositions or surmises.
2 These twelve feoffees were John Morton (d. 1500), archbishop of Canterbury, Thomas Rotherham (d. 1500), archbishop of York, Richard Fox (d. 1528), bishop of Bath and Wells, John de Vere (d. 1513), earl of Oxford, William (d. 1487), earl of Arundel, George Talbot (d. 1538), earl of Shrewsbury, Thomas Stanley (d. 1504), earl of Derby, Sir William Courtenay (afterwards earl of Devon, d. 1511), Sir Reginald Bray (d. 1503), Sir Thomas Lovell (d. 1524) and Thomas Greenfield (d. *c.* 1515), esquire.
3 Moulton, co. Lincoln.
4 Fleet, co. Lincoln.
5 Broughton Asteley (in Astley parish), co. Lincoln.
6 Leesthorpe (in Pickwell parish), co. Leicester.
7 Stobbing, co. Essex.
8 Fairstead, co. Essex.

APPENDIX II

List of the English nobility in the reign of Henry VII (1485–1509)

Dates during which titles were in use are enclosed in square brackets; dates of birth and death are given (in round brackets) after family names. Peerages extinguished between 1485 and 1509 by the failure of male heirs are indicated by [E], and titles forfeited by attainder during that period are marked [A]

DUKES

Bedford
   Jasper Tudor (*c.* 1431–95) [1485–95] [earl of Pembroke, 1452–61; 1470–1; 1485–95]
Buckingham
   Edward Stafford (1478–1521) [1485–1521]
Cornwall
   Arthur Tudor (1486–1502) [1486–1502]
   Henry Tudor (1491–1547) [1502–9]
Suffolk [A]
   John de la Pole (1442–*c*.92) [1463–*c*.92]
   Edmund de la Pole (*c*.1471–1513) [1492–3] Afterwards earl of Suffolk, 1492–1504
York
   Henry Tudor (1491–1547) [1494–1504] Afterwards prince of Wales 1504–9) and King Henry VIII

MARQUISES

Berkeley [E]
   William Berkeley (1426–92) [1489–92]
Dorset
   Thomas Grey (145?–1501) [1475–83: 1485–1501]
   Thomas Grey (1477–1530) [1511–30]: not summoned to parliament before 1509

EARLS

Arundel
   William Arundel (1417–87) [1438–87]
   Thomas Arundel (1450–1524) [1487–1524]
Bath
   Philibert de Chandée (dates of birth and death unknown) [1486–?]
Derby
   Thomas Stanley (*c.* 1435–1504) [1485–1504]
   Thomas Stanley (*c.* 1481–1521) [1504–21]

Devon
   Edward Courtenay (*c.* 1450–1509) [1485–1509]
Essex
   Henry Bourchier (*c.*1472–1540) [1483–1540]
Huntingdon [E]
   William Herbert (*c.* 1455–90) [1479–90]
Kent
   Edmund Grey (1416–90) [1465–90]
   George Grey (*c.* 1440–1503) [1490–1503]
   Richard Grey (*c.* 1478–1524) [1503–24]
Lincoln [A]
   John de la Pole (*c.* 1462–87) [1467–87]
Northumberland
   Henry Percy (*c.* 1449–89) [1470–89]
   Henry Algernon Percy (1478–1527) [1489–1527]
Nottingham [E]
   William Berkeley (1426–92) [1483–92] Afterwards created marquis of Berkeley in 1489
Oxford
   John de Vere (1442–1513) [1464–75: 1485–1513]
Rivers [E]
   Richard Wydevill (*c.* 1450–91) [1485–91]
Shrewsbury
   George Talbot (1468–1538) [1473–1538]
Surrey
   Thomas Howard (1443–1524) [1483–5: 1489–1514] Afterwards created duke of Norfolk in 1514
Warwick [A]
   Edward Plantagenet (1475–99) [1475–99]
Wiltshire [E]
   Edward Stafford (1469–99) [1473–99]
Westmorland
   Ralph Nevill (1456–99) [1484–99]
   Ralph Nevill (*c.* 1495–1549) [1499–1549]

VISCOUNTS

Beaumont [E]
   William Beaumont (1438–1507) [1485–1507]
Lisle [E]
   Edward Grey (1435–92) [1483–92]
   John Grey (1480–1504) [1492–1504]
Lovel [A]
   Francis Lovel (1456–*c.* 92) [1483–5] Before he was created a viscount in 1483, Lord Lovel was a baron, 1465–85

Welles [E]

John Welles (1448–99) [1486–99] He sat as a baron, Lord Welles, in the parliament of 1485–86, and was created a viscount before 8 February 1486

BARONS

Abergavenny
George Nevill (1440–92) [1476–92]
George Nevill (1469–1535) [1492–1535]
Audley [A]
John Tuchet (*c.* 1420–90) [1459–90]
James Tuchet (1463–97) [1490–97]
Beauchamp of Powick [E]
Richard Beauchamp (1435–1503) [1475–1503]
Berners
John Bourchier (*c.* 1464–1533) [1475–1533]
Burgh
Thomas Burgh (1430–96) [1487–96]
Cheyne [E]
John Cheyne (*c.* 1445–99) [1487–99]
Clifford
Henry Clifford (1454–1523) [1485–1523]
Cobham
John Brooke (*c.* 1451–1512) [1464–1512]
Conyers
William Conyers (1468–1524) [*c.* 1506–24]
Dacre of the South
Thomas Fiennes (*c.* 1472–1533) [1483–1533]
Dacre of Gilsland
Thomas Dacre (1467–1525) [1485–1525]
Daubeney
Giles Daubeney (*c.* 1452–1508) [1486–1508]
Henry Daubeney (*c.* 1494–1548) [1508–48] Afterwards created earl of Bridgwater in 1538
De la Warr
Thomas West (*c.* 1456–1525) [1476–1525]
Dinham [E]
John Dinham (*c.* 1433–1501) [1467–1501]
Dudley
John Dudley (1400–87) [1440–87]
Edward Dudley (*c.* 1459–1532) [1487–1532]
Ferrers of Chartley
John Devereux (1464–1501) [1487–1501]
Walter Devereux (*c.* 1489–1558) [1501–58]

FitzHugh
  Richard FitzHugh (1458–87) [1472–87]
  George FitzHugh (1487–1513) [1487–1513]
Fitzwalter
  John Radcliffe (1452–96) [1485–96]
  Robert Radcliffe (*c.* 1483–1542) [1505–42] Afterwards created earl of Sussex
    in 1529
Fitzwarin
  John Bourchier (1470–1539) [1479–1539] Afterwards created earl of Bath in
    1536
Grey of Codnor [E]
  Henry Grey (1435–96) [1444–96]
Grey of Powis
  John Grey (1460–94) [1482–94]
  John Grey (*c.* 1481–1504) [1494–1504]
  Edward Grey (1503–51) [1504–51]
Grey of Wilton
  Reynold Grey (*c.* 1421–94) [1442–94]
  John Grey (1450–99) [1494–99]
  Edmund Grey (*c.* 1469–1511) [*c.* 1494–1511]
Greystoke [E]
  Ralph Greystoke (c. 1414–87) [1436–87]
Hastings
  Edward Hastings (1466–1506) [1483–1506] In the right of his wife, Mary
    Hungerford (d. 1534), Lord Hastings held the baronies of Botreaux,
    Hungerford and Moleyns
  George Hastings (1488–1544) [1506–44] Afterwards created earl of
    Huntingdon in 1529
Hastings of Welles [E]
  Richard Hastings (*c.* 1431–1503) [1482–51] As the widower of the Welles and
    Willoughby heiress, Joan (d.c. 1474), Sir Richard Hastings was summoned
    to parliament [1482–4] as Lord Hastings of Welles, or Lord Welles. After
    restitution was made to the Welles heir male, John (d. 1499), in Henry VII's
    first parliament in November 1485 (see *Welles*), Hastings styled himself Lord
    Willoughby, but he was never summoned to parliament by that title.
    Although he belonged to the English nobility, he ceased to be a member of
    parliamentary peerage on the accession of Henry VII
Herbert
  Charles Somerset (*c.* 1460–1526) [1504–26] Afterwards created earl of
    Worcester in 1514
Latimer
  Richard Nevill (1468–1530) [1469–1530]
Lumley
  George Lumley (*c.* 1442–1507) [1485–1507]
  Richard Lumley (*c.* 1477–1510) [1507–10]

Mautravers
   Thomas Arundel (1450–1524) [1482–71] Lord Mautravers succeeded to the
   earldom of Arundel in 1487
Morley
   Henry Lovel (1466–98) [1476–89]
Mountjoy
   John Blount (*c.* 1445–85) [1475–85]
   William Blount (*c.* 1478–1534) [1485–1534]
Ogle
   Owen Ogle (*c.* 1439–86) [1482–1513]
   Ralph Ogle (1468–1513) [1486–1513]
Ormond of Rochford
   Thomas Butler (*c.* 1424–1515) [1489–1515], earl of Ormond, in Ireland
   [1477–1515]
St Amand [E]
   [Richard Beauchamp (*c.* 1454–1508) was styled Lord St Amand [1483–1508],
   but never summoned to parliament
Scrope of Bolton
   John Le Scrope (*c.* 1437–98) [1459–98] Henry Le Scrope (*c.* 1468–1506) was
   never summoned to parliament
   Henry Le Scrope (*c.* 1480–1533) [1506–33]
Scrope of Masham or *Upsall*
   Thomas Le Scrope (*c.* 1459–93) [1475–93]
   Henry Le Scrope (*c.* 1480–1533) [1506–12] was Lord Scrope of Bolton and
   Upsall, 1506–12
Stourton
   John Stourton (*c.* 1454–85) [1478–85]
   William Stourton (*c.* 1457–1524) [1487–1524]
Strange
   George Stanley (*c.* 1460–1503) [1482–1503]
Willoughby de Broke
   Robert Willoughby (*c.* 1452–1502) [*c.* 1489–1502]
   Robert Willoughby (1472–1521) [1502–21]
Willoughby, or Willoughby de Eresby
   For Richard Hastings (*c.* 1431–1503), styled Lord Willoughby [1485–1503],
   see *Hastings of Welles*
   Christopher Willoughby (1453–99) styled himself Lord Willoughby, but was
   never summoned to parliament
   William Willoughby (*c.* 1475–1526) was summoned to parliament as Lord
   Willoughby by Henry VIII in 1509
Zouche
   John Zouche (1459–1526) [1468–85: 1495–1526]

John Skelton, Cardinal Wolsey and the English nobility

One of the most vivid sources of opinion and information about the role and outlook of the English nobility during the ascendancy of Thomas, Cardinal Wolsey, is the poetry of John Skelton (?1460–1529), whose satires against Wolsey, *Collyn Clout* and *Why Come Ye Nat to Courte?* (both written during 1522) have frequently been mined by historians in pursuit of a lurid quotation. In his ribald account of Wolsey's alleged domination of king, court and country, Skelton refers time and again to the Cardinal's relations with noblemen, and to noble political attitudes in general, with what appears to be knowledgeable insight. But we would be wise to examine such accounts carefully before accepting them at face value.

As I have suggested elsewhere, it is unwise to see Skelton as a spokesman for noble interests in anything but the most indirect sense. For he was not, contrary to received wisdom on the subject, a client of the Howard dukes of Norfolk in this period.[1] But that need not mean that his assertions are without interest for the historian. What follows is an attempt to analyse those assertions from an historical perspective, to see how far they reflect real political conditions, or, conversely, how far they are conditioned by other concerns.

If through nothing else, Skelton's descriptions command attention through their directness and vigour of expression alone. 'Ye are so puffed with pryde,' the poet informs Wolsey in *Collyn Clout*,

That no man may abyde
Your high and lordely lokes.
Ye caste up then your bokes
And vertu is forgotten,
For then he wyll be wroken
Of every lyght quarell
And call a lorde a javell.

A knyght a knave ye make.
Ye boost, ye face, ye crake,
And upon you take
To rule Kynge and Kayser.
And yf ye may have layser,
Ye wyll brynge all to nought.
And that is all your thought. (II. 593–607)[2]

This is the definitive exposition of Wolsey as tyrant; over-proud, violent-tempered and domineering, carrying out a vendetta against the nobility and gentry whose high birth he envies, and intent upon ruling the realm for his own glorification at everyone else's expense. No-one opposes him for they are all either too cowed, too foolish, or beguiled by his subtleties. Thus the realm is turned upon its head, the ruler is himself ruled, and the natural leaders of society are reduced to impotence.

For the lordes temporell,
Theyr rule is very small
Almoost nothynge at all.
Men say howe ye appalle
The noble bloode royall
In ernest and in game.
Ye are the lesse to blame
For lordes of noble bloode,
Yf they well understode
Howe connynge myght them avaunce,
They wolde pype you another daunce.
But noble men borne,
To lerne they have scorne,
But hunte and blowe on horne,
Lepe over lakes and dykes,
Set nothynge by polytykes.
Therefore ye kepe them base,
And mocke them to theyr face.
This is a pyteous case:
To you that over the whele
Lordes must crouche and knele
And breke theyr hose at the kne,
As dayly men may se,
And to remembraunce call:
Fortune so tourneth the ball
And ruleth so over all
That honoure hath a great fall. (II. 608–38)

```
... some of you but late
Hath played so checkmate
With lordes of great estate
After such a rate,
That they shall mell nor make,
Nor upon them take,
For Kynge nor Kayser sake,
But at the pleasure of one
That ruleth the rest alone. (II. 1011–19)
```

This inversion of the social order, in which the tyrannical upstart dominates and degrades a decayed nobility, and thus sows the seed of even greater disorder (by setting a precedent for the commen men who 'may se' and imitate his methods) evokes a common disaster tale of the period.[3]

Yet how seriously should these references to a cowed and humiliated nobility be taken? Grounds for the assertion that early Tudor noblemen preferred the joys of the chase to serious study or the intrigues of politics can be found, as Skelton's most recent editor notes[4] in an anecdote related by Richard Pace, concerning a gentleman who would carry his hunting horn even to the dinner table, and maintained that he would rather his son were hanged than that he should study letters, as 'it better becomes the sons of gentlemen to blow the horn properly, to hunt with skill, to teach and manage falcon. [For] truly the study of letters should be left to the sons of yokels.'[5] Such support as this story offers is, however, far from conclusive, not least because it was a particular habit of the humanists to condemn as lacking learning anyone with whom they disagreed, or at whom they took exception, regardless of their actual education.[6]

Yet this notion of the English nobleman as consciously anti-intellectual had a wider currency. In his treatise, *The Tree of Commonwealth*, Edmund Dudley counselled noblemen to set their sons to school in their own interests:

> for verelie, I fear me, the noble men and gentlemen of Englande be the worst brought up for the most parte of any Realme in Christendome, and therefore the children of poore men and meane folkes are promoted to the promocion and aucthoritie that children of noble bloud should have if they were meete therefore.[7]

Moreover, despite Dudley's apparent fear that England was unique in this respect, the notion of noble indifference (or worse) to learning seems to have had international dimensions. For Joanot Martorell, the aristocratic author of the Catalan chivalric romance *Tirant lo Blanc* (1490) was quite capable of employing the title 'man of letters' as an insult, and declared that writing 'is unworthy of knights and gentlemen and suitable only [for] women and jurists, whose sole defences are their tongues and pens'.[8] Far from concluding the matter, however, this last declaration should alert us that all is not quite as it seems with this account of noble attitudes. For Martorell was, of course, himself an author and 'man of letters', whose work reveals in its many borrowings and adaptations both the extent of his reading and the subtlety of his scholarship. This fact alone must compromise his statements of contempt for learning and its fruits. And elsewhere Martorell is prepared to praise those writers whose labours immortalise the chivalric exploits of the noble class, and thus give substance to the concept of honour.[9] If his attacks upon 'men of letters' have a specific relevance, then it concerns the particular instance of the legal profession, whom Martorell seems to see as attempting to replace chivalric methods of settling grievances with 'unmanly' legal quibbles. Beyond this the assertion seems to bear little relation to noble attitudes in the real world. For, as his own case and that of his co-author, the Valencian knight Marti Joan de Galba, reveals, noblemen and gentlemen were hardly averse to acquiring an education and flaunting its gifts.

And the same is clearly true of English noblemen known to Skelton. Lord John Howard, first duke of Norfolk, for example, seems to have had particularly refined intellectual tastes. When he led the English campaign against the Scots in 1481, he took with him a substantial library of learned French texts, including versions of *The Dictes and Sayings of Philosophres* (translated by Lord Rivers and printed by Caxton in 1477) and Alain Chartier's courtly romance, *La Belle Dame Sans Merci*.[10] And his son, Thomas Howard I, is known to have commissioned the *Introductory to Write/And to Pronounce Frenche* from Alexander Barclay. It is also interesting to note the inscription upon the tomb of *his* son, Thomas Howard II, which noted that the latter was 'in hys yong age, after he had been a sufficient season at the gramer schole, henchman to Kyng Edward the iiii'.[11] The use of the phrase 'a sufficient season' suggests that the need to educate young noblemen to at least a certain standard was more commonly appreciated than Skelton, Pace and Martorell seem to suggest.[12] Similarly it must be recognised that, despite Skelton's disparaging comments, a lack of first-class book learning, coupled with a predilection for hunting, need not bar a man from the possession of political initiative and subtlety. The fourth earl of Shrewsbury, for example, was a keen sportsman who 'hath sette netts and long bows to kyll deare in Ecclesall and hunted dyvers tymes there',[13] yet was no stranger to the snares of court and national politics. His prudent actions during the Pilgrimage of Grace of 1536 reveal him to have been as well, if not better acquainted with the realities of political procedure and manoeuvring than his better-educated advisers.[14]

A predilection for hunting need not necessarily, then, suggest an inaptitude for politics, despite Skelton's assertions. After all the king himself, who studied to convert the sport 'into a martyrdom', [15] could hardly be described as a political *ingénue*, nor, given the evidence of his *Assertio Septem Sacramentorum*, as an intellectual also-ran. Henry, like Shrewsbury, simply followed and, by his example, promoted the fashion for the hunt which was by far the most popular pastime for the noble class. It may well have been that academics such as Skelton and Pace did not appreciate the merits of so boisterous an activity, and so were liable to dismiss its exponents as muscular dullards. But more probably both were simply utilising for their own ends a literary tradition which would be understood and appreciated by anyone acquainted with satirical or 'estates' literature. For the hunting nobleman was as much a medieval literary stock-figure as the gluttonous monk, the lusty young scholar, or the avaricious merchant.

What Skelton is doing in the passage cited above is utilising a number of such literary *topoi* to facilitate a solution to a political dilemma posed by his own arguments. For when he began to attack the lay peers for their unwillingness to oppose Wolsey, the poet moved on to sensitive ground. How was he to explain the fact that the nobility did not act together to unseat the Cardinal? He had suggested that they were simply too cowed to act. But this was not enough, as it would imply that they were collectively seething with resentment at their treatment, whereas experience revealed to both the poet and his readers that this was not the case. But, conversely, he could not simply suggest that the lords were insufficiently outraged at Wolsey's dominance to act against him, still less that they actually accepted it, or his whole portrayal of the Cardinal as a tyrant would be undermined. Hence his recourse to literary convention and the suggestion that the nobility were insufficiently schooled and too busy riding and hunting to notice their abasement. What he is doing is using literary conventions to suggest, in general terms, that the noblemen are failing to act as they should, without his having to examine too closely the political implications of their apparent lack of action. He succinctly conflates two seemingly contradictory functions of riding and hunting in estates literature to provide his solution. First there is the glorious 'out-riding' which was associated with noblemen and knights and which it was quite proper (indeed militarily essential) for them to perform. Such is the sort of riding practised by the Squire in Chaucer's *General Prologue to The Canterbury Tales*, of whom it is said 'Wel koude he sitte on hors and faire ryde'.[16] It is this aspect of horsemanship that is recommended to noblemen in Caxton's translation of Ramon Lull's *Ordre of Chyvalry*, in which the author states that: 'The sayence and the scole of the ordre of Chyvalrye/is that the knyght make his sone to lerne in his yongthe to ride ... And it behoveth/That the sone of a knyght in the tyme that he is squyer can take kepynge of hors.'[17]

Similarly, for noblemen to hunt was entirely honourable. Indeed it was, in addition to their hereditary titles and armorial bearings, one of the chief signs of their membership of an exclusive social elite. For the right to hunt deer, and to do so in specially constructed and enclosed deer parks, was a privilege jealously guarded by the nobility and enshrined in law. Hence the pride in the exercise of hunting skills and the knowledge of hunting lore evident both in noble conduct and in romance literature. In the latter, as J. T. Rosenthal observed, some of the most potent demonstrations of high birth (and frequently the means by which previously disguised characters prove their true lineage) are the ability to speak knowledgeably of the chase, to ride skilfully to hounds, or, in the case of the young Tristan, to carve meat elegantly.[18]

The second, contrary, literary convention which Skelton employs is that in which to describe a character, most obviously a cleric, as indulging a taste for the hunt or for hawking is to suggest an ironic comment upon their possible neglect of other, more worthwhile duties. This was the tradition drawn upon by Chaucer in his description of the Monk in *The Canterbury Tales*, whose lack of interest in his spiritual responsibilities is suggested by the poet's observation that the jingling of his bridle threatens to drown the call of the chapel bell.

> Full many a deyntee hors hadde he in stable,
> And when he rood, men myght his brydel heere,
> Gynglen in a whistlynge wynd als cleere
> And eek as loude as dooth the chapel belle.[19]

It was also the tradition used, less subtly, by Nigel of Langchamps in his *Speculum Stultorum* to castigate the erring bishop who

> spends more time in woods than sacred places
> And values dogma less than the sound of dogs.[20]

Skelton neatly combines these two equestrian conventions to suggest that the nobles *are* failing in their responsibilities, but unwittingly, and only by acting in a manner which befits their class. When he finds himself faced with a political problem, the poet is not averse to seeking a purely literary solution to it.

Yet does such an explanation have any more than a passing similarity to the political reality which the text purports to describe? What *was* Wolsey's attitude towards the nobility and their reaction to him? Skelton was seemingly in no doubt what he wished his readers to think. Again and again he reiterates the point that the lay lords were rendered impotent and humiliated by the cardinal's overbearing dominance.

> ... no man dare rowte;
> Duke, erle, baron, nor lorde,
> But to his sentence must accorde.
> Whether he be knyght or squyre,
> All men must folow his desyre. (*Why Come Ye Nat . . . ?*, ll.341–5)

> ... this madde Amalecke,
> Lyke to a Mamelek,
> He regardeth lordes
> No more than potshordes. ll. 478–81)

> He hath despyght and scorne
> At them that be well borne;
> He rebukes them and rayles,
> 'Ye horsons, ye vassayles,
> Ye knaves, ye churles sonnys,
> Ye rebads nat worth two plummis!
> Ye raynbetyn beggers rejagged,
> Ye recrayed ruffyns all ragged!'
> With 'Stowpe, thou havell!
> Rynne, thou javell!
> Thou pevysshe pye pecked,
> Thou lossell longe necked!'
> Thus dayly they be decked,
> Taunted and checked,
> That they are so wo
> They wot not whether to go. (ll. 599–614)

Is this a reasonable suggestion, or simply the transposition on to Wolsey of all the violent and vicious attributes of the conventional tyrant of medieval drama?[21] The allusions to 'Amalecke', an enemy of Israel from the Old testament,[22] and to Mamelukes (Turks, and also the descendants of slaves, and thus doubly villainous) might suggest that this is merely the influence of tradition at work. Yet Wolsey's public persona, the Wolsey that Skelton would have seen at High Mass and court ceremonies, was indeed a figure on a grand scale, with dukes and lords as his attendants, and with due emphasis laid in the ordering of events on his own superiority as Cardinal-Legate and Lord Chancellor to mere lay lords.[23] Wolsey's retinue was larger and more magnificent than any nobleman's (the measures against retaining and the household ordinances assured as much), and at the banqueting table the Cardinal might enjoy 'nine dishes at his own mess at one meal, besides potages to be served in courses at his pleasure', while dukes, marquises and earls were permitted only seven.[24] Thus, what Skelton and the readers of his final satire saw was a Cardinal who seemed to miss no opportunity to vaunt himself at the expense of his social superiors. That the justification for such a display might have been more diplomatic than personal, that the nobility of the land were symbolically supporting the king's lieutenant in a ceremonial display of national unity before the assembled continental ambassadors – this the poet either failed to see or chose to ignore. For his present purposes it was enough to describe the nobles as humbled, with the implication that they ought to be seething with humiliation and desire for revenge. That they actually were not is deftly employed as a sign of just how complete Wolsey's dominance had become. The poet's purpose here is to revile Wolsey with as many charges of corruption and tyranny as possible. Thus the allegations have to be read with a considerable degree of caution. Because the poet wishes to portray Wolsey as a tyrant at this point, he needs to caricature the nobility as universally subservient. But such logic is entirely *ad hoc*. In a subsequent satire, *Howe the Dowty Duke of Albany* ... , written within a year of the completion of *Why Come Ye Nat* ... ?, for example, the selfsame noblemen who had been so thoroughly reviled in the earlier text as spineless fools are vaunted for their courage and loyalty, purely because Skelton now wished to praise Wolsey and Henry, rather than criticise them, and create the impression of a stable, strong, realm. Thus the cowardly 'shepe' of 1522 become in 1523 'a noble baronage', inspired by the king

> To exploit dedes of armys
> To the domage and harmys
> Of suche as be his foes. (ll. 465–9)

In each case it is the dictates of Skelton's overall strategy, rather than his observation of political reality, which determines the particulars of his argument, As his satiric goals change, so does his analysis of the political situation and the role of the nobility within it.[25]

But might he nonetheless have hit upon the truth almost accidentally? Was there a state of open or covert hostility at court between Wolsey and leading noblemen in the later 1510s and 1520s? A number of critics have suggested that there was. One of the more recent studies of Wolsey's career has concluded that the aristocracy 'never liked him' and that 'among his chief detractors was the Duke of Norfolk, he and his father before him had long harboured distaste for the man from Ipswich.'[26] More generally, Professor Elton has suggested that 'what noblemen and gentlemen might perhaps have taken from the King ... they would not accept from his creature.'[27] But, as I have argued elsewhere, there seems to be no basis in fact for the assertion that Thomas Howard I ever 'harboured distaste' for Wolsey, still less that he actively opposed him. The two were allies on the council in 1513, both favouring an aggressive policy against the French, and the then earl of Surrey's victory at Flodden ideally complemented the then royal almoner's organisation of the French campaign, thus allowing both to gain material rewards at the completion of a job well done. Howard was restored to his father's dukedom, while Wolsey took his first steps on to the ladder of preferment which would lead from the sees of Lincoln and Tournai to the Archbishopric of York and the Cardinal's hat. The two then sat at the head of the council throughout the next decade and co-operated well enough to prompt the Venetian ambassador, Giustiniani, to describe Norfolk as 'very intimate with the Cardinal' in 1519.[28] What evidence there is suggests that Norfolk's was a stabilising rather than a fractious influence at court. When, for example, rumours were circulating about the so-called 'Expulsion of the Minions' in 1519, and allegations of a Wolsey-inspired purge of potential rivals reached the ears of Giustiniani, it was Norfolk who attempted to defuse the situation, suggesting that the changes had been brought about by the king's own desire to 'lead a new life'.[29] Had he harboured any ill-will toward the Cardinal, it would surely have been far easier for Norfolk to have allowed such uncomplimentary and potentially damaging rumours to circulate unchallenged.

That the duke was not associated with any agitation or intrigues against the status quo is further suggested by the fact that, when Henry became concerned at the activities of his noblemen at some point *c.* 1520, and instructed Wolsey to 'keep good watch' on them, he named his close friend Suffolk, and Northumberland, Buckingham and Derby, but Thomas Howard I's name was not on his list.[30]

The notion that Norfolk's son, Thomas Howard II, bore a life-long resentment of Wolsey also seems difficult to square with the existing evidence. For if his ramblings from the Tower when under fear of death are discounted for the mixture of confused memories and paranoid accusations which they seem to be, it seems that only after the Cardinal's fall from royal favour in 1529 did he begin to act in the manner one would expect of a political opponent.[31]

But if there is little evidence to suggest the existence of a lengthy feud between Wolsey and the Howards, does the description of a more general antipathy between the nobility and the Cardinal seem more convincing? Specifically, was (as Professor Elton once suggested) the Cardinal's concern for the poor ... at times ... little more than an animus against the rich and well established'?[32] What evidence there is tends to support the idea that, at least during the early years of his ascendency, Wolsey was genuinely concerned to reform abuses in church and state, rather than to conduct a vendetta against the aristocracy. As Professor Scarisbrick has shown, his efforts to curtail the abuses associated with land enclosure were both prompted by good intentions and impartially administered in practice.[33] And in other legal matters the same seems to have been true.

Edward Hall, a commentator with few good words to say of the Cardinal in other contexts, could find few faults with Wolsey's administration of justice in 1516.

> This yere, by the Cardinal were all men called to accompt that had the occupying of the kinges money in the warres or els where, not to every man's contentacion; for some were found in arrerages, and some saved them selfes by pollicy and brybary and waxed ryche, and some innocents were punished. And for a truthe he so punyshed perjurye with open punyshment and open papers werynge, that in his tyme it was less used. He puniyshed also lordes, knyghtes, and men of all sorts for ryottes, beryng and maytenaunce in their countryes that pooremen lyved quyetly so that no man durst beare for fear of imprisonment, but he himself and his servants were well punished therefor.[34]

Some may have escaped the Cardinal's net, but his intentions seem to strike the chronicler as praiseworthy enough. His only criticism is that once those intentions became known, Wolsey was inundated with fraudulent suits, became disillusioned, and moved his attention elsewhere.[35]

The same conclusion has been reached by modern historians. As John Guy has shown, the Cardinal's concern for impartiality in the administration of the law, both at Westminster and in the localities, was no short-lived or superficial phenomenon. As early as May 1516 he had declared his intentions in an oration to the king and council in which he made open to his [Majesty's] most excellent providence the enormityes usuallye exercised in this his Realme to the derogation of indifferent justice as well as the causes of the continuence of the same enormityes. For the redresse and reformacion whereof the same most reverent father advertised his heighnes in the name of the hole counsellors of certayne provisions by their diligent studye excogitate.[36]

In October 1519 the same message was repeated in another formal oration, and the requirement for the 'indifferent ministration of Justice to all persons aswell heighe as low' was included as part of the oath of office to be taken by the new sheriffs and justices which, along with instructions for jurors to the same effect, was later printed and circulated at Wolsey's behest.[38]

Yet Skelton's satires suggest that Wolsey's legal initiatives were no more than an excuse for his allegedly overbearing behaviour in the Court of Star Chamber. 'He is set so hye,' the poet asserts,

> In his ierarchy
> Of frantycke frenesy
> And folysshe fantasy,
> That in the Chambre of Sterres
> All maters there he marres,
> Clappynge his rod on the borde.
> No man dare speke a worde,
> For he hathe all the sayenge
> Without any renayenge.
> He rolleth in his recordes,
> He sayeth, 'How saye ye, my lordes?
> Is nat my reson good?'
> Good evyn, good Robyn Hode!
> Some say 'Yes' and some
> Syt styll as they were dom.
> Thus thwartyng over thom,
> He ruleth all the roste
> With braggyng and with bost. (*Why Come Ye Nat* ... ?, ll. 184–202)

In this account the Star Chamber becomes a court more in the regal than the legal sense, in which Wolsey's rages and domineering manner have 'all the sayenge'. Although the Cardinal is alleged to make a show of deference to others' opinions, what he 'rolleth in his recordes' and what actually happened were, Skelton claims, very different things.[39] Any agreement reached was achieved purely by intimidation. For, just as Robin Hood can extract a seemingly friendly 'Good evening' from those travelling through his forest, so could Wolsey gain the desired agreement from his fellow councillors through fear of the consequences of opposition. But, if his fellow judges found life with Wolsey difficult, this was nothing, in Skelton's account, to the experience of those noblemen who had the misfortune to appear before him as litigants.

> Our barons be so bolde,
> Into a mouse hole they wolde
> Rynne away and crepe;
> Lyke a mayny of shepe
> Dare nat loke out at dur
> For drede of the mastyve cur,
> For drede of the bochers dogge
> Wolde wyrry them lyke an hogge.
>
> For and this curre do gnar,
> They must stande all afar
> To holde up their hands at the bar,
> For all their noble blode,
> He pluckes them by the hode,
> And shakes them by the eare,
> And brynges them in such feare.
> He bayteth them lyke a bere,
> Lyke an oxe or a bull;
> Theyr wyttes, he saith, are dull;
> He sayth they have no brayne
> Theyr astate to mayntayne;
> And maketh them to bow theyre kne
> Before his majeste. (*Why Come Ye Nat* ... ?, ll. 292–313)

Even if Skelton's descriptions of the treatment of noblemen in Wolsey's courts are metaphorical rather than literal, the picture remains a startling one. Yet the poet's assertions are not entirely the product of his imagination. The seven-year period between Wolsey's acceptance of the Great Seal and Skelton's completion of *Why Come Ye Nat* ... ? is littered with cases in which aristocrats suffered more or less stringent correction in the law courts in general, and from the Cardinal in Star Chamber in particular.

The earl of Northumberland was, for example, tried in Star Chamber before the king on Ascension Day 1516, and was sent to the Fleet as a result, probably for illegal retaining.[40] On 8 June in the same year, Thomas Alen reported to his employer, the fourth earl of Shrewsbury, that 'the

King's Solicitor' had told him that the marquis of Exeter, Lord Hastings, Sir Richard Sacheverell, Lord Abergavenny and Sir Edward Guildford, 'by information put into the King's Bench, are likely to be in great danger for retaining of servants'. Hastings and Sacheverell, he said, were examined because they 'had so many men in a livery' at the meeting of Henry VIII and his sister Margaret, Queen of Scotland, held in Tottenham that May. In the October of that year, Thomas Leeke, Sir George Darcy and Lord Clifford's son and heir, Sir Henry Clifford, were sent to the Fleet, where, after a fortnight's imprisonment, Clifford was said to have 'waxen a sad gentleman'.[41] And on 17 July 1517 Alen informd Shrewsbury that Sir Robert Sheffield was put into the Tower, not for the first time, because of a complaint he had made to the king concerning Wolsey.[42] In addition to such incidents as these, the trial and execution of Edward Stafford, duke of Buckingham, in 1521 is frequently cited as evidence of Wolsey's anti-noble machinations.

Yet need such cases as these betoken an animus on Wolsey's part against the aristocracy? It is important to note that behind many of these examples of Wolsey's alleged hostility there was a royal hand manipulating events, or demanding their manipulation. Indeed, the result of most such trials was not some grand fillip to Wolsey's status, but a potent illustration of royal power and prestige, as those aristocrats who had transgressed the royal prerogative reaffirmed their loyalty through a demonstration of their humility before the fount of royal mercy. This is admirably exemplified in Hall's account of proceedings in Star Chamber during 1519.

In the moneth of November, the Kyng came from Lambeth to the Starre Chamber, and there were before him the Lord Ogle, the Lorde Haward, Sir Mathewe Broune, Sir Willyam Bulmer, and Jhon Skot of Camberwell, for diverse riottes, misdemeanors and offences, & especially *the Kyng rebuked* Sir Willyam Bulmer, Knight, because he beyng the Kynges servaunt sworne, refused the Kynges service, & became servaunt to the duke of Buckingham: saiyng that he would none of his servauntes should hang on another mannes sleve, and that he was aswel able to maintein him as the duke of Buckyngham; and that what might bee thought by his departyng, and what might bee supposed by ye duke's retaining, he would not then declare. The Knight kneled still on his knees criyng the Kyng mercie and never a noble there durst entreate for him, *Ye King was so highly displeased with him.* Yet at the last when other matters were hard, the Kyng moved with pitie forgave thesaid Sir Willyam his offence, saiyng that we wil that none of our servauntes shalbe long to any other person but to us, nor we will not that our subjectes repine or grudge at such as wee favoure, for our pleasure we will have in that case as us liketh, for one we wil favour now, and another at suche tyme as us shall like, and therefor Sir Willyam if you serve us hartely, you shall not be forgotten, and for this tyme we pardon you. Likewise he pardoned the lorde Edmonde Howard, and sir Mathew Broune their offences, which were indicted of riottes, and maintenaunce of bearynges of divers misdoers, within the countie of Surrey: but the Lord Ogle humbly beseeched the Kyng of his mercie to whom he answered: Sir, your matter concerneth murder of our subjecte, whiche greate offence is not onely to us but to god, and therefore we remit you to the common lawe.[43]

Evidently Hall did not perceive this occasion as a public demonstration of Wolsey's power, or of his hatred of the nobility. It is the king who is described as dominating the trial and determining events, not the Cardinal. And it seems that Henry's concern for his own honour was the major issue in his mind rather than any desire to please Wolsey, still less (as has been suggested by some scholars) the need to provide 'a prelude to Wolsey's destruction of Stafford'.[44] The lesser offences Henry pardoned without fuss, having received formal supplication for mercy from the defendants. The personal slight, and still worse the public slight to his beneficence, he treated with far less generosity, venting his anger upon the offender and pardoning him only after making him suffer in uncertainty throughout the proceedings in a public display of royal power and bounty, the message of which was spelt out for all to hear: 'we will that none of our servauntes shalbe long to any other person but to us'. All other prerogatives, all other patrons, must be subservient, and seen to be subservient, to the crown. And what the king willed must be performed, 'for our pleasure we will have in that case as us liketh'.

Such trials were concerned with the endorsement of Henry's position as king and justiciar, not with Wolsey's as master of ceremonies. Skelton might place in the Cardinal's mouth such tirades as,

> Take him, wardeyn of the Flete,
> Set hym fast by the fete!
> I say, lieutenant of the Toure,
> Make this lurdeyne for to loure;
> Lodge hym in Lytell Ease,
> Fede hym with beanes and pease!
> The Kynges Benche or Marshalsy,
> Have hym thyder by and by! (*Collyn Clout*, ll. 1165–72)

and,

> ... have him to the Towre
> *Saunz aulter* remedy!

Have hym forthe, by and by
To the Marshalsy,
Or to the Kynges Benche! (*Why Come Ye Nat . . . ?*, ll. 429–33)

But even if the Cardinal's methods sometimes vaguely resembled these
theatricalities, the point they made would have been, not that he himself
was the source of the power he employed, but that the king, seated in the
throne of state behind him, watching events with a careful eye and
occasionally intervening to exercise his prerogative of mercy, or to
condemn the defendant to further trial, was merely allowing his servant to
express the royal will.

Yet even if Henry and not Wolsey took the leading role on such
occasions, it is still surprising that such noblemen should apparently
succumb so easily to the treatment which Skelton sugests they received. If
they were the independently-minded, strong-willed, intelligent men that
this volume suggests, the 'overconfident and brutal men in the shires'
described by Professor Elton, or 'the greatest and most refractory of Tudor
lords' described by Pollard,[45] they surely would not have simply acquiesced
in their own humiliation. Only thirty years after his father's bloody
usurpation at Bosworth Field, Henry's hold on the throne was not
sufficiently strong to daunt such men from expressing their opposition to
him. Without a male heir and without a standing army Henry was, of
course, both politically and practically vulnerable, and consequently relied
upon the loyalty of his noblemen for the continued stability of his
government. Under such circumstances, to attack some of the most
significant members of the aristocracy for retaining would at first sight
seem a ruinous course of action. Yet were the attacks really as vicious as
Skelton suggests? Henry's language when condemning defaulters was
often fierce, as his treatment of Bulmer eloquently testifies, but only rarely
was his mercy withheld, and then only in cases where the defendant could
not seriously expect it. Lord Ogle, for example, was accused of murder, and
so might expect to serve trial, while Sir Robert Sheffield was finally
charged, not merely with maligning Wolsey, but with harbouring
convicted felons in his household.[46] In such cases it was important for
justice to be seen to be done and, to the crown's credit, the easier path of
pardoning Ogle to ensure his gratitude and loyalty was not taken.
Where a token chastisement was sufficient to prove a point, neither
Henry nor Wolsey seemed interested in imposing further humiliation
(Northumberland's sojourn in the Fleet during 1516, for example, lasted
only twelve days, while Sir Henry Clifford, for all his consequent 'sadness',

was there for only a fortnight). Where the crimes were more serious, the correct channels for indictment and trial were apparently adhered to. Despite the inherent difficulties in Henry's position, it was neither a massacre of over-mighty subjects nor a tyrannous misuse of the royal prerogative which Wolsey oversaw between 1515 and 1522.

For a king in Henry's position, intent upon establishing himself as the sole legitimate ruler, while still aware of the threat posed by the exiled pretender Richard de la Pole, there was a tightrope to be walked between the near-tyrannous over-reaction to such threats which could provoke rebellion, and the over-leniency which could appear as weakness and tend towards the same result. And despite Skelton's caricatures of a tyrannous regime, that tightrope seems to have been walked with notable success. Despite the concern expressed in Henry's order to Wolsey to 'keep good watch on' his leading noblemen, the vast majority of the lay lords both in the shires and at court remained loyal servants of the crown throughout Wolsey's ascendancy and throughout the reign as a whole, despite the provocative religious legislation of the 1530s and the opportunity for rebellion presented by the Pilgrimage of Grace.

It was not, of course, simply selfless loyalty which kept the nobility loyal to the crown. The loyal servant of a generous king might ensure through his obedience and usefulness the steady supply of offices, licences and lands which he needed to reinforce his own status and maintain the loyalty of his clients. Conversely, the civil wars and abortive insurrections of the previous century seem to have served, not as encouraging precedents for a magnate out of favour and anxious to redress the situation by force of arms, but as a potent disincentive to impetuous action. The evidence of familial if not personal memory demonstrated that, whatever the cost of loyalty, the cost of prolonged civil disorder was likely to be far greater.

Perhaps the major reason underlying the nobility's consistent loyalty to Henry VIII has, however, been unconsciously concealed by the very use of the term 'the nobility' itself. For it is misleading to consider the nation's magnates as a unified body with set aims and ambitions. This is an error into which Skelton falls (albeit with mischief aforethought) in his dismissal of the entire nobility, 'Duke, erle, [and] baron' as ingenuous sportsmen more concerned with hunting than with politics. Yet in the final analysis there was little which united the nobility beyond a hereditary title and landed wealth. And often their very lands and wealth acted as barriers between them. There were marriage alliances, certainly, designed to unite houses, consolidate holdings and improve positions. But there were also financial squabbles, disputed entries, law suits and contested wardships.

And in the world of practical politics it was these things which provided the most immediate motives for action, rather than any putative class solidarity.

Neither were magnates united by age. The vagaries of life-span and inheritance meant that even at its highest levels the nobility spanned every generation,[47] while the strict delineation of status within the peerage itself ensured that when lords of similar age did meet together, it was rarely on equal terms. Indeed, given the responsibilities and geographical limitations imposed upon them by their roles as 'princes' on their own estates, and as the representatives of the crown in their shires, the only occasions on which noblemen were likely to meet in significant numbers came during their performance of their crown offices, as justices, or members of the regional councils, or when crown ceremonial required a general aristocratic attendance at court. And on such occasions they gathered less as allies than as potential rivals – for office, for disputed titles, for licences to improve and exploit the resources of their estates, or more generally simply for royal favour. In such circumstances, 'the noble class' split into a host of individual suitors, able to be manipulated by a king who acted with care as circumstances permitted.

Indeed, on closer inspection, what evidence there is suggests that this division of the nobility into rival, and occasionally feuding, groups was more marked in the period between 1514 and 1522 than at other times. The remarks allegedly made by the duke of Buckingham to his chancellor, Robert Gilbert, to the effect that he would bide his time before acting against Henry, are often quoted by historians. But the second part of his observation is rarely emphasised. This stated that he would only act if the other temporal lords would join his conspiracy,as it could only succeed 'if noblemen durst break their minds together, but some of them mistrusteth and feareth to break their minds to other, and that marreth all'.[48] It may well have been that the lords' unwillingness to ally with Buckingham had more to do with the essentially personal nature of his grievances and with his violent temperament and manner with them than with any other preoccupations,[49] but the suggestion that there were suspicions and doubts between the lay peers at this time is an interesting one. It finds support in the testimony of Sir Robert Sheffield who admitted having said that it was unhappy that the lords temporal were at variance at that time, for otherwise my lord Cardinal's head should have been as red as his coat was.[50] Again the more dramatic, second, clause of the sentence usually attracts the most attention, when perhaps the former is the more informative. What precisely this 'variance' involved is open to question.

But there are indications of divisions and rivalries within the nobility which stretch back to 1516 or earlier.

Thomas Alen's reports to Shrewsbury abound with suggestions of feuds and intrigue. On 31 May 1516 he claimed to have heard from 'master comptroller [Sir Edward] Poynges' and Christopher Urswick certain news which, although he had not heard it directly from the cardinal, suggested that,

> everything goeth not forwards as he wold have it ... her is gret snerling among diverse of them yn so muche my lorde cardynall sayd unto Sir Henry Marney that the same Sir Henry had done more displeasur unto the Kynges grace by reason of his cruelnes ayenst the gret estates of this realm then any man lyving.[51]

He concluded his letter with a warning to his absentee employer: '(The saying is, such as be head officers of the King's Household shall give him attendance, and be nigh the King daily, here be so many things out of order) I fer me som ther be wold take a thorn out of theyr own fote and put hit yn yours.' The implication is evidently that Shrewsbury stood in danger of becoming a scapegoat for others currently in disfavour. But quite what the extent of the 'gret snerling' was is difficult to judge. Whether the 'so may things ... out of order' is a description of the political intrigues from which Shrewsbury may have been hiding, or whether the phrase merely referred to the lack of proper order in the court in the absence of its chief officers, is similarly unclear. But the further reference to the notorious occasion on which 'the Lord Marquis, the earl of Surrey, [and] the Lord Bergavenny' were 'put out of the Council Chamber within this few days, whatsoever that did mean', serves to suggest the former, and hints further at a court riddled with division, rumour and doubt.[52]

On 8 June 1516 Alen reported to Shrewsbury the 'great danger' to other lords (interestingly the marquis of Dorset and Lord Bergavenny again) over their keeping of retainers, and remarked that 'there is great trouble between the Marquis, Lord Hastings and Sir Richard Sachaverell', while 'Anthony Babington has complained of Sir Richard to the Council'. Finally he remarked cryptically that, 'Some of the earl's friends think it would be better to stay at home than to come, if he can make excuse, for there are some things come not so well to pass (wherein few were of counsel) as the beginners of the same thought they would have done. I hear some things which are not to be written.'[53] What was this secret enterprise which 'came not so well to pass'? The available evidence is too insubstantial to inspire certainty, but the general impression created is of a disordered and disunited nobility too concerned with its own squabbling to stand against the crown, or to unite against Wolsey, even if it wished to do so (and there is little to suggest that anyone other than the fulminating Buckingham wanted that). At the root of the discontent may well have been the crown's initiatives against retaining,[54] but whether these intrigues were simply the result of noblemen desperately trying to divert royal scrutiny to the most readily available alternative target on an *ad hoc* basis, or whether they were utilising the opportunity to pay off old scores in the process, remains open to speculation.

What is clear, to return to Skelton's account, is that the poet may have correctly described the essence of the political situation at court, in which Wolsey was ascendant and the nobles were largely acquiescent, despite pressure from above upon some of their number. But his interpretation of the causes for, and implications of, this situation are less helpful. His satiric intentions created two contradictory impulses. The first was the need to create as vivid a picture of noble humiliation as possible, in order to substantiate his assertion that Wolsey's domination of the court was tyrannous and unnatural. This the poet achieved through the lurid, and largely fictional, descriptions of the Cardinal's attacks, both verbal and physical, upon the nobility in general. The second imperative, however, ran contrary to the first. For, as I have argued elsewhere, Skelton's major preoccupation at this time was the search for patronage. Certainly the major prospective audience for his later satires was perceived to lie in the City of London, but the poet still maintained the lingering hope of attracting a noble backer.[55] Hence he was forced to provide an honourable explanation for the noblemen's apparent weakness and humiliation, an explanation which did not involve his delving too deeply into the real reasons for their lack of opposition to the Cardinal, in case he should discover either a general acceptance of the *status quo* which would entirely contradict his arguments, or evidence of intrigues between noblemen which lay beyond his limited, scholarly, conception of courtly politics and thus best 'not to be written'. To avoid such difficulties he simply turned to literary conventions for the speciously attractive 'explanation' offered by the stereotype of the hunting nobleman. Skelton's descriptions of an oppressed and foolish nobility thus provide evidence of the poet's mastery of satirical conventions, and of his ability to forge an ingenious argument from initially unpromising material. Unfortunately they reveal little about the complexities of court politics during Wolsey's ascendancy, and still less about the condition and attitudes of the early Tudor nobility.

NOTES

1 G. Walker, *John Skelton and the Politics of the 1520s* (Cambridge, 1988), ch. 1. Alistair Fox (*Politics and Literature in the Reigns of Henry VII and Henry VIII* (Oxford, 1989)) has attempted to resurrect both the notion that Skelton was a client of the Howards and the further claim that this relationship explains the poet's attacks upon Wolsey. Curiously, however, Fox argues that the satires were written, not when Skelton enjoyed Howard support, but at a time when he had lost their favour owing to the family's resentment at a minor poem, *Agaynst Venemous Tongues*, written in 1516. Thus the satires were written, in Fox's view, in an attempt to win back the Howards' patronage. Such logic seems far from convincing, however, and rests upon a number of speculative assumptions of the sort which characterised the earlier biographies of the poet written by H. L. R. Edwards and Maurice Pollet. Primarily Fox's case assumes that Skelton was influential at court. But there is no evidence to suggest that he ever enjoyed access to the king's chambers, still less that he was welcome in the queen's apartments even after he lost royal favour as Fox claims. And the further assertion that the poet was 'in close collusion with the Queen's faction' while he developed his attacks upon Wolsey seems entirely unconvincing, not least as there is no evidence to suggest the existence of such a faction at the time when Skelton was writing. In fact Skelton was never a 'court poet' in the accepted sense of the phrase after 1514. There is no evidence that he could claim 'bouge of court', the right to dine at court which formally distinguished those with an 'official' role there. Nor is there anything to suggest that the poet's work was as influential as Fox's argument requires. Would a passing allusion in a minor poem really have alienated a family as powerful as the Howards? This assumes not only substantial influence on the part of the poet, but also acute perceptiveness on the part of the Howards in their reading of the subtle implications of *Agaynst Venemous Tongues*. And in this context it is interesting to note the reception gained by his later satires, which the poet had to simplify to the point of banality before he gained an appreciative audience for them. If the increasingly clear political allusions of *Speke, Parott* (1521) failed to gain a response at court, is it really credible that the cryptic allusions in the earlier work would have been so readily understood and resented? In more general terms Fox's arguments fail to convince because they assume as a given factor in the political situation a state of sullen hostility between Wolsey and the nobility (and the Howards in particular) which recent scholarship has shown did not exist.

2 All references are to the texts in V. J. Scattergood, ed., *John Skelton: the Complete English Poems* (1982) (hereinafter 'Skelton, *Poems*').

3 See, for example, *Now a Dayes*, ll. 97–100, in F. J. Furnivall, ed., *Ballads from Manuscripts*, Ballad Society (2 vols., 1868), and *The Complaint of the Ploughman*, in T. Wright, ed., *Political Poems and Songs* ... (2 vols., 1859–61), i, 309.

4 Skelton, *Poems*, p. 473, n, 619–23.

5 J. Wegg, *Richard Pace* (1932), p. 46.

6 Cf. Erasmus' criticism of the monastic orders in P. S. Allen, ed., *Erasmus: In Praise of Folly* (Oxford, 1925), P. 126, and of the 'Trojans', the Humanists' opponents in the debate over language teaching, in P. S. and H. M. Allen, eds., *Opus Epistolarum Des. Erasmi Roterdami* (Oxford, 12 vols., 1906–51), iii, no. 948.

7 D. M. Brodie, ed., *Dudley's Tree of Commonwealth* (Cambridge, 1948), p. 37.

8 D. Rosenthal, ed. and trans., *Tirant lo Blanc* (1984), p. ix.

9 *Ibid.*, esp. pp. x–xiv. For praise of poets, see p. xxviii.

10 J. P. Collier, ed., *The Household Books of John, duke of Norfolk and Thomas, earl of Surrey, temp.* 1481–1490, Roxburghe Club (1844), pp. xxvii–ix.

11 J. Weaver, *Ancient Funeral Monuments* (1767), p. 554.

12 For an account of noble education in the previous century, see K. B. McFarlane, *The Nobility of Later Medieval England* (Oxford, 1973), pp. 228–48.

13 G. W. Bernard, 'The fourth and fifth earls of Shrewsbury: a study in the power of the early Tudor nobility', University of Oxford D. Phil. thesis, 1978, p. 309.

14 G. W. Bernard, *The Power of the Early Tudor Nobility: A Study of the Fourth and Fifth Earls of Shrewsbury* (Brighton, 1985), pp. 31–2. See also below, p. 000.

15 *LP*, III, i. 950.

16 F. N. Robinson, ed., *The Complete Works of Geoffrey Chaucer* (Oxford, 1979), *General Prologue*, l. 194. The two functions of noble birth most frequently portrayed in satirical literature were hospitality and charity on the one hand, and horse-riding on the other. Indeed horse-riding becomes almost synonymous with nobility and knighthood in many cases, as it effectively symbolises the elevation of the nobleman above the pedestrian lower classes. To ride to hounds was a doubly effective symbol, as it conveyed both the elevation of the peerage and its freedom to enjoy leisure pursuits. Hence the much-satirised propensity of social upstarts to ape this aspect of the noble lifestyle. See, for example, the treatment of (false) religion in *Piers Ploughman*, who is said to ride with dogs 'as he a lorde were' (W. W. Skeat, ed., *Piers Plowman* (1961), p. 292), and that of worldly abbots in *The Simony* (Wright, *Political Poems*, p. 329), who would 'riden wid hauk and hound' in order to 'countrefeten knihtes'.

17 W. Caxton, *The Ordre of Chyvalry* (*c.* 1484), p. 21.

18 J. T. Rosenthal, *The Nobles and the Noble Life, 1295–1500* (1976), p. 20.

19 Robinson, *Chaucer, General Prologue* ll. 168–71.

20 G. W. Regenos, ed. and trans., *The Speculum Stultorum of Nigel of Langchamps* (Austin, 1959), p. 128. See also John Gower's caricature of the hunting curate in *Vox Clementis* (E. W. Stockton, ed. and trans., *The Major Latin Works of John Gower* (Seattle, 1962), iii, ll. 1507–10): 'The belling from his dogs' mouths as they clamour together, is to him a church bell when God is hymned. Mass is short for him, but lengthy is his devotion in the fields where hounds are appointed his cantors.' John Bromyard makes a similar point in his *Summa Predicantum*, in which sinning rectors are described as 'more ready ... to lead hounds and falcons to the chase than Christians to devotion', as does William de Pagula, who observes in his *Oculus Sacerdotis* that 'many priests are readier to track the footprints of hares or some other wild beast, swifter to collect dogs, than to summon the poor to worship' (cited by E. W. Owst, *Literature and Pulpit in Medieval England* (Oxford, 2nd ed., 1961), pp. 260, 279).

21 For a fuller account of Skelton's use of literary convention, see Walker, *Skelton*, ch. iv.

22 See, for example, Exodus, xvii, Deuteronomy, xxv., 17–19, and Judges, iii, 13.

23 E. Hall, *Chronicle* (1809), pp. 599–600.

24 P. L. Hughes and J. F. Larkin, eds., *Tudor Royal Proclamations* (3 vols., 1964–69), i, 128.

25 That Skelton's assertions may add up to a more coherent and principled view than I have allowed has recently been suggested by Thomas F. Mayer (*Thomas Starkey and the Commonweal: Humanist Politics and Religion in the reign of Henry VIII* (Cambridge, 1989)). Criticism of the nobility provides, for Mayer, a theme which runs throughout Skelton's work, from the earliest extant poem, 'Upon the Dolorous Dethe ... of the Mooste Honorable Erle of Northumberlande', to the Wolsey satires. But this both overstates the case and ignores the very real and practical reasons for the particular treatment of the nobility in each instance. Apart from a brief remark taken from *Magnyfycence*, Mayer's evidence is actually drawn only from 'The Dolorous Dethe' and the Wolsey satires rather than from across the canon, and in each of these cases the portrayal of the nobility is conditioned by the poet's overall strategy. In the former, for example, the poet's comments about the earl's retainers are bound to be critical. These men deserted their lord in the face of a popular rising. Under such circumstances the comments about their 'falsehood' and 'fear' which Skelton offers are entirely *ad hominem* and only to be expected. It would be foolhardy to see them as applying more generally. Similarly the poet's references to noble cowardice in *Why Come Ye Nat ... ?* need to be read in the light of the poem's overall purpose, rather than as free-standing statements of belief. When he claims that 'Our barons be so bold,/ Into a mouse hole they wolde/ Rynne away and crepe' (ll. 292–4), for example, he is referring, not to *all* noblemen, but to those specific northern lords whom he names (Thomas Manners,

Lord Roos; Henry Percy, fifth earl of Northumberland; and Thomas, Lord Dacre of Gilsland), and whom he accuses of failing to resist the incursions of the Scottish army, led by John Stuart, duke of Albany. (For a detailed examination of Skelton's handling of these events, see my '"And Never a Scotte Slayne": John Skelton and the Anglo-Scottish Border Crisis of 1522', *Northern History* XXIV (1988), pp. 56–74.) Again, Skelton's aim is particular, not general. He attacks specific lords for specific failings, and does so at a time when it suits his purposes to do so. His remarks should not be read as evidence of a wider anxiety about noble behaviour generally.

26   N. L. Harvey, *Thomas Cardinal Wolsey* (1980), pp. 29, 105. Since the completion of this chapter P. J. Gwyn's *The King's Cardinal* (1990) has effectively refuted such assertions.

27   G. R. Elton, *Reform and Reformation* (1977), p. 64.

28   R. Brown, *Four Years at the Court of Henry VIII* (2 vols., 1854), ii, 316 (*LP*, III, i. 402).

29   *Ibid.*, ii. 270–1 (*LP*, III, i. 235). For a detailed analysis of this incident, see G. Walker, 'The expulsion of the minions reconsidered', *Historical Journal*, 32 (1989), pp. 1–16.

30   BL Add. MS 19398, fo. 644 (*LP*, III, i. 1). Significantly it was to Norfolk that Henry looked when appointing a regent to administer the kingdom during his absence at the Field of Cloth of Gold in 1520.

31   For Howard's accusations from the Tower, see BL Cotton MS, Titus B i. 94 (*LP*, XXI, ii. 554). A measure of the credibility of these accusations is provided by the sheer variety of people named by the duke as his enemies and persecutors. In addition to Wolsey, whom he implausibly claimed was working against him at the behest of the duke of Suffolk and the marquis of Exeter, he cited Cromwell, Lord Sandys and his own nieces Anne Boleyn and Catherine Howard. For further evidence of good relations between the Howards and Wolsey, see the fulsome letter written to the Cardinal by Lord Edmund Howard, *c.*1515, H. Ellis, ed., *Original Letters Illustrative of English History* (3 series in 11 parts, 1824), 3rd series, i. 160.

32   Elton, *Reform and Reformation*, p. 63.

33   J. J. Scarisbrick, 'Cardinal Wolsey and the Common Weal', in E. W. Ives, R. J. Knecht and J. J. Scarisbrick, eds., *Wealth and Power in Tudor England: Essays presented to S. T. Bindoff* (1978), pp. 45–67.

34   Hall, *Chronicle*, p. 585.

35   See also *LP*, II, i. 1814; III, app. 21; Brown, *Four Years*, ii. 314 (*LP* III, i. 402).

36   J. A. Guy, *The Cardinal's Court* (Hassocks, 1977).

37   Los Angeles, Henry E. Huntington Library, Ellesmere MS, 2655 fo. 10; 2654 fos. 22ᵛ–23, cited in Guy, *Cardinal's Court*, p. 30.

38   Guy, *Cardinal's Court*, p. 32. For evidence of this principle in action, see *LP*, III, i. 1065.

39   The Star Chamber records, which have been the subject of much detailed research by Professor Guy, would seem to give the lie to this assertion. But the citation of apparently contradictory evidence for support is a familiar Skeltonic touch. We might note the similar strategy pursued in his 'Ware the Hauke!', in which the absence of any evidence of the poet's story in 'the offycyallys bokys' is, paradoxically, cited as proof of its veracity.

40   *LP*, II, i. 1861.

41   A. G. Dickens, ed., *Clifford Letters of the Sixteenth Century*, Surtees Society, clxxii (1962), p. 22.

42   *LP*, II, ii. 3487.

43   Hall, *Chronicle*, pp. 599–600, my italics.

44   Guy, *Cardinal's Court*, p. 73.

45   Elton, *Reform and Reformation*, p. 64; A. F. Pollard, *Wolsey* (1929), p. 80.

46   *LP*, II, ii. 3951.

47   In 1509 the 14-year-old Ralph Neville, fourth earl of Westmorland, could have had little in common with the 66-year-old John de Vere, thirteenth earl of Oxford, save a common title.

48   *LP*, III, i. Introduction, p. cxxx.

49   For this suggestion, see Bernard, *Early Tudor Nobility*, p. 2. For Buckingham's rough treatment of Lord Bergavenny and others, see *LP*, III, i. 1284.

50   *LP*, III, ii. 3951.

51   *LP*, II, i. 1959 (Lambeth Palace, Talbot Papers A fo. 39, cited by Bernard, *Early Tudor Nobility*, pp. 20–1).

52   The particular phrase 'whatsoever that did mean' seems to refer to 'within these few days', rather than to the actual 'putting out'. It seems that Alen had news from an informant (possibly Urswick or Poynings again), and that he was either unsure exactly when the Lords were expelled or, more plausibly, unclear as to the duration of their punishment (i.e., how long a banishment 'within these few days' would prove to be).

53   *LP*, II, i. 2018.

54   It may well be that, as George Bernard suggests (*Early Tudor Nobility*, p. 20), Shrewsbury was in self-imposed exile in order to avoid prosecution for retaining. Alen certainly suggested that such an attack might be forthcoming when he warned the earl to 'take heed of' the moves against the marquis of Dorset and his peers, as a servant of his own, one Bulkely, was seen at court in Shrewsbury's livery and had been sent to the Fleet (*LP*, II, i. 2018).

55   Thus the poem is, at least in part, also aimed at a noble readership. Witness the introductory 'Creed': 'All noble men of this take hede', which warned how 'Unto great confusyon/ A noble man may fall/And his honour appall' (ll. 21–3) if society was not reformed.

Henry Bourchier, earl of Essex
(1472–1540)

Studies of individual noblemen must play an important part in any reassessment of the early Tudor peerage. Yet with very few exceptions such studies have focused on two fascinating but unrepresentative minorities among the peers: new men and regional magnates. The new nobles, notably Thomas, Lord Wharton and John, Lord Russell, demonstrate the possibilities open to the crown in promoting loyal and talented members of the gentry to peerages and positions of provincial command, and the risks inherent in such expedients.[1] The regional magnates, the dukes of Buckingham, Norfolk and Suffolk, the earls of Derby, Shrewsbury, Northumberland and Worcester and a handful of others, show the extent to which a combination of noble wealth and dignity and the crown's trust could equip a great man to dominate one or more counties and claim a place in national politics.[2] At some points these two groups even overlap – Russell founded a powerful regional dynasty, while Charles Somerset, earl of Worcester, and Charles Brandon, duke of Suffolk, began their careers as landless courtiers – but neither group furnishes much evidence for generalisation about the bulk of the peerage. Most noblemen were less talented, less ambitious and less insecure than a Wharton, and less wealthy, less powerful and less often in the king's mind than a failed magnate like Buckingham, or a successful one like Shrewsbury. In so small and diverse a group as the early Tudor peerage, no single nobleman could be typical of all his peers, but the attempt to examine in detail a less unusual individual is surely worthwhile.

In several respects Henry Bourchier, earl of Essex, was such a man. The mean taxable income of the peers was £801 in 1523 and £921 in 1534; Bourchier was assessed at £568 11s 2d and £850 respectively.[3] His military retinue in 1513 was more than three times the size of the smallest noble companies, but less than a tenth the size of the largest.[4] He was the second earl of Essex of his line, and the sixth Lord Bourchier: this gave him a title of slightly below-average antiquity among the nine earls of 1509, but a status well above average among the peerage as a whole, since mere barons outnumbered the higher ranks. In Henry VIII's reign, his assiduity in attending court, council and the trials of peers was rather higher than the norm, that in attending parliament rather lower.[5] He received from Henry VIII only rare titbits of patronage in office and land.[6]

For historians, Bourchier's most noteworthy achievement has been to incur fatal injuries falling off a horse on 13 March 1540, thus clearing the way for Thomas Cromwell to be created earl of Essex; he has not even attained the notoriety of spectacular failure in the fashion of his half-brother, Richard Grey, earl of Kent.[7] Such neglect is partly the result of his inaccessibility, for Bourchier is typical of his peers in the unevenness of the evidence that survives about his life. His dealings with the king and his fellow-councillors, his family life and even the details of his finances are largely beyond recovery, yet we know that he had halibut heads for dinner on Ash Wednesday 1534.[8] Such problems make it hard to analyse the sources and manifestations of the earl's social and political power: hard, but not impossible. That power rested on Bourchier's noble title and landed wealth, his relationship with the peers, gentry, towns and religious houses of his native Essex, and his dealings with the crown; but what was the relative importance of these factors, and how did they affect one another?

I

Henry Bourchier was never one of the few noble statesmen who jostled for power with the clerical and legal civil servants and knightly courtiers of the early Tudor court and council. Yet he was the scion of one of the very greatest families of the reigns of Henry VI and Edward IV: his grandfather had been a long-serving lord treasurer and one of the senior statesmen of the Yorkist council, while his great-uncle was concurrently Archbishop of Canterbury. He was first cousin to Queen Elizabeth of York through his mother Anne Wydevill, and this gave him a blood relationship to Prince Arthur, Prince Henry and Catherine of Aragon (the last through his Yorkist grandmother) – a rare distinction, and one of some importance at a time when the honour accorded to the extended royal family had been increasing for several generations.[9] With this background, and as a young nobleman with estates in the home counties, he was ideal material for a Tudor court peer, and such he became. In the later 1480s he seems to have been at court almost all the time, and he took the leading part for which his rank fitted him in the great occasions of the Tudor dynasty, from the coronations of Henry VII and Queen Elizabeth to the queen's funeral and the departure for Scotland of Princess Margaret in 1503; from 1489 he was also repeatedly involved in diplomatic ceremonial.[10]

His role at court was not merely that of a tame earl. From the mid-1490s Essex was a leading light of the circle of young noblemen who graced the jousts and revels with which Henry VII sought to overawe his subjects, impress foreign envoys, and entertain himself.[11] Essex and his fellow-jousters seem to have been friends as well as companions-in-arms: one night in August 1501 Essex, Edmund earl of Suffolk, Thomas Lord Harington and Lord William Courtenay had dinner together in London.[12] But as the reign went on they fell into disgrace one by one. Suffolk fled the country shortly after that dinner in London, and was attainted in 1504. Courtenay was imprisoned in 1502, Harington (having succeeded his father as marquis of Dorset) in 1507; only Essex survived and prospered.[13]

Quite why is hard to say. He constituted less of a dynastic threat than Suffolk, for his Yorkist blood was more dilute by one generation. On the other hand, there is no sign that he enjoyed an especially close relationship with Henry VII. He gave the king a New Year's gift in 1507, but apparently not in 1508 or 1509, while some other earls sent them in all three years.[14] His role in government was limited. He was placed on occasional commissions from 1493 and sat in council from time to time; but unlike Lord Daubeney, the earl of Oxford or the earl of Surrey, he could not be counted a significant councillor.[15] Essex was a trusted and responsible courtier, but a courtier none the less.

Thin though the relevant sources are, they suggest he was often at court, and such assiduous attendance brought him modest but real benefits, as it did to more humble courtiers.[16] Essex did not quite escape the king's rapacity – few noblemen did – but he did manage to owe Henry £160 for twelve years, eventually paying off £50 when chased up by the council learned in the law, and his only share in the punitive fines levied on the peerage for retaining and other offences was the 100-mark price of a pardon for hunting the king's red deer, which he was not called upon to pay before Henry's death.[17] He had to put up with the king's penchant for selling justice, and in 1508 he was robbed of a legal victory when his opponents bought a royal discharge for £800.[18] But these losses were outweighed by a steady trickle of grants from the habitually ungenerous king, including estates forfeited by William Barley of Albury in Hertfordshire and two manors confiscated from his erstwhile friend, the earl of Suffolk.[19] These were temporary rather than permanent additions to his landed estate, but the piecemeal and conditional distribution of Henry VII's patronage may well conceal the existence of other such grants.

Life at court had further advantages. Essex, like other courtier-peers, joined London merchants to stand surety for the Italian traders who borrowed capital from the king; he doubtless received some benefit in return, especially since Lorenzo Bonvisi, for whom he performed this service, had interests in the Essex cloth industry.[20] His London house, in Knightriders Street, became a centre for the education of young courtiers, like the 'vi goodly galaunts of th'erl of Essex, in yellow cercenet, w[ith] many estrich fethers' who led Catherine of Aragon's procession through London in 1501, 'avaunsyng their horsis after the moost coriouse man[er]'.[21] In *c*. 1506 Essex's household included Charles Brandon, the nephew of Sir Thomas Brandon, the king's master of the horse, and Anne Browne, the daughter of Sir Anthony Browne, the lieutenant of Calais Castle, and it was the earl and his council who had to try to sort out the pair's complex marital manoeuvres.[22] Brandon, who served Essex as master of the horse, was typical of the earl's contacts among the younger courtiers who combined service to the ageing king with a chivalrous enthusiasm which caught the eye of the heir to the throne, Prince Henry. Essex, Brandon, the earl's nephew Walter, Lord Ferrers, his half-brother Richard, earl of Kent, Kent's brother-in-law Sir John Hussey, and Hussey's eldest son William shared close links at court, where Kent, Brandon and William Hussey were up-and-coming jousters.[23]

His experiences at the court of Henry VII determined many of Bourchier's friendships and alliances for the rest of his life. Involvement in one another's property settlements between 1504 and 1517 suggests mutual trust between the earl and such leading lights of Henry's court as the jouster Lord Henry Stafford, the captain of the guard Thomas, Lord Darcy, the lord steward George, earl of Shrewsbury, and the lord chamberlain Charles Somerset, Lord Herbert; Sir George Somerset, who became Essex's steward of courts in the 1530s, was the chamberlain's second son.[24] Late in life, Essex still held to his 'old amyte and frendship' with Arthur Plantagenet, Viscount Lisle, brought up at Henry VII's court.[25] The earl was continually helpful in Lisle's efforts to victual Calais, and sent him presents of venison and pheasants; he received large quantities of barrelled fish and good French wine in return, but Lisle's servants were sure that Essex's motives were not mercenary but sprang from his 'unfeigned love'.[26] When the time came to find a husband for Bourchier's very eligible daughter Anne, he looked not to the nobility or courtiers of the 1520s – though there were rumours she might marry

Wolsey's son Thomas Winter – but to the Parr family, veterans of the courts of Edward IV and Henry VII and long trusted by Essex as sureties, feoffees and deputies in office.[27]

On the accession of Henry VIII, Bourchier's courtly credentials stood him in good stead. In November 1509 he was appointed captain of the king's new company of spears, and in February 1510 he organised one of the first large revels of the reign.[28] His servant John Smith, who helped with the revel, became clerk of the spears, but the captainship does not seem to have brought the earl substantial opportunities as a patron.[29] The number of spears from Essex was never disproportionately large – seven at most out of fifty-seven identifiable members of the band between 1509 and 1515 – and the influence of other noblemen was much in evidence in the king's appointments.[30] None of the Essex spears was clearly linked with Bourchier before joining, though their membership may have given the earl useful contacts among the prominent gentry of his home county, and four at least kept up some connection with him after the band's dissolution in 1515.[31] Essex's £100 fee as captain must have been welcome – it continued to be paid after 1515, doubtless softening the blow of the company's demise – and the leadership of such a splendid body surely flattered his self-esteem, for instance when the spears paraded to welcome foreign envoys.[32] But the position was not one of real power, and it symbolised the earl's failure – or lack of ambition – to convert his prominence at court into significant influence with the new king and within the state.

In the first two years of the new reign Essex danced and jousted as much as any of the king's friends, but his age soon began to take its toll. Brandon and his generation, a decade or more younger than the earl, eclipsed him in the king's company and were in turn partially supplanted by still younger intimates. Essex gradually dropped out of the inner circle.[33] He last jousted in June 1517, and while his scoring in the previous year suggests that he was still competent, he was in his mid-forties, the age at which most contemporaries retired from such sports.[34] He was not at court in January 1515 for the obsequies of Louis XII, nor in February 1516 for those of Ferdinand of Aragon.[35] He missed every Garter chapter from 1515 to 1519.[36] He may already have been constricted by the deafness and ill-health which were to afflict him later in life. He may have been discouraged by his evident incapacity to match the administrative and political talents which had won honour and power for his immediate ancestors. Whatever the explanation, he had neither the ability nor, probably, the inclination to make the transition from courtier to elder statesman. Instead, he began a gradual retreat into the life of a country peer.

The tangible benefits of Essex's efforts to keep up with the young king's revels were comparatively thin. In July 1511 he was appointed constable of Windsor Castle, in survivorship with his cousin Sir Thomas Bourchier of Horsley; the post had been in the junior Berners branch of the Bourchier family since 1455, but Essex procured its diversion to the senior line.[37] Sir Thomas died in 1512, and Essex alone then drew the £30 fee for the office. Like many Tudor office-holders, he aimed to account as infrequently as possible in order to use the crown's money which fell under his control as a source of personal credit. In 1496 attempts had been made to encourage the constable to 'bring his bokes of accompt[es] yerly', but Essex managed only one account for 1512–15 and was then found to owe the king £41 *os* 5*d*.[38] From 1515 auditing procedures tightened up, the earl rendered accounts every year, and his financial leeway diminished: he paid the balance of his account for the year ending at Michaelmas 1516 on 14 May 1517.[39] His other important grant in this period came in April 1512, giving him an annuity of 40 marks.[40] Annuities were always welcome – this one raised Essex's cash income from the crown to more than £150 a year, a handsome addition to his revenues – but they were not as welcome as grants of land, and Essex had not done by 1514 what many other courtiers and noblemen had done, namely exploited the new king's generosity to increase his landed inheritance.

Essex did not become a backwoodsman overnight, and his activity at court revived somewhat in the 1520s. The fact that his home country was so near to the usual haunts of the court enabled him to be there more often than many noblemen, for instance when Henry stayed at Beaulieu (New Hall) in Essex in July 1527.[41] He joined more permanent courtiers in buying up spare wine from royal shipments, took up fairly regular attendance at Garter chapters, and attended Bishop Ruthal's funeral in February 1523 as one of the 'lord[es] and knyght[es] beyng at that tyme resident in the court'.[42] He took a responsible part in the ceremonial of the Field of Cloth of Gold (where he was marshal of the English party) and other diplomatic occasions.[43] He even attended the council six or more times between October 1519 and November 1526, and was among the councillors designated to see to the council's legal business in the latter year.[44]

Yet such rates of attendance in court and council marked Essex as a peer of middling importance, but no more; and his retreat (or relegation) from the forefront of the court to its fringes had its costs. He was losing his grip on Windsor by the early 1520s, and in 1524–5 he lost his place completely to Henry, earl of Devon, one of the court's leading peers in a way Essex had been twenty years earlier but was no longer.[45] Essex was partly compensated by the grant of a manor in Somerset from the lands of the fallen duke of Buckingham, and he retained access to other forms of royal patronage.[46] In April 1524 he secured the wardship of John Barrington, and with it at least partial control of £74 of annual income from the Barrington estates in western Essex and Hertfordshire, though he soon granted or sold John's marriage and lands to Thomas Bonham.[47] Essex was not in the wilderness, but he was in a more normal position for the average nobleman than in his golden days at Henry VII's court.

From the early 1530s his importance declined further, and Essex's visits to the centres of politics and government grew rarer. Of the eleven Garter chapters between 1530 and his death, he attended only three.[48] His sense of duty brought him to treason trials and to parliament in 1536 and 1539, though his daily attendances never matched the 57 per cent rate of November–December 1515, and even that had not been a very assiduous performance.[49] In the Reformation Parliament he secured a licence to miss every session.[50] His relationship with the king remained formally good, and they exchanged New Year's gifts throughout the 1530s, Essex sending plate which presumably resembled his earlier present of 'a salte of golde six square w[ith] staves enamylled white and redde' (the Bourchier colours).[51] The summer of 1533 elicited an unusual burst of activity, as he attended discussions with the imperial ambassador and presided at the Garter feast in May, carved Anne Boleyn's food at her coronation banquet in June, led the mourners for the king's sister at her Westminster Abbey obsequies in July, and carried the basins at Princess Elizabeth's christening in September.[52] He did his duty again at Prince Edward's christening in October 1537 and at the king's reception of Anne of Cleves in January 1540, but his enthusiasm even for such great occasions seems to have been waning: he was supposed to lead the new queen to the church for her wedding, but arrived so late that he almost missed the ceremony.[53]

By the 1530s Bourchier was, of course, growing old, as he never stopped reminding Thomas Cromwell. His correspondence paints a picture of sorely comprehensive debilitation. By 1534 fresh air, notably that between home and parliament, made him collapse, start bleeding and fall into a palsy; a few years later he began to 'wexe unwyeldy' and his hearing deteriorated.[54] In January 1539 he was 'acrasyd'; shortly afterwards he felt 'so vexed that my wytt[es] be not my owne', and considered himself 'more lyker unto a beast than a man, for my heryng ys so taken from me, that except a man speake very lowde evyn in my aer, I may not here no whyt'.[55] Yet, as we shall see, he counted himself healthy enough to travel around

Essex and Hertfordshire, to ride young horses, and even to hunt. And when the king's business in Essex demanded that he bestir himself, he could do so. In December 1539 he helped to oversee the trial of the abbot of Colchester, signing writs, riding at the head of the commissioners as they processed to the court, and hospitably keeping 'a very honourable board there for gentlemen'.[56] Serious illness could come and go rapidly in Tudor England, and even during Wolsey's ascendancy Bourchier had once been 'dysseased so that I have this seven dayes cu[m] lytyll out of my hows'.[57] But malingering is suggested by the fact that the affliction of 1534 required a 5s douceur to Cromwell's clerk to be made to sound convincing.[58]

Such malingering was more likely a sign of indifference than of dissidence, especially once the earl decided that his private business in parliament did not require his presence but could be quite satisfactorily carried out by his steward.[59] It is hard to imagine what sort of political motives might justify both absenteeism from the Reformation Parliament and attendance at the Boleyn triumphs of 1533. Essex certainly found some royal policies distasteful, and allegedly went so far as to warn the king that his abuse of Princess Mary, culminating in the enforced resignation of her title to the throne, was 'ung jeu que luy cousteroit la teste'.[60] He had no time for the German protestant ambassadors who came to visit Prince Edward in 1539. Essex had to make the prince laugh to entertain the envoys, and did so by letting the child play with his beard; but when the ambassadors left, Bourchier reminded the prince 'that I am thy father's true manne and thyne, and thiese other be false knaves'.[61] English protestant exiles regarded the earl as a 'cruel tyrant', presumably on religious grounds.[62] Yet Essex's contacts with Mary were no closer than those of many other peers, and there is no evidence to link him with the active conservative politicians of the council and court.[63]

His religion was conventional. He had a chapel with liveried choristers, bells, wax candles and tapers.[64] He exercised his considerable ecclesiastical patronage to a variety of ends, of which the encouragement of learning was not one: of twenty-six priests who owed their livings to Bourchier between 1486 and 1540, only two were graduates, at a time when the overall percentage of graduates appointed to benefices in Essex varied between nineteen and twenty-nine.[65] His household chaplains' abilities as attorneys, feoffees and wartime paymasters were more important to him than their theology, and his ecclesiastical patronage met his duties to his own family (his most loyal clerical servant was one John Bourchier, who duly remembered the earl's daughter in his will of 1558), to the families of his followers among the gentry, and to his family's monastic foundation at

Beeleigh.[66] If it met any ideological demand, it was that of the natural conservatism of an ageing nobleman: the most distinguished of his appointees was a doctor of theology of conservative leanings, and none of his clergy showed reformist enthusiasm.[67]

There is no sign that Bourchier's conservatism extended to an urge to assert the power of the nobility against low-born ministers and a resurgent monarchy. At times he stood on his dignity as a peer, for instance when a London mercer suggested that it was dishonourable of him to default on the payment of a debt: Essex countered by demanding that the council punish his opponent in 'suche maner that ap[er]teyneth to ev[er]y suche light p[er]son to have for the slaunderyng of any of the right honorable lordes of the p[ar]liament'.[68] But in general, bonds with other individuals within the peerage seem to have been more important to Bourchier than a sense of the collective identity of the nobility as a whole. Such bonds might spring from kinship, like those with Lord Ferrers and the earl of Kent, or with Bourchier's cousin, John, Lord Berners, who served him as a feoffee in 1509 and a surety in 1511.[69] Or they might be the product of shared local or regional interests, as the East Anglian supremacy of the Howards led Bourchier to name Thomas, earl of Surrey, Thomas, Lord Howard, and Sir Edward Howard his feoffees in 1509, and to visit Framlingham in 1526-7.[70]

Like many of his contemporaries among the peers, Essex was fulsome in expressing his gratitude and pledging his service to Wolsey, Cromwell, and doubtless to anyone else who might make his life easier. In sending a servant to request one favour, he apologised to Wolsey that he had not 'doon my dewtye to cu[m] to yo[ur] grace my self', assuring the cardinal that 'I have none o[ther] refuge butt to yo[ur] grace in all my caus[es]'.[71] He sent similar excuses to Cromwell, 'my good lorde to whome under the kynge I doo truste mooste unto', kept him sweet with New Year's gifts, and promised that 'in yo[ur] havyng me in yo[ur] good reme[m]brans you bynde me as yo[ur] owne to be at you[r] com[maundment]'.[72] He may have resented the need to abase himself in this way, but he did not resent it enough to do anything: he could not even rouse himself to attend the parliament in which the bones of Wolsey's ministry were to be picked over. This should be no surprise, because Essex was generally able to avoid the potential ill-effects of early Tudor policy.

Wolsey and Cromwell followed Henry VII's lead in utilising noble debt as a political weapon and a fiscal device, yet this never caused Bourchier significant concern. He met both ministers with claims that his debts had been pardoned by the king or discharged by his administrators, and when

in 1539 another attempt was made to recover the £110 due to
Henry VII – now 46 years old – it was only crown legal action against his
sureties that brought it seriously to Essex's attention.[73] The earl was not
incapable of repaying such debts. He produced £40 in cash for Henry VII
in July 1487, and £100 within thirteen days of the start of Wolsey's drive to
collect crown debts in November 1514 – the first instalment of a £1,000
loan from 1509 or 1510, on which he had entirely defaulted in 1513.[74] But
there was no good reason to pay until under pressure to do so, and Essex
took this attitude even to his payments under the 1534 subsidy.[75] Indeed,
debts ignored for long enough might conveniently disappear. The story of
Essex's debts to the crown suggests that, with the right combination of luck
and judgement, early Tudor kingship might be brought to bolster, rather
than to batten upon, the wealth of the average nobleman.

Henry Bourchier was neither one of the few peers who craved a
prominent place in central government, nor one of the few who
mishandled their relations with the crown so spectacularly as to forfeit their
wealth or their local power. Some might count him a failure, as a courtier
who made little impact on politics and did little to enrich himself or his
friends. Certainly he was unfortunate to be a young gallant at the court of
Henry VII and a middle-aged gallant at the more congenial court of Henry
VIII. Yet he escaped the imprisonments and financial penalties of the
former reign, and the executions which struck down more politically active
peers after 1536. Few noblemen can have failed to be attracted by the
chivalrous glamour of the court, and the opportunities for advancement by
conspicuous service to the king which it offered. Yet the court had its
dangers and disadvantages, as courtiers like Wyatt and Bryan were fond of
pointing out, and to a nobleman such as Essex the rival attractions and
importance of the country were very much greater than they would be to a
gentleman-courtier.[76] For power in the country was not merely a
manifestation of power at the centre, and the lasting power of his dynasty
in Essex was at least as important to Bourchier as his own fleeting influence
in the council and at court.

II

For Bourchier, land was the primary source of power. His landed income
was small compared with that of his fellow-earls, but the estates which
generated it were unusually concentrated. The Bourchier inheritance lay
almost entirely in Essex, in a band of manors some twenty-five miles
wide stretching across the county from the Wakerings, Tillingham and

Wivenhoe in the east, through Ramsden Barrington, Broomfield and Halstead in the centre, to Greenstead, Little Hallingbury and the Chesterfords in the west. Even the outlying estates were near at hand, in southern and central Suffolk. Henry's father, grandfather and paternal grandmother died in quick succession in 1483–4, and in the political turmoil that followed the death of Edward IV the Bourchiers lost many of the fruits of their Yorkist partisanship. Henry could not hope to match his grandfather's income of £1,300, and between 1496 and 1498 he dropped the title of lord of Tynedale from his style, recognising that the lordship, lately incorporated into Northumberland, was lost beyond recall.[77] But the Essex inheritance survived, protected by Henry's great-uncle Cardinal Thomas Bourchier and his uncles Sir Thomas and Sir John Bourchier, until Henry came of age and was granted his livery in September 1493.[78]

Henry's immediate ancestors had reserved the compact Essex holdings for the senior Bourchier line, and his father and uncles had made marriages and purchases in Essex and the adjoining counties which reinforced Henry's position still further. They helped to give his uncles the local influence they needed to protect Bourchier interests during his minority: Sir John sat on the commission of the peace for Essex, Sir Thomas for Suffolk and Hertfordshire.[79] They also complemented the main Bourchier holdings, as Henry inherited first, in 1491, Sir Thomas's lands in Hertfordshire, then, in 1503, his own mother's estates in Essex.[80] The dense distribution of Henry's inherited lands probably explains his quiescence on the land market, at a time when many peers were seeking to concentrate their estates by purchase or exchange. He may have made two insignificant acquisitions, but the Bourchier inheritance in 1540 remained almost identical to that shown in the accounts of 1474–5.[81]

Perhaps the concern to maintain the patrimony, so frequently voiced by early Tudor peers, weighed especially heavily on Bourchier, despite the fact that he must have realised at some point that he would have no son to succeed him in the family estate. He seems to have been proud of the grants of land and privilege made to his progenitors, and regularly procured decorated confirmations of their charters.[82] He was keen to maintain all his rights, but fought all the harder in defence of what he called 'my freholde that I and my auncesto[urs]s have hadde tyme owte of mynde'.[83] When King's College, Cambridge tried to remove two boys maintained by the earl at Beeleigh Abbey, he protested vehemently, because it was his duty not to let Beeleigh become 'decayed in my days whyche I wolde be very sory of'.[84] Not only did the names of his manors – Bourchiers in Rivenhall, Tolleshunt Bourchiers, Hallingbury Bourchier – remind him ceaselessly of his forbears, but as he grew to manhood the responsibilities of family leadership were repeatedly brought home to him. When he was 14, his great-uncle left him a 'gret bolle of gold' to pass on as an heirloom to his male successors of the name of Bourchier.[85] When he was 19, his uncle Sir Thomas Bourchier of Leeds died childless, leaving him a bed of blue damask, and at 23 he was named supervisor of the will of his childless uncle Sir John Bourchier of Groby. Sir John requested burial at Beeleigh, and bequeathed to Earl Henry his 'grete Inglishe booke'; four years later, Sir John's widow asked her executors to 'array newly and clenly, John Bourgchier, and so to deliver him to my lord th'erle of Essex'.[86] In 1493 and 1501 the earl lost his two sisters, Cecily, Lady Ferrers, and the unmarried Lady Isabel Bourchier, the latter leaving him half the £200 that their grandmother had left her.[87] Henry Bourchier stood increasingly alone at the head of his house.

Dynastic duty and financial and political practicality combined to make Earl Henry defend the Bourchier estate and seek to expand it in ways which would maintain its coherence. He pressed hard for a grant of Beeleigh Abbey's estates in 1536, but his appeal to his family's rights as founders and his hint that his 'poure servys' to the king might meiit reward could not sway Cromwell when his offer of 1,000 marks for a grant of the lands fell well below the market price.[88] He also made strenuous attempts to regain for the main Bourchier line some of the entailed Essex estates of his cousin John Bourchier, Lord Berners, who died in 1533 leaving a legitimate daughter and three bastard sons; but despite action in parliament and more pleading with Cromwell, some at least of Berners' lands eluded his grasp.[89]

In arranging his marriage, Essex must have thought he was in a stronger position to expand his estates. His chosen bride was Mary, the younger but first-married of the two daughters and heiresses of Sir William Say, a Hertfordshire knight and the son of the first earl's friend, Sir John Say. These family connections, his comital rank and the advantage of having first pick of his father-in-law's estates enabled Essex to write into his marriage contract, settled on 12 March 1497, the promise of a £200 share in the Say lands for himself and his wife. Unfortunately the exact division of the Say estates between Mary and her sister Elizabeth was left almost entirely undecided. The wedding and the associated land settlements then had to be postponed, because Essex was called out to serve the king against the western rebels.[90] The marriage was solemnised soon afterwards, but the disruption caused by the delay enabled Say to marry off his elder – and, dare one speculate, less attractive – daughter, to William, Lord Mountjoy in 1499, under generous terms which clashed with his promises to Essex.

Perhaps Say hoped that his sons-in-law would wait until he died to sort out their wives' inheritances, but by mid-1505 both peers had begun litigation to secure their due.[91] Mountjoy exploited Say's financial weakness – the result of Henry VII's exactions – to negotiate a favourable settlement for himself, but Essex fought on, through arbitration by the chief justices of the king's bench and common pleas in 1512, to mediation by Wolsey in 1515, which finally produced a lasting solution.[92] Bourchier lost Say's manors in Essex, which he had hoped to secure, but gained the more westerly of the Hertfordshire manors and avoided those in outlying counties. By 1540 his share of the Say estates produced £252 0s 10d, well over a quarter of his income, whereas those which passed to Mountjoy's daughter brought in only £153 0s 1d in 1534–5.[93] Essex had had to struggle long and hard to get the best deal out of his marriage, but by and large he had succeeded.

Essex's capacity for litigation in the maintenance and expansion of his landed estate was not exercised solely against the countess's father and brother-in-law, but when dealing with less well-connected opponents he resorted more readily to the standard combination of writ and riot. When John Daniel of Messing, one of the more substantial gentlemen of his corner of Essex, contested the earl's sole ownership of the manor of Knypso in Mayland in 1516, Bourchier sent his trusted servants Thomas Baker and William Spylman to support his farmer Thomas Shoyle in driving off Daniel's sheep and cattle.[94] Meanwhile he conducted another dispute with Daniel, a De Vere client who must have been more vulnerable to Essex following the death in 1513 of the thirteenth earl of Oxford, by a demure action of detinue of deeds in chancery.[95] The same versatile but determined approach was evident in the earl's long-running dispute with St Gregory's College, Sudbury, over his claim that the college owed him an annual rent of 16s 8d. Essex backed up his suit in the court of common pleas with a chancery commission to take evidence locally from vital witnesses of 'greate age impotency & febylnes' and a gang of servants to impound the college's cattle, which he then used unsuccessfully as bait to trap the college into a settlement.[96] The case ran on before the council, where the earl finally won it ten years later, receiving £7 10s in rent arrears, plus £40 for confirmation of the college's tenure of the manor in question at the old rent; he was probably as pleased to have vindicated his ancestral right, as to have made whatever profit remained after the costs of his litigation. Finally, when neither the courts nor brute force brought results, Essex had recourse to arbitration by the learned or powerful, for instance in a dispute of 1521 with the prioress of Wix over a pension, which was referred to four expert ecclesiastical lawyers.[97]

The earl took as much interest in the exploitation of his estates as in their defence. He signed his farmers' petitions for expenses on the repair of buildings, and the copies of court roll which were the title deeds of his copyhold tenants.[98] On occasion his wife even signed – and presumably checked, however perfunctorily – the court rolls themselves.[99] He was eager to profit from the villein status of some of his tenants, including one man who protested to the king that his ancestors were not merely freemen but had even 'entremaried w[ith] gentilmen'.[100] New rentals were produced by his stewards to keep rent-collection efficient.[101] In the case of his manorial demesnes, he was open to a range of alternatives. Some were farmed directly, providing grain, cattle and sheep for the household and for sale to butchers, and hides, fells and tallow for sale at Colchester, Hoddesdon and Halstead.[102] Most were leased, some as part of leases of complete manors. Though no evidence survives that Essex made leases as short as his grandfather's of 5 to 10 years, he leased both whole manors and marshes for terms of 21 or 24 years on occasion.[103] For a favoured candidate, though, or perhaps for a large fine, he would lease for up to 99 years; there could be great advantages in such transactions, especially when they did not impoverish one's descendants, as Bourchier recognised when he granted a 96-year lease, fourteen months before his death, on lands which could not be inherited by his daughter.[104] The relative frequency of long and short leases is impossible to calculate, but whatever the earl's leasing policy, it does not seem to have affected his income too adversely. In 1540 the landed income he left to his daughter and son-in-law was reckoned at £859 17s 10½d; thirteen years later, when many of the manors had been re-leased, Parr's income from the same estates was only £27 0s 8¾d higher.[105] A comparison between 1540 and 1474–5, possible only at the level of individual manors, shows a small increase in most cases, less than that achieved by some landlords in the 1530s, but certainly better than the stagnation or decline suffered by several noble estates over roughly the same sixty-year period.[106]

Whatever his exact position, Bourchier never seems to have been painfully short of money. The park at his country residence, Stanstead Hall in Halstead, contained centenarian oaks in 1553, a sure sign that the earl had not run into serious financial difficulties, and when bidding for Beeleigh Abbey he had envisaged paying out over £200 a year for three years.[107] When he needed cash in a hurry he pawned his plate, but he expected to be able to redeem it readily enough.[108] Like most early Tudor peers he was constantly in debt, but this was not a serious problem.[109] He contracted debts to at least two London mercers, one of which did cause him some difficulties. William Botry sold Essex goods worth £394 9s in the months before April 1510, probably clothes to make a splash at the new king's court, and was still trying to secure full payment twenty-four years and several lawsuits later. Yet in the meanwhile he twice extended further credit to the earl and once stood surety for the earl's debt to a goldsmith and was arrested for his pains.[110] Botry's problem was not that the earl had no money, but that he had better ways to spend it than repaying debts to impertinent mercers.

III

Noble wealth might be converted into power in several ways. First and most obvious was Essex's ability to spend money on an impressive household and an imposing home. Most peers spent between one-third and two-thirds of their income on the household, recognising its importance as a social and political centre: Essex was no exception, devoting £275 8s 1¼d to household expenditure in 1533–4.[111] The result was a direct relationship between wealth, power, and household size, evident among the peers of Essex. The thirteenth earl of Oxford had a household of several hundred servants at the height of his career; in 1533–4, Bourchier, spending less than a third as much as Oxford, employed fifty; in 1523, Lord Marney had an establishment of thirty-two.[112] The earl's household servants were loyal to him, and he to them. When Henry Myddleton, who waited on the earl every day, was imprisoned in Windsor Castle for hunting offences, his first reaction was to ask for Bourchier's help, and the earl gained his release.[113] When Essex wanted reliable troops, he raised them from among his household servants, and when he wanted to repossess the lands of his bailiff in Bildeston, the crowd of eleven local tenants sent to overawe the victim was led by William Clopton, the steward of the household, Clopton's servant John Chaundeler of Halstead, and Alexander Lee, another Halstead resident, who was inserted as the new bailiff.[114] The relationship between the earl's tenants in Halstead and the household was especially close, and families such as the Spylmans, Fullers and Swattocks were prominent in the affairs of the town and the earl alike.[115] Links between the household and the tenantry further afield are harder to establish, though most of the staff in 1533–4 had Essex surnames. The household's provision of hospitality and entertainment for a peer's tenantry and local notables aimed to buy influence and loyalty. Essex repaired, bought and hired plate and other tableware in preparation for the Christmas festivities in 1533, though the identity of his guests is unknown; he also continued his grandfather's patronage of actors and musicians, and employed 'Rychard the mynstrell', who played the viol.[116]

Household expenditure constituted a continuous channelling of income into a display of noble power, while building could pursue the same end with more irregular means.[117] For Bourchier that means seems to have been his wife's income, liberated in 1529 by the death of Sir William Say. It is hard to date precisely the impressive early Tudor rebuilding of Stanstead Hall in Halstead, the Bourchiers' home since the late thirteenth century, but by 1553 it had produced a two-storey brick courtyard house, with ogee-topped corner-turrets, octagonal chimney stacks, and a brick-lined moat over 180 feet square.[118] Substantial work was in progress in the early 1530s, for in 1533–4 there were payments to 'Well[e]s the cast[er] of the mote at Stansted f[or] castyng of the same mote', to craftsmen for glazing the countess's privy closet and panelling the great chamber, and to several labourers for levelling and gravelling-over the outer yard.[119] Essex was doubtless concerned that the Bourchiers should not be left behind in the East Anglian building boom that produced Kenninghall and Westhorpe.[120]

Essex's estates made him powerful, not just because they made him rich, but also because they gave him influence over his tenants. He controlled the markets of Halstead and Bildeston, and through the Say inheritance that of Hoddesdon; he sued out various royal charters to confirm his ancestors' grants of markets and fairs, and successfully defended his rights in Hoddesdon against a *Quo Warranto* in 1534–5.[121] Through the earl's manorial courts minor justice was done to his tenants in his name and by his officers, and in a town such as Halstead this could extend to the fining of those who had hosted late-night games of cards and dice, and even to the use of the cucking-stool on one Alice Trykelowe, who 'kepyth suspesscyous rewle be nyght and causyth dyv[er]s men to kepe syche rewle [that] my lord[es] tenant[es] stond in fere of ther good[es].'[122] As we shall see, the manor courts were also Bourchier's most useful weapon in his struggles with presumptuous gentlemen-farmers, who abused the leases or offices granted them by the earl to waste his demesnes and oppress his tenants.

In serious cases, the power conferred by landlordship was exercised directly by the earl. In December 1537 Ambrose Letyse disappeared from Bildeston. The parish constables and bailiff suspected Philip Wetherick of Letyse's murder, and carried Wetherick off to the local JP, John Spring, who took bail from him on 26 December. Wetherick was tried on 25 March at the Bury St Edmunds assizes, found guilty, and hanged. But in the intervening three months the struggle for Wetherick's life revolved, not around the Suffolk JPs and the judicial structure, but around the earl of Essex. First the parish officers took Wetherick to the earl for examination, presumably in the hope that he would be awed into confession. Wetherick's wife Margery countered with a visit to her uncle, the abbot of St Osyth's, who promised to write to Essex on her husband's behalf. Next the constables threatened Margery with a trip to see the earl, aiming to scare her into betraying her husband. Finally they despatched to Bourchier Wetherick's 11-year-old son Martin, who had agreed to testify that his father killed Letyse and burned the body. With Martin went a collection of bones and ashes found at Wetherick's house – all that was left of Ambrose Letyse, claimed the constables. The earl was presumably convinced, and the boy appeared as the prosecution's leading witness. Essex's impact on the case was an indirect one, but had he been anxious to save Wetherick he could doubtless have intervened. Even Henry VII's council learned in the law accepted that matters concerning a nobleman's tenants might properly be referred to the peer in question, and the people of Bildeston plainly thought the same. That they did so could not have been demonstrated in this instance, had it not emerged in April 1538 that Ambrose Letyse was alive and well and living in Prittlewell, that both the parish officers and his troubled family might have been happier than they claimed to be rid of Philip Wetherick, and that the alleged mortal remains of the victim were in fact those of a pig.[123]

Bourchier's local power to a large extent coincided with and rested on his landlordship. Crown policy reinforced the connection between land-holding and authority by the appointment of peers to the commissions of the peace in counties where they held substantial estates, and the earl was duly named to every Essex and Hertfordshire commission from the mid-1490s to his death.[124] Surviving visual evidence of the earl's power in Essex in the form of Bourchier badges or arms in the decoration of houses and parish churches is not confined to villages where Essex held the advowson or the manor, but it is exclusively concentrated in the areas of the county where his estates lay.[125] The earl's tendency to travel around his manors, though not so pronounced as that of some peers, took him to Ramsden Barrington in the south, Bourchiers in Great Chesterford in the north, and Great Totham in the east, in the last instance 'to hunt the red dere'; such visits must have reinforced his tenantry's familiarity with, and loyalty to, their lord, and the acquaintance of other local inhabitants with one of the great men of their county.[126] In Hertfordshire, where Bourchier's landed interests were small before his wife's accession to the Say inheritance, his efforts to establish his local influence were still more closely tied to his estates. He seems to have made a point of leaving Halstead regularly in the 1530s to stay at houses such as Benington and Baas in Broxbourne.[127] At both manors he self-consciously played good lord to the parish church, presenting Benington with 'a cope w[ith] th'erle of Essex armes' and Broxbourne with 'ij stremers of sarsnet w[ith] egles & Bowsys knott[es]'.[128] Doubtless loyalty to the Bourchiers came rather more readily in the county where their influence had been built up over centuries, than in the new territories on the far side of the Stort and the Lea.

The continuity and concentration of the Bourchiers' landholding in Essex created for Henry a cohesive following among the upper yeomanry and lesser gentry of the areas where his estates lay, a following whose loyalty was reinforced by the earl's employment as estate officers of successive generations of such families as the Gaywoods of Maldon and the Salperwyks of Halstead.[129] Such families might combine into tight local networks like that in the area south and east of Maldon. There, several generations of the Caustons of Latchingdon, Tillingham and Purleigh, the Osbornes of North Fambridge, the Garyngtons of Heybridge and Tollesbury, the Boodes of Burnham, and the Shoyles of Mayland intermarried, witnessed and executed one another's wills, served as feoffees of one another's lands, and took leases of demesnes and other lands from the earl.[130] Linked with the Garyngtons, Caustons, Boodes and Osbornes was Thomas Purfote of Southminster, who served the earl as a feoffee in 1515–17, and was in turn an associate of the Rawlyngs of Great and Little Wakering and of Henry Baker of Eastwood, who also had dealings with Bourchier.[131] Purfote, with over a thousand sheep, and lands valued at £20 6s 8d in his inquisition *post mortem* and thus probably worth substantially more, had grounds to be confident in calling himself a gentleman, but the rest of these men were usually happy to be classed as yeomen. As the leaders of village society they could, at least at moments of crisis, make or break a landlord's power, and they constituted the bedrock of the Bourchier affinity. Yet their co-operation probably sprang as much from the fact that they were the leading families of their restricted area as from any sense of a shared identity as the earl's men, and they were of insufficient standing in county society to contribute greatly to his power in local politics.

Essex had much to offer the more ambitious among them. John Causton of Lovaynes in Latchingdon sought to claw his way to gentility from a taxable landed income of £12 in 1524; Bourchier gave him local office, as bailiff of the Wakerings, and leasehold land, as drainer of a marsh there and as farmer of North Fambridge Hall.[132] To cross the frontier into the gentry proper, Causton had to take leases from many other landlords and begin to buy land, often on doubtful titles.[133] These activities involved him in a flurry of lawsuits in which Essex's influence must have been helpful: Causton's opponents said they feared him partly because he was 'a gret bolsterer & berer of maters' in his own right, but also because, through Bourchier, he was 'a man of great powr & frendshipp w[ith]yn Essex'.[134] A gentleman's or yeoman's place in the Bourchier household – in 1534 the leading yeoman was an Osborne – provided wages of 20s or more a year, and, more important, the chance to petition the earl for the lease of a farm, as John Burtton and perhaps Nicholas Orrell did.[135] For the yeomen farmers who sold wheat, barley and oats to the earl, bought his timber and leased his demesnes, his custom and favour might make the difference between solid prosperity and substantial upward mobility.[136] Essex's estates and the wealth they generated underlay the relationships with the people of his county which made him a powerful man.

I V

Yet even within Essex, Henry Bourchier's landholding could give him no pretensions to the sole leadership of county society. Large blocks of estates were held by the crown, the Bishop of London, and several peers whose main holdings lay elsewhere.[137] More significantly, four concentrations of land in the county were held by other resident noble families during Bourchier's adult life. His most powerful neighbours were the De Vere earls of Oxford. The core of their estates, stretching northwards from the river Colne into southern Suffolk, made the family at least as influential in northern Essex as were the Bourchiers in the centre of the county, and though their Essex holdings were not much more valuable than those of Bourchier, their lands in other counties gave them a total income two or three times the size of his: £1,666 18s 9d in 1498–9, £2,063 3s ¾d in 1540, and £2,914 3s ¼d in 1551–2.[138] The Radcliffes, Lords Fitzwalter and, from 1529, earls of Sussex, were poorer, with an income reckoned at £559 9s 10¾d in Henry VII's reign and £550 in 1523.[139] Their Essex estates were split into an eastern and a western block, and as territorial magnates they could not rival the Bourchiers or De Veres: the De Vere mullet is an even more common sight on late-fifteenth and early-sixteenth-century Essex churches than the Bourchier knot, but the Radcliffe star is prominent only on the south porch of 1523 at Burnham-on-Crouch, where Fitzwalter was lord of the manor.[140] The family's involvement in central politics cost them dear in Henry VII's reign, when Lord John was attainted, but his restored heir reaped the benefits of a close association with the Howards, to gain in wealth and standing at every crisis from 1525 to 1540.[141]

Thomas Butler, earl of Ormond, was another peer active at court and in the council under Henry VII.[142] His Essex estates were scattered across the county, but included a valuable concentration – yielding £286 9s 11½d in 1506–7 and £295 12s 7d in 1509–10 – in its south-eastern extremity around Rochford.[143] It was, not surprisingly, on the new tower of Rochford church that he chose to display his arms.[144] He died in 1515, but his Essex estates passed to Sir Thomas Boleyn, who took the title of Rochford when created a viscount in 1525. Boleyn had been granted lands in Essex by the king as early as 1512, and expanded his holdings during his family's political supremacy in the early 1530s.[145] Sir Thomas and his children probably had too many interests at court, in Kent and in Norfolk to commit themselves fully to the affairs of Essex, but in the years of their greatness they must have provided an important channel of communication between the county and the centres of politics and government.

In a county like Essex, such channels were many and various. Proximity to London and the strength of the cloth industry produced a land-market permeated by merchant capital, and a local power structure with close ties to the city and the court, while Essex lawyers enjoyed successful and profitable careers in litigation and government.[146] Such a lawyer, Lord Chancellor Sir Thomas Audley, constructed from the mid-1530s the fifth great inheritance in Bourchier's Essex, which brought him an income of some £1,038 4s 10⅜d in the year of Bourchier's death.[147] Audley and Richard Rich, who began to follow his example in the later 1530s, were only the most conspicuous of a string of civil servants and courtiers with influence in Essex and Hertfordshire. Thomas Cromwell collected offices in the area, and negotiated a large grant of Essex monastic lands days before Bourchier's fatal accident.[148] Sir Robert Clifford, William Coffin, Sir Anthony Denny, John Gates, Sir Henry Marney, Sir William Petre and Sir Ralph Sadler all settled in one county or the other, and Marney announced his family's rise with a spectacular house at Layer Marney.[149] Sir Francis Bryan and Sir John Cutt spent most of their time in Buckinghamshire and Cambridgeshire respectively, but each had strong interests in Essex and Hertfordshire, and Bryan was demonstrably able to find advancement for his servants in the area.[150]

The influence exercised by such men must have limited any claim by the peers of these counties to local political leadership. It probably increased the competition for crown offices and grants of monastic land in the area to the point where a nobleman like Essex could hope for few or none. What might be achieved was shown by Rich, who used his position in the court of augmentations to found one of the great landed estates of Elizabethan and Stuart Essex, or by Marney, who presided over a remarkable bonanza for his family and friends in the distribution of duchy of Lancaster offices in the months following his appointment as chancellor of the duchy in May 1509.[151] What might have to be done if those further from the centre of government were to reap such benefits was shown by Henry Parker, Lord Morley. From his seat at Great Hallingbury on the Essex–Hertfordshire border, he attended parliament and treason trials with great assiduity, and flaunted successively his servile friendship for Wolsey, Anne Boleyn, Thomas Cromwell, Henry VIII and Mary Tudor, his contempt for the 'Babylonicall seate of the Romyshe byshop' (1539), and his dismay at seditious people who 'denyed the head of the Church, the Popes Holynes' (*c.* 1553). Yet he was not even appointed to the commission of the peace until 1530, when he was well into middle age, and all his obvious loyalty brought him only one stewardship of crown lands, tentative royal assistance in a dispute with the canons of Norwich, and the chance to purchase at the normal price some monastic estates in 1540. The best Morley's epitaph could claim was that he had adorned Essex as 'the most precious jewel in a throng of nobles'.[152]

In Henry VII's reign, the most obvious block to Bourchier's leadership of county society was the thirteenth earl of Oxford. The latter's diehard Lancastrian loyalty was rewarded by Henry VII with a position as one of the most trusted magnates of the realm, a position from which, with the substantial resources of his restored estates to draw upon, he dominated East Anglia in general and Essex in particular.[153] On occasion Bourchier must have thought ruefully of his grandfather's unchallenged dominance in county affairs, and wondered what his own position would have been had the Yorkist regime survived and De Vere remained a landless exile. But Henry VII's debt to Oxford was too great for a prudent rival to do anything other than accept the king's will. When Henry VII wanted something done in Essex, he wrote to John De Vere; when he visited the county, in 1487, 1498 and 1506, he visited John De Vere, and not Henry Bourchier.[154] The king did write to Bourchier on occasion, and on the 1498 progress even deigned to hunt in his park, but for the time being there was little future for Essex as a local magnate, all the more so as Oxford plainly enjoyed influence as a patron at court as well as in the country.[155]

Essex had to work with Oxford, serving under his command in France in

1492, and he showed him proper respect, visiting him at Whitsun 1508 and presenting him with two decorated coverlets.[156] Certainly the common perception must have been that relations between Essex and Oxford were harmonious, for several Essex men chose the two earls to lead their feoffees.[157] Yet it was Oxford's Howard kin, led by Thomas, earl of Surrey, who capitalised on the friendship of the childless earl to claim the succession to his East Anglian satrapy, and at least until Oxford's death in 1513 Essex found it best to turn his attention from a county where he could not shine to a court where he might.[158] Thereafter he seems to have consolidated his position in his native county – probably a natural tendency as his role at court waned – without ever matching Oxford's or his grandfather's dominance there, or competing for a leading role on the wider East Anglian stage.

Under Henry VIII too, Henry Bourchier's relationships with the other great men of his county seem to have been generally harmonious, perhaps precisely because the distribution of power in Essex was sufficiently diffuse to inhibit the development of a struggle between two or three individuals or parties for control of the county. Though Bourchier must have known well most of the courtiers and bureaucrats who lived in Essex, evidence of his dealings with them rarely survives: he twice stayed at Bryan's house at Faulkbourne, trusted Cutt and the Marneys as feoffees, admired Sir Henry Marney enough to vote for his election to the Garter, and appreciated Rich's talents sufficiently to use him as his solicitor at London and Westminster in the early 1530s, but there are no signs of especially close links with any of them.[159]

Essex's relations with the other great peers of his county are rather better documented. He tended not to use them as feoffees. This may have been merely because he foresaw the inevitability of minor land disputes with the De Veres and others, like that against the dowager-countess of Oxford on which he spent £4 3s 11d in 1533.[160] Such tussles did not have to develop into personal feuds – Essex warned the countess when he discovered that the rector of Otten Belchamp had tried to poison her, and in 1534 and 1536 they worked together in ecclesiastical matters – but feoffees who were in no danger of claiming one's estates for themselves or their dependants were a safer choice.[161] Henry VIII certainly expected the peers of Essex to work readily together, to raise taxes, suppress disorder, organise coastal defences and intimidate Princess Mary during her stay at Boreham in 1533.[162] Such co-operation, it seems, was friendly. Audley stayed at Essex's house at Little Easton in August 1539, and at Garter chapters Essex voted once or twice for Audley and the fourteenth and fifteenth earls of Oxford, and three times for Fitzwalter.[163]

Henry Bourchier seems to have been especially close to John De Vere, the fifteenth earl of Oxford. He very willingly gave Oxford his proxy when licensed to miss parliament; in 1534 he visited Oxford's house at Earl's Colne, and later he made a trip to his park at Colne Engaine.[164] Despite Oxford's patronage of John Bale, the two earls seem to have shared religious views of a rather conservative nature, and this made it easy for them to work together in trying to remove the radical John Hilsey as provincial of the Dominican friars, or examining the reactionary abbot of Coggeshall and finding him innocent of any misconduct.[165] They also shared an intense loyalty to the Tudor crown. In November 1533 a priest argued at Maldon that Henry VIII was not rightful king because his father had not been king, but only duke of Somerset; Essex sent the priest and the depositions about his offence to Oxford, evidently expecting his brother earl to agree that 'ther ware no dethe that cowlde be inmagende suffycyent for hys offensus'.[166] The two earls grew old together – Oxford was born in about 1482 and died eight days after Essex – and as they reviewed the county's defences together in spring 1539 they seem to have felt their years. Though Audley assured Cromwell that they had 'taken gret paynes' in the work, they had to admit rather sheepishly that 'it laye not in us to vysy[t] all places w[ith] suche speade as the tenor of the com[m]yssi[on] gave us in comawndement'.[167]

By the 1530s, Oxford was more prominent that Essex in central government, as one of the few peers sitting in the reformed privy council, but they may both have been content to play the great man in local matters and let the profusion of rising Essex courtiers and bureaucrats represent the county at Whitehall and Westminster.[168] The amount of time that an Audley, a Rich or even a Bryan spent at London or at court must have limited their involvement in Essex affairs, and their greatest impact on the county was restricted to the years immediately before and after Bourchier's death, for it was only the dissolution of the monasteries that made it possible for them to accumulate extensive estates. Their efforts as patronage-brokers probably concentrated as much on furthering the careers of their departmental underlings, clerks and other servants in their ministerial households, and contacts from the court, as on the cultivation of a local affinity.[169] And, unlike the great new courtier-magnates of their age, John, Lord Russell, or Charles Brandon, duke of Suffolk, they were not operating at royal command to fill a dangerous local power vacuum. Instead they faced a county where Oxford, Essex and Sussex were powerful landlords at the level of manor and hundred, and respected leaders on the county stage. That all parties accepted the fact explains the apparent lack of conflict or competition between the new men of power and the old.

The balance of power in Essex was reflected in the attempts of religious houses and towns to secure the protection of noblemen and others against their local enemies and, if needs be, against the demands of central government. Abbots paid fees, not only to legal counsel but also, as an official reminded the new abbot of St Osyth's in 1494, to 'other discrete and noble gentylmen not lerned yn the lawes but of gret power yn their contrey and of right sadde disposicyon, of whom the seid abbott[es] ... had good mayntenaunce and rightfull supportacyon yn all their juste and resonable quarell[es] many tymes to their gret comforte.'[170] The monastery with which Bourchier had the closest links was Beeleigh, and in 1536 he wrote to Cromwell to ask a favour for the abbot.[171] At the dissolution, Beeleigh possessed three copes decorated with Bourchier knots, and the earl bought these from the commissioners; among its farmers were several Bourchier tenants and associates.[172] Close behind came St Osyth's, where Essex succeeded Sir George De Vere as chief steward, and had the Bourchier arms and badges displayed on the bishop's lodging, completed in 1527.[173] By 1535 the earl was chief steward of the abbey of Walden too, and of the Essex estates of St Paul's cathedral; until 1527 he was chief steward of Coggeshall Abbey, a post he held jointly with the fifteenth earl of Oxford from that year.[174] Any nobleman might dominate one or two monastic houses, as the earl of Sussex did Dunmow Priory, but by the 1530s Essex's tally of stewardships was impressive, outnumbering those of Oxford and Sussex, paying a total of £11 6s 8d in fees, and giving him military leadership of the monastic tenants.[175] This did not, however, symbolise a significant influence over the houses' affairs, for example, in the appointment of their other officers; and the religious houses of Hertfordshire paid him no discernible attention at all.[176] Indeed, his most noteworthy stewardship, that of the estates of the dean and chapter of Canterbury, was a tribute less to the influence of the earl than to the nepotism of his great-uncle the archbishop.[177] In this way as in many others, Essex could aspire to durable power only on a restricted and local basis. He could not establish more than the shadow of a wider supremacy.

Monastic patronage to a nobleman was hard to revoke. Essex remained steward for life of houses which may have counted on his position at court and within the county remaining strong, while favourable leases could commit a house for longer still: Leighs Priory leased him a manor for ninety-six years in 1515.[178] Towns, which regaled their local peers with presents year by year, could tailor their giving more sensitively to the expected return. The boroughs of Essex made much of the thirteenth earl of Oxford, and Colchester in 1509–10 was especially lavish in its generosity to him.[179] Maldon, too, recognised that Oxford was the king's man in the county, sending him important letters in 1507–8, and a captured 'walshman, ut supponit[ur] a spy' in 1502–3. But in the latter year they entertained Bourchier with a porpoise, three capons and three mallards, and in 1503–4 they gave him 4s 10d worth of wine; he replied by giving the town a buck.[180] In the last decade of Henry VII's reign and even into the 1520s Essex, as a local landowner and a peer about court, was plainly worth knowing, but by the 1530s it was the Radcliffes, resident nearby and visibly more prominent in the king's affairs than Bourchier, who dominated Maldon's entertainment accounts.[181] Others outweighed him in electoral patronage too – the De Veres at Colchester, and the Radcliffes, from 1512 onwards, at Maldon.[182] Had Halstead or Hoddesdon returned MPs, Bourchier might have had a pocket borough of his own; in practice, he was never so dominant in the county nor so powerful at court than towns outside his immediate sphere of influence needed to take more than polite note of him.

V

Henry Bourchier's affinity was an unspectacular affair in comparison with those of his great magnate contemporaries, but served his more limited ends as effectively as theirs sustained their provincial dominance. The success of the thirteenth earl of Oxford, like that of any adept in the politics of good lordship, rested on his relationship with the gentry, both those who were closely bound to his service and those whose vaguer goodwill and co-operation facilitated his regional hegemony.[183] When Oxford made his will in 1509, his executors and annuitants included several of the leading knights of each East Anglian county, and at that date at least one Essex JP in four was closely linked with the De Veres.[184] Lacking Oxford's wealth and obvious power in central politics, Bourchier could not match such a following; he could hope for little more than goodwill from the knights and greater esquires who stood at the head of the gentry community, but such goodwill was valuable. Two families of this status with estates in Essex seem to have been especially well-disposed towards the earl – the Fortescues of Ponsbourne in Hertfordshire (and, between 1508 and 1518, of Faulkbourne in Essex), and the Waldegraves of Smallbridge in Bures, just over the Essex border in Suffolk. John Fortescue and his brother Adrian, Sir William Waldegrave and his son George, served

Bourchier as feoffees and sureties, as did George Waldegrave's son, another Sir William, who was one of the three local knights who sent him presents of fish and game in 1533–4.[185] Yet such men's loyalty to the earl was neither exclusive nor servile. Four of Essex's feoffees in 1509 had served as Oxford's feoffees in 1507; and when Sir Adrian Fortescue was sued by the crown in 1539 as Essex's surety, he was quite prepared to extricate himself by threats to sue the earl on the obligation by which Essex had promised that he would come to no harm.[186]

Greater gentry families whose interests were more exclusively concentrated in Essex had, if anything, even weaker links with the earl. The sparse evidence for the affairs of such men as Sir Roger Wentworth of Codham, John Tyrrell of Heron, and Sir Geoffrey Gates of High Easter shows little contact with Bourchier, though Gates did once sell him a horse.[187] The evidence from the earl's side is equally negative. Only five of the eleven gentlemen who sent him presents in 1533–4 were of sufficient standing to be named as JPs, and only two of those sat for Essex; a sixth had recently been knighted but never reached the bench.[188] Seven Essex justices and many other county gentry were among the forty-five feoffees to whom the earl entrusted four manors in 1515–17.[189] They were doubtless content, perhaps even flattered, to be part of the great man's affairs in this way, but there is no sign that they felt any obligation to him beyond that to serve as honest trustees. Scraps of evidence reveal that such men as Anthony Wingfield, Anthony Darcy and John Pilbarough co-operated with Bourchier in the conduct of the county's business and the local social round, and treated him with respect, but not much more than respect.[190] Henry Bourchier was a great man in his county, but he was not the great man in his county, in the way in which the Stanleys, the Howards or the Percies might claim to be in their counties, and the greater gentry of Essex knew it.

These leaders of Essex and Suffolk gentry society had landed incomes of £100 or considerably more – in 1523–4 Anthony Darcy was taxed on £100, Sir William Waldegrave on £266 13s 4d, Sir Roger Wentworth on £300, Sir Anthony Wingfield on £333 6s 8d – contacts with the court independent of any local peer, and a strong claim in their own right to seats on the bench and in parliament.[191] The men who needed the earl far more were gentlemen in the second rank of county affairs: such individuals formed the most prominent part of the Bourchier affinity, blending at the lower end with the ambitious yeomen tenants – men like John Causton of Lovaynes – who were more naturally bound to the earl. These middling gentlemen were often dominant in their own corner of Essex, but of insufficient wealth, lineage and experience to make a mark on county affairs without the earl's help. The Kynwolmersh family of Great Dunmow, of whom Thomas and William were retained by Essex in 1513, were very prominent in the life of their parish.[192] William Bradbury was almost twice as rich as anyone else in Clavering, with £50 of taxable goods in 1524: he served the earl as a retainer in 1513, as receiver from at least 1519 to 1534, as steward of Chickney in 1524, and as a London agent in 1534.[193] William Clopton, also worth £50, was by far the richest man in Liston in 1524; he was the second son of a Suffolk knight, who married an Essex heiress and became steward of the earl's household.[194] Thomas Bulphan was the earl's bailiff of Asheldham, where he led the list of taxpayers with £285 10s in goods.[195] Bourchier also drew such followers from Hertfordshire, where his auditor Humphrey Fitzherbert of Braughing and his legal adviser Thomas Knighton of Bayford enjoyed taxable landed incomes of £66 13s 4d and £60 respectively.[196]

Bourchier's service attracted these men for various reasons. Their sons could be brought up as gentlemen of his household, as was William Clopton's second son Francis; in 1534 such gentlemen may also have included sons of Thomas Cornewall of Stebbing (taxed at £80) and John Maxey of Great Saling (taxed at £50), and a scion of one of the numerous junior lines of the Tyrrell family.[197] Offices in the earl's household and estate administration paid fees of some significance to men with incomes of around £50: William Clopton earned £5 a year as steward of the household.[198] They also offered minor patronage and delegated power which could help to consolidate a gentleman's local authority. Perhaps for this reason they were attractive to second-generation parvenus, the sons of lawyers or courtiers who had to follow up their fathers' entry into local society without their fathers' advantages: Edward Sulyard of Otes in High Laver, Walter Hobart of Loddon, and perhaps Thomas Clifford of Aspenden would be cases in point.[199]

Essex could offer to exercise on behalf of such men an influence with the king and his ministers which their fathers may have possessed but which they did not. For all these second-rank gentry such assistance was valuable. William Clopton regularly carried letters from the earl to Thomas Cromwell, and several of them included requests for Cromwell's intervention in Clopton's protracted suit to obtain his wife's inheritance.[200] In disputes nearer at hand the earl could lend his influence as an arbitrator, as he did in the 1520s when John Causton of Lovaynes fell out with a servant of Bishop Tunstal of London over the lease of an Essex rectory. Quite apart from any favouritism involved in such arbitration, it was, as Tunstal put it, 'a merytoryouse acte in avoyding of further expensis'.[201] Anything the earl could do to limit the costs or influence the outcome of litigation must have been of great benefit to a man like Causton or to the equally litigious Humphrey Fitzherbert.[202]

What could such gentlemen do for the earl? At the most basic level, they could place their considerable local influence at his disposal. Humphrey Fitzherbert was clearly used to throwing his weight about in Braughing. He had a private pew in the parish church, and when there was talk of arranging 'a play and . . . a drynking . . . for the proffit of the said chirche', the churchwardens respectfully asked his advice. When the vicar quarrelled with his brother, Fitzherbert appeared in the middle of matins with a gang of servants, who picked up the offending cleric to drag him out of church, but were restrained by their master with a gentlemanly 'Horson, lett hym goo, or els I will pull thyn erys from thyn hed'.[203] Anyone within range of Braughing who crossed the earl presumably had Fitzherbert and his men to reckon with.

Many members of the affinity held county office, and this increased their usefulness to Bourchier. William Bradbury (1509–10), Thomas Knighton (1515–16) and John Edmonds (1538–9), to whom Essex leased Asheldham Hall for fifty years in 1536, all held the escheatorship of Essex and Hertfordshire.[204] Robert Plummer (the first earl's right-hand-man) was sheriff in 1494–5, and Thomas Clifford and Thomas Knighton were named on the sheriff roll, though not chosen sheriff, in 1513 and 1520 respectively.[205] These men, together with William Clopton, Humphrey Fitzherbert and Sir George Somerset, served as commissioners to assess taxes, muster troops, and investigate grain stocks, drainage facilities, and infringements of the forest laws.[206] Those of lesser standing might be subsidy collectors, as Thomas Bulphan was in 1523, or borough officers: Thomas Gaywood, Bourchier's steward of North Fambridge, attorney and feoffee, was repeatedly elected one of the bailiffs of Maldon between 1499 and 1518.[207] Others such as Edward Sulyard and Robert Plummer held positions on the crown lands in Essex or Suffolk.[208] The dates of many of these appointments, coinciding with the period when the earl's influence at court was strongest, suggest that he probably helped to secure such promotions for his followers. In return they presumably looked kindly on his interests in the exercise of their power.

The earl could also draw on the special skills often possessed by men on the fringes of the county's governing elite. The gentry saw grammar school education as a means to advancement, as the wills of the Clopton, Edmonds and Bradbury families show, and they saw legal education as a means to further advancement.[209] Walter Hobart, Thomas Knighton, Edward Sulyard, and perhaps William Bradbury attended Lincoln's Inn, and John Edmonds the Middle Temple.[210] Their legal knowledge made them useful councillors, feoffees, and stewards, though when the earl wanted expert legal assistance he turned to the wealth of professional talent that Essex and Suffolk could provide, notably John Jenour, Richard Broke and Humphrey Browne.[211] Accomplished auditors were as useful as lawyers, and it must have been the prospect that his considerable talents would be at Bourchier's disposal that induced the earl to lease three Suffolk manors to John Wren for ninety-nine years in 1522, for Wren had over a decade's experience as auditor of various royal and aristocratic estates.[212]

Bourchier's client gentry supported him in other ways. Though their credit was less substantial than that of a Fortescue or a Waldegrave, they could still stand surety for the earl's debts, as William Bradbury did in 1519.[213] They contributed to the flow of gifts into the household: in 1534 John Causton sent wildfowl on New Year's Day, William Bradbury 'a fatt goose' in Easter week, and Thomas Knighton a crane and a wild goose on Trinity Sunday.[214] They provided a means of contact between the earl and the greater gentry. It was presumably through the good offices of William Clopton that his step-mother granted to the earl the advowson with which he presented one of his household chaplains to the rectory of Ramsden Bellhouse in 1536.[215] When Sir Adrian Fortescue wanted to raise the delicate matter of his suretyship with the earl in 1539, he did so through Thomas Knighton: Knighton was an ideal intermediary, as Fortescue's 'old lovyng & acquayntyd frend' and one of the earl's 'right welbelovyd frynd[es] and counsellours'.[216] As men of some standing who gave the earl service and accepted his good lordship, they contributed to his honour in local society. And in local politics their role in the legal system complemented that of the earl himself, to equip him to serve the crown and protect his own and his followers' interests.

For most of the earl's lifetime there were several of his followers on the commissions of the peace for Essex and Hertfordshire, and the legal knowledge of some of these men secured them a place in the quorum, the inner ring of the commission.[217] The office of justice of the peace was one of increasing importance and flexibility in the local government of early Tudor England. Justices were more active than ever before outside the sessions, in investigating crime, taking depositions from witnesses, and examining suspects, though such activity is hard to document systematically.[218] The number of justices linked with the earl could not compare with that commanded by a great magnate, but his followers made up in assiduity what they lacked in numbers. Robert Plummer missed only three of the sixteen fully recorded Essex sessions between 1489 and 1508, and Edward Sulyard often sat alongside him in the last decade of the reign.[219] When the normal attendance was three or four justices, these were significant records. Sulyard continued to attend regularly under Henry VIII, and he was succeeded among the working justices by Edward Tyrrell, who was apparently well disposed towards the earl and his followers, and then by William Bradbury.[220] Bourchier's friends on the Hertfordshire bench, Thomas Knighton, Thomas Clifford and Humphrey Fitzherbert, were equally hard-working.[221] On occasion the utility of such attendance is obvious: when the Essex bench took indictments under the new livery and retaining statute of 1504, it was very carefully stressed that no blame attached to Essex or Oxford for the illicit wearing of badges depicting Essex's 'Burchyersknotte' and the De Vere 'molette' by a Chelmsford tailor and a Debden husbandman. Among the four justices sitting were Plummer, Sulyard, and Oxford's retainer John Asplond.[222]

The earl himself also exercised his powers as a justice, working closely with his gentry followers. Like Oxford, Sussex, Morley and most other peers, he sat at sessions only occasionally: at Hertford on 9 January 1503, for instance, at Chelmsford on 12 January 1518, and at Colchester on 2 April 1528, having received a letter at his dining table at Stanstead Hall on the previous day, warning that the gaol delivery sessions could not be held 'for lake of justic[es], weropon I inco[n]tyne[n]t made me redy and rode to Colchester'.[223] But he made frequent use of his power to arrest and examine suspects. In December 1507 one of his servants 'brought upe a man' to court, in April 1534 his yeoman of the household Robert Buckeley carried 'John Delyngh[a]m a boy' to Colchester Castle, and in the 1530s he despatched various prisoners to Cromwell.[224] Their crimes are unknown, but other cases of sedition, corruption and robbery investigated by the earl together with his gentry associates – William Bradbury, William Clopton, Richard Waldegrave and John Wren – are documented in detail, often by sheets of depositions signed by Bourchier himself.[225]

Such active involvement in the judicial system could bring trouble, as two cases over the confiscation of stolen goods and the sequestration of property already sold by one Italian merchant to another suggest.[226] Nevertheless, the benefits of judicial responsibility outweighed its in-conveniences. Thus Essex aimed in 1534 to use his authority at the sessions to settle once and for all the problems caused for his friend Lord Lisle by the corrupt customs officers of Colchester.[227] Such benefits extended beyond the earl's own affairs to those of followers like Humphrey

Fitzherbert. Fitzherbert's first recourse in November 1531, when two Braughing yeomen refused to pay his servant for some timber which Fitzherbert had sold them, was to send the servant involved to make a deposition about the matter 'on a boke be fore my lorde of Essex'.[228] Thirteen years earlier, Fitzherbert had called on the earl for more active assistance. Richard and Florence Tyson had disputed Fitzherbert's ownership of a property in Mountnessing for over a decade, and in July 1518 they took occupation of it for the second time in three years. Within five days Fitzherbert not only expelled them, but also 'compleynyd to the ryght honerable Henry erle of Esex & Edward Teryll squyer, beyng ij justysys of the pays', who were conveniently on hand to arrest the Tysons, take them to gaol in Colchester, and oversee their indictment. When a Brentwood man on the jury refused to find the indictments against them, he was, so he later claimed, 'put out and dischargid of the said enquest'.[229]

Normally the earl did not need to be so unsubtle in dealing with juries. A Walden man whom the earl claimed to be his villein, and a Kent gentleman who lost a manor in Hertfordshire when Sir William Say claimed his stepdaughter's wardship and then granted Bourchier her lands, both insisted that the earl's embracery or the people's fear of his power prevented Essex and Hertfordshire juries trying their cases truly.[230] These allegations are merely interesting variations on the standard formulae by which plaintiffs explained their failure at the common law and their need for prerogative justice, but they are substantiated by the comments of the victims of a remarkable anti-courtier riot in Hoddesdon in August 1534. They reposed no trust in the local legal system since the culprits, as Essex's tenants, were assumed to be invulnerable to the normal processes of indictment and jury trial; and they expected the solidarity of jurors and accused to be reinforced by the earl's own efforts to sway Cromwell 'as moche as he can ... to stay the ponysheme[n]t of them'.[231] Essex's powers as a landlord, as a judicial officer, and as a great man in contact with the king and his ministers were mutually reinforcing.

Essex's tenants were instinctively loyal to him and to one another, but for his gentle followers matters could never be so simple. The yeomanry of Essex could readily polarise into separate, tenurially-based, affinities. None of the De Vere farmers or bailiffs of 1488–9 or 1551–2, those of Sir Roger Wentworth in 1514–15, or those of Lord Audley in 1539–40, was connected in any way with Bourchier.[232] A gentleman, in contrast, usually had to take leases from various landowners, or exercise his administrative and legal abilities in the service of more than one master. Thomas Purfote held lands of a number of different lords, and Henry Baker, like many Essex gentry, had been called to Castle Hedingham by the thirteenth earl of Oxford to do homage for lands held of the De Veres.[233] Thomas Knighton, Humphrey Fitzherbert and John Edmonds all put their talents as stewards, feoffees and auditors at the disposal of other landlords beside Bourchier, while the earl's steward at Bildeston, Robert Browne, was first and foremost the servant of Charles Brandon, duke of Suffolk.[234] A gentleman's service to a peer rarely prescribed an exclusive allegiance, though it often defined a primary loyalty.

That loyalty seems to have been more to Bourchier himself than to other members of the affinity. Co-operation between the earl's followers among the gentry can be detected, but it does not seem to have been of much significance in the lives of those concerned. In the mid-1530s William Clopton's younger brother Robert, a priest whom the earl had presented to a living in 1515, used Richard Rich as his counsel in chancery, but cases of the earl's lawyers acting for members of the affinity were rare.[235] In 1529 Thomas Knighton used Richard Rich and William Bradbury as his feoffees in Halstead, and in 1536 another feoffment included Richard Lyrisell of Gray's Inn, to whom the earl gave 7s 6d in June 1534, but in general Knighton chose feoffees unconnected with the earl.[236] Few property transactions or marriage alliances seem to have been contracted between the gentry in Bourchier's service, and they were not often mentioned in one another's wills. Of course the existence of social networks among the gentry which were independent of any connections with peers could be used to advantage by a nobleman in recruiting followers. The Cliffords and the Cloptons, the Knightons and the Says were close to one another before Thomas Clifford or Thomas Knighton was drawn into the earl's service.[237] But an affinity cannot have made much impact on county society – or, perhaps, added much lustre to the reputation of its lord – if it was so loose as to be virtually undetectable in the affairs of its middling-gentry members. Certainly it was a task beyond Essex's abilities to hold his followers to his own conservative religion, if indeed he even tried to do so. John Edmonds left a traditional will in 1544, and William Bradbury's son William thought that the definition of a good priest was one who 'singeth h[is] pleynsong & fabo[ur]don very well'.[238] But Humphrey Fitzherbert died in 1547–8 'trusting in the merit[es] of Christes passion to be one of his electe and chosen children, and to rest with Abraham Isaac and Jacob in the kingdome of God', and John Causton of Lovaynes asked in 1544 that his funeral should feature 'no processione dirige nor soule messe', but a sermon in praise of 'the uttre abholysshinge and extynttynge of the usurpedde and false faynedde power of the romysshe bysshope'.[239]

The bonds between individual Bourchier followers in the Essex gentry seem to have been stronger among those who survived from the affinity of the first earl. Robert Plummer, William Tendring, Thomas Purfote, Edward Sulyard, William Malbon and the John Causton of Lovaynes who died in 1491, worked as one another's executors and feoffees and sold one another land; most were linked with the earl's uncle, Sir Thomas Bourchier.[240] Even this circle was far from exclusive, and its members occasionally served the De Veres or Mowbrays as well as the Bourchiers, but its cohesion is redolent of that of the first earl's affinity in the days when it was the dominant force in Essex politics, when, for example, Plummer, Tendring and Malbon all sat in Parliament as burgesses for Maldon between 1469 and 1478.[241] Though their service to the second earl was doubtless valuable, their loyalties focused more on his grandfather, entombed at Beeleigh. Tendring did name 'my especial good lord Henry, earl of Essex' to supervise his will in 1499, and bequeathed to him a standing cup of silver and gilt, but Malbon, who requested prayers for the first earl and his countess and asked to be buried at Beeleigh in his will in 1505, made no mention of the new earl.[242]

The differences between the affinities of the first and second earls are instructive.[243] The first earl enjoyed more extensive estates and a higher income than his grandson, and a considerable fund of government patronage as lord treasurer. With the De Veres and Butlers respectively under total and partial proscription for their Lancastrian loyalties, and the Fitzwalter heiress married to his friend Lord Dinham, the first earl's leadership in Essex society could go unchallenged. The greater gentry were not subservient to the earl, but took more note of him than their successors did of his grandson; the lesser gentry of the affinity were more numerous, more loyal and more cohesive than those in the service of the second earl. Yet these were not in the main differences between a Yorkist nobleman and a Tudor nobleman. They were rather the result of contingencies in national and local politics: the thirteenth earl of Oxford in Henry VII's reign, or the Howard dukes of Norfolk in Henry VIII's, resembled the first earl of Essex more than did his grandson.

VI

The moment when the growth of the early Tudor state did strike home to a nobleman was when his normal dealings with the gentry and yeomanry broke down. Peers, no less than kings, lived in fear of treason by those whom they had to trust, but it was as hard for noblemen as it was for monarchs to prevent the self-serving abuse of power by those to whom they delegated it, and under the early Tudors the expansion of prerogative justice and the creeping penetration of local society by the patronage networks of the court provided the means for an errant gentleman to fight back against his lord. The earl's response to the reports in June 1514 of misdeeds perpetrated by John Causton of Marshhouse in Purleigh as farmer at North Fambridge is unknown, though his officials thought the matter serious enough to mark the record of Causton's offences 'loqued[um] cum d[omi]no'.[244] Against the crimes of Thomas Wren and Richard Stainsby the earl did take decisive action. When Wren felled 800 oaks at Drinkstone, he was indicted at the assizes and told he had forfeited his lease.[245] Stainsby, a trusted servant of the earl, unscrupulously abused his position as bailiff of Bildeston in the 1520s to augment 'hys lyvyng by his occupacion off clothmakyng' and his taxable landed income of £30, by building up a large farm.[246] In one instance he offered to obtain the lease of a field for another tenant for a reward of 26s 8d, went to the earl to arrange the lease, and returned to announce that he had decided to add the field to his own farm, taunting the original bidder with, 'Howe sayst thowe gyf me twenty noblez for yt?' In this case as in others, Bourchier seemed to connive at Stainsby's self-aggrandisement because Stainsby was his only link with Bildeston: 'my lord belyvyng the seid informac[i]on to be of truthe dyd graunt hym hys desyre'. On 1 September 1533, however, the earl's tenantry presented unanimously in the manorial court that Stainsby had betrayed Essex's trust, felling timber on the demesnes, withholding rents, enclosing parts of the demesne to expand his copyhold lands, and poisoning the atmosphere in Bildeston church by building a private pew with sides so high that no-one could see if there was a Stainsby inside eavesdropping on confessions.[247] Essex used a string of such presentments to justify replacing Stainsby as bailiff and confiscating his copyhold lands, which were rapidly re-let to various other tenants, providing them with an interest in Stainsby's ejection and the earl with £66 15s 10d in entry fines.[248]

In the manorial courts, in the fields of Suffolk and even at the assizes, Wren and Stainsby could not resist the earl and his tenants, though Stainsby did try despairingly to drive a herd of his cattle back into a field while the new bailiff, at the opposite end of the herd, drove them out again.[249] Both sought redress by other means – Wren by an appeal to Cromwell, Stainsby by letters to Cromwell and Archbishop Cranmer and a suit in Star Chamber. Essex found himself forced to protest that he was not handing out rough seigneurial justice, that he was 'verey sory to use any extremyte' against Wren 'or other, but when occasyons constreyne me', and that his only wish was to settle the Stainsby case fairly according to the 'comen lawe, the whiche I and my aunceto[ur]s hathe ben bo[ur]ne unto'.[250] Cranmer pressed him to submit his case against Stainsby to arbitration, and Cromwell can have done nothing to stop Stainsby's Star Chamber suit against the Bildeston tenantry, in which the earl had to spend £10 on his tenants' costs.[251] Stainsby won his case and triumphantly 'entered by the kyng[es] most hon[or]able letters upon hys custum[ar]ye land[es]', and, despite Bourchier's further efforts to remove him, continued to hold them until at least 1542.[252] Similarly, Thomas Wren had his lease at Drinkstone confirmed in 1540.[253] Stainsby, Wren and their kind knew too well how to play on the fears of Tudor kings and ministers that the untrammelled local authority of the nobility was a threat to royal power; in so doing, they gave substance to the fears of Tudor noblemen that an ambitious subordinate might betray them with impunity.

Such cases may have subverted Bourchier's local power, dented his noble pride and forced him to submit his own interests to the demands of his loyalty to the crown. Yet they were few and far between. More usually his pride directed his power into loyal service, never more so than when he was called upon to lead his gentry followers, household servants and tenants to serve the king in war. In 1497 he fought in the force which encircled the Cornish rebels at Blackheath; in 1512 he helped to oversee the mustering of the army at Greenwich, and in 1513 he took Suffolk cavalry and Essex footmen with him to France.[254] There he reviewed foreign horsemen, escorted prisoners, and led a cavalry charge to recover the king's lost artillery.[255] In 1514 he raised 400 men and sent them to Colchester, ready to cross to the defence of Guines, but they were 'countermaunded home ageyne'.[256] Essex did his job as a recruiter and general enthusiastically but, it would seem, without much skill. When the king proposed to give him the command of an expeditionary force in 1521, 'thinkyng hym for hys hardinesse to be ryght mete for that purpose', the necessary qualification was that Bourchier should have 'sad [counsillors] adjoyned to hym'.[257] As a warrior no less than as a courtier, a councillor, or a local magnate, Essex was no better than average. Once again he was gently mocked by the achievements of his ancestors, whose brilliance in previous wars with France had won them the title of count of Eu, which the earl proudly retained in his style to the end of his life.

When Henry Bourchier died, Wriothesley the chronicler could only recount the incident and add a lame epitaph: 'the earle of Essex riding a yong horse by misfortune cast him and brake his necke at his place in Essex, which was greate pittie'.[258] A few years earlier, an anonymous commentator had written him off as 'an old man, of little wit and less experience, without power'.[259] Yet in his very mediocrity, Bourchier was typical: of the twenty leading peers in the scathing anonymous list, eleven lacked wit or wisdom, seven lacked experience, and while only four lacked power, most of those who enjoyed it seemed incompetent in its exercise. In this mediocre typicality, Bourchier is instructive. He readily found a place at court, and even some modest success there; he was prepared to participate in the work of central government, but showed no real aptitude or enthusiasm for it. He cultivated with care both the landed inheritance on which his local power rested, and the relationships with peers, gentry, tenants, boroughs and religious houses through which that power took effect. Yet his affinity was cohesive only at the level of the yeoman tenantry; the upper gentry paid him no great attention, and though he attracted and held the service of men on the fringe of the county's elite, they did not form a very effective social and political unit. Certainly neither his affinity nor his relationship with the king fitted him to be the sole governor of his county. His title and perhaps his royal blood added to the respect due to him both at court and in Essex, but it seems that to be a Bourchier was more important to him than to be a peer. Though its policies slowly eroded the local power of him and his kind, it is unlikely that he resented the monarchy he served so loyally, not least because it can only occasionally have struck him – most conspicuously, perhaps, in his troubles with Richard Stainsby – that his power was under threat. He was less dependent on directly delegated royal authority than the new men amongst the peerage, and less able to implement or obstruct the royal will in his region than the great magnates. In any case, he was quite capable of adapting the government's devices, notably the commission of the peace, to serve his own ends. He was not the man his grandfather had been, but he did what was necessary to pass on the Bourchier inheritance undiminished to his daughter; and, given the choice, perhaps he was wise to risk his neck on young horses rather than risking his head at court.

NOTES

Note: Place of publication is London unless otherwise stated.

1 M. E. James, 'Change and continuity in the Tudor north: Thomas, first Lord Wharton', in his *Society, Politics and Culture: Essays in Early Modern English History*, Cambridge, 1986, pp. 91–147; D. Willen, *John Russell, First Earl of Bedford*, London, 1981.

I am grateful to C. S. L. Davies, M. K. Jones, S. J. Payling, T. B. Pugh, and the editor for their comments on this chapter.

2 B. Harris, *Edward Stafford, Third Duke of Buckingham, 1478–1521*, Stanford, 1986; R. Virgoe, 'The recovery of the Howards in East Anglia, 1485–1529', in E. W. Ives, R. J. Knecht, J. J. Scarisbrick, eds., *Wealth and Power in Tudor England: Essays Presented to S. T. Bindoff*, London, 1978, pp. 1–20; M. J. Tucker, *The Life of Thomas Howard, Earl of Surrey and Second Duke of Norfolk*, The Hague, 1964; S. E. Vokes, 'The early career of Thomas, Lord Howard, earl of Surrey and third duke of Norfolk, 1474–c. 1525', University of Hull Ph.D. thesis, 1988; S. J. Gunn, *Charles Brandon, Duke of Suffolk, c. 1484–1545*, Oxford, 1988; B. Coward, *The Stanleys, Lords Stanley and Earls of Derby, 1385–1672*, Chetham Society 3rd s. XXX, Manchester, 1983; G. W. Bernard, *The Power of the Early Tudor Nobility: A Study of the Fourth and Fifth Earls of Shrewsbury*, Brighton, 1985; M. E. James, 'A Tudor magnate and the Tudor state: Henry fifth earl of Northumberland', in James, *Society, Politics and Culture*, pp. 48–90; W. R. B. Robinson, 'Early Tudor policy towards Wales, parts 1–3', *Bulletin of the Board of Celtic Studies*, XXX, 1962–4, pp. 421–38, XXI, 1964–6, pp. 43–74, 334–67; *idem*, 'Patronage and hospitality in early Tudor Wales: the role of Henry, earl of Worcester, 1526–49', *Bulletin of the Institute of Historical Research*, LI, 1978, pp. 20–36; *idem*, 'The officers and household of Henry, earl of Worcester, 1526–49', *Welsh History Review*, VIII, 1976–7, pp. 26–41.

3 H. Miller, 'Subsidy assessments of the peerage in the sixteenth century', *Bulletin of the Institute of Historical Research*, XXVIII, 1955, p. 18; *Letters and Papers, Foreign and Domestic, of the Reign of Henry VIII* (1862–1932) (hereinafter *LP*), IV, ii. 2972, XI. 139.

4 H. Miller, *Henry VIII and the English Nobility*, Oxford, 1986, pp. 137–41.

5 *Ibid.*, pp. 7, 45, 80–2, 93, 98, 103; H. Miller, 'Attendance in the lords during the reign of Henry VIII', *Historical Journal*, X, 1967, pp. 325–51; *Journals of the House of Lords*, 10 vols., London, 1846, I, pp. 20–125.

6 Miller, *English Nobility*, pp. 203, 215.

7 S. E. Lehmberg, *The Later Parliaments of Henry VIII, 1536–1547*, Cambridge, 1977, p. 86; G. W. Bernard, 'The fortunes of the Greys, earls of Kent, in the early sixteenth century', *Historical Journal*, XXV, 1982, pp. 671–80.

8 Longleat, Devereux Papers (hereinafter DP) 10, f. 9v. References to this volume are to the expenditure section of the accounts unless otherwise specified. I am grateful to the Marquess of Bath for permission to read and cite material from Longleat.

9 R. A. Griffiths, 'The crown and the royal family in later medieval England', in *idem* and J. Sherborne, eds., *Kings and Nobles in the Later Middle Ages: A Tribute to Charles Ross*, Gloucester, 1986, pp. 15–23.

10 A. F. Sutton, P. W. Hammond, eds., *The Coronation of Richard III: The Extant Documents*, Gloucester, 1983, p. 314; J. Leland, *De Rebus Britannicis Collectanea*, ed. T. Hearne, 6 vols., Oxford, 1774 edn, IV, pp. 205, 229, 238, 243–55; J. Gairdner, ed., *Letters and Papers Illustrative of the Reigns of Richard III and Henry VII*, Rolls Series, XXIV, 2 vols., London, 1861–3, I, pp. 390, 392, II, p. 291; F. Grose, T. Astle, eds., *The Antiquarian Repertory*, 4 vols., London, 1807–9 edn, II, pp. 259, 294, 312, IV, p. 658; Leland, *Collectanea*, IV, pp. 259, 266; W. Campbell, ed., *Materials for a History of the Reign of Henry VII*, Rolls Series LX, 2 vols., London, 1873–7, II, p. 474; T. Rymer, *Foedera, Conventiones, Literae et Cujuscunque Generis Acta Publica*, 3rd edn, 10 vols., The Hague, 1739–45, V, iv, pp. 50, 155, 265; J. G. Nichols, ed., *The Chronicle of Calais*, Camden Society, XXXV, London, 1846, p. 3.

11 *Letters and Papers ... Henry VII*, I, pp. 394–9; A. A. Thomas, I. D. Thornley, eds., *The Great Chronicle of London*, London, 1938, pp. 254–6, 313–14; S. Anglo, 'The court festivals of Henry VII', *Bulletin of the John Rylands Library*, XLIII, 1960–1, pp. 30, 36; G. Kipling, *The Triumph of Honour: Burgundian Origins of the Elizabethan Renaissance*, The Hague, 1977, pp. 120–1; G. A. Bergenroth, ed., *Calendar of State Papers, Spanish, 1485–1509*, London, 1862, no. 278; *Antiquarian Repertory*, II, pp. 298–9; S. Anglo, ed., *The Great Tournament Roll of Westminster*, 2 vols., Oxford, 1968, I, pp. 34–40; Leland, *Collectanea*, IV, p. 262.

12 *Letters and Papers ... Henry VII*, I, p. 226.

13 G. E. Cokayne, *The Complete Peerage*, ed. V. Gibbs *et al.*, 13 vols., London, 1910–49, IV, p. 330, XII, i, p. 452; *Chronicle of Calais*, p. 6.

14 Public Record Office (hereinafter PRO), E36/214, fos. 61, 113ᵛ–114ʳ, 115ᵛ–156ʳ.

15 *Calendar of Patent Rolls* (hereinafter *CPR*) *Henry VII*, 2 vols., London, 1914–16, I, pp. 442, 482, II, pp. 29–30, 33, 53, 86, 290, 294, 296, 326, 506 (for the significance of some of these see J. R. Lander, *English Justices of the Peace, 1461–1509*, Gloucester, 1989, pp. 114–15, 124–8); *Rotuli Parliamentorum*, 7 vols., London, 1832, VI, pp. 458, 510; C. G. Bayne, W. H. Dunham, eds., *Select Cases in the Council of Henry VII*, Selden Society, LXXV, London, 1958, pp. 30, 32, 35, 42; M. M. Condon, 'Ruling elites in the reign of Henry VII', in C. Ross, ed., *Pedigree, Patronage and Power*, Gloucester, 1979, pp. 121, 139.

16 *CPR Henry VII*, II, pp. 419, 540; British Library (hereinafter BL), Additional MS 45131, f. 61ʳ; J. Anstis, *The Register of the Most Noble Order of the Garter*, 2 vols., London, 1724, I, pp. 238–64; S. J. Gunn, 'The courtiers of Henry VII', forthcoming in D. Clayton, R. G. Davies, P. McNiven, eds., *Trade, Devotion and Governance in Fifteenth-Century England*.

17 J. R. Lander, 'Bonds, coercion and fear: Henry VII and the peerage', in his *Crown and Nobility, 1450–1509*, London, 1976, p. 292n; PRO: E101/414/6, f. 112ʳ; E101/414/16, f. 90ʳ; E101/415/3, f. 168ʳ; E36/214, fos. 208ʳ, 159ʳ; E36/215, f. 326ᵛ; *CPR Henry VII*, II, p. 596; *LP*, II, ii, p. 1529. The £160 was probably part of the fine for livery of his lands.

18 BL, Lansdowne MS 127, f. 56r.

19 M. Hicks, 'Attainder, resumption and coercion, 1461–1529', *Parliamentary History*, III, 1984, p. 21; PRO, E36/214, f. 158ᵛ; Longleat, North Muniment Room (hereinafter NMR) 489; PRO, SC6/Henry VIII/345, mm. 12–13; Suffolk Record Office, T4374/Box 9/No. 5; PRO, SC12/18/58.

20 *LP*, IV, i. 2065 (28); F. C. Dietz, *English Public Finance, 1485–1558*, Urbana, 1920, pp. 24, 85; W. Page, ed., *The Victoria County History of Essex*, II, London, 1907, p. 382.

21 *Antiquarian Repertory*, II, p. 257. In quotations, punctuation and capitalisation have been modernised, as has the use of i, j, u and v.

22 PRO, C24/28, 29, Haworth and Powis v. Suffolk, *passim.*; Gunn, *Charles Brandon*, p. 28.

23 PRO: C24/29, Haworth and Powis v. Suffolk, deposition of Walter, Viscount Hereford; E36/215, f. 297ᵛ; *Calendar of the Close Rolls* (hereinafter *CCR*) *Henry VII*, 2 vols., London, 1953–63, II, no. 332; W. C. Hazlitt, ed., *Remains of the Early Popular Poetry of England*, 4 vols., London, 1864–6, II, pp. 109–30; PRO, E36/214, f. 184r.

24 Longleat, NMR 185, 1127; *CCR Henry VII*, II, no. 332; *LP*, I, ii. 3049 (20); J. Corder, ed., *The Visitation of Suffolk, 1561*, Harleian Society, n.s. II–III, 2 vols., London, 1981–4, I, p. 92.

25 PRO, SP1/80, f. 8 (*LP*, VI, 1327).

26 M. StC. Byrne, ed., *The Lisle Letters*, 6 vols., London, 1981, I, nos. 31, 94, 173, II, nos. 111, 173, 208, 210, 279, 408, 494.

27 P. G. Bietenholz, T. B. Deutscher, eds., *Contemporaries of Erasmus*, 3 vols., Toronto, 1985, I, p. 180; Anglo, 'Court festivals', p. 40; *LP*, II, ii. p. 1490, VIII, 962 (30); Longleat, NMR 160, 185, 189; PRO: E36/215, f. 327ʳ; WARD9/147; *Complete Peerage*, IX, pp. 669–72; J. G. Nichols, J. Bruce, eds., *Wills from Doctors' Commons*, Camden Society, LXXXIII, London, 1863, pp. 10–11.

28 *LP*, I, i. 244, II, ii, p. 1446; PRO, E36/217, fos. 1–25 (*LP*, II, ii. p. 1490).

29 *LP*, I, ii. 2480 (11); PRO, E36/215, f. 326ᵛ; Longleat, NMR 185.

30 Wistan Browne, Giles Capell, William Fitzwilliam, Geoffrey Gates, William Pyrton, and perhaps Sir Thomas Tyrrell of Heron and William Wyseman: PRO, E36/215, fos. 89ᵛ, 106ᵛ, 118ᵛ; *LP*, I, i. 1453 (v), II, ii. p. 1446; S. J. Gunn, 'Chivalry and the politics of the early Tudor court', in S. Anglo, ed., *Chivalry in the Renaissance*, Woodbridge, 1990, pp. 116–18.

31 For their officeholding, see: *LP*, I, ii. 3499 (12), II, i. 2533, IV, ii. 4194; PRO, E137/11/4, mm. 7–10, 16ᵛ; for links with the earl: Longleat, NMR 185; *The Lisle Letters*, III, p. 428.

32 *LP*, I, ii. 2929, III, i. 1114; PRO, E36/215, fos. 129ᵛ, 156ʳ, 174ᵛ.

33 *LP*, II, ii. pp. 1490–1500; Gunn, *Charles Brandon*, pp. 6–10, 67–70.

34 E. Hall, *Hall's Chronicle*, London, 1809 edn, p. 591; College of Arms, MS Tournament Cheque 1c. I am grateful for permission to read and cite material in the College of Arms.

35 BL, Add. MS 45131, fos. 30ᵛ, 33ʳ.

36 Anstis, *Garter*, I, pp. 270–85.

37 *LP*, I, i. 857 (5); *CPR Henry VII*, I, p. 422; L. S. Clark (née Woodger), 'Henry Bourgchier, earl of Essex, and his family (1408–83)', University of Oxford D.Phil. thesis, 1974, p. 162. I am grateful to Dr Clark for permission to cite her thesis.

38 PRO: E101/414/6, f. 127ᵛ; E36/262, fos. 93–100.

39 PRO: E36/262, fos. 85–92, 144–50; E36/263, fos. 44–52, 70–78, 95–106.

40 *LP*, I, i. 1172 (7).

41 Miller, *English Nobility*, p. 82.

42 *LP*, IV, i. 966; Anstis, *Garter*, I, pp. 287–384; BL, Add. MS 45131, f. 150ʳ.

43 J. G. Russell, *The Field of Cloth of Gold*, London, 1969, pp. 63, 94, 117; Nichols, *Chronicle of Calais*, p. 89; *LP*, IV, i. 614.

44 W. H. Dunham, 'The members of Henry VIII's whole council, 1509–1527', *English Historical Review*, LIX, 1944, p. 209; *LP*, IV, iii, App. 67.

45 PRO, E36/263, f. 110ʳ; *LP*, IV, i. 1298.

46 Miller, *English Nobility*, p. 215.

47 *LP*, IV, i. 297 (21); PRO: WARD9/147; C142/30/18; G. A. Lowndes, 'The history of the Barrington family', *Transactions of the Essex Archaeological Society* (hereinafter *TEAS*), n.s. II, 1879–83, pp. 6–7.

48 Anstis, *Garter*, I, pp. 385–412.

49 Miller, *English Nobility*, p. 59; *Journals of the House of Lords*, I, pp. 43–56, 85–125.

50 Miller, 'Attendance in the lords', pp. 340–1.

51 *LP*, V, pp. 323, 327–8, VI, 32, VII, 9 (ii), XIII, ii, p. 538, XVI, p. 179; E. Trollope, ed., 'King Henry VIII's jewel book', *Reports and Papers of the Associated Architectural Societies*, XVII, 1883–4, p. 171.

52 *LP*, VI, 465, 601, 1111; Anstis, *Garter*, I, p. 392; PRO, LC2/1, f. 175ᵛ.

53 *LP*, XII, ii. 911, XV, 14, 823.

54 PRO: SP1/82, f. 41; SP1/141, f. 134ᵛ (*LP*, VII, 23, XIII, i. 364).

55 *LP*, XIV, i. 131; BL, Cotton MS Vespasian F XIII, f. 170(*LP*, XIV, i. 411); PRO, SP1/146, f. 250 (*LP*, XIV, i. 683).

56 PRO, KB9/545/35, 39; 'The last abbot of Colchester', *Essex Review*, XLIX, 1940, plate facing p. 1: *LP*, XIV, ii. App. 45.

57 PRO, SP1/11, f. 168 (*LP*, II, i. 1147).

58 Longleat, DP 10, f. 37ʳ.

59 *Ibid.*

60 PRO, PRO31/18/2/2, f. 171ʳ (*LP*, XI, 7).

61 J. A. Muller, ed., *The Letters of Stephen Gardiner*, Cambridge, 1933, p. 162.

62 *LP*, XVI, 1204.

63 *LP*, VI, 1540; F. Madden, ed., *Privy Purse Expenses of the Princess Mary*, London, 1831, pp. 3–87.

64 Longleat, DP 10, fos. 37ᵛ, 40ʳ, 46ᵛ.

65 Guildhall Library (hereinafter GL), MSS 9531/7–12, *passim*; Norfolk Record Office, Register 14, f. 176ʳ, second series f. 15ᵛ; Register 16, f. 25ʳ; J. E. Oxley, *The Reformation in Essex to the Death of Mary*, Manchester, 1965, p. 265. For the two graduates, see GL MS 9531/9, fos. 63ᵛ, 83ᵛ; J. and J. A. Venn, *Alumni Cantabrigienses, Part I to 1751*, Cambridge, 1922, I, p. 375, III, p. 42.

66 GL: MS 9531/8, fos. 19ʳ, 110ᵛ, MS 9531/9, fos. 54ᵛ, 62ᵛ; PRO: E101/56/25/20 (*LP*, I, ii. 2480 (13)); E30/1456; Longleat: DP 10, f. 41ᵛ; NMR 185, 403, 1127; H. C. Andrews, 'Rowney Priory', *Transactions of the East Herts Archaeological Society*, VI, 1915–22,

p. 17; Essex Record Office (hereinafter ERO), D/AMR 1, f. 21ʳ; H. E. P. Grieve, 'The deprived married clergy in Essex 1553–1561', *Transactions of the Royal Historical Society*, 4th s. XXII, 1940, p. 151n.

67 PRO, PROB11/34/23; Venn, *Alumni Cantabrigienses*, III, p. 42.

68 PRO, STAC2/26/299.

69 Longleat, NMR 1127; PRO, E36/215, f. 297ᵛ.

70 Longleat, NMR 1127; E. M. Richardson, *The Lion and the Rose*, London, 1922, p. 73.

71 PRO, SP1/11, f. 168(*LP*, II, i. 1147).

72 PRO, SP1/129, f. 134; SP1/141, f. 147 (*LP*, XIII, i. 364, XIV, i. 131); *LP*, XIV, ii. p. 321.

73 PRO: SP1/11, f. 168 (*L*, II, i. 1147); SP1/68, f. 58(*LP*, V, 538); *LP*, VI, 611, XIV, i. 263, 284.

74 PRO: E101/412/17; C54/382, m. 6; E36/215, fos. 295ᵛ, 296ᵛ, 297ᵛ; SP1/9, f. 181ᵛ; SP1/15 f. 71ʳ (*LP*, I, ii. 3483, II, I. 3087); *LP* I, ii. 3499 (47); S. J. Gunn, 'The act of resumption of 1515', in D. T. Williams, ed., *Early Tudor England*, Woodbridge, 1989, pp. 93–4.

75 *LP*, XI, 139.

76 D. R. Starkey, 'The court: Castiglione's ideal and Tudor reality: being a discussion of Sir Thomas Wyatt's *Satire addressed to Sir Francis Bryan*', *Journal of the Warburg and Courtauld Institutes*, XLV, 1982, pp. 232–9; *idem*, 'Court and courtier: how the renaissance came to Sutton Place', in *The Renaissance at Sutton Place*, London, 1983, p. 10.

77 GL, MS 9531/8, fos. 19ʳ, 45ᵛ; A. Luders *et al.*, eds., *Statutes of the Realm*, 11 vols., London, 1810–28, 11 Henry VII, c. 9; M. H. Dodds, ed., *History of Northumberland*, XV, Newcastle, 1940, p. 285; Clark, 'Henry Bourgchier', pp. 191–4, 197–8, 204.

78 Clark, 'Henry Bourgchier', pp. 199–200; *CCR Henry VII*, I, no. 313; PRO, SC6/ Henry VII/1100; *CPR Henry VII*, I, p. 460.

79 *CPR Henry VII*, I, pp. 486, 488, 501.

80 *Calendar of Inquisitions Post Mortem* (hereinafter *CIPM*), *Henry VII*, 3 vols., London, 1898–1955, I, nos. 516, 682–4.

81 P. H. Reaney, M. Fitch, eds., *Feet of Fines for Essex*, IV, Colchester, 1964, pp. 213, 250; Longleat, NMR 1127; Clark, 'Henry Bourgchier', pp. 210–12.

82 Longleat, NMR 148; *LP*, IV, i. 278 (10), V, 278 (9), VI, 196 (6).

83 *LP*, XIV, i. 683; PRO, SP1/82, f. 289 (*LP*, VII, 332).

84 PRO, SP1/69, f. 127 (*LP*, V, 803).

85 L. L. Duncan, ed., 'The will of Cardinal Bourgchier, archbishop of Canterbury, 1486', *Archaeologia Cantiana*, XXIV, 1900, p. 251. The archbishop's executors were reluctant to part with it: PRO, C1/191/72.

86 N. H. Nicolas, ed., *Testamenta Vetusta*, 2 vols., London, 1826, II, p. 405; H. W. King, ed., 'Ancient wills', *TEAS*, n.s. I, 1878, pp. 147–50. John Bourchier may have been the priest mentioned above (p. 141), but this reference suggests someone considerably younger than the earl, whereas John Bourchier, priest, was only one or two years his junior: W. Dugdale, *Monasticon Anglicanum*, ed. J. Caley, H. Ellis, B. Bandinel, 6 vols., London, 1846, IV, p. 345.

87 *Testamenta Vetusta*, II, p. 440; *Complete Peerage*, V, p. 325.

88 Miller, *English Nobility*, p. 229; R. C. Fowler, A. W. Clapham and F. W. Galpin, *Beeleigh Abbey, Essex*, London, 1922, pp. 46–52; PRO, E326/10544.

89 Longleat, NMR 147; PRO, E40/14833; *LP*, VI, 299 (iv), 430, 1271; P. Morant, *The History and Antiquities of the County of Essex*, 2 vols., Wakefield, 1978 edn, I, pp. 250, 299, II, pp. 9, 90; C. Rawcliffe, *The Staffords, Earls of Stafford and Dukes of Buckingham, 1394–1521*, Cambridge, 1978, pp. 141, 194; Harris, *Buckingham*, pp. 145, 236.

90 Clark, 'Henry Bourgchier', p. 154; PRO: C1/281/74–80; E210/10099.

91 PRO: C1/133/81; C1/281/74–80; C1/335/92.

92 H. Chauncy, *The Historical Antiquities of Hertfordshire*, 2 vols., Dorking, 1975 edn,

II, p. 77; BL, Lansdowne MS 127, f. 23ʳ; *CPR Henry VII*, II, p. 606; C. J. Harrison, ed., 'The petition of Edmund Dudley', *English Historical Review*, LXXXVII, 1972, p. 88; *LP*, I, i. 1524 (38); *CCR Henry VII*, II, nos. 228, 549, 628; *Contemporaries of Erasmus*, III, p. 211; BL, Stowe MS 141, f. 16 (*LP*, I, ii. 1849); *LP*, II, ii. 4185; *Descriptive Catalogue of Ancient Deeds in the Public Record Office* (hereinafter *CAD*), 6 vols., London, 1890–1915, I, no. B419; PRO: E326/9012; E315/36/64; C142/51/50; *LP*, II, i. 165, 825. For further adjustments to Say's property, see PRO: E210/10125; E326/5688; E326/12150; perhaps also C54/393, m. 5.

93   *LP*, IX, 481; PRO, C54/418, m. 6.

94   PRO: E179/108/154, m. 8ʳ; STAC2/12/93–5; Longleat, NMR 189, 989.

95   PRO, C1/391/58; W. StJ. Hope, ed., 'The last testament and inventory of John de Veer, thirteenth earl of Oxford', *Archaeologia*, LXVI, 1915, pp. 318–19.

96   PRO: C1/477/43; C1/540/74–7; BL, Add. Charters 8405, 67404.

97   PRO, E40/14012.

98   Longleat, NMR 4437; BL, Add. Charters 4810, 36199.

99   ERO, D/DMj M2, mm. 19ʳ, 20ʳ.

100   Longleat, NMR 1151, 4425.

101   ERO, D/DK M103.

102   Longleat: DP 10, income account, *passim*; NMR 383; K. Mertes, *The English Noble Household, 1250–1600*, Oxford, 1988, pp. 96–101.

103   Clark, 'Henry Bourgchier', pp. 231–2; PRO: C1/503/3; SC6/Philip and Mary/ 503, m. 6; *CAD*, VI, no. C6930.

104   PRO, SC6/Philip and Mary/503, mm. 1, 17; *LP*, XIV, ii. 780 (16).

105   PRO: C54/418, m. 6; SC6/Philip and Mary/503.

106   Clark, 'Henry Bourgchier', pp. 210–12; Gunn, *Charles Brandon*, p. 138; Bernard, *Early Tudor Nobility*, pp. 143–4; J. M. W. Bean, *The Estates of the Percy Family, 1416–1537*, Oxford, 1958, p. 67. Comparisons of income and expenditure for early Tudor peers can never be exact, since different noblemen's accounts were kept in different ways; they rarely provide the figures in which the historian is interested; and they seldom survive in sufficiently complete series to reveal anything more than possibly unrepresentative annual totals.

107   Morant, *Essex*, II, p. 256; *LP*, X, 531.

108   *LP*, VI, 1122.

109   Bernard, *Early Tudor Nobility*, pp. 149–51; Gunn, *Charles Brandon*, p. 225. Buckingham went too far as ever: Harris, *Buckingham*, pp. 133–4.

110   Longleat, NMR 184; PRO: STAC2/187, 214; STAC2/26/299; SP1/46, fos. 253–4 (*LP*, IV, ii. 3929); *LP*, VII, 923 (xxxvii).

111   Mertes, *English Noble Household*, pp. 216–17; Gunn, *Charles Brandon*, p. 64; Longleat, DP 10, f. 47ᵛ.

112   Longleat: Miscellaneous Volume II, fos. 126–35; DP 10, fos. 41ᵛ–42ʳ; PRO, E179/108/154, m. 15ʳ.

113   PRO, C1/335/34.

114   *LP*, IV, i. 1325; PRO, STAC2/20/93; Longleat, DP 10, income account, f. 2ʳ.

115   Longleat: NMR 946; DP 10, *passim*.

116   Clark, 'Henry Bourgchier', p. 243; Anglo, 'Court festivals', pp. 34, 44; *LP*, II, i. 115; Longleat, DP 10, fos. 35ʳ, 36ʳ, 38ᵛ, 39ᵛ.

117   Gunn, *Charles Brandon*, p. 93; M. Howard, *The Early Tudor Country House: Architecture and Politics 1490–1550*, London, 1987, pp. 37–42.

118   Clark, 'Henry Bourgchier', p. 186; Morant, *Essex*, II, p. 256; *Royal Commission on Historical Monuments* (hereinafter *RCHM*), *An Inventory of the Historical Monuments in Essex*, 4 vols., London, 1916–23, I, pp. 146–7.

119   Longleat, DP 10, fos. 35ʳ, 37ʳ, 44, 46ᵛ, 47ᵛ.

120   Howard, *Country House*, p. 211; S. J. Gunn and P. G. Lindley, 'Charles Brandon's Westhorpe, an early Tudor courtyard house in Suffolk', *Archaeological Journal*, CXLV, 1988, pp. 272–89.

121 *LP*, II, i. 4145, III, i. 529 (12), VI, 611, VIII, 962 (6); H. Garrett-Goodyear, 'The Tudor revival of Quo Warranto and local contributions to state-building', in M. S. Arnold *et al.*, eds, *On the Laws and Customs of England: Essays in Honor of Samuel E. Thorne*, Chapel Hill, 1981, p. 284.

122 Longleat, NMR 929, 946.

123 PRO: SP1/131, fos. 199–215; SP1/242, fos. 12–14 (*LP*, XIII, i. 838, Addenda, ii. 1319); R. Somerville, 'Henry VII's "Council learned in the law"', *English Historical Review*, LIV, 1939, p. 441. This became a *cause célèbre*: J. H. Baker, ed., *The Reports of Sir John Spelman*, Selden Society, XCIII–XCIV, London, 1976–7, I, p. 60.

124 Miller, *English Nobility*, pp. 204–5; *CPR Henry VII*, II, pp. 639, 642; *LP*, XV, 282 (20, 61).

125 *RCHM, Essex*, I, pp. 31, 119, 141, 150–1, 163, 182, 229, 267, 314, II, pp. 41, 45, III, pp. 137, 202; G. M. Benton, 'Window in Paglesham church', *TEAS*, n.s. XVII, 1923–5, pp. 203–5; *idem*, 'Medieval graffiti in Steeple Bumstead and other Essex churches', *ibid.*, pp. 259–60; 'Lindsell, Stebbing, Little Dunmow and Barnston', *ibid.*, p. 213. Some of these badges may date from the lifetime of the first earl.

126 *LP*, V, 538; Longleat: NMR 185; DP 10, fos. 18^r, 25^r, 27^v.

127 Longleat, DP 10, fos. 21^v–25^r; *LP*, VIII, 323, X, 531, XIII, ii. 1090, XIV, i. 411.

128 J. E. Cussans, ed., *Inventory of Furniture and Ornaments Remaining in all the Parish Churches of Hertfordshire in the last Year of the Reign of King Edward the Sixth*, Oxford, 1873, pp. 78, 100.

129 ERO: D/DMj M2, mm. 20^r, 21^r; D/DK M91; D/ABW 34/242; PRO, SC6/Philip and Mary/503, mm. 1, 8, 15; Longleat: DP 10, f. 34^r; NMR 189, 821.

130 PRO: PROB11/8/41, 44; PROB11/13/17; SC6/Philip and Mary/503, mm. 3, 4; ERO: D/DMj M2, m. 18^r; D/DK M79, m. 2^r; *CAD*, VI, no. C5813; *Feet of Fines for Essex*, IV, pp. 161, 200, 204.

131 *LP*, I, i. 438 (4, m. 20); *Feet of Fines for Essex*, IV, pp. 91, 116; *CCR Henry VII*, II, nos. 56, 115; *CAD*, VI, no. C6930; LONGLEAT, NMR 185, 186, 902; ERO, D/ABW 28/3; PRO, E150/302/6.

132 PRO: E179/108/160, m. 10^r; C1/481/14; ERO, D/ABW 8/80; *CAD*, VI, no. C6930.

133 PRO: C1/483/48; C1/616/7–8; C1/764/18; C1/996/19; *Feet of Fines for Essex*, IV, pp. 144, 161.

134 PRO: C1/908/5; REQ2/3/12.

135 Longleat DP 10, income account, f. 5^r, expenditure account, f. 41^v; GL, MS 9531/11, f. 36^r.

136 Longleat: NMR 186, 902; DP 10, *passim*.

137 M. K. McIntosh, *Autonomy and Community: the Royal Manor of Havering, 1200–1500*, Cambridge, 1986; R. Somerville, *A History of the Duchy of Lancaster*, I, London, 1953, p. 180; Oxley, *Reformation in Essex*, pp. 17, 94; Harris, *Buckingham*, p. 236; Morant, *Essex*, II, p. 414.

138 ERO, D/DPr 135a, 140; PRO, SC11/919.

139 PRO, SC11/833; *LP*, IV, ii. 2972.

140 *RCHM Essex*, *passim* (IV, p. 19 on Burnham).

141 Lander, 'Bonds, coercion and fear', pp. 274–5; *Complete Peerage*, XII, i, pp. 518–19.

142 *Complete Peerage*, X, pp. 131–3; *Cases in the Council of Henry VII*, p. xxix.

143 Morant, *Essex*, I, p. 290, II, pp. 14, 310, 312, 465; PRO, SC12/1/12; ERO, Film T/A/321.

144 *RCHM Essex*, IV, p. 127.

145 Morant, *Essex*, IV, p. 275, II, pp. 13, 92.

146 S. L. Thrupp, *The Merchant Class of Medieval London*, Chicago, 1948, pp. 279–87; L. Stone and J. C. F. Stone, *An Open Elite? England 1540–1880*, Oxford, 1984, pp. 43–7, 193–210.

147 S. T. Bindoff, *The History of Parliament: The Commons, 1509–1558*, 3 vols., London, 1982, I, pp. 350–3; S. E. Lehmberg, 'Sir Thomas Audley: a soul as black as marble?', in A. J. Slavin, ed., *Tudor Men and Institutions*, Baton Rouge, 1972, pp. 3–31; PRO, LR12/8/259.

148 Somerville, *Duchy of Lancaster*, pp. 604, 606; Miller, *English Nobility*, p. 247.

149 *LP*, I, i. 438 (2, m. 13); *CPR Henry VII*, I, p. 488, II, p. 643; D. R. Starkey, *The Reign of Henry VIII: Personalities and Politics*, London, 1985, pp. 70, 74; W. d'A. Crofton, 'Standon', *Transactions of the East Herts Archaeological Society*, I, 1901–2, p. 280; Bindoff, *Commons*, II, p. 27; N. P. Sil, 'The rise and fall of Sir John Gates', *Historical Journal*, XXIV, 1981, pp. 929–43; Howard, *Country House*, p. 205; F. G. Emmison, *Tudor Secretary: Sir William Petre at Home and at Court*, London, 1961; A. J. Slavin, *Politics and Profit: A Study of Sir Ralph Sadler, 1507–1547*, Cambridge, 1966. I hope to study Marney and other councillors and courtiers of Henry VII and the early years of Henry VIII in a book now in preparation.

150 Bindoff, *Commons*, I, pp. 527–9, II, pp. 57–8; Howard, *Country House*, pp. 201, 204, 206.

151 Bindoff, *Commons*, III, p. 192–5; Somerville, *Duchy of Lancaster*, pp. 393, 402, 423, 426, 587, 601, 604, 606, 608, 611.

152 H. G. Wright, ed., *Forty-Six Lives, translated from Boccaccio's De Claris Mulieribus by Henry Parker, Lord Morley*, Early English Text Society, CCXIV, Oxford, 1943, pp. xvi–xlvii; Miller, *English Nobility*, p. 157.

153 D. N. J. MacCulloch, *Suffolk and the Tudors*, Oxford, 1986, pp. 55–6.

154 PRO: E101/419/19, fos. 15^v–17^r; E101/414/6, *passim*; E101/414/16, fos. 36^v–37^r and *passim*; E101/415/3, *passim*; E36/214, f. 29 and *passim*.

155 PRO: E101/414/6, f. 87^v; E101/414/16, fos. 37^r, 58^r, 124^v, 125^r, 133^v; E101/415/3, fos. 47^r, 85^v, 92^v, 192^v, 284^v; E36/214, f. 160^r.

156 *Chronicle of Calais*, p. 2; PRO, C24/29, Haworth and Powis v. Suffolk, deposition of Sir Anthony Wingfield; 'The last testament ... of John de Veer', p. 322.

157 PRO, C1/335/33; *CIPM Henry VII*, I, no. 759; ERO, D/DU 23/47.

158 'The last testament ... of John de Veer', pp. 305, 315, 322, 333, 335–7, 339–40; Virgoe, 'Recovery of the Howards', pp. 15–16.

159 *LP*, V, 741, VI, 430; Longleat, NMR 185, 1127; Anstis, *Garter*, I, p. 270; Longleat, DP 10, f. 34^r; PRO, SP1/108, f. 42 (*LP*, XI, 699).

160 Longleat, DP 10, f. 34^r.

161 *LP*, VI, 68, VII, 1265, X, 462.

162 *LP*, III, ii. 3504, IV, i. 1321, ii. 4192, VI, 1186, XIV, i. 398; Longleat, NMR 401.

163 *LP*, XIV, ii. 36; Anstis, *Garter*, I, pp. 359, 362, 365, 381, 412.

164 Miller, 'Attendance in the lords', pp. 340–1; *LP*, V. 728, 741, X. 231, XIV, i. 683; *Journals of the House of Lords*, I, p. 58; Longleat, DP 10, f. 40^v.

165 G. Walker, *Plays of Persuasion: Drama and Politics at the Court of Henry VIII*, Cambridge, 1991, p. 170; *LP*, VII, 1265, X, 94, 166; PRO: SP1/238, f. 182^r; SP2/Fol. O, f. 321 (*LP*, Add., i. 883, VI, 1492).

167 *Complete Peerage*, X, p. 247; BL, Cotton MS Otho E XI, fos. 302–3 (*LP*, XIV, i. 615, 682).

168 Miller, *English Nobility*, p. 112.

169 Lehmberg, 'Sir Thomas Audley', pp. 21–4.

170 PRO, SC11/984.

171 *LP*, X, 94.

172 R. C. Fowler, 'Inventories of Essex monasteries in 1536,' *TEAS*, n.s. IX, 1903–6, p. 338; PRO, E315/397, fos. 108–110; SC6/Philip and Mary/503, m. 3.

173 PRO: SC11/200; SC12/23/25; *LP*, XIV, i. 1325 (2); *RCHM Essex*, III, p. 202.

174 J. Caley, J. Hunter, eds., *Valor Ecclesiasticus*, 6 vols., London, 1810–34, I, p. 362, VI, pp. vi, xiii; *The Manuscripts of ... James Round, Esq., MP*, Historical Manuscripts Commission, XIV, ix, London, 1895, p. 276.

175 *LP*, VIII, 865; *Valor Ecclesiasticus*, I, p. 406; Dugdale, *Monasticon Anglicanum*, I, p. 438.

176 PRO: SC6/Henry VIII/1606, 1617; SC11/277; E315/272, f. 62; E315/274, fos. 80–3; SP5/1, fos. 1–43.

177 *Ninth Report of the Royal Commission on Historical Manuscripts*, I, London, 1883, p. 118. He attended Archbishop Warham's enthronement: Leland, *Collectanea*, VI, p. 25.

178 *LP*, XIII, ii. 191 (40).

179 ERO, D/DY 2/3, 6–14.

180 ERO: D/DB 3/1/2, f. 61ʳ; D/DB 3/3/227.

181 ERO, D/DB 3/3/69, 228–30, 233–7.

182 Bindoff, *Commons*, I, pp. 89–90.

183 C. Carpenter, 'The Beauchamp affinity: a study of bastard feudalism at work', *English Historical Review*, XCV, 1980, pp. 514–32.

184 'The last testament of … John de Veer', pp. 318–19; *CPR Henry VII*, II, pp. 638–9; C. Rawcliffe and S. Flower, 'English noblemen and their advisers: consultation and collaboration in the later middle ages', *Journal of British Studies*, XXV, 1986, pp. 160, 165, 171–2; Bindoff, *Commons*, III, p. 183.

185 J. H. Round, 'The descent of Faulkbourne', *TEAS* n.s. XV, 1918–20, p. 51; Longleat: NMR 185, 189, 403, 1127; DP 10, f. 39ʳ; PRO: E36/214, f. 259ʳ; E36/215, f. 297ᵛ; Morant, *Essex*, II, p. 231.

186 Longleat, NMR 1127; BL, Add. Ch. 41711; PRO, SP1/143, f. 53 (*LP*, XIV, i. 263).

187 ERO: D/DRS M1; D/DP A16; PRO, E101/517/18.

188 Longleat, DP 10, *passim*; *LP*, V, 1694, VI, 601 (4).

189 Longleat, NMR 185; *LP*, II, i. 1213.

190 PRO, C24/29, Haworth and Powis v. Suffolk, deposition of Sir Anthony Wingfield; Longleat: NMR 153; DP 10, f. 40ʳ.

191 PRO: E179/108/160, m. 8ʳ; E179/108/163, m. 3ᵛ; S. H. A. Hervey, ed., *Suffolk in 1524*, Suffolk Green Books, X, Woodbridge, 1910, pp. 19, 241.

192 *LP*, I, ii. 2055 (23); Longleat, NMR 185, 403; A. Clark, 'Great Dunmow church antiquities, 1526–1546', *Essex Review*, XXI, 1912, pp. 145, 148–9; *idem*, 'Great Dunmow church organ, 1531', *ibid.*, XXIV, 1915, pp. 131–2.

193 PRO: E179/108/155, m. 15ʳ; SP1/46, f. 253ᵛ (*LP*, IV, ii. 3929); *LP*, I, ii. 2055 (23); Longleat, DP 10, fos. 6ʳ, 34ʳ; ERO, D/DK M103.

194 PRO, E179/108/163, m. 2ʳ; *Suffolk 1561*, I, pp. 24–5.

195 Longleat, NMR 905; PRO, E179/108/160, m. 10ᵛ.

196 PRO, E179/120/133, m. 2ʳ; *LP*, VI, 1545, XI, 699; Longleat, NMR 185, 403, 1127, 4367; H. C. Andrews, 'The Knighton family of Bayford, Herts, and Little Bradley, Suffolk', *Transactions of the East Herts Archaeological Society*, VIII, 1928–33, p. 47.

197 Longleat, DP 10, f. 41ᵛ; PRO, E179/108/163, fos. 2ᵛ, 9ᵛ.

198 Longleat, DP 10, income account, f. 9ʳ.

199 C. F. Richmond, 'The Sulyard papers: the rewards of a small family archive', in D. T. Williams, ed., *England in the Fifteenth Century*, Woodbridge, 1987, pp. 200–10; *idem, John Hopton, a Fifteenth Century Suffolk Gentleman*, Cambridge, 1981, pp. 186–94; 'Norfolk subsidy anticipation, 1523', in W. Rye, ed., *Norfolk Antiquarian Miscellany*, II, 1883, p. 402; Longleat, NMR 2880, 4434; *LP*, I, i. 438 (2, m. 13), ii. 2055 (23); *Longleat*, NMR 403.

200 *LP*, IV, i. 1298, V, 278 (34), 741, VI, 1271, VII, 23, VIII, 543, X, 94; PRO: C1/406/37–8; C1/594/64.

201 Longleat, NMR 384.

202 PRO: C1/310/4; C1/489/20; C1/862/15; C1/871/2; REQ2/3/259; STAC2/15/85–9; STAC2/19/121; STAC2/19/350.

203 PRO, STAC2/19/294, 316, 319.

204 *Tenth Report of the Deputy Keeper of the Public Records*, London, 1849, II, pp. 59–60; PRO: SC6/Philip and Mary/503, m. 1; PROB11/30/16; Bindoff, *Commons*, II, p. 85.

205 J. C. Wedgwood, *History of Parliament: Biographies of Members of the Commons House, 1439–1509*, London, 1936, p. 688; Clark, 'Henry Bourgchier', pp. 273–4; *LP*, I, ii. 2484 (9), III, i. 1042.

206 *CPR Henry VII*, I, pp. 134, 179, 240, 348, II, pp. 181, 373; *Rotuli Parliamentorum*, VI, p. 526; *LP*, III, ii, p. 1367, IV, i, p. 237, ii. 3665 (1), VIII, 149 (49), XIV, i. 275 (M21); *Journals of the House of Lords*, I, p. xxxiii.

207 PRO, E179/108/160, m. 8ᵛ; Longleat, NMR 185, 1127; ERO: D/DMj M2, mm. 20ʳ, 21ʳ; D/B 3/1/2, fos. 64ʳ–89ᵛ.

208 Somerville, *Duchy of Lancaster*, p. 608; BL, Harleian Roll Y 28; *LP*, I, i. 381 (51); Suffolk Record Office, T4374/Box 9/No. 5.

209 *Suffolk 1561*, i. 80; PRO: PROB11/23/17; PROB11/30/16.

210 *The Records of the Honourable Society of Lincoln's Inn*, 2 vols., London, 1896, I, pp. 20, 24, 25, 28; Bindoff, *Commons*, II, p. 85.

211 Longleat: NMR 185, 403, 1127, 4367; DP 10, f. 34ʳ; PRO, C1/272/19; W. C. Metcalfe, ed., *The Visitations of Essex*, Harleian Society, XIII–XIV, 2 vols., London, 1878–9, I, p. 222.

212 PRO, SC6/Philip and Mary/503, m. 17; *LP*, I, i. 132 (117), 381 (90), 749 (8), IV, i. 1941, 1949.

213 PRO, SP1/46, f. 253ᵛ (*LP*, IV, ii. 3929).

214 Longleat, DP 10, fos. 37ʳ, 40ᵛ, 47ʳ.

215 GL, MS 9531/11, f. 34ʳ; Longleat, DP 10, f. 41ᵛ.

216 *LP*, VII, 243; PRO: SP1/108, f. 42; SP1/143, f. 73 (*LP*, XI, 699, XIV, i. 263).

217 Robert Plummer, Edward Sulyard, William Bradbury, John Edmonds and Richard Rich in Essex; Thomas Knighton, Thomas Clifford and Humphrey Fitzherbert in Hertfordshire. *CPR Henry VII*, II, pp. 639, 643; *LP*, I, ii. p. 1538, III, i. 278 (27, 29), ii. 3586, IV, iii. 6803 (12); PRO, SP2/Fol. M, fos. 132ᵛ, 135ʳ.

218 J. G. Bellamy, *Criminal Law and Society in Late Medieval and Tudor England*, Gloucester, 1984, pp. 8–53; M. L. Zell, 'Early Tudor JPs at work', *Archaeologia Cantiana*, XCIII, 1977, pp. 133–5.

219 PRO, E137/11/3.

220 PRO: E137/11/4, mm. 1–10, 13–19; E150/301/5; PROB11/18/18; STAC2/29/85; *LP*, VI, 1595 (17).

221 PRO, E137/16/1.

222 A. Cameron, 'The giving of livery and retaining in Henry VII's reign', *Renaissance and Modern Studies*, XVIII, 1974, p. 27 (though this example is rather suggestive of the local constraints on the king's policy than of its ambitions and successes); PRO, KB9/434/9; 'The last testament . . . of John de Veer', p. 319.

223 PRO: E137/11/4, m. 13ʳ; E137/16/1, mm. 1ᵛ, 4ʳ; KB27/1095, Rex m.9; SP1/47, f. 164 (*LP* IV, iii. 4129); Zell, 'Early Tudor JPs', p. 138n; Condon, 'Ruling elites', p. 121.

224 PRO: E36/214, f. 108ᵛ; SP1/78, f. 109; SP1/90, fos. 148, 179 (*LP*, VII, 1526, VIII, 237, 268); Longleat, DP 10, fos. 40ᵛ, 41ᵛ.

225 PRO: SP1/47, fos. 164, 176; SP2/Fol. O, f. 321; SP1/108, f. 42; SP1/140, f. 125 (*LP*, IV, ii. 4129, 4145, VI, 1492, XI, 699, XIII, ii. 1090); STAC2/23/276; *LP*, XIII, ii. 74.

226 *LP*, VII, 1526; PRO: SP1/23, fos. 156–7; SP1/233, fos. 268–9 (*LP*, III, i. 1870, Add., i. 399); *LP*, VI, 1702, Add., i. 874; Longleat, NMR 188.

227 *LP*, VII, 1390.

228 PRO, SP1/81, fos. 6–7 (*LP*, VI, 1545).

229 PRO, STAC2/29/85.

230 Longleat, NMR 1151; PRO, REQ2/4/312.

231 *LP*, VII, 1084, 1120; PRO, SP1/85, f. 207 (*LP*, VII, 1180); J. A. Tregelles, *A History of Hoddesdon*, Hertford, 1908, pp.318–22; M. K. McIntosh, 'Some new gentry in early Tudor Essex: the Cookes of Gidea Hall, 1480–1550', *TEAS*, 3rd s. IX, 1977, pp. 312–13.

232 ERO: D/DPr 139, 140; D/DRs M1; PRO, LR12/8/244.

233 PRO, E150/302/6; ERO, D/DPr 145, f. 29ʳ.

234 *Feet of Fines for Essex*, IV, pp. 107, 151, 165, 166; *Herts Genealogist and Antiquary*, I, 1895, pp. 77–9, 83–4, 138, 140; PRO: C1/944/37; C1/982/12; C1/989/54; Gunn, *Charles Brandon*, pp. 87, 166; Longleat, NMR 2880.

235 GL, MS 9531/9, f. 62ᵛ; *Visitations of Essex*, I, p. 179; PRO, C1/766/44.

236 *Feet of Fines for Essex*, IV, pp. 173, 203; *Herts Genealogist and Antiquary*, I, pp. 9, 84; Longleat, DP 10, f. 43ʳ; PRO, E150/318/4.

237 E. L. Conder, *Church of the Holy Trinity, Long Melford, Suffolk*, London, 1887, pp. 83, 85; Andrews, 'The Knighton family', p. 43, *CCR Henry VII*, II, p. 239.

238 PRO: PROB11/30/16; LR9/4/584.

239 PRO, PROB11/32/20; ERO, D/ABW 8/80.

240 *Feet of Fines for Essex*, IV, p. 91; PRO: PROB11/8/41; C1/269/2–7; C1/360/62; C1/343/23; C1/484/3; *CAD*, VI, no. C6184; *CIPM Henry VII*, II, no. 250; Richmond, 'The Sulyard papers', pp. 210, 214; *Suffolk 1561*, I, p. 111; ERO: D/DMb M22; GL, MS 9531/7, f. 207ᵛ; MS 9531/8, fos. 6ᵛ, 16ᵛ.

241 PRO, C1/343/23; *CAD*, VI, no. C5310; *Herts Genealogist and Antiquary*, I, pp. 2, 3; *CIPM Henry VII*, II, no. 250; *CCR Henry VII*, I, no. 777; Richmond, 'The Sulyard papers', p. 210; Clark, 'Henry Bourgchier', pp. 269–79; Wedgwood, *Commons*, pp. 4, 688, 844.

242 G. M. Benton, ed., 'Essex wills at Canterbury', *TEAS*, n.s. XXI, 1933–4, pp. 259–60; H. W. King, ed., 'Ancient wills', *TEAS*, n.s. I, 1878, pp. 150–2.

243 Clark, 'Henry Bourgchier', 261–79.

244 ERO, D/DMj M2, m. 23ᵛ; PRO, PROB11/8/44.

245 PRO: SP1/129, f. 134; SP1/141, f. 218 (*LP*, XIII, i. 364, ii, App. 11).

246 Longleat, NMR 2880, 2895; PRO, STAC2/20/93; *Suffolk in 1524*, p. 157; *LP*, VII. 332.

247 Longleat, NMR 2895; PRO, STAC2/20/93.

248 PRO, SP1/82, f. 289 (*LP*, VII, 332); Longleat: NMR 4422; DP 10, income account, f. 4ᵛ.

249 PRO, STAC2/20/93.

250 *LP*, VI, 1272–3; PRO: SP1/82, f. 289; SP1/129, f. 134 (*LP*, VII, 332, XIII, i. 364).

251 PRO, STAC2/20/93; Longleat, DP 10, income account, f. 3ᵛ; *LP*, VII. 375.

252 Longleat: NMR 2895; DP 10, f. 40ᵛ; PRO, SC6/Philip and Mary/503, m. 18.

253 *Ibid.*, m. 17.

254 D. Hay, ed., *The Anglica Historia of Polydore Vergil AD 1485–1537*, Camden Society, 3rd s. LXXIV, London, 1950, pp. 94, 96–7; *LP*, I, i. 1170 (7); Miller, *English Nobility*, p. 139.

255 Hall, *Chronicle*, p. 540; *LP*, I, ii. 2053 (6, iii), 2391.

256 PRO, SP1/231, f. 230 (*LP*, Add., i. 126).

257 *State Papers, King Henry the Eighth*, 11 vols., London, 1830–52, I, p. 32.

258 C. Wriothesley, *A Chronicle of England*, I, ed. W. D. Hamilton, Camden Society, n.s. XI, London, 1875, p. 113.

259 *LP*, XIII, ii. 732.

Henry Percy, sixth earl of Northumberland, and the fall of the House of Percy, 1527–1537

Most historians would now agree that the relationship between magnate and early Tudor monarch was one which operated to their mutual and reciprocal benefits.[1] The older perspective – that the Tudors were antagonistic to the higher nobility because they saw them as rivals for political power – has disappeared in the face of the work of the most recent generation of historians like autumnal mist before the rising sun. If some nobles fell spectacularly – Buckingham in 1521, Surrey and Norfolk in 1546, the northern earls in 1569–70 – they did so because they placed themselves beyond the tacit bounds of the permissible in sixteenth-century politics. When Henry VIII withdrew his trust from a noble, then his fall was perhaps inevitable, but on other occasions early Tudor policy recognised the need for nobles to act as viceroys in the English counties. The king who destroyed Buckingham established Charles Brandon, duke of Suffolk in Lincolnshire and John Russell, Lord Russell in the West Country. In a clear reference to Yorkist precedent, Henry established (or rather re-established) councils and courts for his daughter, the Princess Mary, and his illegitimate son, Richmond, in Wales and the North. Nobles continued to fulfil a supervisory role in the counties; they were not the jewels of the state but its very pillars. Precisely because they were a working peerage, individual incapacity, whether through youth or mental or physical breakdown, presented government with severe problems of administration and oversight. In this chapter we consider such an instance.

The sun has not yet penetrated every corner. This chapter is concerned with the life and experience of Henry, sixth earl of Northumberland, who died, having surrendered his estates to Henry VIII, a pensioner of the king in June 1537. The outlines of his story are familiar: the interpretation to be placed on the basic facts is unclear. Over his short life there remains a bank of mist. Previous historians of the Percys – writing in an older tradition – tended to regard the sixth earl as the victim of a hostile and avaricious monarch, engaged in achieving a long-standing Tudor ambition of removing the Percys from their estates. Professor Bean saw the sixth earl as a 'weak and gullible character, the willing victim of greedy favourites and the skilful diplomacy of a hostile Crown', portraying the earl as both flawed and preyed upon.[2] Dr James's discussion of the sixth earl is coloured by the assumption that it was a long-term ambition of the crown to exclude the family from their offices on the borders and dispossess them of their lands. In his essay on Sir Thomas Wharton, James wrote of 'the policy of securing the Percy lands to strengthen the Crown's authority in the North, which was almost certainly conceived by Wolsey, but which did not begin to be implemented until after Cromwell's appointment to the Council'.[3] Another writer has spoken of the 'strategy by which ... the Percy's northern patrimony was dismantled and transferred to the Crown' and more recently still, two American historians have claimed that with the death of Sir Ingram Percy in 1538, the crown had 'accomplished the ruin of a family that had rivalled it for two centuries'.[4]

The fall of the Percys has also been placed in a larger context by Dr Steven Ellis who, writing from an Irish perspective, has pointed to the fall of a number of noble houses in the mid-1530s – Kildare in Ireland, Dacre on the north-western Anglo-Scottish border, the marquis of Exeter in south-western England, and Northumberland on the north-eastern Anglo-Scottish border – which 'appeared to mark a major shift in Tudor policy from the Crown's traditional reliance on local magnates in governing outlying regions to more bureaucratic methods'.[5] Ellis warns us against welding the separate experiences of these nobles into a general pre-conceived policy, but the question of whether the crown set about undermining these individuals or whether their fall was accidental and even unwelcome needs to be asked of each one.

Other recent writers have expressed their agnosticism over the issue of the crown's ambitions for the Percy patrimony, regarding the earl as being merely incompetent or gullible,[6] but have failed to work out a full interpretation of the reasons why he abdicated before his premature death in 1537. A new assessment of the earl's life is required to take into account, but also test, the new orthodoxy. And the study can be further justified by the discovery of new sources which, while clarifying his actions, still leave the personality of the man an enigma.[7]

I

Henry, sixth earl of Northumberland, head of the Percy family from 1527 to 1537, has not had a good press.[8] Later generations of his own family gave him the sobriquet of 'the unthrifty earl' to distinguish him from his father, 'the magnificent'. Percy was born about 1502–3 and died in 1537. He was educated in Wolsey's household where about 1522 or 1523 he formed his attachment to Anne Boleyn.[9] In the aftermath of this entanglement he was sent to the borders where he impressed the earl of Surrey with his enthusiasm and was considered a candidate for the wardenship of the Middle and Eastern Marches. In the event he had to wait until after his father's death to become warden. In 1524–5 he married Mary Talbot, daughter of the fourth earl of Shrewsbury. The marriage was unhappy and their only issue was a stillborn child. By 1529 the earl believed the countess was spying on him on behalf of Norfolk, and it was she who communicated the information of the earl's early interest in Anne Boleyn to the king in 1532, doubtless seeing in this a way to procure her own divorce. By this time the couple had separated and the earl ceased to support his wife some years before his death.[10]

Northumberland was not preferred to the borders in 1524, but became warden late in 1527. He owed his appointment to the inability of Sir William Eure to capture Sir William Lisle, a Northumberland gentleman in the service of the earl's father. Following a dispute with the sheriff of Northumberland, Lisle escaped from gaol in Newcastle in August 1527, crossed into Scotland and from there pursued a career of border banditry. Northumberland obtained Lisle's submission but was unable to secure his pardon, and at the king's insistence he was executed at Alnwick in early 1528.[11] In his conduct of border business in the following ten years, and in his behaviour in the Anglo-Scottish war of 1532–3, Northumberland appears to have been active, competent and when necessary, ruthless in the maintenance of order on the borders. He received several tokens of royal favour: the Garter in 1531, a commission of array in Yorkshire which made him the *de facto* President of the northern council in 1533, and he had a grant of the shrievalty of Northumberland in February 1534. It is not clear whether or not his request to make knights in the war of 1532–3 was granted.[12]

Northumberland, it is true, was treated appallingly by both his father and Wolsey while a young man: the old earl would allow his newly-wed son and his bride practically no comforts or income, and Wolsey interfered in his household, attempting to intrude his own servants to control the earl. While this has given the earl a reputation for being pliable, it would be a mistake to assume that contemporaries saw him as being weak or incapable. If anything the evidence points the other way, but throughout his adult life he was prone to periods of serious ill health. As early as 1529 he reported the return of his 'old disease' and expected to die. He was ill in late 1532 and early 1533 and again in mid-1534. In February 1536 he wrote that he had not been outside his chamber at Topcliffe for a year because of his illness (although this overlooks a trip to Newcastle made the previous autumn). He was taken ill at the Garter Feast in May 1536 and again at the trial of Anne Boleyn. By the time of the Pilgrimage he was physically broken and he died in his mid-thirties.[13] The nature of his illness is unknown. It is no coincidence that both Northumberland's doctors, Stephen Thomasson and Thomas Wendy, were handsomely rewarded by him.[14]

But the most striking features of Northumberland's life are his sales and gifts of land and the eventual disinheritance of his brother, Sir Thomas Percy, in favour of the king. Northumberland stands accused of destroying his estates in two ways. In the first place he is charged with making gifts or sales of lands to a variety of men (including the king) which represented poor or foolish bargains. Secondly, by giving annuities, some of considerable size, and by granting leases at reduced rents to a coterie of favourites, many of whom were members of his household, he further reduced the income of the earldom. This 'orgy of liquidation' stripped the earldom of its lands outside Yorkshire, Cumberland and Northumberland: the earl sold lands in Somerset, Dorset and Devon, Sussex, Lincolnshire, Wales and elsewhere in the south of England. The result was that where in 1489 the lands of the earldom were worth about £4,000, the rental of the estates remaining on the earl's death in 1537 came to only £2,840, of which £1,906 had been given away by the earl in the form of fees, annuities and cheap leases.[15] These sales drew criticism from within the earl's own circle. By 1532 the earl had dismissed his auditor in the south-west, Thomas Twesell, who had evidentally engaged in too much plain speaking.[16] Cromwell's agent Robert Southwell, employed to survey the estates in 1537 after the earl's death, reported that he had 'never ... seen a finer inheritance more blemished by the follies of the owner and the untruth of his servants'. Professor Bean accepted this, and blamed the dissolution of the estates on the inadequacies of the owner rather than on inherited indebtedness.

The identity of the earl's beneficiaries and their relations with him are therefore crucial in attempting to understand his actions. They can quickly be divided into two groups. The first and smaller contains those who by the time of the earl's death had bought parts of his estates, sometimes in place of annuities. None was in any sense a member of the earl's household. Virtually all of those in the second and larger group, the earl's annuitants and lessees, were household servants in the earl's northern houses. Given the differing character of these groups and the rewards that association brought them, it is convenient to treat each separately before turning to Northumberland's relationship with the crown.

With the exception of his sales to the crown, Northumberland's dissolution of his southern estates falls into two phases and was mostly completed by mid-1532.[17] The first phase consists of the sales that the earl made to Thomas Arundel (later Sir Thomas, executed in 1552) in 1528–9. Arundel, the son of a Cornish squire, had been a contemporary of Northumberland's in the Cardinal's household. The two were certainly on close terms, for in the late 1520s Northumberland was in the habit of addressing Arundel in his letters as 'his bedfellow'.[18] On his succession to the earldom in 1527, Northumberland appointed him receiver of his estates in the West Country and by 1530 Arundel was also serving as constable of the castle of Stoke Cursey and chief steward in Devon, Somerset and Dorset, drawing from the estate fees totalling £42 0s 8d.[19] By indentures of late July 1528 Northumberland granted Arundel an annuity of £60 from the manors of Slapton and Torbrian for life, £40 of which was to be continued to be paid to his widow. The same day Arundel had the earl's grant of the manor of Kingesdon in Somerset. Early in the following year Northumberland covenanted to convey the manor of Slapton to Arundel, who subsequently paid the earl £800 in consideration of the grants of Kingesdon and Slapton. But these were not ordinary sales: they were made not only for a pecuniary consideration but also for 'the manifold kindnesses and goodness at many times before this time by the said Thomas Arundel shown the earl'.[20] One wonders if the 'manifold kindnesses' included Arundel lending to Northumberland. On one occasion in 1528 Arundel is known to have lent the earl £50 to pay off an existing debt to the London merchant, Richard Gresham, but beyond this it is impossible to say. Other fragmentary evidence reveals that the revenues of his west country manors were, in 1529–30, being used by the earl to fund the repayment of debts of at least £780 to the king and London merchants.[21] In November 1529 Percy mortgaged manors in Kent to Sir William Sidney for £3,400.[22]

The second phase of Northumberland's sales falls in the year after midsummer 1531. In July 1531 he granted the manor of Staple in Somerset to Henry Pole, Lord Montague and leased manors in Sussex to the earl of Wiltshire for sixty years. The following summer he granted his remaining estates in Somerset and the reversion of two manors in Dorset to feoffees for the marquis of Exeter, and mortgaged further manors in Sussex to Sir Edward Seymour for £1,600.[23]

In these years Northumberland appears to have been deliberately liquidating manors which were peripheral to the main Percy interest in the North. Contrary to Professor Bean's suspicion, these transactions were sales rather than gifts, and some followed established networks of borrowing. As he pointed out, some of these sales were made to extinguish grants of annuities out of the same or other manors. The sale of Slapton to Arundel is a case in point. Montague had Staple for the surrender of an annuity of £40 out of the earl's lands at Petworth. There is evidence that Northumberland had been charging his southern manors with annuities in the years before 1531/2. The Somerset manors granted to Exeter in 1532 bore outgoing annuities totalling £115 of which £40 was paid to Arundel as an officer, £33 6s 8d to other estate officers, and the balance to various annuitants, including Lord Mountjoy who had £20.[24]

Some explanation of Northumberland's apparent generosity with annuities is required. In terms of their size, they were far in excess of those usually granted for friendship, as, for instance, by monastic houses on the eve of the dissolution. There is every sign that, in common with the debts repaid from the west country manors in 1529–30, they constitute a disabling legacy of borrowing contracted in the years before the earl inherited. The relationship of borrowing to annuities is revealed in his indenture with John Cowpland of London, merchant tailor, of March 1525. In return for £100 paid to Percy, and for previous loans of £280, Percy agreed that within twenty days of his marriage (if he married in the lifetime of his father) he would grant an annuity of £10 to Cowpland, his wife and son for their joint lives. If the old earl died first, Percy was to grant Cowpland, his wife and son an annuity of £20 for their lives.[25] Borrowing on the promise of a future grant of an annuity was surely ruinous, but as an heir without assets to be offered as security it was perhaps the best that Percy could do. It is not impossible that some of the other large annuities out of the estates, possibly those to Arundel and other nobles – certainly the £15 6s 8d paid annually to Thomas Kitson of London, merchant, in 1529 – were offered in recompense of similar loans. There is other evidence that Percy was kept short of money at about this time. Late in 1524 he was forced to turn to his brother-in-law, Lord Clifford to borrow funds to take part in a court tournament for 'my lord my father will do nothing for me but would be glad to have me put to lack'.[26] The outcome of this financial desperation was the sale of lands in 1528–32.

In other respects these grants were not quite what they might seem. The grants made to Arundel in 1528, Montague in 1531 and Exeter in 1532 were not absolute, but were made to the heirs male of the grantees with reversion to Northumberland or his heirs. There was therefore a reasonable chance that the lands would finally return to the Percy family. But more importantly, the Exeter grant was made in fee farm. Exeter was to pay £20 rent immediately, but his rent was to increase as annuities granted out of the Somerset manors ceased, finally reaching a total of £115. The Dorset manors were to pay a rent of £70 from the time Exeter entered possession. The earl therefore reserved a considerable financial interest in these manors.

Northumberland entered into similar arrangements elsewhere. In 1531 he surrendered two manors in Wales to Thomas Perrot in return for an annual rent of £80 p.a. and the surrender of his family's hereditary (but vague) claim to the earl's west country inheritance.[27] Most interestingly, in August 1532 he granted the Percy Fee in Craven to feoffees for his nephew, Henry Lord Clifford, conditionally on the earl's death without issue.[28] In the grant the earl reserved to his own heirs the customary rents of the manors concerned. In all these cases the earl was selling one type of property, the fee simple, with its associated perquisites of franchises, offices, local standing and the leading of men, whilst retaining if not the entire financial interest in every case, then at least a substantial one for his own family. And he further considered the larger family interest by retaining the reversion of some of the lands he granted away. Immediate financial needs rather than gullibility prompted these sales, from which the earl retained more than has been recognised.

Different considerations influenced the granting of leases and annuities to Northumberland's servants. Although no household accounts are extant, we are fortunate in the survival of the texts of a large number of grants made by the earl, mostly in the form of copies enrolled by officials of the Court of Augmentations after the earl's lands passed into their charge. The earl's privy seals are especially helpful in that the recipients are normally described by their office, so permitting the compilation of detailed lists of the membership of the Percy household and council.[29] The majority of the earl's recorded grants are unexceptional appointments to bailiffships and keeperships and other estate positions, but there are also leases, mostly modest, of lands on the estates.[30]

Our concern on this occasion is with the major household figures named, and as far as possible, identified, in the Appendix to this chapter. One striking feature of the list is the absence of Northumbrian gentry save the Carnabys, all sons of William Carnaby of Halton, and Nichasius Heron. Lascelles, Norton and Middleton were all of Yorkshire families. Wharton was of Westmorland, but perhaps a honorary Yorkshireman through his marriage to a daughter of Sir Brian Stapleton of Wighill in the West Riding, and in any event, Wharton became a Yorkshire landowner of some importance. Given that the earl spent much of the period before the establishment of the Anglo-Scottish peace of 1534 on the eastern borders, the absence is all the more surprising.

But this is not to say that Northumberland's wider circle was bereft of support from amongst the Northumbrian gentry. John Widdrington of Widdrington was appointed constable of Alnwick Castle and master forester in Alnwick lordship in 1530. He was replaced by Sir William Heron of Ford in 1534, at whose death the following year the earl's brother Sir Ingram became constable.[31] Sir John Heron of Chipchase was made constable of Warkworth Castle and master forester in 1534: in 1532 his son, John Heron, had been granted an annuity of £10 by the earl until he could be offered some better preferment.[32] John Ogle of Ogle Castle only appears in the circle on his appointment in February 1535 as a deputy in the Middle Marches: John Horsley of Skranwood, appointed a deputy warden in August 1535, had been reappointed master forester in Rothbury Forest and officer in the lordship of Alvisham in 1527 and had a lease of the lordship in 1536.[33]

Even within the earl's small household coterie, not all prospered and some may even have left the earl's service. Roger Lascelles of Breckenbrough Hall (Yorks.) had been in the service of the old earl who, in 1526, had made him constable of Prudhoe Castle and steward of the lordships of Topcliffe and Spofford. One of the young earl's first steps had been to appoint Lascelles to the stewardship of the house and he gave him a new patent of the stewardships he held, in survivorship with his son, Christopher. From then onwards, he never appears as a grantee in the earl's surviving privy seals. In 1531 he was supplanted in the constableship of Prudhoe by the earl's son Sir Thomas. Although he was a captain of a force of Northumberland's tenants in the war of 1532, he was the king's and not the earl's appointee.[34]

John Norton of Norton Conyers near Ripon similarly only appears as a grantee early in the earl's life. In July 1528 he had an annuity of £20, and in November a lease of the cornmill of Topcliffe. In July 1529 he was made master forester throughout Yorkshire with a fee of £13 6s 8d. In about 1529 or 1530 the earl pressed Norton's interest on the countess of Derby for a lease of Kirkby Malzeard, but after this date Norton appears not to have featured as the subject of any reward.[35] Named as treasurer of the earl's household in 1528–9, by 1535 that office was held by Sir Thomas Johnson.[36] Likewise, his son, Richard, who was to lead the Nortons to destruction in 1569, only appears as a grantee in 1529 when he was given an annuity.[37] Thomas Middleton is another who obtained little – minor offices in Spofforth and a lease of Spofforth mills, the rent of which Middleton was to keep to pay his fees. There are some signs that offices held by the Middleton were, by 1536, being granted to Johnson.[38]

It should not be thought that the earl was wholly profligate with his gifts. The truth is that he discriminated amongst those who surrounded him in favour of three men – Sir Reynold Carnaby, Sir Thomas Johnson and Sir Thomas Wharton. The common feature of these men was their comparative youth. Wharton was certainly the eldest of the three, for he was married in 1526, but Johnson was only wed in 1529 and Carnaby not long before 1536, and his children were only born in 1540–2.[39] Carnaby and Wharton both came from gentry backgrounds and were in fact cousins, but nothing is known about Johnson before his first mention as a gentleman of the earl's chamber in late 1528. Each will be treated in turn.

Sir Reynold Carnaby never received lands in fee, but rather leases and offices.[40] In all, the earl made him ten grants, one in 1530, four late in 1532, two in 1533 and one in 1534, of which five were made jointly to Carnaby and either his father or a brother. Five were of offices, and of the remainder only two were leases of substantial areas of land; of the demesnes of Langley in November 1532 (where Carnaby was constable of the castle and master forester) and of the manor of Corbridge in 1535, both for ninety-nine years.[41] Carnaby's profits were drawn from the difference between the true rental value of the lands and the rent reserved by the earl. The lease of Ovingham fishery had a reserved rent of £3 6s 8d, but had been let previously for £13 6s 8d. The lease of Corbridge reserved a rent of £26 although Augmentation's auditors reported that it had been previously rented at £36.[42] By September 1536 Northumberland was rooting for a grant of the lands of Hexham priory for Carnaby, a grant which was made to him after the earl's death in 1538.[43]

The gifts the earl made to Carnaby were modest compared to those received by Sir Thomas Johnson. The first reference to Johnson in the earl's service comes in a remarkable indenture of covenants of 28 December 1528 by which the earl, in effect, undertook to make him a gentleman. (His marriage licence calls him a member 'of the family of the earl of Northumberland' which underlines his dependency.) Firstly, and with her consent, he was to marry Isabel Palmes of Lindley in Wharfedale, the widow of one of the earl's lawyers, Brian Palmes, who had died the previous winter.[44] To support the couple, Northumberland undertook to grant to them and Johnson's male heirs the manor of Leathley and an annuity of £24, together with £200 for the newlyweds to set up their house. He promised to procure for them, at his own expense, the wardship of Isabel's son, Francis. Furthermore, Johnson was to be appointed steward and master forester of Spofforth, a promise fulfilled a few weeks later but at the cost of depriving Lascelles (who had been granted the same offices in 1527). In 1535 Johnson had a further grant in fee from the earl of the manors of Walton Head near Spofforth and Arrow in the Yorkshire Wolds, and he also obtained manors in Somerset, although it is uncertain whether these transactions were gifts of the earl's or purchases by Johnson.[45]

The general outlines of the earl's generosity to Sir Thomas Wharton, his comptroller, are familiar, but will bear a fresh rehearsal. In May 1528 Wharton was appointed steward of Tadcaster and Healaugh in the West Riding, and in December of that year he had a grant of an annuity of £20. But it was with three grants made on 18 October 1530 that the earl transformed Wharton's standing and abdicated to him the traditional Percy authority in Cumberland. In the first, Wharton was granted the lieutenancy of the Honour of Cockermouth with the accustomed fees, not for life, but to him and his heirs. To this was added a grant of the herbage of the park at Cockermouth, a handful of mills in Cumberland, a coal mine and six manors at a rent of £72 (itself less than their rental value), to be held to Wharton and his heirs male. In the third grant the earl gave Wharton and his heirs male an annuity of 100 marks from his lands in Cumberland, but Wharton was to pocket the rent of his newly-acquired lands in recompense for his annuity.[46] The creation of Wharton was made at the cost of demoting John Lamplugh, one of the fifth earl's servants, whose tenure of the lieutenancy (and of other offices in Cumberland not granted to Wharton) had been confirmed as recently as June 1527.[47] To the gifts in Cumberland was added the manors of Healaugh and Catterton in Yorkshire, the grant of which the earl acknowledged by fine in 1531.[48]

What was the earl trying to do with these grants? In the case of Johnson there is little sign that his intention was anything other than to ease an intimate into the gentry by making a marriage for him at his own expense. In the cases of Wharton and Carnaby more serious purposes can be detected, although their treatment differed in important respects.

Two suggestions for explaining Wharton's rise in the earl's service can be discounted. James's argument that the grant of Cockermouth was an attempt to perpetuate the Percy influence in Cumberland during an expected period of eclipse supposes a fatalism on the part of the earl and determination by the crown for which, as will be shown below, no evidence exists.[49] Nor, as might be thought, was Wharton created in order to spite or to diminish Clifford influence in the Western Marches. It is true that the 1540s saw serious disputes between the second earl of Cumberland and Wharton, but in the early 1530s Wharton still moved within the Clifford circle.[50] In 1534 he was the Cliffords' steward and master forester of Mallerstang in Westmorland. His letters to the earl of Cumberland from this time reveal a cordial relationship between the two, with Wharton well aware of the ambiguity of his position.[51] In a letter of September 1532, after reporting the arrangements he had made in Westmorland for the mustering and preparation of the earl's tenants, he continued

> Ande sore I am that I maye not accordyng to my dewtye attend this and other yor lordshyps serwes as I am bowndon, most humble besuchyng yor lordshyp to consydre now my serwes to my lorde [Northumberland] frome whome I have beyne long abcent. And yff ther be any serwes ther or elles wher your lordshyp wyll commande me [and] I shall attende the sayme ...

No explanation can be offered for the planting of Wharton and Carnaby in which the earl's ill-health does not play a part. Wharton was 'mine own hand' in a period of illness in 1535: neither he nor Carnaby could be spared by the earl.[52] Both Wharton and Carnaby were created to be military leaders in the border. Wharton was given the military office in Cumberland, but not the stewardship. Carnaby was made constable of Langley castle. The earl's letters of 1533 make particular play of their activities against the Scots.[53] In 1534, after the fall of Dacre, Northumberland is found trying to obtain the captaincy of Carlisle for Wharton.[54] He, of course, went on to become a ruthless and aggressive warden of the West Marches. When the earl secured for Carnaby a grant of additional arms in 1534, the patent explained that they were 'for the true, faithful and laudable service to the said earl done as well in war as peace, as also now of late in Scotland at the burning and casting down of many towns and fortresses, there the said Sir Raynold Carnaby hardly and manfully showing himself in the presence of the said earl', and then demonstrated in the most public fashion the 'great love and favour' which the earl owed Carnaby by conferring on him the right to use a parcel of the Percy arms. Carnaby was regarded sufficiently seriously by the crown to be appointed keeper of Tynedale in 1537, but his reputation never recovered from his capture and ransom by his own charges in 1540, and he died prematurely in 1544.[55]

Northumberland's motivation must therefore be seen in terms of a perceived need to establish two of his intimates as independent forces on the borders. His analogous grants to the Cliffords, of the stewardship of Kirkby Malzeard to the first earl and the reversion of the Percy Fee in Craven (where the Cliffords already held the stewardship) suggest a similar attempt to build up the Cliffords' military strength at the cost of his own. Northumberland was acting as pelican to his intimates.[56] But Johnson appears not to have been a credible military figure: he, rather than Carnaby, should be identified as the earl's whim.

This, without question, was to the detriment of the earl's two younger brothers, Thomas and Ingram. The earl ultimately disinherited the pair, but this should not be taken as evidence of total neglect. Thomas Percy, although he complained that his brother had delayed providing for him until the time of his marriage, was granted the manor of Kildale in Yorkshire, and on 28 August 1529 was granted an annuity of 100 marks from the manors of Prudhoe, Corbridge and Langley. In May 1530 the earl made him steward of his tenants in Tyndale with a fee of £6 13s 4d. A further grant to Thomas and his infant sons Thomas and Henry (the future seventh and eighth earls) in October 1531 made them constable of Prudhoe Castle, lessee of the demesnes of Prudhoe (rent free) and steward of Prudhoe.[57] These arrangements were upset by the earl's lease of Corbridge to Sir Raynold Carnaby in December 1534 which, being underrented, produced a shortfall in Percy's annuities out of the manor. The earl took Carnaby's side in the subsequent wrangle over Corbridge, the possession of which Sir Thomas seized.

The dispute took on wider ramifications during the following summer. Percy's brother-in-law, Sir Thomas Clifford, captain of Berwick, spoke to the king on Percy's behalf – perhaps reporting the earl's treatment of his brother, but possibly advancing Percy's confessed ambition to join the king's service – and at the warden court held in late July, the earl indicted a number of Clifford's gentlemen in retaliation and ordered his own servants to ostracise Clifford. At about this time Percy wrote his famous memorial to Cromwell in which he complained of Carnaby's divisive influence over the earl and stated his own desire to enter the royal service.[58] Relations between the two brothers were still poor the following autumn when Aske tried to effect a reconciliation.[59]

Sir Ingram retained the earl's affection for a longer period, but by 1536 he too had been removed from favour. Ingram had the grant of an annuity of 100 marks in 1528. By 1532 he was drawing £176 13*s* 4*d* annually from the estates, 100 marks in annuity, 50 marks as steward and master forester in Northumberland, and £76 13*s* 4*d* towards the cost of his house. In November 1534 he was appointed vice-warden of the Eastern Marches and undersheriff of Northumberland; in November 1535 he became constable of Alnwick Castle with a fee of £20. He was removed from the vice-wardenship during the summer of 1536 for reasons which are unknown.[60]

The Percy brothers were of some influence and authority until relatively late in the earl's life. Northumberland clearly took Carnaby's side against Sir Thomas, and it was Wharton, rather than Sir Thomas or Sir Ingram, for whom Northumberland was trying to obtain the captaincy of Carlisle in 1534. But even before 1534, neither brother seems to have had the first claim on Northumberland. This may be reflected in their marriages. Sir Ingram died a bachelor; Sir Thomas married a co-heiress of the Harbottle family, hardly the match of the brother of an earl (and heir to an earldom). Both brothers could reflect, and doubtless did, that Wharton, Carnaby and Johnson were favoured over them. It comes as no surprise that in the general breakdown of order which accompanied the Pilgrimage of Grace, both took the opportunity to attack the Carnabys and destroy their property.

II

It was not only the sixth earl who failed to further the interests of the Percy brothers, but also Henry VIII and his servants. As the largest purchaser of the earl's estates before 1536 and the beneficiary of his death, Henry's attitude to the earl and his brothers requires the fullest attention. The general outline of the earl's dealings with the king can be stated thus. In 1531 Henry received a part of the estates for the settlement of debts, and in the following year forbade the earl to dispose of any further part of his estates. In 1535 the settlement of 1531 was renegotiated with the crown and additional lands were surrendered. In early 1536 the earl announced his intention to make the king his heir, and this arrangement received statutory confirmation in the parliament of 1536. In 1537 the earl went a stage further and surrendered his estates for a pension, although he died before this could be put into effect. Various questions can be asked. Why was the settlement of 1531 renegotiated? Why did the crown attempt to curtail Northumberland's freedom of action in both 1532 and 1536? Did the idea that the earl should make the king his heir arise with the earl, or was he persuaded to do so by the king or Cromwell? At first sight, it appears that a powerful case can be made for Northumberland's being harrassed into surrendering his estates, but on a closer scrutiny the evidence looks less sure.[61]

The earl's initial problems with the crown arose from the need to settle substantial debts. On 7 July 1531 the earl granted the honour of Cockermouth and all his other estates in Cumberland to the king in return for the quashing of bonds worth £8,062, contracted by the earl on behalf of a failed Italian merchant, Anthony Bonvisi.[62] This was not an outright sale as Bean assumed: the indenture allowed for the redemption of the lands, but there is no evidence that the earl was able to take advantage of this. The transaction may well have been oppressive, but does not of itself give any indication that the crown was interested in seizing the whole or any part of the estates: it was merely settling debts.[63]

That this settlement needed to be renegotiated in late 1534 and a new indenture sealed on 3 February 1535 arose from a number of matters.[64] For one, the agreement of 1531 had not included all the earl's debts. By 1535 the earl owed the king £703 including £316 for his livery. To this was added a mortgage for £1,604 secured on the earl's Sussex estates which the crown purchased from Sir Edward Seymour.[65] It might be that the king had set his face on having Petworth for himself.[66] And, as the indenture itself explained, experience had proved how the tenants of Cockermouth were better ordered by the earl than by any royal official and so should be placed anew under his command. Now here the indenture was less than honest. Cockermouth was returned to the earl because he had shown himself incapable (or unwilling) to effect its redemption. (In the 1532 indenture he was licenced to sell lands to do so.) The exchequer may well have pressed for a new agreement because, having been charged with Wharton's grants in 1530, the honour was worth considerably less than its rental value. From the earl's point of view the surrender of Cockermouth in 1531 was a masterstroke: it did relatively little to reduce his revenues (and Wharton's income was unaffected), but because Wharton had the grant of the lieutenantship in perpetuity (and here the indenture's justification is revealed as particularly threadbare), the surrender made no difference to his (or Wharton's) military control of the district.[67] In 1531 Northumberland had sold the king a pup: in 1535 the earlier indenture was abrogated and Bonvisi's debts revived. For the cancellation of these and the other accumulated debts and a cash payment of £4,000, Northumberland surrendered his honour of Petworth, the manor of Hackney in Middlesex, his lands in Lincolnshire and Wales, and the reserved fee farm of the lands in the West Country sold to the marquis of Exeter in 1532. And the earl again covenanted not to sell any of his lands in Yorkshire, Cumberland or Northumberland except to his kin.[68]

This may seem to be a veritable persecution of the earl, but other noblemen were under pressure at about this time to clear debts including the duke of Suffolk, the earls of Shrewsbury and Derby, and Lords Audley, Darcy and Mordaunt.[69] Debt collection was a part of the normal business of the executive: it was pursued with greater vigour at times when the exchequer lay exhausted (as it was in 1529–32).[70]

The scale of the crown's intervention in Northumberland's affairs is unusual but not unprecedented. It is true that there is no other instance of the crown purchasing a nobleman's debts. The king paid off the Seymour mortgage and bought other debts contracted on bond.[71] But there is no sign that the king bought up the debts in order to pressurise the earl. Before buying the mortgage, Cromwell intervened with Seymour on the earl's behalf and obtained a respite for him.[72] The earl was grateful for this, and if the crown's other dealings are analagous, it seems the purchase of the earl's debts was to protect him from his creditors.

Likewise it was with the intention of saving the Percy estates that the earl entered into covenants with the king in July 1532, whereby he undertook to let the balance of the estates in Northumberland, Yorkshire, Lincolnshire, Somerset and Dorset descend to 'one person bearing the name of Percy and of the blood of the said Percy'. The earl was permitted to sell lands in Lincolnshire and Wales to the value of £331 10s ½d to redeem the honour of Cockermouth, but once redeemed, the honour was to be subject to the same restraints on alienation as the other lands of the earldom.[73]

The chronology of the earl's sales in 1531–2 serves to explain the purpose of this agreement. It appears that no such covenants were regarded as necessary at the time that the 1531 settlement was drawn (or else the indenture of 1532 would have been unnecessary). But in the summer of 1531 the earl had energetically sold land, as he was to do again in 1532. The indenture of 1532 was therefore a response to reports from the previous summer that the earl was selling. It was designed to save him from himself. A similar clause was added to the 1535 indenture. He ignored them both.[74]

The obvious parallel to be drawn here is with the similar treatment of Richard Grey, third earl of Kent, in the last years of Henry VII's reign. Another peer, Thomas Lord Vaux, was bound to make no more sales and had his conveyances resumed in 1535.[75] In each case, the nobleman was bound because of alarm at his dissipation of his estates. In its treatment of Northumberland between 1532 and 1535, the crown trod a road between the irreconcilable objectives of collecting debts, both its own, but also others bought to save the earl, whilst ensuring that the earldom was not damaged by injudicious sales. In the lands that the crown took in settlement and allowed the earl to sell, a clear appreciation emerges that Northumberland was first and foremost seen as a northern landowner. Indeed, it could even be suggested that lands might be exchanged with him to strengthen his Northumberland estates.[76]

After the indenture of February 1535, the Percy earldom was shorn of virtually all its estates outside the three northern counties. But the indenture should have provided the conditions for the earldom's survival. The earl should have been free of major debts and had undertaken not to alienate further lands. Yet, within a little more than a year, he had agreed to disinherit his brothers and make the king his heir. At the end of a further year he agreed to resign his lands and shortly after he was dead.

Throughout the year after February 1535 the earl was absent from London. By 10 April he was at Topcliffe, and save for a period in July and August when he visited Newcastle and Northumberland, he remained in and around Topcliffe until at least late February 1536.[77] In December 1534 he had told Cromwell that he was too ill to settle his affairs with the king. When he was called to London in late February 1536, he claimed to have been kept in his chamber for the past year by sickness.[78] This may not have been the case, but it may be taken that for most of 1535 his health was poor.

In the earl's extant correspondence of that year, there is no mention of any further settlement of the estates. The question of the inheritance first arises in letters of 2 February 1536 to Cromwell and the king. Addressing himself to Cromwell, he began by saying that as he was continually sick and that as his marriage was unlikely to be fruitful, the king had permitted him to nominate one of his kin (of the Percy name) as his heir. 'Perceiving the debility and unnaturalness of those of my name', he had determined to make the king his heir. The earl did this, he claimed, because of his sickness and the youth of his wife. The accompanying letter to the king was couched in similar terms.[79]

This bombshell passed unnoticed in the earl's next letter to Cromwell (22 February), but by a letter of 17 February he was called to London. Replying on 26 February, he promised to travel when his illness allowed.[80] It was not until March that he set out, and it was a Newark (in the 'Queen's Chamber' of the White Hart) on 20 March that the earl had the conditions of his grant drawn up and witnessed by a notary. He added his own seal, and the following day sent it on in advance from Stamford.[81]

The Newark articles envisaged the earl entirely surrendering his property to the king save for lands worth £500. He was in addition to be empowered to grant a jointure out of the lands worth 500 marks, and have liberty to grant annuities worth in total £100. His sales of lands to the crown, his gifts of leases, lands and annuities were to be confirmed by statute made in the parliament then sitting. This was more than the letters had offered. In proposing these terms the earl was in effect announcing his withdrawal from his public offices on the borders.[82]

The statute which followed gave the king much less than the earl volunteered in the Newark articles. In effect it guaranteed the Percy estates to the earl for life, and then to the heirs of his own body: it ignored the claims of the other members of the Percy family except in so far as they, with innumerable others, secured the addition of provisos to the act protecting their own gifts or purchases from the earl.[83] To all appearances, the gift of the estates to the king was Northumberland's own doing. There is no evidence that it was enjoined upon him by the king or any royal servant. Rather, if any motivation can be guessed at, it must be that the earl, crushed by illness, deliberately decided to disinherit Sir Thomas as a punishment for his challenge to Sir Raynold Carnaby. Northumberland's proposals became more extravagant between the original proposal and the making of the Newark articles. The bill which was submitted to parliament, which was doubtless drawn after discussions between Northumberland and the king, represented a retreat from the position taken by the Newark articles. This must be read as indicating that in March and April 1536 the king and Cromwell worked to moderate the earl's intentions, perhaps to avoid having to find a new warden.

The interest which was neglected in all of this was that of the earl's brothers. It might be thought surprising that the estates were left unentailed by the fifth earl, but it appears that this was so. The sixth earl therefore had an unusual degree of freedom in the disposition of his lands, but as he lived and died without issue, the eldest of his siblings was his common law heir. The covenants of 1532 and 1535 were drawn in an extremely wide fashion and make no reference to the brothers and seem to envisage a situation where at the earl's death, the estates might be bequeathed one way whilst the title descended another. The 1536 act deliberately disinherited Sir Thomas Percy. If the analysis offered before is accepted, then the crown, even if it thought to protect Sir Thomas's rights in the matter, might have been unable to do so because of the *earl's* determination to deprive Sir Thomas of his rightful expectations – which is not to say that if the earl had died before the Pilgrimage rather than after, Sir Thomas would not have been granted the estates as an act of munificence to support the title.

111

Between the settlement of 1536 and the resignation of 1537 came the cataclysm of the Pilgrimage of Grace. Northumberland stayed in London throughout the summer of 1536, returning to the North only when news reached him of the rising at Hexham (where the monks and townspeople had resisted the suppression commissioners). Subsequently he remained at Wressle, ill, eager to avoid the indignity of capture and willing his own death.[84] He was back in London by early February 1537. By 12 March he had been deprived of, or had resigned, his wardenships.[85] It is impossible to avoid offering some assessment of the role of the Percys in the rebellion.

The belief that the Pilgrimage of Grace was in some way a pro-Percy or Percy-inspired movement is often met but has never been worked out at length.[86] To make such a claim is to imply that the rebellion was organised from above and dedicated to promoting specific political aims. This, I would contend, is to misunderstand grossly the character of the Pilgrimage, the dynamic of which came, not from gentry or alienated courtiers, but from below. The oft-made claims that gentry were captured and compelled to join the rebels must be read as literally true. Both the sixth earl and Sir Thomas Percy were the objects of coercion. The body of men who gathered at Wressel Castle crying 'thousands for a Percy' did so in the expectation that the earl would lead them along the lines they expected, indeed demanded. Sir Thomas Percy's account of trying to flee from his mother's house at Seamer (near Scarborough), being stopped, recognised (or so he believed), threatened and then waiting to be impressed by the Pilgrims is one at a piece with every other account of the movement's early days.[87] Both the earl and Sir Thomas, in common with other gentry (and certainly in common with Darcy and Hussey) were the prisoners of a movement that was not of their making and which they could only control by aligning themselves with its aims. Sir Ingram Percy was at Alnwick at the time of the Yorkshire rising, and whilst his reasons for accepting the Commons' oath later in October are far from clear, he used it to gather the support of other Northumberland gentry to further his dispute with Sir Raynold Carnaby.[88]

From early November, both Sir Thomas and Sir Ingram were in

Northumberland. Both seized control of the wardenships and used their *de facto* authority to restrain the men of Tynedale and Redesdale whilst pursuing their vendetta against the Carnabys. On one occasion Sir Thomas expressed himself confident that it was safe to engage in factional conflicts in the expectation that the Pilgrims would secure a general pardon.[89] Neither brother was present at the York or Pontefract conferences, making it clear that the concerns of the Pilgrims were not their own. On the evidence of the sealing clauses of his privy seals, the sixth earl remained in Yorkshire throughout the Pilgrimage and was actually in York on 26 November and 9 December and a number of days in between.[90] There is no evidence that he played a part in the York conference and all the witnesses agree that he was ill. Nonetheless he had the stamina and courage to defend the king and Cromwell in front of Sir Thomas Percy and reprimand his brother for denouncing them.[91]

None of the Percy brothers were at the centre of the movement. Nor were the earl's household officers. Johnson and Lascelles were at the Pontefract council, but there is no reason to believe that they contributed anything very special.[92] Wharton was in hiding in Westmorland.[93] Carnaby was a refugee from the attentions of the younger Percy brothers.

But then there is Aske. Aske, it is well known, was a Grey's Inn lawyer. We may therefore assume that he knew everyone and everyone knew him. The belief that he was a servant of the earl's turns upon a single instance of Aske acting as the earl's 'servant', receiving cash and disbursing petty sums for household expenses, in 1527.[94] Servant is a notoriously vague term and no other reference to Aske in the earl's service has come to light. There is no sign whatsoever that he was one of the earl's lawyers or learned stewards. That said, it would be quite inconceivable in the small-town society of sixteenth-century England if the earl and Aske did not know each other. Aske's family was settled only a few miles from Wressle in an area dominated by the earl. His brother Christopher was the right-hand-man of Northumberland's brother-in-law, Cumberland. Aske's own brother-in-law, William Monckton, a signatory to the proclamation which called out the Marshland at the head of the Humber on 10 October, was named as one of the sixth earl's gentlemen of his chamber in 1534 when he had a lease of the demesnes of Wressle.[95] And Aske was well enough known to both the earl and Sir Thomas Percy to attempt to bring about their reconciliation during the Pilgrimage. The strength of the association may not be doubted. But there is no sign that Aske attempted to press Sir Thomas Percy's case either in the rebellion itself or in the brief moment of peace between the conditional surrender at the second Doncaster conference and the outbreak of Bigod's rising when he (at least) thought himself to be of real influence. There can be few manifestos as wide ranging (or inchoate) at that drawn up at York in late November, but neither Aske nor anyone else thought it worth including within it any clause concerning the Northumberland estates.

Arguing a negative case is never satisfying, but cumulatively it is impossible to see that the Pilgrimage was pro-Percy or that it relied on the Percys or their officers for leadership. It does not assist our understanding of the rebellion or the fall of the house of Percy to assume that it was.

IV

If the Pilgrimage destroyed Sir Thomas Percy, the sixth earl came out of it strangely untouched.[96] It was not until some months after the suppression of the Pilgrimage that the question of surrender was spoken of again. From the earl's letter to Cromwell of 2 May, it appears that Wriothesley had visited him at Newington Green and relayed a royal demand that Northumberland should immediately surrender his lands to the king. The earl wrote that he was willing to do so, but asked Cromwell to secure for him some pecuniary compensation. On 11 May the earl sent a 'bill of articles' to Cromwell. At the end of the month the matter was still unsettled and the earl wrote again, objecting to accusations that he had delayed the finalisation of the conveyance.[97] It appears that he was trying to secure some concession from the king and it makes sense to view the earl's request for lands worth £500 for life and eight years subsequently, with a further annuity charged on the customs of London, as dating from this time.[98]

The earl's requests, whatever form they took, were received coolly, and on 3 June the earl again wrote to Cromwell, withdrawing his conditions and offering the whole estate to the king with only the request that some provision be made for him. He died at the end of the month before his donation had been accepted.[99]

It seems clear that it was Henry who decided in April 1537 that he wished to come to a new arrangement akin to that originally proposed by the earl the year before. It is Northumberland who appears to have tried to negotiate concessions out of the king rather than the opposite: on this occasion the Tudor was trying to dispossess the Percy.[100] Why the haste remains unclear. It is possible, though unlikely, that after the earl's resignation from his border offices, the king required his lands to form the endowment of a new warden. This option is not amongst those canvassed in the memoranda of the time, nor was it put into effect. It is more likely that the crown, having before it reports of Northumberland's sales of woods and even his houses for building materials, decided to move to secure the estates before the earl wasted their assets further.[101] The earl was not unwilling to assign his estate, but Henry refused to concede his demands and forced from him an unconditional resignation.

It appears that his death was expected. The heralds' accounts of his funeral, to which attention has recently been drawn by Broce and Wunderli, show that he died at Hackney on 29 June, and was interred *outside* the church there on the same day.[102] The observances were far from impromptu, proper regard being paid to the status of the deceased, although the ceremonies were rather reduced in scale. Broce and Wunderli use the account of the ceremonies to illustrate the 'triumph of the Tudors over the Percies, and so a performance in changed political relations'.[103] This may be criticised on two grounds. For one, whilst the funeral was held in the absence of most of Northumberland's household officers, this is surely to be explained by the decision to bury him immediately and at Hackney rather than at one of the ancestral burial places in the North. Wharton and Carnaby were absent, but there is no great mystery about this; both held military offices in the North and the early summer of 1537 saw an invasion scare. Instead, one is impressed that forms were observed and that some individuals of importance in the earl's life, including William Stapleton, three members of the Carnaby family and Richard Gresham, were present. The chief mourner was Lord James Butler, son of the earl of Ossory; the other mourners included Lord Burgh, Ralph Sadler, Sir Anthony Wingfield and Richard Cromwell. Notwithstanding the urgency of his burial, the decision was obviously taken to have him buried with respect.

It is this very urgency which is particularly interesting. Broce and Wunderli's assumption that this symbolised the conquest of the Percys by the Tudors may be challenged. It may just as well be read as an economy; it may also be seen as an answer to a practical problem. The funeral of an aristocrat was the occasion at which the estate passed from generation to generation. With a corpse but no heir and little family, a full funeral would have lacked its most vital actor. But in their eagerness to take the funeral as an illustration of Tudor triumphalism, Broce and Wunderli never consider whether its form did not in fact reflect Percy's own wishes. Immediate burial, in Hackney rather than with his ancestors at Beverley, and outside the church too – may this not be seen as a final self-effacement, a definitive rejection of family and status, a logical conclusion to his life?

V

An account of the earl's short life can be organised about two features which run through it as weft and warp. The first is debt; the other is illness. It is true that the earl inherited a relatively light burden of debt and died leaving not negligible, but hardly spectacular borrowings. Previously it was suggested that in his youth he ran up, if not debts, then promises. There is clear evidence that he was borrowing heavily in about 1530–2. The settlement with the crown in 1535 brought him £5,200 in cash and he had £1,000 towards his expenses in 1536. Yet by the spring of 1537 he was without the money to pay his deputies in the Marches, and in the weeks before his death he lived by borrowing where he could. Wolsey's judgement that the young earl had no sense with money and therefore needed to be controlled by those who had might, in retrospect, seem shrewd, but we need to ask how the earl spent so much money.

In the absence of expenditure accounts, it is possible to do little more than speculate. Obviously his income was severely reduced by his sales of lands, and his gifts of annuities came to take up a great deal of what remained. It is though too easy to use the earl's own acts to explain his illiquidity. It is worth recalling that apart from the earl, his estates supported four other members of his family (five if he actually maintained his wife while she lived apart from him): his mother, the dowager-countess (annuity of £413 6s 8d in lieu of her jointure); his uncle, Sir William Percy (£104 6s 8d), and his brothers (who had about £250 in fees and annuities between them). These sums are those paid in cash: if the value of the lands assigned to Sir William and Sir Thomas Percy is included, then the earl carried charges of £8–900 in supporting his family.[104] Otherwise the earl is not known to have been profligate in his personal lifestyle. Nor did he invest in building except at Warkworth Castle, but not even the most flint-faced clerk of the Augmentations could object to the re-edification of a border castle in time of war.[105]

But the charge remains, and cannot be refuted, that the earl diminished his estates in order to further the interest of his favourites. Many servants received an annuity or a lease, but few received munificent gifts. The sole recorded grant to George Finch, one of the grooms of the earl's chamber, of an annuity of 66s 8d, is far more in character than the gifts to Wharton, Carnaby and Johnson.[106] Nonetheless the earl can be seen being generous to his close associates. While Johnson's marriage presents are unparalleled, Henry Whiteraisen, an usher of the chamber, had the grant of an annuity of £20 at the time of his marriage. The earl's attorney, William Stapleton (who wrote the account of the earl's illness at Wressle in the autumn of

1536) had the grant of an annuity of £13 6s 8d as his wedding present. The young earl agreed to contribute 40s a year towards the education of Henry Tenant, the son of the earl's signet clerk, Robert Tenant.[107] Instinctively, one feels that the earl's need to reward arises from his own insecurity, from his need to bind people to him, and that this in turn arises from his illness. The 'wasteing of his estates' therefore fulfilled a deep need in his character rather than any 'gullibility' or 'folly'.

Of the earl's illness nothing is known. It is not even certain if 'the old disease' was a physical ailment or a psychological depression (as if the two could ever be entirely distinguished in a man chronically and persistently sick). If the need to reward is a dimension of illness, is perhaps the creation of Wharton and Carnaby another? Earlier I argued that they were intended to fulfil a military function. Is it the case that they were intended to take the place of the earl on the borders in times of illness? But if so, why not build up the earl's brothers into his lieutenants?

The question of why Sir Thomas and Sir Ingram's claims were ignored by the earl remains unresolved. The facile assumption that the division between elder brother and siblings was of long standing appears not to be true. While Sir Thomas possessed a grievance over the speed with which the provisions of his father's will had been put into effect (perhaps because the earl chose to economise on his brother's well-being – another facet of poverty?), he held offices and favour until the first part of 1535, and there is no evidence of Sir Ingram's fall from authority until he was relieved of the deputyship in mid-1536.[108] But what did the earl mean when he proposed to make the king his heir because of the 'debility and unnaturalness in those of my name'? This is strong language if it refers to no more than a dispute amongst the Percy brothers over the correct place of Sir Raynold Carnaby. May it not be read as an allusion to illness, and so to say that some illness was present in other members of the Percy family besides the earl, and that he planned to terminate the line for this reason?

This is speculative and perhaps far-fetched. The argument is not assisted by our ignorance of the physical well-being of any other members of the family. But a history of chronic disease would explain much about the fortunes of the family in the sixteenth century. If the fifth earl suffered in some way, it might offer a clue as to why he was never appointed to border office. If illness dominated the sixth earl's life it would explain something of the way he handled his estates and disinherited his brothers.

No-one could claim that this chapter finally exposes the earl in his true colours or provides a verifiable explanation for the pattern of his life. Occasionally we have glimpses of deeper currents, caught like the flash of a solitary card in the hand of another player. In December 1528 the earl was the subject of a blackmail attempt. His councillor John Lamplugh was addressed by Sir William Gascoigne at Gascoigne's house at Gawthorpe (Yorkshire) in these words:

> John Lampleu, thou hast byn my frynd and y [*sic*] have byn thyn. I pray you recemend me to my lord besechyng hym to be my good lord. It is no honor to hym to do me displesure nor ytt no worshipp to me to do hym dishonor, besechyng hym to be my good lord. And yf he do me no good to me nor harme, prayyng hym to call to hys remembruance such writynges as he wrott in my lord hys fathers dayes when he was lord Percy and yf I be compelyd therunto I shall shew them before the Kynges Councell the wiche shall nott be to my lord honor.[109]

We cannot even begin to guess what these letters contained that might be so much to the earl's danger. Even if the man remains an enigma, perhaps some points have been clarified. The earl's distribution of patronage was not as wild as some have supposed and those who benefited mostly did so for logical reasons. The rift between the earl and his brothers came late in the earl's life. In his relations with the king, Northumberland enjoyed a great deal of favour: his settlements with Henry show no trace of victimisation. On the contrary, the crown strove to keep the inheritance together and it was the earl's idea, not the king's, that his brothers should be disinherited. Of course Sir Thomas Percy was executed, but this was not out of any intention to dispose of claimants to the Percy patrimony (and remove the embarrassment of an impecunious earl of Northumberland), but an impulsive and irrational urge by Henry VIII to try and execute a representative sample of the Pilgrims of Grace. There was no strategy to dispossess the Percys.

This is to suggest that the life and fortunes of the sixth earl can be incorporated within the bounds of the new orthodoxy of mutual benefits which has emerged in the last generation. It offers no solace to those who wish to see 'an integrated policy of "Cromwellian reform" in the borderlands'.[110] Nonetheless there are similarities in the roles played by the earls of Northumberland and Kildare in the British polity and their misfortunes in the mid-1530s.[111] Both families were the dominant landowners in frontier areas of strategic importance where they held crown offices which extended their control. Both families were excluded for periods from the offices they normally held (and were best equipped to exercise) through the substitution of other, more favoured royal servants – in the case of the Percys by the long Dacre wardenship, the Kildares by the

Butler earl of Ossory and others. Both fell at much the same time: indeed the major claimants to both earldoms were executed within a matter of months in early 1537. The removal of the Kildares was followed by open rebellion, designed to prove their indispensability. The fall of the Percys was accompanied by the Pilgrimage of Grace which some have seen as a pro-Percy movement (although this, as I have argued earlier, is not an acceptable view).

Resemblances there are, but they cannot be pressed too far. It is far from clear what innovations in the government of Ireland the king and Cromwell were planning in 1533–4; but it did not extend to depriving the Kildares of their estates. The decision by the Kildares to engage in open revolt was theirs and theirs alone, and it was that miscalculation, coupled with the overt papalism of the Geraldines, that led to their defeat and execution. Likewise the surrender of the Percy estates and the disinheritance of the earl's brother arose not from any campaign plotted by Cromwell, or Henry, but was a decision taken by the sixth earl. The crucial similarity between the history of the two families is simply that it was their decisions which forced a reaction from government. In Ireland the removal of the Kildares forced the garrisoning of the pale and its administration by expatriate viceroys with consequences that were worked out over the remainder of the century (and perhaps longer). In the North the consequences were, by comparison, small beer: the refoundation of the Council of the North, a piece of *ad hoc* planning whose survival for 100 years would have surprised its architects. It is hard to detect Henrician government pursuing a forward policy of intruding itself into the provinces. It is much easier to see government being obliged to step into the voids created by the calculations and miscalculations of individual nobles. And that leads us to the final coincidence. Both families were restored – at much the same moment – at times of military calamity when their respective frontier areas were judged indefensible.[112] Both restorations were expedient, and neither family ever recovered the status it possessed before the 1530s. But the fact of their recreations might lead us to ponder upon the continuing reliance of government on noble in the mid-sixteenth-century British state.

NOTES

Note: Place of publication is London unless otherwise stated.

1　I am grateful to Mr C. S. L. Davies, Dr S. G. Ellis, Dr S. J. Gunn and the editor for their comments on earlier drafts of this paper without necessarily wishing to commit them to its conclusions. All manuscript sources are (unless otherwise noticed) lodged at the Public Record Office, Chancery Lane.

2 J. M. W. Bean, *The Estates of the Percy Family 1416–1537* (1958), p. 157. Bean says relatively little about the earl's personality or his circle, being mostly concerned with the dispersal of the estate.

3 Dr James never wrote at length on the sixth earl, but there is much material in his essays on the fifth earl of Northumberland (1966) and the first earl of Cumberland (1965), conveniently brought together (but unrevised) in his collection, *Society, Politics and Culture: Studies in early modern England* (1986). For the present quotation p. 101, but also see p. 171. For an older statement of this view, see R. R. Reid, *The King's Council in the North*, (1920, repr. 1975), pp. 118–20.

4 Diarmaid MacCulloch, *Suffolk and the Tudors. Politics and Religion in an English County 1500–1600* (1986), p. 70; Gerald Broce and Richard M. Wunderli, 'The funeral of Henry Percy, sixth earl of Northumberland', *Albion* 22 (1990), p. 201.

5 S. G. Ellis, *Tudor Ireland* (1985), p. 129.

6 H. Miller, *Henry VIII and the English Nobility* (1986), p. 221.

7 The new material is a large body of indentures and conveyances scattered through the ancient deeds in the Public Record Office. In all fairness to Professor Bean and Dr James, it must be recorded that this material was not available for consultation when they were engaged in their research in the 1950s and early 1960s. Much of the chapter is based on a fuller analysis than has been undertaken previously of the so-called Book of Grants at Alnwick (hereinafter cited as Alnwick, Grant Book), described in n. 29 below.

8 For previous accounts of the sixth earl of Northumberland, E. B. de Fonblanque, *Annals of the House of Percy* (2 vols., 1887), i. ch. 9; Bean, *Estates of the Percy Family*, pt. 3, ch. 3; and James, *Society, Politics and Culture, passim*.

9 The account which follows is mostly based on Fonblanque, *Annals*, i, ch. 9 except where noted. The fullest account of the Boleyn–Percy liaison and its aftermath is E. W. Ives, *Anne Boleyn* (1986).

10 Fonblanque quotes the main sources. See also G. W. Bernard, *The Power of the Early Tudor Nobility* (1985), pp. 153–4.

11 James, *Society, Politics and Culture*, pp. 56–62.

12 *Letters and Papers, Foreign and Domestic, of the Reign of Henry VIII* (1862–1932) (hereinafter *LP*), V, 1635.

13 *LP, IV, ii.* 4202; IV, iii. 5497, both of the same date and probably 25–26 April 1528 rather than 1529. (In one the earl refers to falling ill on Easter day which was on 12 April in 1528 but 28 March in 1529, and there is evidence that the earl was in London in both March and April 1529). R. W. Hoyle (ed.), 'Letters of the Cliffords, lords Clifford and earls of Cumberland, *c*. 1500–*c*. 1565' (an edition to appear in the *Camden Series* in 1992), nos. 74–5 (of November 1532 and March 1533); *LP*, VII, 896 (June 1534), *LP*, VIII, 100, 166, 266; J. Anstis (ed.), *The Register of the Most Noble Order of the Garter* (2 vols., 1724), i. p. 402 (which I owe to Dr Gunn); Ives, *Anne Boleyn*, p. 388; M. E. and R. Dodds, *The Pilgrimage of Grace 1536–7 and the Exeter Conspiracy 1538* (2 vols., 1916, repr. 1971), i. pp. 283–4; *LP*, XII, ii. no. 165 (June 1537).

14 Alnwick, Grant Book, pp. 72, 75–6, 91, 122–3. At the end of his life, the earl was rooting for monastic leases for Wendy. *LP*, XI, 529; XII, i. 1121.

15 Bean, *Estates of the Percy Family*, p. 129, 145; SC11/959.

16 E321/40/82 and cf. *LP*, V, 1574. I owe both of these references to Dr Gunn. William Worme, the fifth earl's auditor, was detained against his will at Alnwick for at least five years, possibly for communicating the earl's affairs to Wolsey: *LP*, IV, ii. 4603: C1/919 no. 39.

17 This discussion of the earl's sales treats only with those where indentures are known to survive. For others, known only from feet of fines, see Bean, *Estates of the Percy Family*, pp. 147–8.

18 For Arundel see *Dictionary of National Biography*. The form of address is clearly most unusual between men but hardly amounts (as some have believed) to evidence of homosexuality.

19   E326/9051; SC6/Henry VIII/6306.

20   E326/9048; 8665, 11759; E329/405, 427; E315/54 no. 52. Cf *LP*, IV, ii. 3119 (2).

21   E314/79, Arundel file, warrant, 20 Dec 20 Henry VIII; SC6/Henry VIII/6306, also E315/427 fos. 58–60; SP46/162 fo. 276.

22   C54/404 nos. 64–5 (which can be found more conveniently at E315/163 fos. 28ʳ–33ᵛ).

23   E40/3223; E326/11700; E328/283, 90, 210 (the last duplicates).

24   Recited in E328/283.

25   E328/178. Cowpland was later in receipt of the annuity promised him which is mentioned as a charge in E305/7/D65.

26   Hoyle, 'Clifford letters', no. 47.

27   Bean, *Estates of the Percy Family*, p. 150. Bean is critical of Percy for entering into this arrangement, but it must be remembered that Northumberland needed the Perrots to abandon their claim to the estates to allow him to sell them, which he did during this and the following summer.

28   James, *Society, Politics and Culture*, pp. 169–170; R. W. Hoyle, 'The first earl of Cumberland, a reputation reassessed', *Northern History* xxi, (1986), pp. 81–2.

29   The chief source is Alnwick Castle, Mss of the duke of Northumberland, Letters and Papers no. 2 (described briefly in Historical Manuscripts Commission, *Third Report* (1872), pp. 46–7) and available, with permission, on microfilm 280 in the manuscript reading room of the British Library. (I have cited this volume subsequently as Alnwick, Grant Book.) This volume is a Land Revenue auditor's enrolment book identical in form and content to those remaining in the Public Record Office, LR2 *passim*. Other grants of the earls were enrolled in augmentations, mostly in E315/92. E314/55 contains a full listing of grants of lands and annuities made by the earl in the North, again the product of the augmentations administration of the estates. Unfortunately charges out of and leases of lands subsequently sold by the earl are much less well documented.

30   I hope to discuss the Percy retinue further in a subsequent article.

31   Alnwick, Grant Book, pp. 25, 12, 57; *LP*, IX, 65.

32   Alnwick, Grant Book, pp. 15, 22.

33   Alnwick, Grant Book, pp. 160, 22, 217–18.

34   Alnwick, Grant Book, pp. 31–2, 139–40; SC11/959; E314/55, fo. 10ʳ; Hoyle, 'Clifford letters', no. 7.

35   Alnwick, Grant Book, pp. 93, 129–130; James, *Society, Politics and Culture*, pp. 162, 166–7.

36   Alnwick, Grant Book, pp. 129–30, 141.

37   E315/92 fos. 66ᵛ–67ʳ.

38   Alnwick, Grant Book, pp. 63, 70–1. For the rivalry over Spofforth, see E212/10543.

39   Wharton, see James, *Society, Politics and Culture*, p. 104; for Johnson's marriage, see below. Carnaby, E. Bateson *et al.* (eds.), *A History of Northumberland* (hereinafter *NCH*) (15 vols., 1893–1940), x, pedigree opposite p. 408.

40   It is not the case that he acquired the Kent estates from the earl. They were mortgaged to Sir William Sidney in 1529 (C54/406 nos. 64–5) and made the subject of an absolute sale in 1532 (E328/90, 210). In 1533 Sidney sold them to Carnaby, at the latter's insistence (C54/407, no. 9).

41   Alnwick, Grant Book, *passim*, but see *NCH*, x, for materials based on this source.

42   E314/55 fos. 1ʳ, 1ᵛ. Bean provides considerably larger figures drawn from other augmentations sources. Bean, *Estates of the Percy Family*, p. 148.

43   *LP*, XI, 449; XIII, ii. 967 (53).

44   E210/10192; 'Testamenta Eboracensia', iii, (*Surtees Society*, xlv, 1864), p. 375 for the licence, and 'Testamenta Eboracensia', v, (*Surtees Society*, lxxix, 1884), p. 264 for Palmes's will.

45   E210/10192, 10492; E326/12863; E211/259; Alnwick, Grant Book, pp. 130–2; 'Yorkshire feet of fine Tudor', i, *Yorkshire Archaeological Society Record Series*, ii, 1887, p. 72; Bean, *Estates of the Percy Family*, p. 149.

46 Bean, *Estates of the Percy Family*, pp. 146–7; James, *Society, Politics and Culture*, pp. 105–6; Alnwick, Grant Book, pp. 191–2, 196–8. To this was later added the fee of Wharton's brother Christopher, made bailiff of Allerdale, the lieutenant's deputy, in 1534. The bailiff's fee was charged to the receiver of Cumberland although it had previously been a charge on the lieutenant. Alnwick, Grant Book, p. 51; E101/519/23.

47 Alnwick, Grant Book, p. 81.

48 'Feet of fine Tudor', i, p. 60.

49 James, *Society, Politics and Culture*, p. 106.

50 I hope to discuss the circumstances of their estrangement and eventual reconciliation in another place.

51 Chatsworth, Mss of his Grace the duke of Devonshire, Bolton Abbey books 8 fo. 23ᵛ; Hoyle, 'Clifford letters', no. 73.

52 *LP*, VII, 896; VIII, 80, 255.

53 *LP*, VI, 124–5, 322, 409.

54 *LP*, VIII, 896.

55 *NCH*, x, pp. 400–1, 408.

56 Hoyle, 'First earl of Cumberland', pp. 78–83.

57 E315/327 p. 144; Alnwick, Grant book, pp. 3–4; E314/55 fos. 1ᵛ, 10ʳ, 11ᵛ, 12ᵛ.

58 *LP*, VIII, 1143.

59 Dodds, *Pilgrimage of Grace*, i, pp. 283–4.

60 Alnwick, Grant Book, pp. 2, 5, 46; E315/92 fo. 63ᵛ–64ʳ; *LP*, VII, 1358; J. Raine (ed.), 'Memorials of Hexham', i, *Surtees Society*, xliv, 1864, p. cxxxvi.

61 For another discussion of these events with which I differ on many points, see Bean, *Estates of the Percy Family*, pp. 151–4.

62 Bean, *Estates of the Percy Family*, p. 156. Why Bonvisi failed to satisfy his obligation to the crown is unclear.

63 The indenture is not extant, but is recited in the 1535 indenture.

64 Renegotiation was afoot in September and December 1534, *LP*, V, 435 (misdated); VII, 1550.

65 For a list of these debts see *LP*, V, 395 (misplaced in *Letters and Papers*).

66 Miss Helen Miller has recently shown how the king could (and did) demand that his nobles surrender to him lands and houses which he fancied, see *Henry VIII and the English Nobility*, pp. 218–220. For the grounds for this suggestion, see *LP*, V, 435, misdated, of 1534.

67 Indeed, one could go beyond this to suggest that Wharton's grants were made in the knowledge that Cockermouth would be surrendered to the crown in the following year. It is not wholly impossible that the grants of October 1530 were conditional on a tacit agreement that they would be offered up when the earl came back into possession. But this is finally unevidenced speculation – if rational behaviour!

68 E305/7/D63 (original deed); C54/403 no. 17 (enrolment); E315/162 fo. 31ʳ–37ᵛ (registered copy). By an indenture of 18 January Northumberland sold his Sussex manors to the king. On 9 March he conveyed other manors (Duncton and Sutton in Sussex, Oxnall (Gloucestershire) and the Lincolnshire manors) to the king. C54/403 nos. 11–17, more conveniently E315/162 fos. 38ᵛ–42ᵛ; *LP*, VIII, 362.

69 S. J. Gunn, *Charles Brandon, duke of Suffolk, 1484–1545* (1988), pp. 135–6; Bernard, *Power of the Early Tudor Nobility*, p. 150; Lancashire Record Office, DDK 4/7; *LP*, V, 612, 875, 955, 1715; VII, 714–15, 885; XII, ii. 186 (62).

70 D. Starkey *et al.*, *The English Court from the Wars of the Roses to the Civil War* (1987), p. 96.

71 *LP*, V, 1169; VII, 215. Cf. VII, 1550.

72 *LP*, V, 435.

73 Alnwick, Syon Ms D.I.8a.

74 In 1532 the earl undertook to assure the descent of the lands of the earldom within two years. This was never done. The grant of the Percy Fee in Craven to feoffees for Henry

Lord Clifford, made within weeks of the 1532 settlement, was clearly contrary to the terms of the indenture, as were other grants made before 1536.

75   G. W. Bernard, 'The fortunes of the Greys, earls of Kent, in the early sixteenth century', *Historical Journal* 25 (1982), esp. pp. 675–8; Miller, *Henry VIII and the English Nobility*, p. 185.

76   *LP*, VII, 885.

77   The earl's movements can be traced from an analysis of the dating clauses of the grants in the Alnwick Grant book.

78   *LP*, VII, 1550; VIII, 266 (both misdated).

79   *LP*, VIII, 166 (misdated); X, 150.

80   *LP*, VIII, 255, 266 (both misdated).

81   E328/31; *LP*, X, 509.

82   Because of this the letter was probably received with horror in London.

83   27 Henry VIII c.47 (printed, *Statutes of the Realm* iii. pp. 611–19); the provisos were apparently added on the floor of the house. S. E. Lehmberg, *The Reformation Parliament 1529–1536* (1970), p. 244.

84   *LP*, XII, i. 392 at p. 192 (Stapleton's account). He was in York at the time of the York conference, *ibid.*, and see Alnwick, Grant Book, pp. 22, 189 for grants dated there at that time.

85   *LP*, XII, i. 328, 609, 636.

86   See, for instance, G. R. Elton, *Reform and Reformation* (1977) p. 265 (although the role of the Percys is not emphasised in his subsequent article, 'Politics and the Pilgrimage of Grace', in his *Studies in Tudor Politics and Government*, iii. (1983), pp. 183–215).

87   Dodds, *Pilgrimage of Grace*, i, pp. 230–1.

88   *Ibid.*, i, pp. 198–201.

89   *Ibid.*, i, p. 285; ii, pp. 42–3. The major source for their activities is the deeply hostile remembrance in *LP*, XII, i. 1090.

90   Alnwick, Grant Book, pp. 29, 154, 189.

91   Dodds, *Pilgrimage of Grace*, i, p. 284.

92   *Ibid.*, i, p. 345.

93   Wharton's movements are unknown: S. M. Harrison, *The Pilgrimage of Grace in the Lake Counties* (1981), pp. 108, 133, but he did get word of his predicament to his brother-in-law Stapleton (the earl's lawyer) who tried to get Wharton a safe-conduct from Aske. *LP*, XII, i. 392 at p. 193.

94   BL, Add. Ms 38,133 fo. 9 (a commonplace book said to be Aske's), printed by H. I. B. in *Notes and Queries*, 11th Ser., iv (1911), pp. 442–3. It is not self-evident that the Robert Aske who kept this account is the same as the lawyer and rebel. Aske's elder brother John, the head of the family, called his eldest son Robert and it is this Robert who is the Robert younger who signed the proclamation raising the Marshland on 10 October 1536. J. Foster (ed.), *The Visitation of Yorkshire made in the years 1584–5* by Robert Glover (priv. printed, London 1875), pp. 118–19; Dodds, *Pilgrimage of Grace*, i. p. 148.

95   Dodds, *Pilgrimage of Grace*, i. p. 148, ii. pp. 32–3; Alnwick, Grant Book pp. 127–8; R. W. Hoyle, 'Land and landed relations in Craven, Yorkshire, *c.* 1520–1600' (University of Oxford D.Phil. thesis, 1987), pp. 247–8.

96   That the earl had allowed Aske to make his base at Wressle was judged to be high treason in one paper and the earl sought to defend his actions. *LP*, XII, i. 849 at p. 382, 1062.

97   *LP*, XII, i. 1121, 1176, 1304.

98   *LP*, VII, 1550 (2). Another bill, whereby Northumberland asked for £1,000 per annum, a cash payment of £1,000 to clear his debts, with the promise of £1,000 to pay for his funeral and either £500 or 500 marks towards the setting up of his house, may date from earlier in May, but seems more in tune with the proposals the earl made in February 1536. *LP*, VIII, 363.

99   *LP*, XII, ii. 19, 165.

100   There also survives the text of an unconditional grant of all his estates to the king

made by the earl on 31 August 1536. The purpose for which this was made is far from obvious; it was not put into effect. E315/162 fo. 45ᵛ.

101 *LP*, XII, i. 609, 1173. They may not have known that on 2 May, the day Wriothesley visited him, the earl leased the demesne lands of Wressle to a yeoman of his wardrobe, Stephen Stamford. E315/52 no. 127.

102 The section which follows is based on Broce and Wunderli, 'Funeral of Henry Percy'. I have not seen the original mss. A tomb was erected. D. Lysons, *The environs of London*, ii, *Middlesex* (1795), pp. 469–70.

103 Broce and Wunderli, 'Funeral of Henry Percy', p. 215.

104 The two annuities are mentioned in the 1536 act assuring the estates to the king, 27 Henry VIII c. 47, sect. x and xi. The annuities to the Percy brothers can be traced through the Alnwick Grant Book. Ingram had a grant of 100 marks in 1528 (p. 2): it is not clear if this was superseded by a grant of August 1531 (confirmed in November 1532 and perhaps also in June 1534) of £176 13s 4d (p. 5, E314/55 fo. 12ᵛ). Thomas had the grant of two manors in Yorkshire and an annuity of 100 marks in 1529, which was regranted to him and his two children in 1531 (Alnwick, Grant Book, pp. 3–4; E314/55, fo. 12ᵛ).

105 *NCH*, v, pp. 55–6.

106 Alnwick, Grant Book, p. 48.

107 Alnwick, Grant Book, pp. 134–5, 215; E315/92 fos 112ᵛ–113ʳ.

108 Above, pp. 191–2.

109 CP40/1064 (Hilary 21 Henry VIII) m. 341. The form of words given here are those admitted by Gascoigne which are fuller than those claimed by Northumberland, but in Northumberland's version Gascoigne finished by saying 'and bid hym answer to them as he will at his jeparde and perell'. The earl sued for damages of 1,000 marks.

110 Ellis, *Tudor Ireland*, p. 130.

111 For the most readily accessible study of the Kildare ascendency in Ireland, see Ellis, *Tudor Ireland*, chs 4 and 5.

112 The eleventh earl of Kildare was restored in May 1554, the seventh earl of Northumberland in May 1557. Both men were, by further coincidence, aged 29.

APPENDIX

Senior household officers and councillors of the sixth earl of Northumberland

Note: All page references are to Alnwick, Grant Book.

STEWARD

(Sir) Roger Lascelles of Breckenbrough Hall, NRY: steward to the fifth earl and reappointed by the sixth earl, 7 July 1527, fee 20 marks (p. 140). Had grant (with son Christopher) of the stewardship of the manors of Spofforth (WRY) and Topcliffe (NRY), and master forestership of game, fee £13 6s 8d, 22 July 1527 (pp. 139–40).

TREASURERS

John Norton of Norton Conyers, WRY: named as treasurer in grants of 1528–9 (see below) possibly in succession to William Worme, so named in 1527 (Fontblanque, *Annals*, i, p. 382). Had lease for life of the corn mill at Topcliffe, 20 November 1528, rent £20 (pp. 129–30); appointed chief master forester in Yorkshire, with fee of 20 marks and gift of deer during pleasure, 11 January 1529 (p. 129).

Sir Thomas Johnson of Lindley, par Otley, WRY: named as treasurer in letter of 10 July 1535 (*LP*, VIII, 1013–14) and in grant of 3 November 1535 (p. 141). Died 1542 ('Testamenta Eboracensia', vi, pp. 203–5). For Johnson's career, see text, pp. 188–9.

COMPTROLLER

Sir Thomas Wharton of Wharton, Westmorland and later Healaugh, WRY: named as comptroller in grants of May 1528 (p. 136) and October 1530 (pp. 191–2): knighted 1528, baron 1544, d. 1568. For his service to the sixth earl, see text, pp. 189–90 and for his career generally, James, *Society, Politics and Culture* pp. 91–147 and *History of Parliament 1509–1558*, ed. S. T. Bindoff (3 vols., 1982), iii, pp. 597–9.

GENTLEMEN OF THE CHAMBER

Note: The Carnabys are all sons of William Carnaby of Halton, Nlnd (Cf. pedigree in *NCH*, X opp. p. 408).

Cuthbert Carnaby: named as such in 1534 when had the lease of the pannage of Newsham Park, NRY and in 1536 when had the lease of Birks and Middlesmore in Langstrothdale, WRY (pp. 60–1, 286–7).

Lionel Carnaby: named in April 1537 when had the grant of annuity of £13 6s 8d with his younger brother Lancelot (pp. 228–9).

(Sir) Raynold Carnaby: the eldest of the brothers. Named as gentleman in grants of 1530 of the bailiffship of the lordship of Hayden Bridge, Nlnd, fee 60s 8d, and 1532 of the offices of constableship, master forestership with lease of the demesne lands of Langley, Nlnd (pp. 44, 14, 179–80) but not in grants of December 1533 and December 1534 (pp. 17–18, 27–8). Knighted 1532–4. Had grant of Hexham Abbey 1538: keeper of Tynedale 1537–9. Died 1543.

Thomas Carnaby: named as gentleman in grant of 1534 of the stewardship and master forestership of Rothbury, Nlnd (p. 122).

Nichasius Heron: named when appointed bowbearer of the Forest of the West Ward in Cmld, November 1536 (p. 108). Described as one of the chamber in 1535 (pp. 56–7). Bailiff of Wressle (ERY) and keeper of the castle and parks there, 1535 (pp. 54–5). Probably a cadet of one of the Nlnd Heron families.

(Sir) Thomas Johnson. See above: named as a gentleman of the chamber in January 1529 (pp. 130–1).

Thomas Middleton: named as gentleman in grants of April 1530 of the bailiffship of Spofforth and keeper of woods there (p. 63); June 1530 of the bowbearership of Spofforth and keepership of Spofforth Park and woods (p. 70) and of a lease of Spofforth mills in 1532 (p. 71). Called servant in 1535 (*LP*, VIII, 1013–14). Son of Sir William Middleton of Stockeld WRY: d. 1548–9 in the lifetime of his father when resident at Spofforth Park ('Testamenta Eboracensia', vi, pp. 278–9).

COUNCILLORS

Edward Edgore, auditor in the North. Described as councillor in 1536 (p. 79). Previously auditor to the duke of Buckingham (C1/441 no. 2).

Thomas Kelke: named as councillor and sewer for the earl's body in grant of bailiffship of Leconfield and of the offices of the keepership of Leconfield Parks in 1530 (p. 87). Described by the fifth earl in 1526 as sewer of the earl's board when had grant of the bailiffship of the manor of Byker (Nlnd) and a lease of the manor in reversion (p. 21): still sewer in June 1537 (p. 125). Acted as one of the earl's commissioners to lease lands, 1534, E315/47 no. 224; 54/no. 52. Origins unknown, but doubtless the heir of Christopher Kelke whose wardship was in contention in c. 1524 (*LP*, IV, i. 420): dead by June 1538 (*LP*, XIV, i. 1355 (p. 593)). His son living in Seamer, NRY in 1546 (*Yorks. Arch. Soc. Rec. Ser.*, cii, p. 110).

Sir Thomas Johnson: see above. Named as councillor and treasurer in the grant of the keepership of the Little Park of Topcliffe in November 1535 (p. 141).

(Sir) John Lamplugh: of Lamplugh, Cmld gent. Servant of the fifth earl's: had grant of the lieutenantship of Cockermouth and master forester in Wasdalehead and Eastdalehead in Cmld with the deputy stewardship of St Bees in July 1527 (p. 99). Superseded in Cmld by Wharton. Date of knighthood unknown.

(Sir) Roger Lascelles: see above. Called councillor in grants by the fifth earl in 1526 and the sixth earl in 1527 (references as above).

William Maunsell: of York, lawyer. Named as councillor when had a fee of 4 marks in 1535 (p. 142). For his career, see *Yorks. Arch. J.* xli (1971), pp. 373–4.

John Norton: see above. Named as councillor in grant of 1529 (p. 129).

The downfall of Sir Thomas Seymour

If families had been political factions, then Sir Thomas Seymour, Lord Seymour of Sudeley, and his older brother Edward Seymour, earl of Hertford, who in a coup on the death of Henry VIII in January 1547 became duke of Somerset and Protector of the realm, might have been expected to work closely together. Like his elder brother, Sir Thomas Seymour had served in the king's privy chamber, in diplomacy and on the battlefield, though less prominently: he was ennobled and appointed Lord High Admiral at the same time as his brother became Protector. But far from co-operating, Seymour and his brother quarrelled bitterly, and in March 1549 Sir Thomas Seymour was executed for treason. A study of his activities between January 1547 and March 1549 makes an exciting story,[1] but it is much more than that. Seymour's career shows the possibilities open to ambitious noblemen: more broadly still, it shows where power lay, or was thought to lie, in mid Tudor England.

What then did Seymour do? Marriage with a member of the royal family was an obvious source of power and advancement: the Seymours had of course greatly benefited from their sister Jane's marriage to Henry VIII. Seymour followed her example. In June 1547 the French ambassador reported rumours that he had considered making suits to Princess Mary or Anne of Cleves;[2] a later French account suggested that he had tried for Princess Elizabeth.[3] What Seymour in fact did was to marry Henry VIII's widow, Catherine Parr. Catherine had apparently been interested in Seymour before Henry had taken a fancy to her. She told Seymour that she would not have him think that her honest goodwill towards him proceeded from 'any sodayne motyon or passyon', because 'as truely as god ys god my mynd was fully bent the other tyme I was at lybertye, to marye you before any man'.[4] According to the possibly extravagant Leti, she had been very unhappy in her marriage with Henry – he had, she felt, done her great wrong to marry so young a woman – and she was not displeased to marry someone young and vigorous. Leti added that Seymour made overtures to her the day after she was widowed, that they were soon kissing shamefully, and that they were married thirty-four days after Henry's death.[5] Vertot suggested that Catherine had not been a widow for a month when Seymour declared his love for her.[6] Such speed is not implausible. One of the charges against Seymour in 1549 was that he had married the queen so abruptly after Henry had died that if a child had come soon it would have been difficult to tell whether it was his or the king's.[7] Another charge accused Seymour of having first married the queen secretly and of then concealing the marriage.[8] Undated letters between Catherine and Seymour, presumably from early 1547, suggest that Seymour was putting pressure on Catherine to mourn the king for two months, not two years.[9] But Catherine was clearly very much in love. She asked Seymour not to be offended that she sent sooner to him than she had said: 'for my promys was but ones in a fortened howbeyt the tyme ys well abrueyated by what meanes I knowe not excepte the weakes be schorter at Chelsey than in other places'.[10] Seymour noted that 'it hath pleased your highnes to be the furst breker of yor a poynttement'.[11] Soon he was visiting Catherine at her suggestion early in the morning and leaving by 7 o'clock, 'so I suppose ye may come without suspect'. Evidently they discussed how best to win Somerset's acceptance of their marriage. 'Your Brother hathe thys Afternoone a lytell made me warme', wrote Catherine. 'Yt was fortunate we war so muche dystant, for I suppose els I schulde have bytten hym. What cause have they to feare havyying suche a Wyff?'[12] She thought Seymour was 'in sum fere how to frame my lord your brother to speke in your fauour' and felt he should not 'importune for hys good wyll, yf yt cum nott frankely at the fyrst, yet schalbe suffycyent ones to haue requyre yt, and after to cesse'. She suggested getting letters from the young king in their favour and also seeking 'the ayde and furtherance of the most notable of the counsell'.[13] Seymour appealed unsuccessfully to Mary for her support. Mary reacted to the 'strange newes concernyng a sewte you haue in hande to the quene for maryage': if Catherine was keen, Mary could do but small pleasure; if Catherine was not keen, 'if the remembrance of the Kynge mayestye my father (whose soule God pardon) wyll not suffre her to grawnt your sewte, I ame nothyng able to perswade her to forget the losse of hyme, who is as yet very rype in myn owne remembrance'. But she excused herself for advising on 'woweng matters ... wherin I being a mayde am nothyng connyng'.[14] According to Leti, Mary was horrified, but thought Catherine more to blame than Seymour. She appealed to

Elizabeth, but her half-sister told her they lacked credit at court and so they should suffer what they could not prevent.[15] He did make efforts to win over the king. He took up Catherine's idea and got Edward to write her a letter whose contents he evidently dictated. Dated 25 June, this letter made the marriage appear as Edward's request to Catherine. 'We thank you hartely, not onlie for your gentle acceptatione of our sute moved unto you, but also for your lovinge accomplishinge of the same,' it read. It added an assurance that Somerset would not trouble her about the marriage: 'Wherfore ye shal not nede to feare anie grefe to come, or to suspecte lake of ayde in nede; seing that he, being mine uncle, is so goode an nature that he will not be troblesome'.[16] But Seymour had run into difficulties in trying to obtain this letter. Earlier he had asked John Fowler of the king's privy chamber to discover what the king thought about his marriage plans: unhelpfully Edward had suggested that Seymour should marry Anne of Cleves or Mary. Possibly an earlier letter from Edward to Catherine shows that Edward had been put off writing to Catherine and that Somerset was taking great care that no interview between Edward and Catherine took place. Seymour at some point did manage to see Edward in person: possibly that is when he got Edward to write.[17] The king's journal leaves no doubt that Somerset was angry at the marriage: 'the lorde Seimor of Sudley maried the quene, whos nam was Katarine, with wich mariage the Lord Protectour was much offended'.[18] Did he unwittingly further it? One of the charges against Seymour was that he had deceived his brother, persuading him to ask Catherine to bear her favour towards Seymour, to suggest that she made a marriage that had already been consummated.[19] If Somerset did for a while then accept the *fait accompli*, the marriage led to friction between the brothers and their wives. Seymour tried to secure certain jewels previously given to Catherine by Henry VIII and now held by Somerset. He took legal advice and was very agitated about this matter throughout 1547 and 1548. He asked his servant Wightman to find out whether the jewels and household stuff which Henry had had delivered to the queen were 'by waye of Gift or Lone', and to ask divers gentlemen 'as neare they coulde' to tell him 'the verye Woords his Majestye spake at the sending of such Jewells or Household Stuffe unto her'. He wrote to nine or ten lawyers asking what judgement they would give. Even after Catherine's death in September 1548, Seymour carried on his campaign. Catherine's will, significantly because unnecessarily, bequeathed to Seymour all her manors and goods that she had, or, a notable addition, 'of right ought to haue had'.[20] He appealed to Princess Mary for her support and her testimony 'howe and after what sorte the Kinges maiestie vsed to departe with thinges vnto her, and namely those iewelles whiche his hieghnes delivered her against the Frenche Admiralles cooming in': were they gifts or just temporarily lent?[21] There were difficulties as well over Catherine's lands.[22] Just how strongly Seymour felt about these supposed injustices can be seen in his trust that the baby that Catherine was carrying 'wyll revenge such wroonges as nether you nor I can at this prisent'.[23] Most seriously, Seymour's marriage provoked the bitter jealousy of Somerset's wife, Anne Stanhope. Who had precedence – Anne as the Protector's wife or Catherine as Dowager Queen? A later writer thought that Seymour responded by trying to disinherit Anne's children in favour of Somerset's children by his first marriage.[24] Seymour's marriage did then immediately raise his status, but it also created problems.

Seymour's interest in the royal family also included Princess Elizabeth. But if Seymour was flirting with Elizabeth, it does not follow that his marriage with Catherine had broken down. By early 1548 she was pregnant and gave birth in September 1548: a few days later she died. It is most unlikely that Seymour had poisoned her.[25] Later he spoke of his shock and confusion 'in a tyme when partelye with the Quenes Highnes deathe, I was so amased that I had smale regard eyther to my self or to my doinges'.[26] And it is worth recalling the obvious pride and affection with which Seymour had written about 'my lettell man' when Catherine was pregnant.[27] Nevertheless there is much evidence of the familiarity between Seymour and Elizabeth while she was living with Catherine and him. Seymour sometimes came to her chamber alone.[28] For a while he used 'to com up every mornyng in his nyghtgown, barelegged in his slippers, where he found commonly the Lady Elizabeth vp at hir Boke. And then he wold loke in at the galery dore, and bid my Lady Elizabeth god morrow, and so go his way.'[29]

> He wold com many mornyngs into the said Lady Elizabeths chamber, before she were redy, and sometyme before she did rise. And if she were up, he wold bid her good Morrow, and ax how she did, and strike hir vpon the bak, or on the buttocks famyliarly, and so go forth through his lodginge . . . And if she were in hir bed he wold put open the curteyns, and bid hir good morrow, and make as though he wold come at hir: And she wold go further in the bed, so that he could not com at hir; And one mornyng he strove to have kissed her in hir Bed.[30]

On another occasion, when Elizabeth (with Catherine) was walking in the garden, Seymour 'wrastled with hir and cut hir gown in c peces': 'sche was so tremed', said her servant Kate Ashley who remonstrated with her;

Elizabeth claimed that Catherine had held her while Seymour cut her gown.[31] Ashley thought that Seymour 'loved her but to well, and hadd so done a good while' and that 'the Quene was jelowse ouer hir and him, in somoche that, one tyme the Quene, suspecting the often accesse of the Admirall to the Lady Elizabeth's Grace, cam sodenly vpon them, wher they were all alone, (he having her in his Armes)'.[32] Was it Catherine's jealousy, or wish to prevent a scandal, that explains why Elizabeth was sent away in June or July 1548? Or was it just Catherine's pregnancy?[33] Seymour allegedly told John Seymour, who was bringing Elizabeth to Hatfield, to ask her 'whither her great Buttocks were grown eny les or no?' And Elizabeth wrote in veiled terms to Seymour, possibly at this time, that he did not need to send an excuse to her 'for I coulde not mistruste the not fulfillinge of your promes to prosede for want of good wyl, but only oportunite serveth not': 'I am frende not wonne with trifels, nor lost with the like.'[34] Much of the evidence of Seymour's relationship with Elizabeth comes from statements made by Kate Ashley, Elizabeth's servant, when Seymour was under investigation in early 1549 and may have been secured from Ashley through psychological torture. Yet it is difficult to see why it should have been invented. Elizabeth was certainly sent away.[35] And, if Ashley's testimony is believed, Elizabeth was certainly pondering the chances of a marriage with Seymour after the death of Queen Catherine. 'You may haue hym yf you will,' Ashley told Elizabeth, adding that Elizabeth would not refuse him if Somerset and the council agreed to it. But Elizabeth kept denying it. On another occasion when Elizabeth was playing cards, she drew Seymour 'and chast hym a way': Ashley told her she would not refuse him if Somerset and the council did bid her, 'and she sayd yes by her troth'.[36] If at another time Elizabeth said she would not have him 'because that she, that he had before, ded so Myskary', that shows rather just how seriously Elizabeth was thinking about it all. Is it significant that after Seymour's execution his close servant John Harrington gave Elizabeth his portrait with a pretty verse written on it, a picture which in the 1580s was hung in the gallery at Somerset House?[37]

After Catherine's death, Seymour was clearly interested in proposing to Elizabeth: that is the impression from a complex series of letters and messages between Elizabeth, Seymour, Ashley and Thomas Parry, the queen's cofferer. Seymour was very interested in Elizabeth's lands, boasting to Lord Russell how much they were worth, and inquiring about their location, values and conditions, and making suggestions for exchanges.[38] He asked Thomas Parry 'of the state of her graces howse, and how many persons she kept', 'what howses she hadd and what landes'; 'if it were good landes or no'; 'what state she had in the lands, for terme of lief, or how'; 'whether she hadd out her letters patentes or no'.[39] Elizabeth, anxious to have somewhere to stay in London, asked Seymour to be a suitor to Somerset on her behalf for Durham Place; Parry wrote and delivered the letter; Seymour replied that Durham Place was going to be turned into a mint but offered Elizabeth his own household. Or was this just a ploy? Parry suspected 'they used me but for an Instrument, to serve their purposes to be brought to passe, and to have entered farther, under the pretence of the Sute for a House, and such like affayres'.[40] Vertot and Leti both suggest that Seymour quickly proposed to Elizabeth.[41] 'Men did thynk that my Lord Admirall kepes the Quenes maydens together to wait vpon the Lady Elizabeth, whom he entended to mary shortly, as the bruyt went.'[42] There are hints that Somerset or the council banned Seymour from marrying Elizabeth and there were fears of another secret marriage. Lord Russell warned Seymour, 'if ye go abowte any soche thinge, ye seke the meanes to vndo your selfe', adding, 'yt is cleane agayne the kinges wille.'[43] Seymour told the marquess of Northampton 'he was credibly informed, that my Lorde Protector had said he wold clappe him in the Tower if he went to my ladie Elizabeth'.[44] A later French account suggested that Somerset got parliament to pass a bill declaring anyone who tried to marry the princesses without telling the protector and without the approval of the council guilty of *lèse-majesté*.[45] Possibly Seymour took note: when Ashley asked him if he wanted to marry Elizabeth, he replied that 'I loke not to lose my life for a wife. It has been spoken of, but it cannot be.'[46] Or possibly, as we shall see, Seymour had wider intentions.

Seymour was from the start highly dissatisfied with his standing in the regime. A would-be contemporary historian of these years wrote that 'the cause of the falling owte of the Proctector and the Admyrall was the ambytion of the Admirall and the envy he hadd that his brother should be more advaunced then he'.[47] He was incensed that his brother should be both protector of the realm and governor of the king: those functions should, he claimed, be divided and he should have one. According to Sir William Sharrington, 'he thought yt was not the Kinges will that dead ys, that eny oon man sholde haue bothe the gouernement of the King that now ys, and also the Realme. And that in tyme past, yf ther were two Unkills, being of the mothers syde, thoon sholde haue thoon, thother thother.'[48] Seymour confessed that he had searched through chronicles for precedents and discovered 'that there was in England at one tyme one Protectour and an other Regent of Fraunce and the Duke of Exeter and the Busshopp of Winchester, Governours of the Kinges persones'.[49] Two sources suggest that it was John Dudley, earl of Warwick, who put Seymour up to this, promising him his support if he raised the matter in council; when Seymour did so, Somerset rose without saying a word and the council meeting ended.[50] Other sources suggest that Seymour was dissuaded from pressing the point after it was pointed out to him that he had signed the instrument making Somerset Governor of the king's person with his own hand.[51] Somerset explained his reluctance to accept his brother's demand by pointing to the dangers of repeating the discord between Humphrey, duke of Gloucester, and Cardinal Beaufort.[52]

Certain sources hint that Seymour was not satisfied and began intriguing. During the Scottish military campaign in summer 1547, Seymour, despite his office of Admiral, stayed in London while his brother went north to fight: 'howe being admirall he would not goe in person in the iorney againste Scotland'.[53] (A year later he again failed to serve, staying at Sudeley and just sending out orders.)[54] Somerset won a smashing victory at Pinkie but then left the borders very hastily without pursuing his military advantage. Almost certainly that was in order to counter his brother's plotting. Somerset rushed back because 'il apprit, par un courier qu'on lui dépêcha exprès, que l'amiral son frère formait à la cour un puissant parti contre lui, et qu'il avait pris des mesures secrètes avec le roi même; pour lui enlever la charge de gouverneur de ce jeune prince'. In Somerset's absence Seymour had won over men in the privy chamber.[55] In 1549 it was claimed against him that 'by corrupting with gieftes and faier promises diverse of the privie chamber he went about to allure his highnes to condescend and agree to the same his most heynous and perillous purposes'.[56] Some of the privy chamber, a later source suggested, had become Seymour's 'pensioners'.[57] Seymour confessed that 'he gave money to ii or iii of them which were about the King' and also to the grooms of the chamber.[58] Seymour's chief man in the privy chamber was John Fowler. They chatted together repeatedly, with Seymour frequently asking Fowler to remember him to Edward. 'Many and sundrie tymes,' testified Fowler, Seymour 'wolde com into the privie Buttrie and drinke there alone and aske me whether the kyng wold say any thing of him.'[59] Fowler got the king to write to Seymour when his uncle was away in the country and often told him to be grateful for Seymour's gifts. It was probably at this time in Somerset's absence that Seymour was able to see the king, play with him and spoil him; it was at this time that he got the king to write a letter in support of his marriage. He tried to persuade Edward that the responsibilities of protector and governor were incompatible – when the protector was away with the army, there was no governor for the king –

and possibly prepared a letter which he hoped Edward would sign stating that Seymour should be governor. Seymour was also helped by John Cheke and Thomas Wroth. Fowler, Cheke and Wroth were blamed after the plot of summer 1547, though Fowler and Cheke at least soon recovered their standing.[60] Seymour's contacts with them show his awareness of the importance of gaining influence, if not control, over Edward: even a king who was a minor was potentially influential and could sign letters and grants. If Somerset's return was enough to halt Seymour's immediate hopes, he nonetheless continued to try to persuade Edward to agree to his plan to secure the governorship. He urged Edward to take upon himself the ruling of his kingdom. He told him that within four years he would be sixteen, and 'Rewler of his own thynges'; that he trusted that by that time the king would himself help his men with such things as fell within his gift. Edward testified how Seymour said 'I was to bashfull in myne owne matters, and asked me, why I dyd not speak to beare rule as well asother kyngs do. I sayd, I neded not, for I was well enough.'[61] Undaunted by Edward's reticence, Seymour asked Fowler 'to put the kinges majeste . . . in mynde' if Somerset criticised him to the king, and to inform Cheke and Wroth.[62] He attempted to get him to sign a letter on his behalf for the parliament that was meeting in autumn 1547. He sent John Cheke to take it to the king. It read: 'Mi Lordes I prai yow fauor my Lord Admiral mine vncles sute which he wil make vnto yow.' But on Cheke's advice, Edward refused to sign it. Edward said that during the parliament Seymour had come to him asking him to write a thing for him, claiming it was nothing ill but for the queen. Edward responded with precocious discretion that if Seymour's suit were good, the lords would allow it; if it were ill, then he would not write.[63] That all this related to Seymour's ambitions is suggested by his later confession that just before he drew up that bill, he 'cawsed the King to be moved by Mr Fowler whether he coulde be contented that he shulde have the governaunce of him as Mr Stanope had'.[64] Sir Michael Stanhope, Somerset's brother-in-law, was loyally guarding the king. But Somerset was sufficiently worried by all this intriguing to have the letters patent declaring him protector and governor confirmed in parliament. Perhaps that is also why Somerset chose to have special precedence in the House of Lords, sitting alone 'upon the myddes of the bench or stole stondyng nexte on the right hand of our siege reall'. It is not surprising in turn that Seymour said 'he mislyked that he was not placed in the parlament howse as woon of the king his unkylls'.[65] He continued to discuss the possibility that he might become governor. He talked of advancing Edward's age of majority. He boasted to the marquess of

Dorset and the earl of Rutland that within a year (or two years, or three years) the king should rule his own affairs. But Seymour did not have that much contact with the king. Fowler saw him far more often than Seymour: that is why he was so important for Seymour. Seymour saw Edward in summer 1547, just before and during Somerset's absence on the Scottish borders; he saw him again during parliament later that year. The various conversations that Seymour had with the king may well all date to those periods: but even if they took place at other times as well, nonetheless the impression is that they were scattered and intermittent. Somerset evidently largely succeeded in keeping his brother away from the king. Seymour continued to exploit his contacts with Fowler and Cheke to send money to Edward, although it cannot be established exactly when. On several occasions sums of £5 and £10, and as high as £40, were given by Seymour to Fowler and Cheke for giving to the king. Seymour encouraged Edward to write to him for money which he did, for example, in on 26 June 1548: 'My lord send me for Latimer as much as ye think good and deliver it to Fowler.'[66] Seymour had told the king 'ye are a beggarly king ye haue no monie to play or to geue'.[67] He described how Edward moaned 'my Unkell off Sumerset deylyth very hardly with me and kepyth me so strayt that I cane not have mony at my wylle but my Lord Admyrall both sendes me mony and gyves me mony'.[68] Whether that was true or not, Seymour was clearly trying to use Edward's understandable desire for more spending money to insinuate himself into his favour. If Seymour and Edward had lived longer, such a relationship might have seen significant developments.

As we have already noted, Seymour believed that he could use parliaments to further his purposes. He tried to recruit several noblemen to support his various causes, often speaking with them on their way to or from parliament: the marquesses of Dorset and Northampton, the earls of Rutland and Southampton, Lords Russell and Clinton. For example, Seymour told Clinton that he intended to put a bill into parliament. 'He ment to get som auctoryte that waye whyche he thought otherwyse he could not attayne.' After he had been in the parliament chamber for an hour 'he callyd me owte and after he had talkyd with some of the lordes ther he requyred me agen to gyue my consent to the byll and make hym as many frendes as I cold'.[69] Was Seymour the keener to lobby because he was 'an il speker himself'?[70] He also attempted to assemble a group of associates and servants in the Commons.[71] In autumn 1547 he threatened to disrupt the parliament. He was accused of saying: 'I haue herd spekying of a black parlament and they vsse me as they doo begyn by goddes preshios soule I wyll make the blakiste parleament that euer was in England.'[72] Somerset's letters patent of 12 March 1547 had confirmed Henry VIII's alleged oral appointment of Somerset as governor and protector: now Seymour made a great fuss over the bill confirming those letters patent in the light of the noble victory that God had given Somerset over the Scots, presumably disguising his real reasons for opposing it by 'surmysing that he [Somerset] would therby geve away Callies': our source went on to note 'what sturre was in the parliament by that meanes'.[73] There are hints that such a bill ran into difficulties. Read three times in the Lords between 1 and 9 November, it was replaced by another bill which was read in the Lords on 19 November, and sent to the Commons 'cum provisione eidem connectenda'. There it was read four times between 22 November and 12 December. Seymour and the marquess of Dorset dissented when it returned to the Lords on 14 December.[74] Very likely it was to block this bill that Seymour tried to get a letter from the king.[75] According to the charges in 1549, Seymour 'wrote a lettre with his own hande, whiche lettre the kinges majestie shuld haue subscribed or writen again after that Copie to the parliament howse'; then he had resolved to take that letter into the Commons himself, 'and there with his fauvorers and adherentes before prepared to haue made a broile or tumulte and vprore'.[76] He seems also to have been angry at the repealing of an act for speaking of words – presumably the Treason Act – 'wherin my lord admirall wold a had a promyse that men shold not haue had lyberty to a spokyn any thing ayenst the quene'.[77]

Seymour was very much aware of the need to build local support. The advice he gave those noblemen whom he hoped to recruit to his cause is an eloquent account of the operation of landed power. Northampton said how in early 1548 Seymour had advised him 'to go and set vpp howse in the Northe countrey where as my landes laye thinkyng it to be muche for my commodite'.[78] Doreset told how in the late summer of that year 'thadmyrall diuising with me to make me stronge in my countrey, aduised me to kepe a good house'.[79] Seymour himself allegedly boasted 'it is good abiding at home, and to make mery with our neighbors in the contry', telling Northampton 'he liked well' country life.[80] To Dorset he gave more detailed advice. He should not trust the gentlemen of the county too much 'for they have sumwhat to loose'. Instead,

> I wold rather aduise you to make muche of the head yeomen and frankelyns of the cuntreye, specially those that be the ringleaders, for they be the men that be best hable to perswade the multitude and may best bring the number and therefore I wold wishe you to make muche of them, and to goo to their houses, nowe to oon and nowe to an other, caryeng with you a flagon or two of wyne,

and a pasty of veneson, and to use a familiaritie with them, for so shall you cause them to love you, and be assured to haue them at your commaundemente.

'This maner (I may tell you),' Seymour continued, 'I entende to vse mieslf.'[81] He said much the same to Rutland, advising him 'to make moche of the gentilmen in my countrey, but more of suche honeste and welthy yemen as were ringleaders in good townes ... as for the gentilmen ther is no gret trust to be had to them, but for the other making moche of them and somtymes dyning lyke a good fellow in one of their houses I shuld by that gentill enterteynment allure all their good willes to go with me wither I woolde leade them.'[82] Seymour's conception of local power was competitive. He advised Dorset 'to kepe my house in Warwikeshire ... because yt war a cuntrey full of men, but chiefly to match with my lorde of Warwike, so as he should not be hable to matche with me there'.[83] Rutland said Seymour 'thought me to be so frended in my country as I was hable inough to matche with my lorde of Shrewesbury'.[84] One of the charges against Seymour was that 'he hath parted as yt were in his imaginacion and entent the Realme, to set noble men to contervale suche other noble men as he thought wolde let his devilishe purposes and so labored and travelid to be strong at all his devises'.[85] Sir William Sharington testified how Seymour

> wold divers tymes loke vpon a charte of England which he hath and declare vnto this Examinate how strong he was and how far his lands and domynions did stretche; and how it lay all to gither betwene his house and the Holt and what shire and places were for hym; and that this way he was emong his frends; so notyng the places and when he cam to Bristow, he wold say; this is my Lord Protectors; and of other, that is my Lord of Warwikes; to the which two, this Examinate knoweth he had no great affection.

Riding from the marquess of Dorset, Seymour 'vsed sondry tymes to shewe me as we rodde togithers the cowntrees rounde about sayeng all these which dwell in thes parties be my frendes'. 'And so he did vaunt ... that he had as great a nombre of gentlemen that loved hym, as eny noble man in England.' 'And further said that he thought that he had more gentlemen that louved hym than the Lord Protector had and vpon that he said he was happye that hath freends in this world what so ever shuld chaunce'.[86] Such evidence was echoed in the charges against him: 'he hath parted as yt were in his imaginacion and entente the Realme, to set noble men to contervale suche other noble men as he thought wolde let his devilishe purposes'; 'he ment to have matched and sett one Noble man against such an other Noble man, as he thought he cowlde never compasse and wynne to assent to his factyon and false conspiracye.'[87] Talking about his office of Lord Admiral, he boasted that 'nowe I shall haue the rule of a good sort of shippes and men.' 'And I tell yow it is a good thing to haue the rule of men.'[88] Discussing his lands in the Marches with Parry, Seymour boasted how they were 'of goodly manredde'.[89] In the light of such boasts, it is not surprising that he was accused of retaining. It was alleged that 'he hath reteynid yonge gentlemen and hed yemen to a great multitude and farre above suche nomber as is permitted by the lawes and statutes of the realm or were otherwise necessarie or convenient for yor service, place, or estate to the fortifyeng yor self towardes all yor evill ententes and purposes.'[90] Moreover, 'he hath not onely studied and imagined how to haue rule of a nombre or men his handes, but he hath attempted and gotten diverse stuardshipps of noble mens landes, and the manredes to make his partie stronge for his purposes.'[91] And he 'especially moved the noble men and who he thought not to be contented to departe into ther contreys and make them selfes strong'.[92] All this offers remarkably vivid insights into a world of lordship often thought to have disappeared by the mid sixteenth century. But how far were Seymour's boasts matched in reality?

Seymour undoubtedly tried to create a following among other noblemen: as one of the charges put it, 'he hath labored and gone about to combyne and confederate him self with som persones to haue a parte and faction in a redynes'.[93] Henry Grey (executed 1554), marquess of Dorset was won over by Seymour's promise to marry his daughter, Jane, to the king. Harington, Seymour's servant, came to him immediately after Henry VIII's death, and told him how Seymour was likely to hold great authority and that being the king's uncle 'and placed as he was', he might 'doo me much pleasure', urging him to go to him and 'entre a more frendeship and familiaritie with him'. If he agreed to put his daughter Jane in Seymour's household, he would secure her marriage to the young king, was the gist of Harington's message, but it was conveyed by hints. He described Jane 'as handsom a lady as eny in England, and that she might be Wife to eny prince in christen, and that, if the kinges Majestie, when he came to Age wold mary within the realme, it was as likely he wold be there, as in eny other Place'; he continued that if she were in Seymour's household 'she were as like ... to haue a gretter and better turn, then he wold thynk; and that he durst not tell what it was; and that beyng kept in my lord's hows, who was vncle to the Kyng, yt were never the wors for hyr; and that my Lord wold be right glad, if the king's majestie could like eny in his howse'. So Dorset went to Seymour within seven days and heard similar arguments from him.

Harington did not deny having seen Dorset or having urged him to be friendly with Seymour, but claimed he did it without any instruction from Seymour.[94] Jane was duly sent to Seymour's household. At the same time Seymour lent Dorset money, sending £500 as soon as he despatched Jane, and taking no bond – except Jane herself.[95] Seymour may have fancied her himself: he told Thomas Parry 'ther hath bene a talke of late (no Force) they say now I shall mary my Lady Jane'; adding to it 'I tell you this but meryly, I tell you this but meryly'.[96] Immediately after Queen Catherine's death Seymour, distraught and fearing he would have to dissolve his whole household, sent Jane back to Dorset, but very soon was anxious to have her back. Dorset testified how shortly afterwards Seymour 'came to my house himself and was soo ernestly in hand with me and my wief that in the end because he wold haue no naye, we were contented she shoulde againe returne to his house'. Sir William Sharington 'travailed as ernestly with my wief' as Seymour had with him. On that occasion, said Dorset, Seymour 'renued his promise vnto me for the mariage of my doughter to the kinges majeste'.[97] Later in autumn 1548 Jane became another cause of contention between Seymour and his brother. Seymour told Harington that there would be 'muche ado' for her since Somerset and his wife would do what they could to persuade the marquess to give her to them.[98] Looking back, Dorset said that he 'was so seduced and aveugled by the said Lord Admirall, that he promised him that except the kinges Majesties Person only, he wold spend his lief and bloode in his the said Lorde Admiralles parte against all men'.[99] But Harington said that when asked whose part he would take if Somerset and Seymour fell out, Dorset had replied that 'he wold take his Part, that toke the kinges Parte'.[100] Earlier, Dorset had joined Seymour in dissenting from the bill confirming Somerset's letters patent as Protector in November–December 1547.[101] Dorset remained close to Seymour until Seymour's arrest at Seymour's house in the week before, riding with him from parliament on the day of his committal.[102] Seymour also tried to recruit the earl of Rutland, the marquess of Northampton and the earl of Southampton. William Parr (d. 1571), marquess of Northampton, brother of Seymour's wife Catherine Parr, testified how in early 1548 Seymour, supposing that he was not content (possibly because of the way his wish to remarry while his wife, who had left him, was still alive was being handled), 'vsing me also very freendly . . . aswell in dedes as also in wordes, saying I shuld lacke nether money nor any other thing that he had', gave him 'a certaign specialtie of good valewe' and 'shewed me muche freendshipp and gentleness'.[103] Just before his arrest Seymour confided his fears in Northampton and wanted him to take a message to

Somerset in which Seymour set out his terms for answering the council's questions.[104] Thomas Wriothesley (d. 1550), earl of Southampton, testified how on their way to dinner during parliament, 'after a litle comen talk' Seymour said to him, 'ha my lord of Southampton, you were well handeled touching yor office. Why shuld you not haue it again?'[105] That must have referred to his surrender of the Lord Chancellorship and unsuccessful resistance to Somerset's seizure of the protectorate in January–March 1547; and Southampton would again be prominent when Somerset fell in autumn 1549.[106] Seymour clearly attempted to win over noblemen. In his defence, however, Harington declared that while Seymour might 'peradventure' say to him that he or he was his friend, 'but to say, that eny Man were his assurid, or that I have this, or this Man assurid, or eny Thyng foundyng to makyng a Party, he never hard hym speke such Thyngs in his lief'. And according to Robert Tyrwhit, Seymour recognised his dependence on the crown, asking 'ame not I mayd by the Kyng? Hav not I all that I hav by the Kynge?'[107]

What of Seymour's country living? Since 1536 he had been steward of Holt, Chirk, Bromfield and Yale in the Welsh Marches, and in 1547 he had received further grants of land there and in adjacent counties, including the lordship of Sudeley, Gloucestershire, and the manor of Bewdley, Shropshire. He also received ex-Howard lands in Bramber and other parts of Sussex.[108] (Is it significant that these grants were made on 19 August, just before Somerset left for the Scottish borders? Was Strype right to suggest that Somerset was trying to bridle his brother with liberality?[109]) The patent rolls for 1547–8 suggest vigorous buying, selling and leasing of lands. Soon he was building at Sudeley Castle, Gloucestershire, and at Bromham. More significantly still, Seymour was fortifying Holt Catle, Denbighshire, 'a goodly castel', at a key crossing point on the Dee and astride 'the gateway from north Wales to the south'. In a survey most probably made during the reign of Henry VIII, it was described as 'beyng more strongly builded with stone and tymber then stately lodgeing or convenyant', with a 'towre very strongly builte upon a rocke' and surrounded by a moat 150 feet broad connected to the river. Within the castle there were 'all howses of office mete for a prynce to kepe his house yn'. It could serve as a focus for the prosperous gentry of Flint and Denbighshire and for tenants holding their lands by semi-military tenures, in an area rich in men.[110] Here Richard Fitzalan (d. 1397), earl of Arundel, had held out for six weeks against Robert de Vere in 1387 and defied John of Gaunt in 1393; here Sir William Stanley (executed in 1495) and William Brereton (executed in 1536) had both made their base.[111] The potential was significant. But did Seymour succeed in creating an affinity? John Harington remained loyal to Seymour even after Seymour's arrest: 'He labors to haue byn in the towre with the Lord Admyrall,' dryly noted Petre under his answers.[112] In 1582, for the benefit of his son he

> wrote with his owne hand the names of those who were then living of the old Admiraltie (so he called them that had bene my lords men and there were then xxxiiii of them living) of which many were knights and men of more reverence than himselfe, and some were but meane men, as armorers, artificers, keepers, and farmers, and yet the memorie of his service was such a band among them all of kindnesse as the best of them disdained not the poorest and the meaner had recourse to the greatest for their countenance and ayd in their honest causes.[113]

And his son then saluted Seymour's memory in verse: 'Temp'rate at home, yet kept great state with staie / And noble house that fed more mouthes with meet, / Than some advanced on higher steppes to stande.'[114] Yet one must suspect the exaggerations of nostalgia here. Elsewhere various of Seymour's neighbours complained to Somerset about Seymour's activities.[115] And there is virtually no detailed evidence that Seymour seriously attempted to create a following in North Wales or the Marches, whatever his dreams, whatever his boasts that he could raise ten thousand men.[116]

Did he try to turn those dreams into reality in late 1548 and early 1549? On 24 November 1548 he ordered his steward Edward Rous to make preparations for beer to be taken to Bewdley where he was intending to keep his house from the following May into summer: Rous was to prepare 'all the housys ther sayinge that for the tyme of his contynewance ther he wolde kepe as great a house and of large expences as he did in the quynes lyffe tyme'.[117] Was he exploiting his office as Admiral to get money? He was accused of maintaining pirates and taking a share of their spoil.

> Diverse of the hed pirates being brought vnto yow, yow have let the said pirates go agayn free vnto the seas, taking away from the takers of them not onely all their commoditie and profit, but from the true owners of the shipps and goodes all suche as ever cam into the pirates handes, as though yow were authorised to be the chief pirate, and to have all the advauntage thei could bring vnto yow.

Goods taken by pirates were daily seen in Seymour's household where they were distributed amongst his servants and friends.[118] He asked Sir William Sharington, under-treasurer of the mint at Bristol, who had been manufacturing testoons for his own pocket, and was possibly hoping to be protected from the consequences by high-placed friends (Seymour had described him as 'my frend' in 1547 and Sharington had sat in parliament for Bramber later that year, probably as a result of Seymour's influence),[119] whether he could coin money for him. He asked him 'how muche money will find ten thousand men a moneth, and vppon that accompting a whill with himself, he dyd cast that after the rate of vi^d a daye for a man, x$^{m\ li}$ or thereaboutes wold serve'.[120] According to a charge in the draft list of accusations but not retained in the final list, Seymour 'removed also his howse to the Holt at Christmas last past'.[121] In the act of attainder it was claimed that Seymour had put the king's castle of Holt 'wherof he had the keping even nowe a late in a redynes, and there cawsed to be prepared a great furnyture of wheat malte bestes'.[122] Some light on what Seymour was planning appears in the part of this charge that was retained. Seymour's deputy, steward and other officers at Holt had

> against Christmas last past at the saide Holte made suche provision of wheate, malt, beefes and other suche thinges as be necessarie for the sustenaunce of a great nomber of men, making also by all the meanes possible a greate masse of money, in so much that all the countray dothe greatly marvaile at yt, and the more becausse your servantes have spred rumours abrode that the Kinges Majeste was ded; wheruppon the countrey is in a great m... dowbte and expectacion, loking for some broile, and wolde have bene more if at this present by your apprehension it had not bene staied.[123]

What this shows are suspicions that Seymour was planning to use Holt Castle in Denbighshire as a strongpoint from which he could defy his brother. Perhaps he also had in mind the Isles of Scilly and Lundy as a final refuge.[124] What was Seymour hoping to do? A later French account offers an answer. he 'résolut de tout hasarder pour se rendre maître de la princesse et du gouvernement'. Secretly he assembled his friends; 'on convint qu'il falloit enlever le roi et la princesse; que l'amiral l'épouseroit aussitot aux yeux du prince, dont la présence tiendroit lieu de consentement et qu'il se serviroit ensuite de son autorité pour détruire celle du duc et pour lui enlever la régence'. It was to Holt Castle that he hoped to take Edward and Elizabeth.[125] Significantly when in custody Seymour denied 'that euer I went about to take the kyng from my lord my brother by force; I never ment it, nor thought it.'[126] If he had hoped to have custody of the king it was only with the consent of the realm.[127] Yet Fowler testified how Seymour had once come to St James's at 9 a.m. and voiced his surprise that there were so few people there: 'a man might stele away the king now for there cam more with me than is in all the howse besides.'[128] And Seymour himself admitted that about Easter 1548 he had said to Fowler 'that if he might have the King in his custodie ... he wolde be glad, and that he thought that a man might bring him through the Galery to his chamber, and so to his howse,' but this, Seymour insisted, 'he spoke merely meaning no hurte.'[129] Interestingly, when Seymour was persuading Dorset to send back his daughter to his household, he told Dorset that 'he durst warraunt me' that Edward would marry Jane, 'if he might ones get the kinge at libertye.'[130] If Seymour was indeed plotting to kidnap Edward and Elizabeth, marry Elizabeth and have himself made Protector in place of his brother, it is not surprising that he was arrested and tried once his plans were discovered. How was he found out? One letter offers a clue. This was written by John Burcher in Strasbourg to Henry Bullinger on 15 February 1549. Burcher had most horrible intelligence to pass on. Seymour 'has attempted, by an unheard of treachery and cruelty, to destroy with his own impious hands, in the deep silence of the night, our innocent king.' Burcher went on to describe how Seymour obtained from one of the king's chamberlains who knew his plans a key which opened into the royal bedchamber. Seymour went there at dead of night together with some servants. But then things went wrong. In the space between the door through which he entered and the king's chamber was a little dog, 'the most faithful guardian of the youth', who had that night been accidentally shut out of the chamber. When the dog saw Seymour moving towards the door of the king's chamber, 'he betrayed the murderer by his barking'. Seymour killed the dog and was on the point of killing Edward when one of the king's guards, roused by the noise, came out after waking the other bodyguards. When he saw Seymour he asked him what he was doing: Seymour said he was checking that the prince was securely guarded. But that excuse was unavailing, and the next day Seymour was in the Tower.[131] Was Burcher's intelligence in part inaccurate? Was not Seymour trying to kidnap rather than to murder the king, for which he could have no motive? Or is this fanciful evidence? Wightman, Seymour's servant, testified that a week before his arrest, Seymour 'vsed ... diuers nightes to repayre frome his house to the courte after nyne of the clocke at night', leaving Dorset and Huntingdon behind at his house. Was he preparing a kidnap?[132]

From Dorset's and Northampton's depositions, it appears that Seymour was committed to the Tower after Henry (1526–63), second earl of Rutland, had first been examined by Somerset and then made a declaration against Seymour to the council. What Rutland said and why remains obscure. Seymour had talked to him the previous summer about advancing the declaration of the king's majority and denounced Somerset's bill confirming his letters patent, hoping that he would in due course have Rutland's voice in the parliament.[133] And Seymour told Dorset about 'such comunicacion' that there had been between Rutland and himself, 'where of he made a longe discourse'. What they talked about is unknowable. Had Rutland been so shocked by Seymour's schemes that he had gone to the council? Did he give evidence that Seymour was planning to kidnap the king, and did this reinforce that interpretation of Seymour's nightime visits to court? However that may be, Seymour seems to have got wind of Rutland's statement from one of his servants whose brother was a servant of Rutland. Just before he was committed to the Tower, he told Northampton that he would be called before the council that day to answer articles that Rutland had declared against him. Seymour said he was willing to answer all things if left at liberty and if the Lord Privy Seal (John (d. 1555), Lord Russell) and Mr Comptroller (Sir William Paget (d. 1563)) were sent to him, but would not answer if shut up, presumably if he were imprisoned. He struck Dorset, who visited him at his house after dinner, as 'muche afrayed' of going to the council and he appears to have thought of securing Mr Comptroller as a pledge, claiming defiantly that otherwise he would not go to the council. It was left to Dorset's brother Thomas to advise Seymour rather to trust Somerset, since he was 'a man of muche mercy' and, in any case, 'if he list to have you, it is not this house that canne kepe you, though you had x tymes so many men as you haue'.[134] Possibly he refused to come to the council when summoned: one of the charges against him was how 'being sent for by thauthoritie to answere to suche thinges as were thought to be refourmed in him, he refused to com, to a verie evill example of disobedience'.[135] That day Seymour also called Sharington to him, thinking that the council were going to see if they could get anything out of him. Had Sharington's arrest for coining led to the discovery of any agreements between the two men and particularly of Seymour's grand plans for manufacturing testoons to pay a private army? Was that what had led to conciliar inquiries?[136] Seymour was arrested on 17 January 1549.[137] Examined on 25 January, he wrote an abject submission to Somerset on 27 January. Many were interrogated: several noblemen, of whom the earl of Rutland had been one of the first (he was examined by Somerset and then declared certain articles against Seymour to the council); Elizabeth's servants, Thomas Parry and Katherine Ashley. The Lord Great Master (William Paulet (d. 1572), Lord St John, later marquess of Winchester) and Mr Denny (one of the chief gentlemen of the king's privy chamber) came to interrogate Parry, who was terrified.[138] Both Parry and Ashley were put in the Tower.[139] Elizabeth was interrogated by Paget, Denny and Tyrwhit.[140] Tyrwhit was convinced that 'ther hayth beyne some secrett Promys, betwyne my Lady, Mestrys Aschley, and the Cofferer, never to confesse to deythe': only the king or Somerset would extract it from her.[141] Meanwhile Parry confessed in the Tower,[142] prompting Elizabeth to condemn him as a 'false wretche, and sayd he had promyssed he wold never confesse yt to Deyth'.[143] Ashley also confessed in part.[144] 'They all synge onne Songe, and so I thynke they could not do, vnles they had sett the nott be for.'[145] But Elizabeth would not confess and claimed forgetfulness, protested against the unpleasant things said against her and asked for a proclamation against such rumours.[146] But what was admitted then by Ashley, Parry, and by several noblemen and servants of Seymour largely provides the evidence for Seymour's activities over the previous two years. Some members of the council were clearly turning this information into articles against him. Seymour was examined on 18 February; the council disussed the matter on 22 February; Seymour was examined again on 23 February, but refused to answer unless his accusers stood before him, and would not even subscribe the answers he had earlier begun to make. On 24 February the councillors reported to the king, Somerset 'declaring how sorowfull a case this was unto hym', but regarding his duty to the king greater than that to his brother. The councillors sent once again to Seymour, who would answer no more than three of the articles. On 25 February a bill was introduced into parliament, unopposed in the Lords (Somerset was allowed for natural pity's sake to be absent), but 'very much debated and argued' in the Commons, in which lawyers declared that Seymour's offences 'were in the compasse of High Treason'. On 5 March the bill was passed, the Commons 'being marvailous full almost to the number of iiii^c persons, not x or xii at the most giving their nays tharunto'. On 19 March, Seymour was executed.[147] To the end Seymour continued his plotting. A later writer noted 'howe yt was saied he hadd writen with cyfre of an oriege in paper, and saved hytt in his shooe and being on scaffold willed his men to remember what he saied, to him, whoe dysclosed yt'.[148] Latimer denounced Seymour in a sermon.

> The man beyng in the tower wrote certayne papers whyche I saw miselfe. They were two lyttle ones, one to my Ladye Maryes grace, and an other to my Lady Elizabeths grace, tendynge to thys ende, that they shoulde conspyre agaynst my Lord Protectours grace ... [these two papers] ... were founde a showe of hys. They were sowen betwene the solles of a veluet showe. He made his ynke so craftely and with suche workemanshyp as the lyke hath not sene ... He made his pen of the aglet of a poynte that he plucked from his hosse, and thus wrought these letters so sedytiouslye.

Latimer accused Seymour of religious indifference. When Queen Catherine had ordained twice daily prayers in her household, Seymour 'gets him out of the way like a mole digging in the earth'. He continued by casting doubt on Seymour's subsequent fate.

> And as touching the kind of his death, whether he be saved or no, I refer that to God only. What God can do, I cannot tell. I will not deny, but that he may in the twinkling of an eye save a man, and turn his heart. What he did, I cannot tell. And when a man hath two strokes with an axe, who can tell but that between two strokes he doth repent? It is very hard to judge. Well, I will not go so nigh to work: but this I will say, if they ask me, what I think of his death, that he died very dangerously, irksomely, horribly ... He was a man the farthest from the fear of God that ever I knew or heard of in England.[149]

How far should the conventionally pious verses supposedly written by Seymour before his death mitigate Latimer's harsh judgment?

> Forgetting God to love a kynge
> Hath been my rod, or else nothynge
> In this frail lyfe, being a blaste
> Of care and stryfe till yt be paste;
> Yet God did call me in my pryde
> Leste I shulde fall and from hym slyde
> For whom he loves he must correct
> That they may be of his electe.
> Then deathe haste thee, thou shalt me gaine
> Immortally with Hym to raigne.
> Lord! sende the kinge in years as Noye
> In governinge this realme in joye
> And after thys frayl lyfe such grace
> That in thy bliss he may find place.[150]

Was Seymour brought down by his brother? Was their relationship marked by discord, then suspicion and finally extreme hatred?[151] Was Somerset pushed into reluctant hostility by his wife or by 'makebates' or some 'crafty merchant'?[152] Elizabeth later thought on these lines. 'I have harde in my time of many cast away, for want of comminge to the presence of thir Prince'. She had heard Somerset say that 'if his brother had been suffered to speak with him, he had never suffered; but the persuasions were made to him so great, that he was brought in belief that he could not live safely if the Admiral lived, and that made him give his consent to his death.'[153] But Elizabeth may not have been an impartial witness. More is known about Seymour's feelings than Somerset's. Seymour claimed just before his arrest that Somerset was very jealous of him and increasingly frightened, recently going 'better furnisshed with men aboute him than he was wont'.[154] Seymour seems, however, to have feared the council more than Somerset – 'I am suer I can have no hurt, if thei do me right; thei can not kyll me, except thei do me wrong' – and appeared confident that Somerset would never commit him to the Tower.[155] On the day before Seymour's arrest the council had 'great secret conferences ... in the garden'; and it is striking how full a part the council took in the examinations, discussions and decisions of mid-late Febuary.[156] Just how large a part was Somerset playing in all this? Leti's account, in which Somerset is seen as merely reacting to teach Seymour a lesson, but being pushed into harsher courses by other councillors and by the sheer weight of information emerging against Seymour, seems worth pondering. Was the earl of Warwick behind Seymour's fall? Has he been jealous of Seymour since he had relinquished the Admiralty to him in early 1547? Seymour boasted how 'he was as glad of that office as of any office within the realm and that no man shuld take that office from him but that he shuld take his lif also'.[157] Had Warwick felt his loss as strongly? Had he provoked the quarrels between the two brothers by encouraging Seymour's ambitions to become Governor? Seymour confessed how 'he *harde*, and uppon that sought out certain precedentes'.[158] There is evidence that there was no love lost between them: Seymour wanted Dorset to keep house in Warwickshire to match with Warwick; there were rumours that they were not friends; they quarrelled over Stratford-upon-Avon. A later would-be historian noted 'howe Warewick was lodged with Somersett in his howse for feare of his brother the Admerall'. Some lines written after discussions between Seymour and Rutland were delivered to Warwick, and perhaps Warwick urged that Seymour be struck down hard in 1549.[159] Clearly there was strong pressure on the judges to deal with Seymour firmly. According to a would-be historian's notes, when the examination of Seymour's treason was committed to Montagu, the king's serjeant and attorney, and Gooderick and Gosnall, the latter two doubted whether Seymour's offences involving Sharington were treason. Montagu told them not to stick on that point. Gooderick retorted that he should then be tried by the common law. Montagu thought it better done by parliament, lest if Seymour were condemned by common law they should be blamed when the king came of age: if it was done by parliament, they would be discharged.[160] What that suggests is a sense that Seymour's behaviour had been treasonous even if it would be difficult technically to convict him of treason in particular points: it was his plans and boasts, more than his actions, that condemned him. More telling still than any fratricidal bitterness or any factional stirring seems to be quite simply what was found out about Seymour's activities and ambitions during the investigations in January and February 1549. He had done and said quite enough to have provoked not only his brother, but all his fellow councillors. 'After divers examinacions of those whiche for suspicion and maters laied against them in the lorde Admiralles case were committed to the Tower', it appeared to Somerset and 'all' the council that the divers and sundry articles of high treason sorely charged against him 'semid so manifestly proved against him by diverse wais that it appearid not able to be avoided but he shulde be giltie of them'.[161] If in addition he had been caught in the act of kidnapping the young king, it becomes even less necessary to seek out 'factional' motives for his downfall.

What then is the significance of Seymour's behaviour? What his actions and boastings vividly show is where power lay, or was thought to lie, in mid Tudor England. At one level that remains true even if Seymour was in fact innocent. He married a dowager-queen and perhaps hoped to marry a royal princess. He sought a position close to the king and exploited his friendship with several members of the privy chamber. He tried to abuse the youthful goodwill of the king by giving him money and getting him to write letters in his favour. He used parliaments to stir up opposition against his brother and to recruit noblemen to his cause. He was keen to acquire lands and jewels and money. He fortified his castle at Holt. He spoke vividly of retaining and leading men. Finally he attempted, in a gambler's last throw, to seize Edward and Elizabeth. Seymour in the event failed. He tried to do too much too quickly and there was as much rhetoric as action. He won insufficient support among his fellow counsellors: even if Dorset, Northampton, Rutland and Southampton were keener than they allowed themselves to appear in their interrogations, Seymour never won any wholehearted commitment. He hardly had any coherent programme, even if he agreed with his wife's criticism of the distribution of crown lands[162] or attacked Somerset's Scottish invasion of 1547 for risking the loss of a great number of men and for costing 'a great summ of Money in vayn'[163] or suggested that Somerset would give up Calais to the French,[164] or declared generally that 'he myslyked the procedinges of the Lord Protector and counsayle' and sought 'the alteracion of the state and ordre of the Realme'.[165] Yet suppose that he had delayed his plots until the autumn of 1549, and he might have gathered more support after the continuing military difficulties and the serious popular rebellions of the summer. Seymour moved too soon. And his failure was as much a matter of temperament. It was very difficult, and it had always been very dangerous, for a nobleman to risk launching a rebellion. Dissident nobles might talk of joining in, but just like the gentry they could not be greatly relied upon because 'they have sumwhat to loose'.[166] A successful politician in the mid sixteenth century needed a more subtle aproach: Seymour should have been more patient. Wightman, his servant, testified how 'if he had oones conceyved opynion by his owne perswasions, neyther Lawyer nor other could tourne him'.[167] His fiery nature and his soaring ambition told against him. 'This day,' said Elizabeth on hearing of his execution, 'died a man with much wit, and very litle judgment.'[168]

NOTES

I should wish to thank Dr S. Adams, Mr C. S. L. Davies, Mr P. J. Gwyn, Dr R. A. Houlbrooke, Mr T. B. Pugh, Mr H. James and Mrs J. Loach for their comments. I should also wish to record my thanks to the British Academy and the Faculty of Arts, University of Southampton, for grants towards the cost of the preparation of this paper. *Note:* Place of publication is London unless otherwise stated.

1   Earlier accounts include L. B. Smith, *Treason in Tudor England: Politics and Paranoia* (1986), pp. 20–35; R. L. Davids and A. D. K. Hawkyard, sub Seymour in S. T. Bindoff, ed., *The History of Parliament: The House of Commons 1509–1558* (3 vols., 1982), iii. 297–301; B. N. de Luna, *The Queen Declined: An Interpretation of Willobie his Avisa* (Oxford, 1970), pp. 47–54, 137–52 (though the relationship of the text to Seymour is speculative) (I owe this reference to Mr H. James); W. K. Jordan, *Edward VI: The Young King* (1968), pp. 368–82 (Jordan's chronology is often inaccurate); J. E. Neale, *Queen Elizabeth I* (1960 edn), pp. 25–33; J. Strype, *Ecclesiastical Memorials* (3 vols. in 6 parts, 1822–4), II ii. 191–209; G. Burnet, *The History of the Reformation of the Church of England* (ed. N. Pocock, Oxford, 6 vols., 1865), ii. 1146, 181–6.

2   G. Lefèvre-Pontalis, ed., *Correspondance politique de Odet de Selve* (Paris, 1888), no. 176 pp. 152–5.

3   Abbé de Vertot, ed., *Ambassades de Messieurs de Noailles en Angleterre* (Leiden, 5 vols., 1763), i. 102–3. (The first volume of this edition of ambassadors' correspondence includes an anonymous account of politics in the reign of Edward VI: I am very grateful to Miss P. Tudor for showing me the significance of this account.)

4   E. Dent, *Annals of Winchcombe and Sudeley* (1877), pp. 162–3.

5   G. Leti, *Historia Overo Vita di Elisabetta regina d'Inghilterra* (Amsterdam, 2 vols., 1693), i. 180 (also accessible in a French translation, *La vie d'Elizabeth reine d'Angleterre* (Amsterdam, 2 vols., 1694), i. 165–6). Gregorio Leti, born a catholic in Milan in 1630, died in Amsterdam in 1701 as a calvinist. He wrote many works of history as well as treatises against the catholic church, several of which were placed on the Index. In his preface, Leti tells how for thirty years he had thought of writing the life of Elizabeth. He had talked to many English lords, including some knowledgeable in history, but found that opinions were too polarised, the protestants seeing Elizabeth as an angel, the catholics as a devil. But when business again took him to England, he met Lord Anglesey who encouraged him to write his lives of Elizabeth and Cromwell. The French translator commented in his preface that Leti 'a trouvé en Angleterre par le moyen d'un seigneur considerable de ce pais-la, des memoires particuliers que Camden, le plus exact de tous les auteurs qui ont parlé de cette reine, n'avoit jamais vus'. The seigneur in question might have been Arthur Annesley, first Earl of Anglesey (1614–86) whom the *Dictionary of National Biography* describes as 'perhaps the first peer who devoted time and money to the formation of a great library', which was, however, sold

on his death. The difficulty with Leti's text is that he does not give references for some remarkable letters which he prints in full or for several unusual stories. It is possible that these are inventions – and Leti published a whole volume of letters supposedly by Paolo Sarpi which is regarded as largely spurious (*ex inf.* Professor J. I. Israel) – but usually they seem sufficiently plausible to be worth adding to the body of evidence on which an account of Seymour must rest. (I am very grateful indeed to Dr P. J. Holmes for his help in pursuing Leti.)

6 Leti, *Historia Elisabetta*, i. 178 (164); Vertot, *Ambassades*, i. 101–3.

7 British Library (hereinafter BL), Harleian MS, 249 fo. 38ᵛ (19b).

8 BL, Harleian MS, 249 fo. 38ᵛ (19C).

9 Bodleian Library, Ashmole MS, 1729 fo. 5; Public Record Office (hereinafter PRO), SP10/1/43.

10 Dent, *Annals*, between pp. 162–3.

11 PRO, SP46/1 fo. 14.

12 S. Haynes, *A Collection of State Papers at Hatfield* (1740), pp. 61–2.

13 Bodleian Library, Ashmole MS 1729, fo. 5.

14 BL, Lansdowne MS, 1236 fo. 26.

15 Leti, *Historia Elisabetta*, i. 182–6 (167–70).

16 J. G. Nichols, *Literary Remains of Edward the sixth* (Roxburghe Club, 2 vols., 1857), i. no. xlvi p. 45; Jordan, *Edward VI*, p. 370, citing Strype, *Ecclesiastical Memorials*, II i. 208–9, takes Edward's congratulations at face value.

17 PRO, SP10/6/10.

18 Nichols, *Literary Remains*, ii. 215.

19 BL, Harleian MS, 249 fo. 38 (19C); Vertot, *Ambassades*, i. 101–3; Letti, *Historia Elisabetta*, i. 186–7 (169–71)

20 PRO, PROB11/32/19.

21 BL, Hatfield Microfilms, M485/39, vol. 150 fo. 126 (Haynes, *State Papers*, p. 73). I am grateful to the marquess of Salisbury for permission to consult and to cite passages from the Cecil Papers.

22 *Ibid.*, pp. 84, 71–2.

23 PRO, SP10/4/14.

24 J. Hayward, *The Life and Raigne of King Edward the Sixth* (1630), p. 82; Vertot, *Ambassades*, i. 132; J. A. de Thou, *Histoire universelle* (11 vols., 1740), i. 497 n. 4; BL, Add. MS, 48023 fo. 350ᵛ; Lefèvre-Pontalis, *Correspondance*, no. 304, p. 287.

25 Burnet, *History of the Reformation*, ii. 181. Cf. S. E. James, 'Queen Kateryn Parr (1512–1548)', *T[ransactions of the] C[umberland and] W[estmorland] A[ntiquarian and] A[rchaeological] S[ociety]*, lxxxvii (1988), pp. 115–18.

26 BL, Hatfield Microfilms, M485/39, vol. 150 fo. 119 (Haynes, *State Papers*, p. 77).

27 PRO, SP10/4/14.

28 BL, Hatfield Microfilms, M485/39, vol. 150 fo. 74 (Haynes, *State Papers*, p. 93).

29 BL, Hatfield Microfilms, M485/39, vol. 150 fo. 86 (Haynes, *State Papers*, p. 100).

30 BL, Hatfield Microfilms, M485/39, vol. 150 fo. 85 (Haynes, *State Papers*, p. 100).

31 PRO, SP10/6/21; BL, Hatfield Microfilms, M485/39, vol. 150 fo. 85ᵛ (Haynes, *State Papers*, pp. 99–100).

32 BL, Hatfield Microfilms, M485/39, vol. 150 fo. 80ᵛ (Haynes, *State Papers*, p. 96).

33 T. Hearne, *Titi-Livii Foro-Juliensis viat Henrici Quinti, regis angliae, accedit sylloge Epistolarum, a variis angliae principibus scriptarum* (Oxford, 1716), pp. 165–6; PRO, SP10/2/25.

34 Hearne, *Titi-Livii*, pp. 211–12.

35 BL, Hatfield Microfilms, M485/39, vol. 150 fos. 85–8 (Haynes, *State Papers*, pp. 96, 100); Hearne, *Titi-Livii*, pp. 165–6).

36 PRO, SP10/6/19, 10/6/22.

37 R. McNulty, ed., *Ludovico Ariosto's 'Orlando Furioso' translated by Sir John Harington, 1591* (Oxford, 1972), p. 217; R. Hughey, *John Harington of Stepney: Tudor*

Gentleman: his life and works (Ohio, 1972), pp. viii, 52 (I owe this reference to Dr S. Adams).

38 PRO, SP10/6/16; BL, Hatfield Microfilms, M485/39, vol. 150 fo. 81ᵛ (Haynes, *State Papers*, p. 97).

39 BL, Hatfield Microfilms, M485/39, vol. 150 fo. 81ᵛ, cf. fo. 84 (Haynes, *State Papers*, p. 97; cf. pp. 98–9).

40 BL, Hatfield Microfilms, M485/39, vol. 150 fos. 79–84, esp. 83–84ᵛ (*ibid.*, pp. 95–8).

41 Vertot, *Ambassades*, i. 137; Leti, *Historia Elisabetta*, i. 190–1 (173–5).

42 BL, Hatfield Microfilms, M485/39, vol. 150 fo. 87ᵛ (Haynes, *State Papers*, p. 101, cf. p. 72).

43 PRO, SP10/6/16; cf. BL, Hatfield Microfilms, M485/39, vol. 150 fo. 44ᵛ (Haynes, p. 69).

44 PRO, SP10/6/14.

45 Vertot, *Ambassades*, i. 138.

46 H. James, 'The fall of Thomas, Lord Seymour, Lord Admiral, and North East Wales', citing J. A. Froude, *History of England from the Fall of Wolsey to the Death of Elizabeth* (12 vols., 1893 ed.), iv. 369. (I am grateful to Mr H. James for showing me this unpublished paper.)

47 BL, Add. MS, 48023 fo. 350ᵛ. Fos. 350–369ᵛ in the bound volume BL, Add. MS. 48023, part of the Yelverton Manuscripts, are in the same hand. Fos. 350–351ᵛ deal with Edward VI's reign; fos. 352–369ᵛ with the years 1559 to 1562, interrupted by interludes treating the siege of Exeter in 1549 and the loss of Calais in 1558. The later folios are quite full, and from fo. 359ᵛ are set out in the form of a diary under monthly headings. The folios dealing with the reign of Edward VI are often brief jottings, sometimes memoranda for further work, rather like the working notes of a would-be historian. Unfortunately the author has not been identified, but on his own account he knew several royal officials, took a considerable interest in foreign and economic affairs, and was keen to report gossip. He writes in similar vein as the anonymous eye-witness of BL Add. MS, 48026 fos. 6–16 about the quarrels between Somerset and Warwick.

48 BL, Hatfield Microfilms, M485/39, vol. 150 fo. 71 (Haynes, *State Papers*, p. 90).

49 J. R. Dasent, *Acts of the Privy Council* (hereinafter *APC*) (32 vols., 1890–1907) ii. 259. Seymour's allusion is to the minority of Henry VI. John, duke of Bedford, one of Henry VI's uncles, became regent of France (on the refusal of the duke of Burgundy). Another, Humphrey, duke of Gloucester, was appointed 'Protector and Defender of the realm and church in England and principal councillor of the king' for the duration of Bedford's absence overseas by the Lords in parliament on 5 December 1422. But he had also wanted to be regent or have the governance of the realm. He supported that claim not just by his birth, but on the grounds that when in the codicil of his will, the dyng Henry V had granted him the principal tutorship and defence ('tutelam et defensionem ... principales') of the baby king, he had meant by that phrase to confer on Duke Humphrey the government of the kingdom itself. But the Lords, after searching the 'precydentes of the governaill of the land in tyme and cas semblable', found Duke Humphrey's desire 'not according with the lawes of this land'. A king, they claimed, could not devise such powers by will without the assent of parliament. They accordingly refused to call him Tutor, Lieutenant, Governor or Regent, but settled, 'to appese you', for the description of Protector and Defender 'which emporteth a personell duetee of entendance to the actuell defense of the land' against enemies abroad and rebels at home. Gloucester did not then demur. (In the light of the Lords' reasoning (which we know from the Lords' reply to Gloucester's later request in 1428), it seems unlikely that Henry V had meant by the phrase 'tutellam et defensionem ... principales' simply the responsibility for the personal property of the king.) In 1426, as part of his broader complaints against Henry Beaufort, cardinal bishop of Winchester, the most influential councillor in the mid-1420s, Gloucester put forward a further claim: he was the one 'to whom, off alle persones or that shulde be in the londe, by the wey off nature and birthe yt belongeth to se unto the

governaunce of the kynges persone'. It is not entirely clear who had had the day-to-day keeping of the young Henry VI. Henry V's codicil had distinguished between the 'tutelam et defensionem . . . principales' of the king, granted to Gloucester, and the 'persone sue regimen et gubernationem' which Henry entrusted to Thomas Beaufort, duke of Exeter. Most likely it was indeed Exeter who had undertaken that task: but possibly he shared the responsibility with his brother Henry Beaufort. Gloucester's bid for the governorship evidently failed. Next, on 3 March 1428 he asked the Lords in parliament for a definition – presumably he meant an enlargement – of the scope of his power and authority as Protector, but the Lords simply reminded him of his agreement to their decisions in 1422. Seymour was thus justified in arguing that responsibilities had been divided in the minority of Henry VI and that no-one had held so great a combination of powers as Somerset did in the minority of Edward VI: the repeated rejection of Gloucester's claims, even though Gloucester's title of Protector conferred far less on him than the same title did on Somerset, would have further encouraged him. (For this complex episode see J. S. Roskell, 'The origins of the office and dignity of protector of England, with special reference to its origins', *English Historical Review*, lxviii (1953), esp. pp. 194, 198, 200, 203–7, 210, 216, 218, 220, 228; P. and F. Strong, 'The last will and codicils of Henry V', *English Historical Review*, xcvi (1981), p. 85; R. A. Griffiths, *The reign of Henry VI: The Exercise of Royal Authority 1422–1461* (1981), pp. 17–22, 51, 70–81; G. L. Harriss, *Cardinal Beaufort: A Study of Lancastrian Ascendancy and Decline* (Oxford, 1988), pp. 115–17, but note crucial criticism by R. G. Davies, *English Historical Review*, cv (1990), p. 399; T. B. Pugh, *Henry V and the Southampton Plot* (Southampton, 1988), pp. 144–5; *Rotuli Parliamentorum*, iv. 175, 326; C. L. Kingsford, ed., *Chronicles of London* (Oxford, 1905), p. 77. (I am grateful to Dr R. G. Davies and Mr T. B. Pugh for advice.)

50 BL, Add. MS, 48023 fo. 350; BL, Add. MS 48126 fos. 6–7; and cf. Paris, Bibliothèque Nationale, MS Ancien Saint-Germain, Fonds Francais, 15888 fo. 186ᵛ.

51 *APC*, ii. 259.

52 BL, Add. MS, 48126 fo. 6; Griffiths, *Henry VI*, pp. 31, 70–81; Harriss, *Beaufort*, pp. 136–44, 150–2.

53 BL, Add. MS, 48023, fo. 350ᵛ.

54 Vertot, *Ambassades*, i. 104. Does the charge that Seymour 'did withdraw yourself from the Kinges Majestes service, and being moved and spoken unto for your owne honour and for thabilitie that was in yow to serve and aide the Kinges Majestes affaires and the Lord Protectour, yow wolde alwais draw back and feyn excuses, and declare plain that yow wolde not do yt' refer to Seymour's failure to fulfil his military duties? (*APC*, ii. 252 (22).)

55 Vertot, *Ambassades*, i. 129–31; cf. Burnet, *History of the Reformation*, ii. 84, 114–16; BL, Add. MS., 48023 fo. 350ᵛ.

56 *APC*, ii. 260.

57 Vertot, *Ambassades*, i. 129–31.

58 *APC*, iii. 259; cf. PRO, SP10/6/27.

59 PRO, SP10/6/10 (5).

60 PRO, SP10/6/10 (7).

61 BL, Hatfield Microfilms, M485/39, vol. 150 fos. 64ᵛ, 51 (Haynes, *State Papers*, pp. 79, 87–8, 74).

62 BL, Harleian MS, 249 fos. 29–29ᵛ.

63 PRO, SP10/6/26; BL, Hatfield Microfilms, M485/39, vol. 150 fo. 51 (Haynes, *State Papers*, p. 74).

64 *APC*, iii. 260.

65 Nichols, *Literary Remains*, i. cxx; R. H. Brodie, ed., *Calendar of Patent Rolls: Edward VI* (6 vols., 1924–9), i. 217; BL, Hatfield Microfilms, M485/39, vol. 150 fo. 71ᵛ (Haynes, *State Papers*, p. 91).

66 PRO, SP10/4/31; SP10/6/10 (10).

67 Bodleian Library, Ashmole MS, 1729 fo. 9.

68 BL, Hatfield Microfilms, M485/39, vol. 150 fo. 112 (Haynes, *State Papers*, p. 75).

69 PRO, SP10/6/11.

70 PRO, SP10/6/26.

71 R. J. W. Swales, 'The Howard interest in Sussex elections, 1529–1558', *Sussex Archaeological Collections*, cxiv (1976), pp. 49–60; Bindoff, *House of Commons*, iii. 299–300 (somewhat speculative); J. Loach, *Parliament under the Tudors* (Oxford, 1991), pp. 90–1.

72 PRO, SP10/6/7 (10, 11); BL, Hatfield Microfilms, M485/39, vol. 150 fo. 61 (Haynes, *State Papers*, p. 85); BL, Harleian MS, 249 fo. 34 (5).

73 *Cal. Pat. Rolls, Edward VI*, ii. 96–7; BL, Add. MS, 48023 fo. 350ᵛ.

74 *Lords' Journals*, pp. 295–99, 307, 313; *Commons' Journals*, p. 2.

75 BL, Hatfield Microfilms, M485/39, vol. 150 fo. 51 (Haynes, *State Papers*, p. 74).

76 BL, Harleian MS, 249 fo. 34 (4).

77 PRO, SP10/6/11; BL, Hatfield Microfilms, M485/39, vol. 150 fo. 113 (Haynes, *State Papers*, p. 76).

78 PRO, SP10/6/14 (1).

79 PRO, SP10/6/7 (6).

80 PRO, SP10/6/13 (16); SP10/6/14 (2).

81 PRO, SP10/6/7 (6); cf. SP10/6/12.

82 PRO, SP10/6/12; cf. BL, Harleian MS, 249 fo. 35ᵛ (14).

83 PRO, SP10/6/7 (7).

84 PRO, SP10/6/12.

85 BL, Harleian MS, 249 fo. 35 (13).

86 BL, Hatfield Microfilms, M485/39, vol. 150 fo. 93ᵛ (Haynes, *State Papers*, p. 105); PRO, SP10/6/13 (5, 6, 7).

87 BL, Harleian MS, 249 fo. 35 (13); *Statutes of the Realm*, iii. 63.

88 PRO, SP10/6/13.

89 BL, Hatfield Microfilms, M485/39, vol. 150 fo. 84 (Haynes, *State Papers*, pp. 97, 99).

90 BL, Harleian MS, 249, fo. 35ᵛ.

91 *Ibid.*, fo. 35ᵛ (15).

92 *Ibid.*, fo. 35 (12).

93 *Ibid.*; cf. *Statutes of the Realm*, iv. 62; Vertot, *Ambassades*, i. 132; Leti, *Historia Elisabetta*, i. 193 (176–7).

94 PRO, SP10/6/7 (1–3); BL, Hatfield Microfilms, M485/39, vol. 150 fo. 53–53ᵛ (Haynes, *State Papers*, p. 83).

95 BL, Hatfield Microfilms, M485/39, vol. 150 fo. 115 (Haynes, *State Papers*, p. 76).

96 BL, Hatfield Microfilms, M485/39, vol. 150 fo. 84ᵛ (Haynes, *State Papers*, p. 98).

97 BL, Hatfield Microfilms, M485/39, vol. 150 fos. 119–20 (Haynes, *State Papers*, pp. 77–9); PRO, SP10/6/7.

98 PRO, SP10/6/14 (3).

99 BL, Hatfield Microfilms, M485/39, vol. 150 fo. 115 (Haynes, *State Papers*, p. 77).

100 BL, Hatfield Microfilms, M485/39, vol. 150 fo. 54ᵛ (*ibid.*, p. 83).

101 *Lords' Journals*, p. 307.

102 BL, Hatfield Microfilms, M485/39, vol. 150 fo. 43ᵛ (Haynes, *State Papers*, p. 68); PRO, SP10/6/7 (11).

103 M. A. R. Graves, *The House of Lords in the Parliaments of Edward VI and Mary* (1981), pp. 115–16; PRO, SP10/6/14 (2). Cf. S. E. James, 'A Tudor Divorce. The Marital History of William Parr, Marquess of Northampton', *TCWAAS*, xc (1990), pp. 199–204.

104 PRO, SP10/6/14.

105 PRO, SP10/6/15.

106 R. Grafton, *Chronicle; or History of England* (1809 edn), pp. 499–500; Strype, *Ecclesiastical Memorials*, ii. app. HH, p. 109; BL, Add. MS, 48126 fos. 6–16; BL, Add. MS, 48023, fos. 350–51ᵛ; BL, Harleian MS, 249 fos. 16–18; D. E. Hoak, *The King's Council in the reign of Edward VI* (Cambridge, 1976), pp. 43–5, 231–9; A. J. Slavin, 'The fall of Lord

Chancellor Wriothesley: a study in the politics of conspiracy', *Albion*, vii (1975), pp. 265–86.

107   Haynes, *State Papers*, pp. 82–3; BL, Hatfield Microfilms, M485/39, vol. 150 fo. 103ᵛ (Haynes, *State Papers*, p. 104).

108   *Cal. Pat. Rolls, Edward VI*, i. 25–33; cf. H. Miller, 'Henry VIII's unwritten will: grants of lands and honours in 1547', in E. W. Ives, R. J. Knecht and J. J. Scarisbrick, eds., *Wealth and Power in Tudor England: Essays Presented to S. T. Bindoff* (1978), pp. 102, 104.

109   Strype, *Ecclesiastical Memorials*, II ii. pp. 194–5.

110   James, 'Seymour and North East Wales', citing L. T. Smith, ed., *Itinerary of John Leland*, 5 vols. (1906–8), iii. 69; A. Palmer, 'The town of Holt, Denbighshire', *Archaeologia Cambriensis* lxvi (1907), pp. 313–14.

111   James, 'Seymour and North East Wales', citing R. R. Davies, *Lordship and Society in the Marches of Wales 1282–1400* (Oxford, 1978), pp. 56–8, 72; and I. D. Thornley and A. H. Thomas, eds., *The Great Chronicle of London* (1938), p. 258, Cf. also R. R. Davies, 'Richard II and the principality of Chester 1397–9', in F. R. du Boulay and C. M. Barron, eds., *The Reign of Richard II* (1971), pp. 256–79; J. L. Gillespie, 'Richard II's Cheshire archers', *Transactions of the Historic Society of Lancashire and Cheshire*, cxxv (1974), pp. 8, 12; M. K. Jones, 'Sir William Stanley of Holt: politics and family allegiance in the late fifteenth century', *Welsh History Review*, xiv (1988), pp. 1, 10.

112   BL, Hatfield Microfilms, M485/39, vol. 150 fo. 57 (Haynes, *State Papers*, p. 85).

113   McNulty, *Harington*, p. 217.

114   H. Harington, ed., *Nugae Antiquae* (2 vols., 1804), ii. 330.

115   PRO, SP10/5/1.

116   PRO, SP10/6/13 (5, 6, 7); cf. BL, Harleian MS, 249 fo. 35ᵛ; *Statutes of the Realm*, iv. 62.

117   PRO, SP10/6/8.

118   BL, Harleian MS, 249 fos. 37–37ᵛ (24–26) and cf. 37ᵛ–38 (27–28); BL, Add. MS, 48023 fo. 350ᵛ; Leti, *Historia Elisabetta*, i. 196 (178).

119   PRO, SP10/1/43; BL, Harleian MS, 249 fo. 36ᵛ (21, 22); Swales, 'Sussex elections', pp. 54–6 (though the impressive-looking evidence is in fact rather tentative: three connections seem certain); C. E. Challis, *The Tudor Coinage* (Manchester, 1978), pp. 100–3.

120   PRO, SP10/6/13 (9).

121   BL, Harleian MS, 249 fo. 39ᵛ (I am grateful to Mr H. James for drawing my attention to this point).

122   *Statutes of the Realm*, iv. 63.

123   *APC*, ii. 255–6 (I am grateful to Mr H. James for this reference).

124   *APC*, ii. 247–56 (23). Seymour visited the Scilly Islands in 1547 and may have taken the initiative in fortifying them the following year (H. M. Colvin, ed., *The History of the King's Works, Vol. iv, 1485–1600 (part ii)* (1982), p. 588).

125   Vertot, *Ambassades*, i. 139–40.

126   BL, Hatfield Microfilms, M485/39, vol. 150 fo. 99ᵛ (Haynes, *State Papers*, p. 106).

127   BL, Hatfield Microfilms, M485/39, vol. 150 fo. 101ᵛ (*ibid.*, p. 108).

128   PRO, SP10/6/10 (6).

129   *APC*, ii. 258–9; PRO, SP10/6/27.

130   PRO, SP10/6/7.

131   H. Robinson, ed., *Original Letters Relative to the English Reformation*, Parker Society (2 vols., 1846–7), ii. no. ccci p. 648 (I owe this reference to Dr A. D. M. Pettegree).

132   BL, Hatfield Microfilms, M485/39, vol. 150 fo. 43ᵛ (Haynes, *State Papers*, p. 68).

133   PRO, SP10/6/12 (5); BL, Hatfield Microfilms, M485/39, vol. 150 fo. 64 (Haynes, *State Papers*, p. 87); PRO, SP10/6/14 (6), 10/6/7 (11).

134   PRO, SP10/6/7 (11); CF. HAYNES, *State Papers*, pp. 107, 84–6; PRO, SP10/6/14 (5, 6).

135   BL, Harleian MS, 249, fo. 34 (6).

136   Jordan, *Edward VI*, pp. 373–4.

137   Dorset testified that Seymour and he rode from parliament together on the day that Seymour was committed (PRO, SP10/6/7 (11)); the last day that Seymour was marked as present in the House of Lords was 17 January (*Lords' Journals*, p. 332). Instructions to search Seymour's house are dated 18 January (PRO, SP10/6/2).

138   Haynes, *State Papers*, pp. 70–1.

139   *Ibid.*

140   *Ibid.*

141   BL, Hatfield Microfilms, M485/39, vol. 150 fo. 70 (Haynes, *State Papers*, pp. 88–9.

142   BL, Hatfield Microfilms, M485/39, vol. 150 fo. 79–84 (Haynes, *State Papers*, pp. 94–5).

143   BL, Hatfield Microfilms, M485/39, vol. 150 fo. 78 (Haynes, *State Papers*, p. 95).

144   PRO, SP10/6/19 (BL, Hatfield Microfilms, M485/39, vol. 150, fos. 85–8) (Haynes, *State Papers*, pp. 99–100); PRO, SP10/6/20.

145   BL, Hatfield Microfilms, M485/39, vol. 150 fo. 91 (Haynes, *State Papers*, p. 102).

146   Bodleian Library, Ashmole MS, 1729 fo. 11 Arch F. c. 39; BL, Lansdowne MS, 1236 fos. 33–33ᵛ (Ellis, *Original Letters*, 1st series, ii. 155–8), fo. 35 § (*Original Letters*, 1st Series, ii. 153–5).

147   *APC*, ii. 246–7, 256–8, 260.

148   BL, add. MS, 48023 fo. 351.

149   *Latimer's Sermons, temp. Edward VI* (1549), sig. M. iiᵛ–iii; Nichols, *Literary Remains*, i. cxxiii–iv; G. E. Corrie, ed., *Sermons and Remains of Hugh Latimer, Parker Society*, xvi, xx 1844–5, pp. 161–5; cf. Hayward, *Edward VI*, pp. 83–4.

150   Harington, *Nugae Antiquae*, ii. 328–9 R. Hughey, ed., *The Arundel Harington Manuscript of Tudor Poetry* (Columbus, Ohio, 2 vols., 1960), i. 341–2.

151   J. Pratt, ed., *The Acts of Monuments of John Foxe* (8 vols., 1877), vi. 283.

152   Hayward, *Edward VI*, p. 82; Foxe, *Acts and Monuments*, vi. 283; Latimer, *Sermons* Sig-M iiᵛ-iii.

153   Dent, *Annals*, p. 193, citing Ellis, *Original Letters*, 2nd series, ii. 256.

154   PRO, SP10/6/14 (5).

155   BL, Hatfield Microfilms, M485/39, vol. 150 fo. 56ᵛ (Haynes, *State Papers*, p. 84).

156   PRO, SP10/6/14 (5): *APC*, ii. 246–7, 256–8, 260.

157   PRO, SP10/6/13.

158   *APC*, ii. 259; CF. PRO, SP10/6/27.

159   PRO, SP10/6/7 (7); Vertot, *Ambassades*, i. 140; Haynes, *State Papers*, pp. 83–4, 107; PRO, SP10/6/13 (4); BL, Add. MS, 48023 fo. 351ᵛ (cf. BL, Add. MS, 48126 fo. 7).

160   BL, Add. MS, 48023 fo. 351.

161   *APC*, ii. 246–7.

162   Haynes, *State Papers*, p. 104.

163   Bodleian Library, Ashmole MS 1729 fo. 9.

164   BL, Add. MS, 48023 fo. 350ᵛ.

165   BL, Hatfield Microfilms, M485/39, vol. 150 fo. 60ᵛ (Haynes, *State Papers*, p. 85); BL, Harleian MS 249 fo. 34 (4).

166   PRO, SP10/6/7 (6).

167   BL, Hatfield Microfilms, M485/39, vol. 150 fo. 45 (Haynes, *State Papers*, p. 70).

168   Dent, *Annals*, p. 193; Leti, *Historia Elisabetta*, i. 201 (182).

The Dudley clientèle, 1553–1563

At some point in 1567 Sir William Cecil composed a well-known memorandum on the greater suitability of the Archduke Charles of Styria as a consort for Elizabeth I rather than Robert Dudley, earl of Leicester. Fourth in the list of arguments against Leicester was the danger that 'he shall study nothing but to enhance his own particular friends: to wealth, to offices, to lands and to offend others'. As if to illustrate the point Cecil then added the names of nineteen individuals.[1] The possible significance of the members of this Dudley faction has not gone unnoticed. Conyers Read and Wallace MacCaffrey have drawn attention to their prominence in the Newhaven (Le Havre) expedition of 1562–3.[2] David Loades has observed that Cecil's list 'reads like a roll call of the rebels and conspirators of the previous reign'.[3] Nicholas Canny discovered that many of the Newhaven survivors accompanied Sir Henry Sidney to Ireland in 1565–6, and saw in their presence there the victory of Leicester in a factional struggle with the third earl of Sussex.[4] In the best of the three recent biographies of Leicester, Derek Wilson has argued that his association with the former conspirators gave him a greater political importance in the first years of Elizabeth's reign than has been previously appreciated.[5]

There is, however, a further, and less-discussed, aspect to this Dudley faction. David Loades also noted that many of the leaders of the Wyatt and Dudley conspiracies had 'held office in the previous reign'.[6] This point deserves further attention. If these men had indeed been followers of John Dudley, duke of Northumberland, then their association with his son in Elizabeth's reign could be seen as the reforming of an earlier Dudley clientèle rather than the creation of a new faction.[7] Two very interesting hypotheses would then arise. The participation of these men in the Marian conspiracies would suggest that as a group they retained a certain cohesion between 1553 and 1558. Secondly, their allegiance to Lord Robert in the new reign may not have been solely the result of his prominence at court. The reverse may well have been the case. His personal closeness to the queen may have derived some of its notoriety from his leadership of an existing faction.

If these hypotheses can be proved, they would add a new dimension to the politics of the first years of Elizabeth's reign. Lord Robert's position at court would make possible a restoration of the lands and offices the Dudley family and its clients had lost after 1553. The extent to which such a restoration occurred has never been explored. This chapter will examine the evidence for and ramifications of both the continuity of the Dudley clientèle from 1553 to 1563 (a terminal date suggested by the Newhaven expedition), and the Dudley restoration. Its first section will establish more clearly the identities of the clientèle of the early 1560s and trace, where possible, their Edwardian connections. Its second section will reconstruct Lord Robert's activities in the reign of Mary. Its final section will assess the place of the Dudley clientèle in a wider 'Edwardian restoration' in 1559.

I

The great majority of the nineteen names that Cecil noted in 1567 are easily identified. Relations by blood or marriage formed a central group: Leicester's brother Ambrose, earl of Warwick, the master of the Ordnance, his brother-in-law Sir Henry Sidney, president of the Council in the Marches of Wales and lord deputy of Ireland, Sir Francis Jobson, who married his father's half-sister, and John Appleyard, half-brother to Amy Robsart. Four cousins were also included: Sir James Croft, Sir Henry Dudley and the brothers Thomas and John Dudley.[8] Thomas Wilson, Henry Killigrew, Henry Middlemore, Edward Horsey and Thomas Leighton had already served Elizabeth in either a civil or a military capacity, and would do so more prominently in future. Robert and George Christmas, Anthony Forster and Richard Ellis were, like the Dudley brothers, among Leicester's men of business. Only four prove more elusive. 'Colshill' may be either Robert, the gentleman pensioner, or his brother Thomas, surveyor of the customs. 'Wysman' was probably Thomas, son of the Exchequer official John Wiseman. 'Mollynex' was probably Sidney's future secretary Edmund Molyneux, rather than either of the MPs in the 1563–6 parliament.[9] 'Middleton' has been tentatively identified as Richard, the captain of Denbigh Castle.

The main reason for the obscurity of the last four is the fact that they were not otherwise prominent among Leicester's followers. This raises doubts about the accuracy of Cecil's list, which are reinforced by some obvious omissions. Why, for example, were his other brother-in-law Henry Hastings, earl of Huntingdon, and Sir Nicholas Throckmorton, widely regarded as his political brain at that time, not on the list, when Throckmorton's cousin Middlemore, for whom he was constantly soliciting office, was there?[10] Cecil's motive in compiling the list was clearly to reinforce the argument that a domestic marriage for the queen would create factions. He had already advanced it at an earlier stage in the revived negotiations with the Archduke Charles, when he told an agent of the duke of Württemberg in 1564 that the English nobility feared that a royal consort drawn from their ranks would 'favour his family and oppress others'.[11] It may simply have been the case that these were the first names that came to mind, possibly because Leicester had recently given his assistance to suits they had submitted.

The list is not therefore a definitive guide to Leicester's following. To establish its wider membership, other methods must be employed. In doing so it should first be noted that, with the exception of immediate household servants, Leicester and his brother Warwick employed the same pool of officers, lawyers and 'men of business' throughout the first three decades of Elizabeth's reign. This was a Dudley clientèle, rather than Leicester's personal following.[12] In the absence of a satisfactory study of the duke of Northumberland, let alone his household and clientèle, the previous history of these men is not always easy to trace.[13] It is simplest to proceed through a series of categories relevant to both father and son.

The immediate households present the fewest difficulties. The survival of two volumes of Robert Dudley's household accounts (20 December 1558–20 December 1559 and 22 December 1559–30 April 1561), wages and livery lists for 1559–60, together with a number of tradesmen's bills and other financial documents from the period 1558–66, makes it possible to identify the members of his household and his chief men of business in those years.[14] Neither Northumberland's nor Ambrose Dudley's household accounts have been discovered, but we do possess the records of the crown's commissioners who wound up Northumberland's estate after his execution, which can be supplemented by some miscellaneous correspondence.[15] The surviving wardrobe inventories of his heir, John, Viscount Lisle (earl of Warwick from 1551 to 1554) also give some idea of the persons in the Dudley entourage between 1545 and 1550.[16]

Robert Dudley's household in the early 1560s appears to have been fairly fluid in structure; formal offices are not encountered until the end of the decade, possibly because his estate did not assume its full shape until the period 1563–72. Only Richard Ellis, compiler of the second volume of accounts, is described in passing as Dudley's 'paymaster'.[17] William Chauncy, who drew up the first volume, is not encountered again after 1559. There was, however, a distinct group of men of business dealing with Dudley's affairs at Elizabeth's accession, most of whom remained in his service on a permanent basis for the rest of their lives. Chauncy's account was audited by John Dudley, William Kynyat and Richard Horden. Thomas Blount of Kidderminster, Anthony Forster, two Chester lawyers – William Glasier and John Yerwerth – and two men of Norfolk background, the lawyer William Grice (clerk of the Stables by 1564) and the London merchant William Hogan or Huggins, were the most prominent of their colleagues in 1559.[18] After 1562 Horden disappears; Dudley's wages account for 1559–61 was audited by Kynyat, Ellis, Blount, and the otherwise unknown Richard Overton. In the period 1564–6 the auditors were Dudley, Kynyat, Blount, Forster, Glasier and George Christmas.[19] Dudley, Kynyat and the lawyer Thomas Rolfe were the surveyors of the lands granted to Robert Dudley by Elizabeth in 1563; Dudley, Kynyat, Glasier and Yerwerth for those of 1566. Blount and John Somerfield were the attorneys for the livery of seisin of Kenilworth in 1563; Dudley, Rolfe, Glasier and Yerwerth were the commissioners in the settlement with the tenants of the lordship of Denbigh in the following year.[20]

Two of these men had been among Northumberland's leading household officers. Blount (whose position under Leicester appears to have been a similar one) was his comptroller in 1553.[21] Kynyat was one of his three general surveyors in 1548–9, and was described retrospectively as his auditor.[22] John Dudley and Hogan can be identified as his servants; Somerfield was a cousin of the duchess of Northumberland and an executor of her will; Forster and Ellis had some form of association with his household.[23] Grice, whose father Gilbert (bailiff of Great Yarmouth) had some connection to Northumberland, is referred to in Lisle's wardrobe inventory.[24] Glasier cannot be traced directly to Northumberland, but he was doing business with Robert Dudley on the eve of Edward VI's death.[25]

Several of Northumberland's household officers in 1553 – John Holmes, his secretary, Charles Tyrell, his master of the horse, or Henry Brooke, his general receiver, for example – are not encountered among his son's servants. It is therefore possible that we may be giving those who survived to the 1560s a greater retrospective importance than they deserve. By the same token many of Northumberland's household servants may have obtained a more independent stature by Elizabeth's reign, and their relationship to Leicester would have become a less formal one. Only one man is found in both the list of the gentlemen of Northumberland's household in 1553 and Robert Dudley's wage and livery lists for 1559–61: John Dudley's younger brother Thomas, Leicester's comptroller by 1571.[26] Another of the household gentlemen of 1553, Henry Killigrew, was a secretary to Sir Nicholas Throckmorton in Paris in 1559.[27] The Lisle wardrobe accounts refer to Killigrew, Blount, Grice, one of Dudley brothers, one of the Aglionbys, Sir Richard Verney and Sir George Blount.[28] Other sources identify at least three further men associated with Leicester in the 1560s as Northumberland's servants in 1553: Sir John Throckmorton, his brother Clement, and the captain of Bewcastle in Cumberland, Simon Musgrave. The career of Thomas Wilson, the future secretary of state, also spans both households.[29]

As in any other sixteenth-century affinity, the family formed the core. Northumberland's brother Sir Andrew, who died unmarried in 1559, was prominent in his entourage. So too was Jobson, whose wife Elizabeth was the daughter of Northumberland's mother through her second marriage to Arthur Plantagenet, Viscount Lisle. Northumberland's other half-sister, Bridget, married the brother of Sir Thomas Cawarden. Sidney and Hastings were brought into the Dudley connection by Northumberland's marriage manoeuvres for his children in the last years of Edward's reign. John Appleyard was the main figure to enter Robert Dudley's clientèle through the Robsart marriage. However, the example of William Hogan, whose sister was married to Appleyard, reveals that a clear distinction cannot be drawn between Northumberland's clientèle and Robert Dudley's Norfolk connection.[30]

Given the extent of intermarriage among the mid Tudor political nation, the importance to be assigned to cousins can be exaggerated. The case of Sir James Croft, however, provides clear evidence of the role it played in the formation of Northumberland's military clientèle. In his 'autobiography' Croft records how, as a relative of Dudley's wife, he was invited by him to serve in the expedition to Leith in 1544 'as a private man'; later in the year he was given the command of 100 of Dudley's household men at the siege of Boulogne. Thereafter he became an officer of the garrison (water-bailiff and under-marshal), and then obtained further rapid promotion in the military service of the crown.[31] It is probable that the military career of the notorious Sir Henry Dudley (son of John Sutton, Lord Dudley, of the senior branch of the family) followed a similar pattern. Thomas and John Dudley came from a junior branch, domiciled at Yanwath in Cumberland.

The Worcestershire Blounts (Thomas of Kidderminster and Sir George of Kinlet), always addressed as cousins, were probably related to Northumberland's mother. However, it is not clear how important family connections were to other prominent members of Northumberland's clientèle, Sir Nicholas and Sir Ralph Bagenal or Sir Henry Gates, for example.[32]

The officers of the Boulogne garrison, where he was lieutenant in 1544–5, were possibly the most significant element in Northumberland's military clientèle. The garrison was the first substantial body of English troops to be armed extensively with arquebuses. The officers were therefore the most professional the mid Tudor period could boast.[33] Their later careers are of equal interest; for both Sir Henry Dudley and many of the central figures of Wyatt's rebellion (Sir Thomas Wyatt himself, Croft, Sir George Harper, Sir Nicholas Arnold, Cuthbert Vaughan and Alexander Brett) were former Boulogne officers. It was precisely the element of a military coup rather than a provincial rising which distinguished the Marian conspiracies from the other rebellions of the century, with the significant exception of Essex's revolt. The senior officers of the Newhaven garrison of 1562–3 were also veterans of Boulogne: both the first knight-marshal, Sir Adrian Poynings, and his successor, Sir Hugh Paulet, the treasurer (Sir Maurice Dennys), the comptroller (Cuthbert Vaughan) and the clerk of the council (the later puritan activist, Thomas Wood). Croft was expected to have joined them, but his appointment was blocked by the duke of Norfolk.[34]

The Boulogne connection suggests that to label the Wyatt rebels and the Newhaven officers as 'gentlemen adventurers' is to miss the point. They were in fact key figures from the Edwardian military establishment who had enjoyed the benefits of Northumberland's patronage. Lord Robert's involvement in the preparation of the Newhaven expedition (and the expectation that he would command it) made possible their re-employment by Elizabeth, for only a few of the former Edwardian officers had served in the expedition to Scotland in 1560. Newhaven provided the occasion for the revival of Dudley military patronage, with which Leicester would be identified until his death. No list of appointments specifically made by him survives, but a number of Dudley followers can be found among the sixty-two men who held either captaincies or staff appointments in the expedition.[35] This total excludes the earl of Warwick and those who, like Sidney, Sir Richard Lee and Sir Francis Knollys, were sent to Le Havre for brief periods of inspection, but does include Sir Thomas Finch, who drowned in the sinking of the *Greyhound* en route, and Killigrew and

Leighton who commanded the companies sent to Rouen in October 1562. Apart from the senior officers already referred to, four of the men on Cecil's list were among them: Killigrew, Leighton, Edward Horsey, and John Appleyard. William Saule, lieutenant of the ordnance, and Arthur Heigham, the water-bailiff, are both found in Dudley's 1559–60 livery lists.[36] Nicholas Maltby (Warwick's secretary), John Fisher of Packington (the gentleman porter), and Edward Driver can also be definitely identified as Dudley clients.[37] Together they constitute about a quarter of the total.

Two further aspects of the Newhaven expedition deserve consideration. It also served to expand and consolidate the Elizabethan Dudley clientèle, for not all the officers later associated with the Dudleys had been among Northumberland's immediate followers. Horsey, for example, had originally been a client of Lord Clinton.[38] Moreover, the Edwardian military establishment had been bitterly divided by the fall of the duke of Somerset. William, Lord Grey de Wilton's treatment of Northumberland at his surrender in 1553 is well known. William Pelham, Wyatt rebel, captain of the pioneers at Newhaven and Warwick's lieutenant of the Ordnance from 1567, had left England for the service of the queen of Hungary in the Netherlands after Somerset's arrest in 1551, and did not return until after Mary's accession.[39]

The simultaneous assembly of the parliament of 1563 made the Newhaven officers and the MPs mutually exclusive bodies. Since many of the Newhaven survivors would sit in later parliaments, the Dudley clientèle present in the House of Commons in 1563 may have been smaller than it otherwise would have been. Nevertheless, Blount, Glasier, Grice, Yerwerth, Wilson and John and Thomas Dudley, Lord Robert's leading men of business, were all to be found in the House. With the exception of Blount they sat for boroughs, in some cases with the possible patronage of Dudley himself. Also in the House was a group of older Dudley followers: Jobson, Ralph Bagenal, Clement Throckmorton, Ellis Price, Arnold, Gates and Croft. They, on the other hand, sat for counties or for boroughs where they possessed their own influence; most of them had been MPs either in 1559 or before.[40]

II

The fifty-odd men identified above do not represent the whole of the Dudley clientèle of the early 1560s, let alone that of Northumberland. But it is doubtful that many of the significant Elizabethan figures have been excluded. They are not easy to trace in Mary's reign, for the slightly paradoxical reason that the disaster of July 1553 had only a limited impact on most of Northumberland's followers. If the duke himself, Sir John Gates and Sir Henry Palmer were executed, and his sons and several peers imprisoned and attainted, the others suffered mainly loss of office or (later) former episcopal lands. Wyatt's rebellion, by contrast, had far more widespread consequences. These, however, the Dudley brothers, with the exception of the unfortunate Lord Guildford, were able to escape. The research of Richard McCoy has now established that Lord Robert and Lord Ambrose took part in one of the Anglo-Spanish tournaments of the winter of 1554–5.[41] A petition to Philip drafted by Roger Ascham for Lord Ambrose's wife, Lady Elizabeth Tailboys, on 8 November 1554 reveals that he alone was still in the Tower by then. His brothers were probably released in October, immediately prior to the death of the eldest, John, earl of Warwick, at Penshurst on the 21st.[42] There is no reference to them as prisoners in the privy council registers after September 1554, and no contemporary source includes them among those released ceremoniously on 18 January 1555. With the exception of Sir Andrew Dudley, the latter were all former Wyatt rebels.[43]

As the well-known passages in her will reveal, the duchess of Northumberland had made considerable efforts to obtain the release of her sons. In her campaign she was assisted by Sir Henry Sidney, who later claimed to have joined the embassy to Spain of his brother-in-law Viscount Fitzwalter (the future third earl of Sussex) at the beginning of 1554 for that purpose.[44] It is also not impossible that some of Mary's councillors, Sir Thomas Cornwallis, Lord Hastings of Loughborough, and Lord Paget in particular, may have regarded their case with sympathy. Despite Northumberland's role in Paget's disgrace in 1552, good relations between the families had continued. Robert Dudley was a close friend to Sir Henry Paget (the future second lord), and later informed the third Lord Paget that he had loved his father and brother 'as dearly as any friends as ever I had'.[45] As Dudley frequently acknowledged, however, the key role was played by the new king.[46] Charity was not Philip's only, or even his primary, motive. It was in his interest to win over both the Dudleys and the former Wyatt rebels by a gesture that gave him a claim to their future personal loyalty and service. For Croft and Edward Randolph, release was followed by inclusion in his list of pensioners, with, in the case of Randolph, the significant rank of colonel.[47]

Philip's benevolence is of central importance to the participation of both the Dudley brothers and many of the other former prisoners in the St Quentin expedition of 1557. This expedition was both mounted at Philip's request and financed by him.[49] Its members 'went out to serve the king', their service being less the rallying to the crown of a 'deeply divided ruling class', than the honouring of a personal debt.[49] It is revealing that the unpardoned rebels then in France (Sir Henry Dudley, Henry Killigrew and Edward Horsey, for example) did not return.[50] What has further complicated the issue has been the persistent belief that Robert Dudley was a member of Philip's household in Brussels after 1555.[51] This has been derived from a single reference in Henry Machyn's diary to Dudley's arrival at the court on 17 March 1557 with letters 'from King Philip from beyond the sea' advising of his impending departure from Calais on his final visit to England.[52] There is also evidence that Dudley met both Cardinal Granvelle and Lazarus von Schwendi prior to 1559, but he probably did so at St Quentin.[53] He was not a member of Philip's English household, nor can an extended absence abroad be deduced from other sources.[54] His presence at Calais in March 1557 can be explained by membership in the entourage of the earl of Pembroke, who had been sent to inspect the fortress in December 1556 and remained there to escort the king to England.[55]

Several months after their release, the former prisoners were pardoned: the Dudley brothers on 22 January 1555, the others during the following spring.[56] But their attainders were not repealed, nor was their property automatically restored. However, the Dudleys thereafter received several further demonstrations of royal generosity, culminating in their restitution in blood in the parliament of 1558.[57] The latter may be explained by the death of Lord Henry in the assault on St Quentin. The reasons for the earlier are less immediately obvious, though they may have been inspired by the same motives that underlay the kindness that Mary showed to the duchess of Northumberland in 1553–4. They also made possible the initial rebuilding of the Dudley clientèle.

It is important at this point to resolve the confusion that has arisen over Lord Robert's claim to the Robsart estate: the Norfolk manors of Syderstone, Bircham Newton and Great Bircham, and the Suffolk manor of Bulkham. Under the terms of the marriage settlement made between Sir John Robsart and Northumberland on 24 May 1550, Robert and Amy Dudley would inherit the Robsart estate only after the deaths of both Sir John and his wife. To support the young couple, Northumberland obtained from the crown the lands of the former priory of Coxford which had been confiscated from the third duke of Norfolk.[58] They lay close to the Norfolk manors of the Robsart estate, and Northumberland intended that when the two were combined Robert Dudley would possess a substantial landed interest in the county. In 1553 he added the manor of

Hemsby near Great Yarmouth, so that his son 'might be able to keep a good house in Norfolk where he had married him'.[59] These lands were lost in Dudley's attainder, and therefore on his release he was propertyless. Sir John Robsart had died on 8 June 1554, but his widow, Lady Elizabeth, was alive as late as the winter of 1557–8.

About the time her sons received their pardons, the duchess of Northumberland herself died.[60] Through a series of exchanges with the queen, she had been able to retain a life interest in part of her jointure and an estate of inheritance composed of properties inherited from her own family, together with the lands of the former monastery of Hales Owen in Worcestershire and Shropshire.[61] Under the terms of her will (drafted in the months between her sons' release and their pardon) Hales Owen was to descend to Lord Ambrose, with fifty marks' worth of other lands to both the surviving younger brothers. As attainted traitors, however, they were unable to inherit, so Hales Owen was left to her executors (Sidney, Sir George Blount, John Somerfield and the Warwickshire lawyer Thomas Marrow) to be used for the benefit of her children.[62]

On 4 May 1555 the queen, in the first of her further acts of generosity, waived her rights to the estate and permitted Ambrose Dudley to inherit it despite his attainder.[63] This in turn made possible a remarkable family compact. On 20 November 1555 the duchess's executors, Lord Ambrose, Lord Henry and Sir Andrew Dudley agreed that Lord Robert, 'left with nothing to live by and having most need of [ ] friendly and brotherly [love?]', could inherit the whole of Hales Owen in exchange for the settlement of the duchess's debts, provision of an estate of fifty marks p.a. for Lady Katherine Hastings, and payments to Lord Ambrose of £800 and Sir Andrew of £300.[64] This agreement was confirmed and livery of seisin performed on 6 March 1556.[65] In those involved the first stage of the Dudley restoration can be detected. Lord Robert's attorneys were his men of business William Glasier and William Grice. The attorneys for the tenants were Northumberland's former servants Thomas Blount and George Tuckey, who had been granted extensive leases of lands from the Hales Owen estate during the 1540s. Tuckey was also the bailiff of Hales Owen, and Lord Robert appointed Blount its chief steward.[66]

This is not the place to attempt a reconstruction of Robert Dudley's tangled finances. However, one or two points should be noted. By the summer of 1557 parts of Hales Owen had been heavily mortgaged. Dudley borrowed £400 from the London merchant William Bird in December 1556, and then another £340 from the brothers William and Robert Bowyer on 31 May 1557.[67] There is some evidence these loans may have been used to repay earlier debts, as one bond made in May 1556 was cancelled in February 1557.[68] The same may also be true of the mortgage of all of Hales Owen to Anthony Forster on 11 July 1557, which appears to have been employed to redeem the earlier one to the Bowyers.[69]

Dudley's decision to exploit Hales Owen in this manner may have been influenced by a second act of royal favour. On 30 January 1557 both Hemsby and his rights of inheritance to the Robsart estate were restored to him despite his attainder, together with such of his chattels still in the possession of the crown.[70] It was probably as a consequence of this grant that he persuaded Lady Elizabeth Robsart in May 1557 to permit him to sell the outlying Robsart manor of Bulkham to Robert Armiger under the condition that his wife was assigned certain lands of the Hales Owen estate for her jointure.[71] The reasons for the large-scale raising of money between May and July 1557 cannot be fully established. It may have been intended to equip a retinue for the St Quentin expedition.[72] The contemporary rumours that Dudley supplied Elizabeth with money during Mary's reign remain unconfirmed.[73]

In 1558 his position underwent a further transformation. At some point during the winter of 1557–8 Lady Elizabeth Robsart died, and by the summer the three Norfolk manors of the Robsart estate had descended to Dudley and his wife. Thanks to the letters patent of January 1557, the descent of the Robsart estate did not depend on the restitution in blood in the first session of the parliament of 1558, though the latter did restore to Northumberland's four surviving children their full rights of inheritance.[74] The inheritance of the Robsart estate probably lay behind the decision to sell Hales Owen to Blount and Tuckey on 27 March 1558 for £3000.[75] Despite the formal processes gone through, there is some reason to suspect the sale was a fictitious one, but it enabled Dudley to raise the capital to repay Forster.[76] More decisive was the further sale of Hales Owen to John Lyttleton of Frankley for £2000 by Blount and Tuckey on 22 October, a sale in which Dudley clearly had a hand.[77]

The traditional picture of Dudley greeting the accession of Elizabeth as a Norfolk squire is therefore very much a myth. The manor house of Syderstone was uninhabitable, and Sir John Robsart himself had lived at Stansfield, a house in which his wife had been left a life interest by her first husband, Nicholas Appleyard. On her death it descended to John Appleyard, her son by that marriage. Dudley faced his father-in-law's difficulty in the summer of 1558, and his earliest surviving letter (22 July) deals with the possible purchase of the manor of Flitcham 'if I am to live in that country'.[78] Between 1556 and 1558 Hales Owen was given as his residence on legal documents, though there is no evidence that he ever lived there.[79] He probably spent most of the time in one or other of two houses in London: Sir Andrew Dudley's in Tothill Street, Westminster, and the mansion of Christchurch in the liberty by St Bartholomew the Grand, which Lord Henry Dudley's wife had inherited from her father.[80] Other than that, he may have been peripatetic until Elizabeth granted him the house at Kew on 29 December 1558.[81] Amy Dudley's own roamings at the beginning of 1559 from Lincolnshire to Denchworth and then Cumnor in Berkshire may not therefore have had any sinister implications.[82]

The Hales Owen estate did, however, make possible a continued Dudley connection with the West Midlands during the reign of Mary. It is revealing that the two leases of Robert Dudley's to survive were both to former servants of Northumberland.[83] If the mutual support the members of the immediate Dudley family provided for each other might have been expected, the continued association of Sidney, Blount and Forster, whose own interests might appear to have been better served by distancing themselves from so discredited a cause, is the more noteworthy.[84] Less clear is the political significance of the connection during Mary's reign. Wyatt's Rebellion caused a substantial dispersal of the clientèle, for many of those who, like Killigrew, went abroad in 1554 did not return until the accession of Elizabeth. Nor is the extent to which they maintained a correspondence known.[85] The best-known reference to some form of 'political' association is the report of the Venetian ambassador in July 1555 of the lord chancellor's order that the Dudley brothers and the released Wyatt rebels should leave London.[86] The possible connection between these gatherings and the Dudley Plot of 1555–6 remains obscure. In April 1556, immediately after the conspiracy was broken and the first arrests made, the French ambassador reported a rumour that 'les enfans du duc de Northumberland sont tous fugitifs et que l'on a fait une grande diligence pour les prendre'.[87] Arnold and Cawarden were temporarily arrested, and Killigrew, Leighton and Horsey (then in France) were implicated. Anthony Forster was tried in July 1556 (and pardoned in January 1557) for misprision of treason.[88] John Appleyard was placed under a recognizance in May.[89] The threat of misprision frightened Sir Nicholas Throckmorton into fleeing to France, and possibly Sir Ralph Bagenal as well.[90] Sir Henry Sidney's decision to serve in Ireland at this point, 'neither liking nor liked as I had been', may not have been unrelated.[91]

Misprision was probably the significant aspect. If anything the plot was focused about Edward Courtenay, earl of Devon; it may have been less the case that the Dudleys and their immediate friends were actively involved in the conspiracy, than that their natural associations were with those who were.[92] Robert Dudley's later connection to the former Marian conspirators was not confined to those on Cecil's list. Six captains had led the 'white-coats' who defected to Wyatt at Rochester in January 1554. The three who survived Mary's reign (William Pelham, Brian Fitzwilliam and Robert Perceval) all received Dudley's patronage in the years that followed.[93] It is also revealing to encounter Dudley dining in May 1559 at Arundel's, the tavern opposite St Lawrence Eastcheap which Croft had made his headquarters at the end of 1553 and where the Dudley plotters met in late 1555.[94]

III

It was not until April 1559 that the extent of Dudley's personal closeness to Elizabeth I became open knowledge, but on the eve of the accession he was included among those expected to form the inner circle of her court.[95] There are one or two hints that he had had some contact with the household at Hatfield before then, and he was certainly part of the new court by the time of the move to London on 22 November 1558. He was proposed by Cecil as a possible ambassador to Philip II to announce the accession, but on being given responsibility for the Stables was replaced by Lord Cobham.[96] His family was soon equally well entrenched in Elizabeth's court. Mary Sidney was a gentlewoman of the privy chamber 'without wages' by the time of the coronation. Lord Ambrose was named master of the Ordnance by the end of 1558, though he did not receive his letters patent until the beginning of 1560. Sidney himself become lord president of the Council in the Marches after his return from Ireland in the middle of 1559.[97]

Dudley's membership of the new court was seen from the start as part of Elizabeth's general rejection of Mary's household and return to the former Edwardians. In recent work the 'Edwardian' influence on the religious settlement of 1559 has been accorded much greater importance than it has in the past.[98] The wider political dimension deserves similar attention. The use of the 1552 prayerbook as the basis for that of 1559, and the refusal of the Marian bishops to accept the royal supremacy, which left the crown with no alternative but to recruit a new episcopate from the middle ranks of the Edwardian hierarcy, made the Edwardian influence on the new church relatively straightforward. Yet there were also two further aspects to the 'restoration of religion' of no less significance. The first was the attempt in the parliament of 1559 to obtain restitution by statute for those 'bishops and spiritual persons' deprived under Mary.[99] The second was the demand encountered both in 1559 and later for the punishment of the bishops associated with the Marian persecutions, particularly Edmund Bonner: 'by his willing cruelty no few number of the saints of God hath lost their lives ... yet through her mercy he liveth at such liberty as he himself considering his own cruel faits I think could not have hoped for'.[100]

The twin themes of restoration and revenge are central to any discussion of the Edwardian influence on the politics of the accession. It has been suggested that Sir Thomas Cawarden's intervention in the Surrey election of 1559 may have been inspired by revenge for his treatment by Lord Howard of Effingham after the discovery of the Dudley Plot.[101] In April 1560 Lord John Grey of Pirgo (another significant figure) criticised Elizabeth's failure to purge the former Marians from her privy council.[102] It is now clear that most of leading members of the new royal household, both male and female, came from the household at Hatfield. It is also probably the case that support for Elizabeth during Mary's reign lay behind the choice of those retained from the previous court and council.[103] Yet the appointment of Cecil as secretary of state was also seen by one correspondent as a return to 'your old room'.[104] Similarly, Lord Robert's appointment as master of the horse could also be considered a restoration, for his brother Warwick had held the office in 1553.[105]

The Dudley family could expect to be central figures in an Edwardian restoration. Yet the process took much longer than might have been expected, particularly when Edward Seymour was restored to the earldom of Hertford and William Parr to the marquessate of Northampton at the coronation. Not until December 1561 were the viscountcy of Lisle and the earldom of Warwick restored to Ambrose Dudley, or, as Robert Dudley put it, Elizabeth 'restored our house to the name of Warwick'.[106] He himself readopted the celebrated device of the bear and ragged staff in the following spring, but his own entry into the peerage was delayed until September 1564.[107] Nor was there an immediate restoration of Northumberland's estate. Except for Knebworth Beauchamp in 1559, Warwick did not receive anything until 1562 and 1564. Robert Dudley obtained the house at Kew at the beginning of the reign, and the site and demesne lands of the former priory of Watton in the East Riding of Yorkshire in 1560, but no substantial grants until 1561 and 1563.[108] In the meantime he began negotiating the purchase of the stewardship of the borough of Warwick from Sir Robert Throckmorton and (less successfully) revived his father's old campaign for the lands of the Suttons, Lords Dudley.[109]

The clientèle had an equal interest in a Dudley restoration. Lord Robert's surviving correspondence for 1559–60 contains frequent references to suits of old Dudley servants, such as the unnamed 'gentleman's widow, whom my lord your father (whose soul God pardon) favoured well', recommended by Croft from Berwick in April 1559, or Lady Joan Poyntz's request for a prebend for 'my man Freeman, the which was once servant to my lord your father, whom I think your lordship knoweth well'.[110] On one level this was expected filial piety, similar to his private gift 'to a poor woman that named herself your lordship's father's nurse', but there was also a political aspect.[111] In the West Midlands the Dudley reforming proceeded the restoration of Northumberland's lands. Lord Robert's tenure of the lord-lieutenancy of Warwickshire (jointly with Sir Ambrose Cave) and Worcestershire in 1559–60 saw Thomas Blount, John Fisher of Packington and Sir Richard Verney rise to prominence in local administration.[112] A similar process occurred in the East Riding of Yorkshire, where Simon Musgrave offered to 'provide your lordship yearly of three or four geldings as I did to my lord's grace your father' in return for his 'patent of Beverley', a suit obtained when Lord Robert was granted the lordship of Beverley in 1561.[113]

The Dudley connection was also the key to Lord Robert's religious patronage in 1559–60. Two prominent former Edwardians, Edwin Sandys and John Aylmer, both of whom may have had some association with Northumberland's household, were the main recipients.[114] Sandys became bishop of Worcester (a possibly significant choice of diocese); Aylmer, whose participation in Wyatt's rebellion may have been regarded suspiciously, only obtained the archdeaconry of Lincoln. More revealing, perhaps, were Dudley's household chaplains: Thomas Willoughby in 1559 and the émigré Scot Alexander Craik in 1560.[115] Both appear to have been Marian exiles, but equally importantly, both had been chaplains to Northumberland.[116] Their household service to Lord Robert was followed by promotion in the church, Willoughby to be a canon of Canterbury and Craik the bishop of Kildare.

More controversial was the question of episcopal lands. In the summer of 1559, following the deprivation of the bishop of Durham, Ralph, Lord Eure wrote to Dudley to request the restoration of a stewardship to some of the bishopric's temporalities he had held under Edward VI, 'for that it may appear to my countrymen that the queen's highness hath me in no less estimation than her majesty's brother had'.[117] Better known, thanks to the work of N. L. Jones, were the attempts in the parliament of 1559 to regain episcopal estates obtained under Edward and forfeited under Mary. Both

Sir Francis Jobson and Sir John Throckmorton had been forced to surrender lands to the bishop of Worcester, and Jobson to the bishop of Durham as well. Thomas Fisher had similar interests in Coventry and Lichfield.[118] It is revealing of the way in which the Dudley restoration was pursued that Robert Dudley later obtained episcopal leases for Jobson (and possibly Throckmorton also) in compensation for the failure of their bill.[119]

The Bagenals advanced an equally awkward demand for restitution. Immediately after Elizabeth's accession Sir Ralph Bagenal petitioned the privy council for restoration of his former Irish lands and offices. These he claimed he had lost through his opposition to the re-establishment of papal authority in the parliament of November 1554.[120] His brother, Sir Nicholas, took up the case in a letter to Dudley in July 1559, requesting as well the restoration of his own marshalcy of Ireland, which he had lost to Sir George Stanley in 1553–4.[121] Restoring the Bagenals, however, would involve undercutting the earl of Sussex's administration in Ireland. It did not occur until Sidney's appointment as lord deputy at the end of 1565, which was thus as much an aspect of the Dudley restoration as a revolution in Irish government.

The Dudley clientèle were not alone in seeking restitution. Other former Edwardians, Sir Ralph Sadler and Sir Thomas Smith, for example, submitted similar requests or held similar expectations on Elizabeth's accession.[122] However, the potential ramifications of the Dudley restoration were considerably greater and they account for much of the tension surrounding Lord Robert's relationship to the queen. When he left London for Cambridge in July 1553, Northumberland was said to have warned the privy council: 'If ye meane deceat, thoughe not furthwith yet hereafter, God will revenge the same'.[123] Would his son be the instrument of that revenge? Pius IV heard something to this effect in 1561:

> the greater of part of the nobility of that island take ill the marriage which the said queen designs to enter into with the Lord Robert Dudley. His father was beheaded as a rebel and usurper of the crown and they fear that if he becomes king, he will want to avenge the death of his father, and extirpate the nobility of that kingdom.[124]

Domestic echoes can also be detected. In the same year Thomas Trollope proposed to Dudley to publish a tract to 'take away the infamies passed against your father and grandfather', and with 'a probable reason to prove their unjust and innocent deaths procured through envy and malice'.[125]

The death of Northumberland was not the only potentially contentious issue. There was also the older question of Northumberland's role in the fall of Somerset, a subject that exercised several minds in the early 1560s.[126] The danger that factional disputes arising from old quarrels and revenge for old injuries might tear apart the new court was thus very real. In this context an otherwise cryptic comment of Elizabeth reported by Sir Humphrey Ratcliffe in November 1560 takes on considerable significance: 'I learned of a friend of mine in secrecy that the queen's majesty should in commendation of my Lord Robert upon questions moved say that he was of a very good disposition and nature, not given by any means to seek revenge of former matters past, wherein she seemed much to allow him'.[127] Other contemporary references to Lord Robert's open nature and generosity may therefore reflect more than sycophancy or compliment. The extent to which Dudley may have made a conscious effort to let bygones be bygones and to bury old quarrels is an aspect of his career in the Elizabethan court that still needs exploration. He certainly appears to have have sought good relations with the Seymours, as his efforts to mitigate the queen's anger against Hertford for his marriage, his later patronage to Pelham and Arthur, Lord Grey, and his kindness to John Hales reveal.[128]

The political fears created by the threat of a Dudley restoration may account for the long time it took Elizabeth to grant Northumberland's lands to his sons. They may also have inspired Cecil's reflections on the archducal marriage. Yet by the time Cecil compiled his list, many of the men included (the main exception being Sir Henry Dudley) had become established figures in Elizabethan governing circles. They were neither a faction of outsiders, nor even enemies of his. He enjoyed very good relations with Sidney and Thomas Wilson, and Henry Killigrew (albeit after some initial hostility on Cecil's part) became his brother-in-law. Dudley was on similar friendly terms with former Edwardians like Smith or Sadler, who are normally regarded as allies of Cecil. The impression Cecil's list gives of a distinct faction may well be a distortion.

The significance of the Dudley clientèle is possibly best explained by its social composition. The Dudley family itself is revealing. For all their claims of descent from the Suttons, Lords Dudley and the Beauchamp earls of Warwick (through Northumberland's mother, Elizabeth Grey), their prominence was the result of legal and military service to the crown. The background of their clients was quite disparate. If their connection included some members of established gentry families (the Blounts, Sidney or Croft), the social antecedents of others (the Bagenals, Forster or Jobson, for example) were highly questionable. Cawarden, like Sir Nicholas

Arnold and Sadler, had originally been a member of Thomas Cromwell's household. Nor should the military bias obscure the importance of the lawyers and men of business found among them, many of whom (like Glasier or Grice) were also important local political figures. The wide geographical base is equally striking: the connection extended to Cumberland, Chester, the East Riding, East Anglia and Cornwall, as well as the West Midlands. Essentially we are seeing the initiation of a third phase in the post-Reformation reshaping of the social basis of the Tudor political nation. The first began with Thomas Cromwell in the 1530s, the second took place in the court of Edward VI: the early years of Elizabeth's reign saw its consolidation.

The Dudley clientèle was thus a curious hybrid. The impressive degree of mutual loyalty displayed after 1553 was not dissimilar to that found in other affinities. If the clients provided support (financial as well as moral) in bad times, they would expect their reward in prosperity. Yet because 1559 saw a Dudley restoration rather than the formation of a new faction, there were bounds to their ambitions. To regain offices and lands they had lost, or to obtain compensation for them, was their immediate aim. Furthermore, because they were as much a section of a former governing elite as a personal faction led by Lord Robert, they were rapidly integrated into Elizabethan government. Lord Robert's direct influence cannot be discounted, as, for example, in the Newhaven expedition, but given the central role the Dudley clientèle had played in the reign of Edward VI, they could not be excluded in an Edwardian restoration. Lord Robert was as much the spokesman for their interests as they were the supporters of his.

NOTES

Early versions of this chapter were delivered to seminars at the Universities of Durham and York and the Institute of Historical Research. The research was made possible by generous grants from the British Academy, the Carnegie Trust for the Universities of Scotland, the Wolfson Foundation, and the Universities of Wales and Strathclyde. I should like to thank the Most Honourable the Marquesses of Bath and Anglesey for permission to employ the Dudley MSS at Longleat and the Paget MSS. The microfilms of the Cecil MSS at Hatfield House deposited at the British Library are used with permission of the Marquess of Salisbury.

Note: Place of publication is London unless otherwise stated.

1 Hatfield MS 155, art. 28, printed with the omission of 'Wilson' in S. Haynes (ed.), *A Collection of State Papers . . . left by William Cecil, Lord Burghley* (1740), p. 444. Haynes dated the memorandum April 1566, though it was endorsed by Cecil Anno 90 Eliz.
2 C. Read, *Mr Secretary Cecil and Queen Elizabeth* (New York, 1955), p. 260; W. T. MacCaffrey, *The Shaping of the Elizabethan Regime* (Princeton, NJ, 1968), pp. 96–7 and 129–30.

3 D. M. Loades, *Two Tudor Conspiracies* (Cambridge, 1965), pp. 246–7.

4 N. Canny, *The Elizabethan Conquest of Ireland: A Pattern Established 1565–1572* (Hassocks, Suss., 1976), pp. 42–3, 70–1.

5 D. Wilson, *Sweet Robin: A Biography of Robert Dudley, Earl of Leicester, 1533–1588* (1981), pp. 104–5, see also the comments on pp. 318–19.

6 Loades, *Two Tudor Conspiracies*, p. 16. A stronger connection is drawn in K. R. Bartlett, 'The English exile community in Italy and the political opposition to Queen Mary I', *Albion*, xiii (1981), 223–41.

7 A point made by Wilson, *Sweet Robin*, p. 105, though he sees the resort to Leicester as a consequence of his prominence at court.

8 Cecil's note can be read either Tho or Jho Dudley, but since both the brothers were Dudley's service both are included here.

9 For the controversy surrounding Molyneux, the MP who moved the linking of the petition on the succession to the subsidy bill in the parliament of 1566, see P. W. Hasler (ed.), *The History of Parliament: The House of Commons, 1558–1603* (1981), iii, 60–3, and G. R. Elton, *The Parliament of England 1559–1581* (Cambridge, 1986), pp. 365–6.

10 For Throckmorton's advancing of Middlemore, see J. E. Neale, 'Sir Nicholas Throckmorton's advice to Queen Elizabeth on her accession to the throne', *E[nglish] H[istorical] R[eview]*, lxv (1950), 91.

11 V. von Klarwill, *Queen Elizabeth and Some Foreigners* (1928), p. 190.

12 Discussed in more detail in S. Adams, 'The Dudley clientèle and the House of Commons, 1559–1584', *Parliamentary History*, viii (1989), 217, n. 6.

13 I am very grateful to Mr A. J. A. Malkiewicz of the University of Edinburgh for his generous help and advice on the sources for Northumberland's followers. R. C. Braddock, 'The composition and character of the duke of Northumberland's army', *Albion*, vi (1974), 342–55, refers in passing to one or two of the men discussed here.

14 The accounts are now [Longleat], Dudley MSS XIV, XV; the wages list Dudley MS III, fos. 2–17v; the bills and the livery lists are found in Dudley Box V, the livery lists being fos. 280–3.

15 P[ublic] R[ecord] O[ffice], L[and] R[evenue Office] 2/118; S[tate] P[apers] 46/163/53–74.

16 Bodl[eian Library], MS Addit[ional] C. 94.

17 Dudley MS III, fo. 114, bill of Hans Frank (pre-1564). In his account of receipts for December 1559–February 1561 (*ibid.*, fo. 27ᵛ), Ellis is simply styled servant.

18 All of them appear in Chauncy's account, Dudley MS XIV. For Grice, Blount, Yerwerth and Glasier, see Adams, 'Dudley clientèle and the House of Commons', 221, 224–5; for Hogan nn. 24, 30 below.

19 Based on a study of the bills found in Dudley Box V. George Christmas died on 23 February 1566. His brother Robert was Leicester's treasurer in 1570–1, see Adams, 'Dudley clientèle and the House of Commons', 227.

20 The two surveys are now Dudley MSS XVI–II; for the seisin of Kenilworth see Dudley Box II, art. 11; for the Denbigh commissioners, S. Adams, 'The composition of 1564 and the earl of Leicester's tenurial reformation in the lordship of Denbigh', *Bulletin of the Board of Celtic Studies*, xxvi (1976), 481, 491.

21 J. R. Dasent (ed.), *A[cts of the] P[rivy] C[ouncil]* (32 vols., 1890–1907), iv, 323–4.

22 See *ibid.*, p. 330; C[alendar of the] P[atent] R[olls], *Philip and Mary* (4 vols., 1936–9), ii, 116; PRO, SP 46/124/77 and C[hancery] 78/17/10 (Robert Dudley vs. High Ellis, decided on 27 November 1559); B[irmingham] R[eference] L[ibrary], [Lyttleton of] Hagley Hall MSS 351597–8. In T. Kemp (ed.), *The Black Book of Warwick* ([Warwick], 1898), p. 8, he is described as auditor to Ambrose Dudley in 1565.

23 The duchess's will is PRO, PROB 11/37/194–5; much is omitted in the synopsis published in A. Collins (ed.), *Letters and Memorials of State … written by Sir Henry Sidney* (2 vols., 1746) [hereinafter *Sidney Papers*], i, 33–6. For John Dudley and Northumberland, see his will, PRO, PROB 11/63/117ᵛ–8; for Hogan, B[ritish] L[ibrary], Harleian MS 353, fos.

121–2ᵛ. Clear references for Forster and Ellis are not available, though Ellis's brother Hugh is identified as a servant of Northumberland's in PRO, C 78/17/10.

24 See Adams, 'Dudley clientèle and the House of Commons', 235, n. 35. Bodl. MS Addit. C 94, fo. 2.

25 Glasier and Dudley received a grant of miscellaneous lands on 27 June 1553, see PRO, SP 10/18/49 (a draft) and *CPR, Edward VI* (5 vols., 1924–9), iv, 221. This was enrolled in Chancery by Dudley on 1 April 1555 (PRO, C 54/509).

26 PRO, LR 2/118 and Dudley Box V, fo. 282. He also served in the household of the duchess of Northumberland in 1553–5 and was left an annuity of £5 in her will (PRO, PROB 11/37/194ᵛ). In 1560 he was receiving one of £6/13/4 from Lord Robert (Dudley MS XV, fo. 10). See also Adams, 'Dudley clientèle and the House of Commons', 236, n. 61.

27 He was referred to as 'next the queen's majesty wholly your lordship's' in Dudley MS I, fo. 116, Throckmorton to Dudley, 27 February 1560.

28 For Edward and Thomas Aglionby and Sir George Blount, see Adams, 'Dudley clientèle and the House of Commons', 224, 228.

29 See Adams, 'Dudley clientèle and the House of Commons', 223 (John Throckmorton), 224 (Clement Throckmorton), 237, n. 81 (Musgrave). I should correct here the implication in the above that Clement Throckmorton's connection with the Dudleys included office-holding at Kenilworth. He was in fact appointed constable of Kenilworth by Mary on 19 September 1553, following the deprivation of Ambrose Dudley. However, John Throckmorton was receiver of the castle under Dudley. See PRO D[uchy of] L[ancaster] 42/23/97 and 29/464/7594–5. For Wilson, see the dedicatory epistle to *A Discourse Uppon Usurye* (ed. R. H. Tawney, 1925), p. 185. In December 1560 he was expected to become Dudley's 'chancellor' (PRO, SP 70/21/61).

30 Hogan was a son of Robert Hogan of East Bradenham and brother to Thomas, the servant of the fourth duke of Norfolk, and Robert, the servant of Philip II who acted as an English intelligencer in Spain during the 1560s. Edmund, the Spanish and Barbary merchant, was also a member of this family. Like the Ellises, the Hogans were related to Sir Thomas Gresham, whose own career reveals the difficulties of distinguishing a metropolitan from an East Anglian nexus.

31 See R. E. Ham (ed.), 'The Autobiography of Sir James Croft', *Bulletin of the Institute of Historical Research*, l (1977), 50.

32 For the Bagenals and the Dudleys, see Adams, 'Dudley clientèle and the House of Commons', 236, n. 46.

33 Discussed in S. Adams, 'The Dudley clientèle and the earl of Leicester's expedition to the Netherlands, 1585–1586', in *The Dutch in Crisis, 1585–1588. People and Politics in Leicester's Time* (Annual Symposium, Sir Thomas Browne Institute, 27 November 1987: Leiden, 1988), pp. 9–10. For the identities of the Boulogne officers see C[alendar] of S[tate] P[apers], Foreign [series], Edward VI (1861), pp. 292–355, and PRO, SP 68/15/191.

34 For Croft, see 'Autobiography', p. 56. Warwick also wanted Thomas Wilson at Newhaven (PRO, SP 70/44/163). I intend to re-examine the early life of Thomas Wood in a further essay.

35 Derived from Hatfield MS 154, art. 47, 'Names of such as served at Newhaven Anno 1563', supplemented by the correspondence in SP 70/40–61 and SP 12/24–29.

36 For Heigham, see PRO, SP 70/47/140; for Saule, SP 70/49/87.

37 For Maltby, see PRO, SP 70/44/37. He had been associated with the exiles in France in 1554: [Paris], A[rchives du] M[inistère des] R[elations] E[xtérieures], C[orrespondence] P[olitique], A[ngleterre], IX, fo. 271. Fisher is discussed below, nn. 84, 111. For Driver, see PRO, SP 70/54/92.

38 P. Forbes (ed.), *A Full View of the Public Transactions in the Reign of Elizabeth* (2 vols., 1740–1), i, 161, Throckmorton to Cecil, 13 July 1559.

39 For Pelham, *APC*, iii, 391. C[alendar of] S[tate] P[apers], Span[ish], 1553 (1916), pp. 351–2, 354. For Grey, AMRE, CPA, XII, fo. 40ᵛ, Noailles to Henry II, 20 July 1553.

40 See Adams, 'Dudley clientèle and the House of Commons', 224–5.

41 R. C. McCoy, 'From the Tower to the tiltyard: Robert Dudley's return to glory', *H[istorical] J[ournal]*, xxvii (1984), 425–35. The Dudley brothers appear on an undated tournament score cheque. There were four major Anglo–Spanish tournaments, dated 14 and 18 December 1554, 23 January and 25 March 1555 by McCoy, and 4 and 8 December, 24 January and 25 March by A. Young, *Tudor and Jacobean Tournaments* (1987), p. 31. It has not been possible to establish the one to which it belongs. David Loades, 'Philip II and the government of England', in C. Cross, D. Loades and J. J. Scarisbrick (eds.), *Law and Government under the Tudors* (Cambridge, 1988), p. 193, assigns it to that of 23 January.

42 J. A. Giles (ed.), *The Whole Works of Roger Ascham* (3 vols., 1865), i, 419–20. For Warwick's death, see J. G. Nichols (ed.), *The Diary of Henry Machyn* (Camden Society, xlii, 1848), p. 72 and AMRE, CPA, XIII, fo. 270ᵛ, Noailles to Henry II, 26 October 1554.

43 *APC*, v, 72. Lists of those released can be found in *Machyn's Diary*, p. 80; *APC*, v. 90–1; AMRE, CPA, IX, fo. 635ᵛ and XII, fo. 320; and J. Stow, *The Annales of England* ([1592]), p. 1061. The Dudley brothers were first included by John Strype, *Ecclesiastical Memorials* (3 vols., 1721), iii, 208, to whom the error can be traced. Cf. McCoy, 'Tower to tiltyard', 425.

44 PRO, PROB 11/37/194–5 *passim*. For Sidney's role, see his 'Memoir' of 1 March 1583, in *Calendar of the Carew Manuscripts* (6 vols., 1867–73), ii, 359; it is also commented upon by Noailles in his letter of 26 October 1554, see n. 42 above.

45 [Plas Newydd], Paget MSS, X, art. 12, 25 May [1574]; Paget in turn referred to the affection the duchess had borne him (*ibid.*, art. 57). She left gifts to the first lord and his wife in her will. The possible role of Cornwallis and Hastings is suggested by Dudley's help for them in 1559: see Dudley MS I, fos. 16, 54.

46 See, *inter alia*, PRO 31, 3/3/25, fo. 134, Paul de Foix to Catherine de Medici, 23 January 1565; *CSP Span., Elizabeth* (4 vols., 1892–9), ii, 314; [Brussels], A[rchives] G[énérales du] R[oyaume], P[apiers d'] E[tat et de l'] A[udience] 361, fo. 156, Champigny to Requesens, 15 February 1576.

47 Copies of the cedulas are now in A[rchivo] G[eneral] de S[imancas], C[ontaduría] M[ayor de] C[uentas], Primera Epoca, leg. 1345, n.f. The original of Randolph's is now BL, Stowe MS 142, fo. 19.

48 See D. M. Loades, *The Reign of Mary Tudor* (1979), p. 373. Loades's surmise is confirmed by the account of Philip's paymaster, see AGS, CMC, Iª Epoca, leg. 1231.

49 PRO, SP 11/11/12. Cf. Croft, 'Autobiography', p. 54, 'divers Elected persons were chosen thereunto', and J. M. Osborn (ed.), *The Autobiography of Thomas Wythorne* (Oxford, 1961), p. 85, Lord Ambrose Dudley 'waz kalled to serv the prins in her warz'. The argument of C. S. L. Davies, 'England and the French War, 1557–9', in J. Loach and R. Tittler (eds.), *The Mid-Tudor Polity c. 1540–1560* (1980), p. 163, overlooks the personal nature of the relationship to Philip.

50 As noted by Loades, *Reign*, pp. 470–1, and K. R. Bartlett, '"The misfortune that is wished for him": the exile and death of Edward Courtenay, earl of Devon', *Canadian Journal of History*, xiv (1979), esp. 19–21.

51 Most recently in McCoy, 'Tower to tiltyard', 430, from Wilson, *Sweet Robin*, p. 71.

52 *Machyn's Diary*, p. 128.

53 The letter of recommendation for Philip Sidney sent to an unnamed German on 23 July 1573 (Cambridge University Library, University Archives, Letters 8, p. 160), recalling 'nostra benevolentia recordatione iam inde a Sancti Quintini obsidione', was undoubtedly addressed to Schwendi. In his letter to Requesens of 15 February 1576 (AGR, PEA 361, fo. 156v), Champigny reports Leicester's references to courtesies received from 'Monsr. d'Arras lequel il avait cogneu avant qu'il fut Cardinal'.

54 He is not found in any of the lists of Philip's English household, e.g. AGS, CMC, Iª Epoca, leg. 1184, or E[stado] 811, fo. 122.

55 For Pembroke's visit to Calais, see AMRE, CPA, XX, fo. 349, F. to A. de Noailles, 20 December 1556, and C[alendar of] S[tate] P[apers]. Ven[etian], vi (2) (1881), p. 835.

56   *CPR, Philip and Mary*, ii, 150–1, 158–9. Sir Andrew Dudley did not receive his pardon until 5 April (p. 42), Sir Nicholas Arnold until 4 March (p. 47).

57   4 & 5 Philip and Mary c. 12. On the subject of reversal of attainders, see Elton, *Parliament of England*, pp. 303–5.

58   Dudley Box II, art. 12, published in J. E. Jackson, 'Amy Robsart', *Wiltshire Archaeological and Natural History Magazine*, xvii (1878), 81.

59   Quoted in Robert Dudley vs. Hugh Ellis (PRO, C 78/17/10).

60   The date of the duchess's death is not clear: the inquisitions post mortem give 15 January 1555, her funeral monument in Chelsea Old Church, 22 January. See G. E. Cockayne, *Complete Peerage* (rev. ed., 13 vols., 1910–49), ix, 726.

61   Northumberland obtained Hales Owen from the crown in 1538 and settled it on his wife in 1539. The duchess received further jointures in 1546 and 1552. See BRL, Hagley Hall MS 351609 and *CPR, Edward VI*, iv, 431. For the settlement with Mary, see Edinburgh University Library, Laing MS 634/2 AND *CPR, Philip and Mary*, i, 129. The manorial court of Hales Owen was held in her name in 1554, BRL, Hagley Hall MS 357332.

62   PRO, PROB 11/37/194. Marrow was an MP for Warwickshire in October 1553. The overseers included Jobson and Sir Thomas Cawarden.

63   *CPR, Philip and Mary*, ii, 121. Lady Tailboys petitioned Philip for the restoration of her own estates on 22 February 1555; Giles, *Works of Ascham*, i, 429–30.

64   BRL, Hagley Hall MS 351613, badly damaged by damp. Lord Henry apparently wanted nothing. His generosity may be attributed to the fact that he was married to a major heiress, Margaret, daughter of Thomas, Lord Audley, whose lands the queen permitted them to inherit when Margaret came of age in July 1556. See *CPR, Philip and Mary*, iii, 11. Dudley MS XX [Schedule of Evidences], fo. 55v, refers to a release by a further executor, the minor Gloucestershire gentleman, Gabriel Blike. He is not mentioned in any of the other Hales Owen muniments, but did have a later association with Leicester, see Adams, 'Dudley clientèle and the House of Commons', 235, n. 34.

65   BRL, Hagley Hall MS 351614. The view of frankpledge was taken in Lord Robert's name in April 1556, MS 346500.

66   For Tuckey's lease of the manor house of Hales in 1549, see BRL, Hagley Hall MS 351598. He was one of Northumberland's household gentlemen in 1553 (PRO, LR 2/118). Blount is identified as chief steward in two of the Hales Owen court rolls of 1556: Hagley Hall MSS 346501 and 346869.

67   William Bowyer, keeper of the records in the Tower in the 1650s, wrote an *Heroica Eulogia* in 1567 to celebrate Robert Dudley's creation as earl of Leicester. This is now [San Marino, Calif.] Huntington Library MS HM 160. The recognizances for the loans from the Bowyers are PRO, C 54/529, m. 26, and 531, mm. 32 and 44; from Bird, C 54/533, mm 8, 20.

68   PRO, L[ord] C[hamberlain's Department], 4 [Recognizances]/188/287.

69   PRO, C 54/546, m. 6. See also n. 76 below. Forster may have leased the estate back to Dudley on the 16th, see Dudley XX, fo. 58ᵛ.

70   *CPR, Philip and Mary*, iii, 250–1.

71   PRO, C[ommon] P[leas], 40 [feet of fines, enrolled deeds]/1170/17, 1171/9ᵛ–10; CP 26/1/94; C 54/531, m. 45. See also C 78/68/11, Arthur Robsart vs. John Lyttleton and George Tuckey, 1578.

72   For his raising of money on 16–17 July 1557, see PRO, LC 4/188/369ᵛ–70. M. Waldman, *Elizabeth and Leicester* (1944), p. 60, refers to a sale of lands to equip a retinue that failed to assemble, but provides no evidence. Cf. Wilson, *Sweet Robin*, pp. 71–2.

72   They are discussed in Wilson, *Sweet Robin*, p. 73.

74   Their petition of 20 January 1558 (PRO, C 89/6/5) referred to their disablement from inheriting lands of their father, their wider family or their ancestors.

75   The indenture of sale is BRL, Hagley Hall MS 351493; the licence to alienate (24 March), *CPR, Philip and Mary*, iv, 345.

76 See the release of Forster of his interest in Hales Owen, 28 March 1558, BRL, Hagley Hall MS 351494; the bill for the redemption of the mortgage, PRO, C 54/546, m. 6; and the related recognizances, LC 4/188/415–ᵛ, 432. The argument for a fictitious sale is made in N.D. Fourdrinier, 'Amy Robsart' (unpublished typescript, c. 1957, now Norfolk Record Office, MS MC 5/33), p. 135.

77 For the date, see BRL, Hagley Hall MS 351621; for the licence to alienate (3 November 1558), *CRP, Philip and Mary*, iv, 440–1. Some idea of the circumstances can be found in the badly worn response of John Lyttleton (PRO, C 3/50/120), the only document from the case of Dudley vs Lyttleton (1560) to survive.

78 BL, Harleian MS 4712, fo. 273, to John Flowerdew.

79 His coat and conduct money for the St Quentin expedition was paid to and from Hales Owen: see BL, Stowe MS 571, fos. 101–ᵛ, 121.

80 *CPR, Philip and Mary*, iii, 10–11. Robert Dudley had books delivered to Christchurch in 4 Mary (1556–7), Dudley Box V, art. 3, and belongings moved from in early 1559, Dudley MS XIV, fo. 6ᵛ. For Sir Andrew Dudley's house, see his will (drafted on 21 July 1556), *Sidney Papers*, i, 30.

81 For the grant of Kew, *CPR, 1558–1560* (1939), p. 60.

82 Her movements can be traced through references in Dudley MS XIV.

83 BRL, Hagley Hall MSS 351612, 351619.

84 Sidney and John Fisher of Packington also stood surety for Lord Ambrose in the reign of Mary, see the bonds enrolled in PRO, C 54/505 and 539.

85 Thomas Wood referred to corresponding with Croft from Germany while the latter was in the Tower in 1554. PRO, SP 70/45/5ᵛ, to Cecil 17 November 1562.

86 *CSP Ven.*, vi(i), 137. See Loades, *Two Tudor Conspiracies*, pp. 177–8.

87 AMRE, CPA, XII, fo. 502, avis au roi, 29 April 1556. See also *APC*, v, p. 263, an order on 18 April to stay the process of seizure of Ambrose Dudley's goods.

88 *CPR, Philip and Mary*, iii, 453.

89 *APC*, v, 274–5.

90 See Throckmorton's letters of 30 September 1556, BRL, Baker MS 2/2, n.f.; for Bagenal, Loades, *Two Tudor Conspiracies*, p. 214. It is worth noting that the French wished the English exiles to use a cover story that they were fleeing their creditors. See AMRE, CPA, IX, fo. 609, Montmorency to Noailles, 21 March 1556.

91 'Memoir', *Cal. Carew MSS*, ii, 359.

92 On Courtenay, Bartlett, '"Misfortune"', pp, 19–21.

93 Pelham was identified as a follower of Leicester's in 1568 ([Paris], Bibliothèque Nationale, fonds français 15971, fo. 143, La Fôret to Charles IX, 19 July). For Fitzwilliam, see Bodl, MS Carte 56, fo. 194, Leicester to Sir W. Fitzwilliam, 21 October 1573, for Perceval, PRO, SP 70/49/158, 60/97, Sir T. Smith to Cecil, 2 January, 19 July 1563. Of the other three, Alexander Brett was executed following Wyatt's Rebellion and William Sturton after the Dudley Plot, while Sir George Harper appears to have died between 1555 and 1559.

94 Dudley MS XIV, fo. 10.

95 M. J. Rodríguez-Salgado and S. Adams (eds.), 'The count of Feria's dispatch to Philip II of 14 November 1558', *Camden Miscellany XXVIII* (Camden Society, 4th ser., xxix, 1984), pp. 332, 341n. For his position as favourite, AGS, E 812, fo. 28, Feria to Philip II, 18 April 1559.

96 'Feria dispatch', p. 341n. For Dudley's associations with Hatfield, see Dudley MS I, fos. 27, 26, Sir Nicholas Bagenal to Dudley, 12 July 1559, Sir Thomas Benger to Dudley, 23 July.

97 For Mary Sidney, see the 'coronation roll': PRO, LC 2/4/3, fo. 104. The young countess of Huntingdon does not appear to have been as close to Elizabeth at the beginning of the reign as she was in the 1590s.

98 W. S. Hudson, *The Cambridge Connection and the Elizabethan Settlement of 1559* (Durham, NC, 1980); N. L. Jones, *Faith by Statute: Parliament and the Settlement of Religion 1559* (1982).

99   See Elton, *Parliament of England*, p. 121, and Jones, *Faith by Statute*, pp. 156–7.

100   Dudley MS I, fo. 90, the duchess of Suffolk to Dudley, [? October 1559]. For later examples see J. E. Neale, *Elizabeth I and her Parliaments, 1559–1581* (pb. ed., 1965), pp. 121, 180.

101   C. G. Bayne, 'The First House of Commons of Queen Elizabeth', *EHR*, xxiii (1908), 467–8. See also the petition he submitted to Elizabeth on her accession for compensation for damages suffered under Mary: A. J. Kempe (ed.), *The Loseley Manuscripts* (1835), pp. 140–4.

102   PRO, SP 12/12/1; Haynes, *Burghley Papers*, p. 295, to Cecil, 1, 20 April 1560.

103   S. Adams, 'Eliza enthroned? the court and its politics', in C. Haigh (ed.), *The Reign of Elizabeth I* (1984), pp. 64–5. Loades, *Reign of Mary Tudor*, pp. 459–61.

104   PRO, SP 63/1/12, J. Alen to Cecil, 16 December 1558.

105   The staff of the Edwardian Stables were still in post in 1559. Compare BL, Stowe MS 571, fo. 37^v and PRO, E 101/427/8–^{v} (the establishments of 1552 and 1553) with the household subsidy rolls for 1559 (BL, Lansdowne MS 3, fo. 200) and 1564 (PRO, E 179/69/81).

106   E. Lodge (ed.), *Illustrations of British History* (3 vols., 1791), i, 347, Dudley to the earl of Shrewsbury, 27 December 1561.

107   BL, Addit MS 35831, fo. 32, R. Jones to Sir N. Throckmorton, 25 May 1562.

108   These were all lands formerly held by Northumberland, with the exception of Kew and some of the manors granted to Robert Dudley in 1563 and to Warwick in 1564. See *CPR, 1558–60*, pp. 86, 288, *1560–63* (1948), pp. 189–90, 291–3, 534–43, *1563–1566* (1960), p. 59. For Watton, see also A. G. Dickens (ed.), 'Archbishop Holgate's Apology', *EHR*, lvi (1941), 456–8, and Dudley MS I, fo. 44, Yerwerth to Dudley, 19 July 1559.

109   For the stewardship of Warwick, see Adams, 'Dudley clientèle and the House of Commons', n. 33. Northumberland had bought out John Sutton, Lord Dudley in the reign of Henry VIII; these lands were restored to Edmund, the fourth lord, by Mary (*CPR, Philip and Mary*, ii, 22–3, iii, 34–7). For Robert Dudley's efforts to purchase them, see Dudley MS I, fos. 84, 108, 171, Lord Dudley to Dudley, [? Aug] 1559, 30 January, 25 November 1560.

110   Dudley MS I, fos. 13, 74, Croft to Dudley, 10 April, Poyntz to Dudley, 29 August 1559.

111   Dudley MS XIV, fo. 15. The rewarding of old Dudley servants was an extensive process, see, for example, the correspondence over 'my dear lord and father-in-law's old servant' Hugh Shadwell, Dudley MS II, fo. 131, Sidney to Leicester, 2 March 1573.

112   Dudley MS I, fos. 36, 121, 158, Cave to Dudley, 16 July 1559, Fisher to Dudley, 18 March, 29 August 1560.

113   Dudley MS I, fo. 118, 6 March 1560. See Humberside R.O., B[everley] C[orporation Records], II/7/2 [Minute Book of the Governors, 1558–1567], fos. 66, 76^v, tolls paid to Mr Musgrave, 1564–65.

114   For Aylmer, Dudley MS I, fos. 106, 172. For Sandys, *ibid.*, fo. 139, and BL, Addit. MS 32091, fo. 185. The 'list of divines' dated 1559 in Historical Manuscripts Commission, *Report on the Pepys MSS* (1911), p. 2, relates to the Vestiarian Controversy and should be assigned to 1565–6.

115   Dudley MSS XIV, fo. 15, XV, fo. 24^v. For Craik, see also Greater London Record Office, P92/Sav/1957, Craik to Dudley, 10 January 1562. How this letter strayed into the St Saviour's parish records is a mystery.

116   For Willoughby, see Dudley MS I, fo. 70, Ambrose to Robert Dudley, 17 August 1559. For Craik and Northumberland, see PRO, SP 10/14/144, Northumberland to Cecil, 11 December 1552. I am very grateful to Dr John Durkan of Glasgow University for information about Craik.

117   Dudley MS, I, fo. 28.

118   See N. L. Jones, 'Profiting from religious reform: the land rush of 1559', *HJ*, xxii (1979), 287–8.

119   PRO, SP 15/12/88, Sir John to Sir Nicholas Throckmorton, 29 December 1565.

For Jobson's claims in the bishopric of Durham, see also SP 12/20/62, Bishop Pilkington to Cecil, 14 November 1561.

120 PRO, SP 63/1/20.

121 Dudley MS I, fos. 27–8.

122 For Sadler, see PRO, SP 15/12/109 and Dudley MS I, fo. 181, to Dudley, 24 January 1561; for Smith, *CSP Foreign, Elizabeth*, vi, p. 186.

123 J. G. Nichols (ed.), *The Chronicle of Queen Jane* (Camden Society, xlviii, 1850), pp. 7, 9. At his trial, Sir Thomas Palmer accused his judges of being equally guilty of treason, *CSP Span, 1553*, p. 185.

124 To the cardinal of Ferrara, July 1561, printed in J. H. Pollen (ed.), *Papal Negotiations with Mary Queen of Scots* (Scot. Hist. Soc., xxxvii, 1901), pp. 60–1.

125 Dudley MS I, fo. 207. William Hayworth took up the same theme in 1573: 'how Judasly your dear father was betrayed by trusting too much to the children of man'. *CSP Scotland, 1571–74* (1905), p. 631.

126 Notably the anonymous compilers of the 'histories' of Edward VI's reign now BL, Addit. MSS 48023, fos. 350–69ᵛ, and 48126, fos. 6–16.

127 BL, Cottonian MS Titus B XIII, fo. 28, to the earl of Sussex. The first page has disappeared, obscuring the immediate circumstances of the remark.

128 For Grey, see *Sidney Papers*, i, 282, Sidney to Grey, 17 September 1580; for Hales, BL, Addit MS 32091, fo. 248, Hales to Leicester, 28 July 1571. Northumberland is said to have sought a reconciliation with Somerset's sons on the eve of his own execution: see *CSP Span. 1553*, p. 185.

Power and duty in the Elizabethan aristocracy: George, earl of Shrewsbury, the Glossopdale dispute and the Council

Geoffrey Elton once exhorted historians to study situations rather than trends.[1] Hugh Trevor-Roper too has advised that we should look not at men, but at men in their circumstances. Sadly, not all of us can obtain grants to illuminate the *mentalité* of the Balinese cock-fight. But we can at least seek to turn the spotlight on particular events and episodes, of limited duration and of no great historical moment, but from which, with a certain amount of digging, we may be able to gain some insight into men's self-image and their relations one with another.

Among the disorganised and widely scattered papers of the Elizabethan Talbots, earls of Shrewsbury, are numerous documents which refer to a dispute between George, the sixth earl, and his tenants of Glossopdale in Derbyshire. In the course of that dispute the scene shifts back and forwards between small Peakland villages and the court in London, and the *dramatis personae* range from the queen and Lord Burghley to nameless subsistence farmers. By piecing together the fragments it is possible to shed some new light, through the experiences of the sixth earl, on a number of issues: in particular, on the nature of the changing relationship, social and economic, between great lord and tenant, and on the attitudes, skills and effectiveness of those who formed the queen's council; and so to reach towards some conclusions on the extent of noble power enjoyed by an Elizabethan nobleman, and the restraints upon it.[2]

In 1536 the Statute of Absentees enabled the crown to confiscate the Irish landholdings of the fourth earl of Shrewsbury. In recompense, letters patent of October 1537[3] granted the Talbots the manor and rectory of Glossop in the High Peak, with other Derbyshire lands. All of these had formerly belonged to the suppressed monastery of Basingwerk, in County Flint. Dr George Bernard has shown that this and other such royal grants consolidated Talbot holdings in Derbyshire; rewarded their sterling service during the Pilgrimage of Grace; and budgeted for the future, the crown seeing 'the enhancement of [the Talbots'] local power as a guarantee of their continued loyalty and of stability in their country'. Henry VIII's generous treatment of Lord Wharton in the North and the Russells in the West Country performed much the same function.[4] Forty years later, the Elizabethan crown still had an indirect interest in nearly three-quarters of the manors in Derbyshire – including Glossop – as Duchy of Lancaster lands, and farmed about twenty-six manors itself. But the Talbots were a considerable force too, the sixth earl and his wife, Bess of Hardwick, possessing between them about thirty-seven manors, chiefly in the north and north-west of the county. The region has been described as 'a vast extent of rough grazing', suffering from 'harsh winters, short, cool summers and sixty inches of precipitation': unforgiving territory, in which the jury of a court of survey could not 'conveniently soe distinguish between the arable, meadow and pasture as is required, by reason that the most part ... is used for all the said purposes of plowing, mowinge and pasturage as occasion and necessite doth urge the occupyers'. On the small hill farms, mostly run by family labour, and the common pastures which fed unshepherded flocks, 'mere subsistence rivalled stock-breeding as the great object of husbandry'.[5] It was against this stern background that the Glossopdale dispute took place.

I

By the late 1570s and early 1580s financial problems were pressing hard on the Talbots. Earlier, scant trouble with minorities, fecklessness or attainder had left them one of the wealthiest aristocratic families in Tudor England. The consolidation and acquisition of estates had compensated for 'a period of stagnation, if not decline' in the real value of some of those they already held. At the sixth earl's succession in 1560, contemporary figures on income suggest that they were at least holding their own. Dr Bernard has even suggested that 'possibly the Talbots were just so rich that inflation at its mid-century level appeared to pose no threat.'[6] But by 1579 the Talbot papers are full of doom and gloom. The persistent indebtedness of Gilbert Talbot, Shrewsbury's second son, and the increasing rapacity of Bess of Hardwick, account for many of these references. More specifically, Shrewsbury complains, for example, that the 'fenyshere' of his house in London lays on charges apace, and orders him sent away. Alderman Pullyson is to be refused any more lead until he settles his debts, for at present all the money the earl has and can borrow will not suffice him. The lack of news from a trading voyage makes Shrewsbury weary of such enterprises.[7] Mrs Pierrepont, his step-daughter, is twice asked to forbear half her annuity for a time, since he cannot pay it immediately 'for want of money'. Shrewsbury's London agent, Thomas Baldwin, complains that he is charged with more payments than his receipts can cover, and is ordered to pay a debt to a glazier before tackling the needs of Bess of Hardwick – a scheduling of debts which must have taken some nerve. By late 1580 a creditor is asked to accept for a year only the interest on a loan, because the earl has so many other demands on his money, and so many break promises with him in the country.[8] Clearly, the Talbots were suffering from a cash-flow problem at the very least.

But the burden of royal service, less widely shared by Shrewsbury's noble contemporaries than these issues of building, business and family provision, vastly exacerbated this. As President of the Council in the North, the third earl of Huntingdon's heavy expenses and static fee, eroded by inflation and paid in very dilatory fashion, reduced him to embezzling money intended by Elizabeth for the King of Scots. A similar story is told of the third earl of Sussex.[9] For fifteen years, between 1569 and 1584, Shrewsbury was keeper of that deeply tedious woman, Mary Stuart. We all know of *her* experiences; no-one seems to have cared much about the effect on her unfortunate captor. Shrewsbury's allowance for the 'Scotch Queen's diet' was frequently delayed – by October 1580 it was a year overdue. He claimed that it did not cover half his expenses in any case, forcing him into heavy borrowing.[10] He had to victual a noble household including over thirty of Mary's entourage: he estimated in July 1580 that wine, spices and fuel alone 'commethe not under one thousande poundes by the yeere'; replacing plate, pewter and other household stuff the Scots 'wilfully wasted' cost another thousand; annuities to servants to keep them honest £400 more; and the extra soldiers needed would not live on the 6*d* per day the queen allowed them. This was no doubt exaggeration, but when Elizabeth halved even this inadequate allowance desperation set in. As Shrewsbury noted sadly, 'the worlde must nedes thinke that eyther my desertes have ben very small, or els her Majestie doth make very small accompt of me'.[11] In the light of this, by 1581 he was asking Baldwin – for public consumption at any rate – to find out 'what olde plat yeldes the ounce, for I wyll not leve me a cuppe of sylvare to drink in butt I wyll see the next terme my creditors payde'. The earl of Leicester even rebuked him for keeping Mary 'very barely for hir dyett': on Easter Day 1581 she had had 'so fewe dysshes, & so badd meat in them, as yt was to to bad to se yt'. Apparently Shrewsbury had told her he was 'cutt of of [his] allowance, &

therfore could yeald hir no better'. Even these shock tactics produced no sympathy; only a warning that the queen would 'much myslyke' it.[12]

Shrewsbury's experiences and perceptions provide further material for any reassessment of Lawrence Stone's economic crisis of the aristocracy as a whole. Like other noble families in difficulties, the Talbots saw their troubles not in Stone's terms of rising expenses, fuelled by extravagance and inflation, outstripping inflexible land revenues,[13] but rather as a collection of immediate and disparate problems, more personal than general, more traditional than new, and (perhaps) more psychological than real. Certainly, Shrewsbury continued to live in great style. What mattered, however, was that like others he *felt* poor. What makes Shrewsbury unusual and historically valuable is that he was keener than most of his mid-Elizabethan contemporaries to do something about it.

It is indeed odd that before the 1590s many, perhaps most large landowners seem to have done little effective to preserve their financial stability. Like their fifteenth-century forebears, they saw the practicalities of estate management as a dirty business, fit only for lesser mortals and not particularly rewarding anyway.[14] Dr Hassell Smith writes of the fourth duke of Norfolk's 'benevolent estate management' – which presumably means a policy of do-nothing. The Petres cut household costs and abandoned the expensive court rather than raise rents. The earls of Worcester *did* carry out a number of manorial surveys; but these were 'designed more to confirm ... existing rights and services ... than to provide an accurate basis on which calculations of future yields could be made'. Their activities were sporadic, and new land purchases and a court boycott did most to keep them solvent.[15] Lord Darcy boasted complacently, 'I have lived as my father did before me, of the old rents of my land.' So did the earl of Westmorland.[16] In the 1580s both the desperate earl of Huntingdon and the ninth earl of Northumberland used the 'beneficial lease' – high entry fines in return for low annual rents – to make money in haste and repent at leisure. In the Chalk country, the Thynnes too concentrated on raising entry fines.[17]

Stone has described how this short-term expedient remained popular into the 1590s, though in an age of inflation it benefited the tenant at least as much as the landlord. Only from the 1590s, he suggests, did landlords realise that higher rents were the long-term answer to their economic troubles. Thus, by 1609 the earl of Northumberland had seen the light, turned to estate management, and doubled his land income with his 'books of surveys, plots of manors and records'.[18] The time-lag between the onset of financial difficulties for many in mid-century and positive remedial action only in the 1590s was damaging indeed. I tend to agree with Stone and others that R. H. Tawney, perhaps too prone to seek for victims, exaggerated the amount of conflict between sixteenth-century landlord and tenant. Few peers other than the third earl of Sussex and the first earl of Cumberland seem to have been a hissing and a byword to their tenants for their exactions. The earlier sixteenth-century Talbots seem more typical, with 'a traditional form of administration ... not legalistically exploited'. Dr Bernard notes (perhaps a touch regretfully?) that there is little evidence that they had serious disputes with their tenants.[19] That conflict was 'occasional and spasmodic' rather than inevitable[20] is, in fact, a profound criticism of the aristocracy's collective lack of will to survive. All too often great Elizabethan landowners seem to be suffering from a wilful myopia as to their danger, or, at least, from a reluctance to act other than via traditional, short-term expedients. Shrewsbury's experiences during the Glossopdale dispute help to explain why.

Shrewsbury's response to *his* problems was far more vigorous than that of others. In the traditional way, he devoted more attention to exploiting his offices, advancing a claim to outlaws' goods in the Peak. He began negotiations with the crown about a fee-farm for his services. More originally, from the 1570s he became the largest lead producer in Derbyshire, playing a highly personal and active role 'of the utmost significance' in the growth and technological development of the industry – including, notably, its revival in the High Peak.[21] But, above all, he realised that he had 'no other helpe towards his maintenance & discharge of his greate debts but his lands'. Mary Stuart kept him tied to his Midlands estates for fifteen years; ironically, this cause of his impoverishment led him to the potential solution: the 'great deal of personal attention to the problems of estate management' that Stone so commends in him.[22] Irish history is full of myths, one being the unmitigated evils of absentee landlordism. The tenants of Glossopdale, at any rate, would have given much not to have had a bored, straitened landlord on the spot.[23] As a result, the next four years saw a prolonged and deliberate attempt by a ruthless, modernising landlord to raise rents, and convert money tithes into kind; above all, to attack custom and security of tenure, to seek to change the very nature of the tenurial bond. What follows seeks to prove these assertions.

II

There is some evidence that Shrewsbury had always been a tough and inventive landlord. As early as 1563 he had tried to obtain an aid from his

Hallamshire tenants on the marriage of his eldest daughter, causing some anguish.[24] There was friction too with his High Peak tenants some time before they lurched into open conflict. In 1575 'clamoruse people' from the area complained of his great extortions, both in London and when the matter was heard in the Duchy. In 1576 Gilbert Talbot wrote from the court that he had missed 'those of the Peak Forest', for after they had delivered their supplication to one of Burghley's clerks they never came again. He dismissed them lightly as 'but two simple fellows'.[25] In October 1578, however, their grievances became more explicit. Two of Shrewsbury's servants, George Scargill and Richard Roberts, report from Glossop that at his command they have spoken to his tenants individually and have made offers concerning the 'encreasing of their Rents according to their Rates'. Almost all the tenants have agreed, and the officers hope that the earl will approve when he sees their book. In fact, far from needing more people, they will be able to send home some of those they already have.[26]

At first it seems that Shrewsbury was simply renegotiating the terms of his tenants' twenty-one year leases, apparently expiring at Michaelmas 1578. Certainly the Derbyshire JPs, meeting at Chesterfield in April 1579, noted that he had offered to 'continue [his tenants] still in suche reasonable sorte as the[y] oughte to have bene contented with all'. But it is difficult to square this picture of business as usual with the fact that the JPs met 'uppon complainte latelye made unto us of the Ryotous behaviour of dyvers your L[ordship's] Rude and uncyvill tenaunts of Glossoppedale'.[27] In nearby Symmondley the tenants were walking their grounds with bills, long pikes and staves; four were coming to see Shrewsbury and threatened, if they did not get 'a good answere', to fetch the rest and so go altogether to London.[28] In any case, such 'renegotiation' would have hardly required the accompanying force which the earl's men obviously had in October, nor explain their surprise that there had been no trouble.

One can only assume that the tenants had at first been intimidated, misled or simply stunned, for within days they were in London – despite Gilbert Talbot's attempt to head them off at Barnet – and the nature of their plight rapidly became apparent. On 18 April 1579 a formidable Privy Council meeting of Burghley, Leicester, Lincoln, Bedford, Hunsdon, Walsingham, Hatton, the treasurer and the comptroller heard four of the tenants, led by one Harry Botham, present a bill against Shrewsbury. The Councillors were told that George Scargill and William Dickenson, the bailiff of Sheffield, had demanded four marks for every 12*d* of old rent, such high rents being 'requyred to be payde at the last Ladyes day for one quarter or els to departe'. Leicester, in a private letter to Shrewsbury, reported the tenants' accusation that the two officers 'have delt very hardly with them', warning them 'ether to pay an other exstreame rent such as they have [as]cessed upon them, or ells to be quyte putt fro[m] ther lyvings'. Tenants paying around ten groats at the old level were now assessed at £14, £15 or £16 per annum, and all the rest rated likewise.[29] One man who had paid 4s-odd for less than twenty acres now had to pay £14. Subsequently the tenants were to claim that Shrewsbury had trebled the rent reserved in their old leases, even though most of the ground would bear no other corn but oats, so that collectively they had paid £470 more than was right.[30]

Both the tenants' initial readiness to negotiate, and Shrewsbury's frequent claims to be willing to do so,[31] suggest that the leases were indeed arbitrable on renewal for fines though probably not for rents. But Shrewsbury knew that Mary Stuart was unlikely to be soon removed from his care. His recognition that he therefore needed a *continuously* increased annual income (which fines could not deliver) was perhaps fifteen years ahead of its time in seeing *rent*-raising as the main priority. Thirty years later Gilbert Talbot, as seventh earl, was to attempt a similar redressal of the fines/rent ratio in Staffordshire, when such a policy had become more common: the Glossopdale men would undoubtedly have agreed with the tenants' response in 1609, that they 'had rather smart one year than every year'.[32] Of course, Shrewsbury did not ignore fines altogether. An undated letter to the Council contended that he had nothing with which he could make so much money towards paying his debts, and condemned the Glossopdale tenants' offer of ten years' rent for a fine as much less than they had ever offered before.[33] But it was not a priority. The presence of a 'tithe controversy' in the dispute gives further evidence that long-term gain was the target. In February 1581 a Talbot officer demanded tithes in kind, as well as rents, but the tenants refused to pay any rent at all unless they were discharged of their tithes. The tenants said that tithes in kind would be 'to the overthrowe of two and fiftie ploughes', utterly undoing more than 500 people.[34] Secretary Wilson was to ask Shrewsbury to let them pay their tithe in money as they had done to Shrewsbury's father; the Council asked that they 'might enjoy their tithes in their kinds paying money for them'.[35] Tithes in kind would not only have reduced the impact of inflation on Shrewsbury's expenses in general. Glossop was only twenty miles from Sheffield, and tithes of food, coal and the like were certainly used to lighten the Scottish burden there.[36]

But it is Shrewsbury's ruthlessness as much as his methods which is significant. The rent rises were so vast that the tenants, in their innocence, at first believed – even told the Council – that Scargill and Dickenson must have misled their lord into thinking that their yearly rent was only 2*s* per acre: it was exceedingly above it, and Shrewsbury must have 'bene very evell dealt with all'. Gilbert Talbot reported that even the more hard-bitten Council could not believe rises of four marks for every shilling. Leicester said they had thought it 'impossible any such rate could be sett uppon so smale lyvings'. They had even wondered if these huge rises were really fines, but had been assured that they were yearly rents. Indeed, the tenants had said that 'yf that had byn so ther ys none of us but wold have held ourselves to our shirts to have satysfyed his L[ordship]'. How could any man, Leicester asked, 'make so much of so few acres of that countrey soyll', barren as it was?[37] They awaited an answer.

Shrewsbury's reply, backed up by Gilbert Talbot on the spot, must have shattered any illusion held by tenants or Council that he was the blissfully ignorant victim of over-enthusiastic officials. He stoutly defended their actions. Whilst he was prepared to have the rents mitigated if they seemed too hard 'by vewe of indyfferent gentlemen by [the tenants] themselves to be chosen', in fact, he claimed, the tenants owned great waste and commons, and several fertile pastures for tillage or hay. A far greater sum could be raised, and they paid no tithe or custom except their rents. Later he was to add that the tenants were of good wealth, and that he did not see why he should not raise his rents as his farms increased in value, and as his farmers raised the prices of the commodities they had thereby.[38]

Perhaps there was some justification for higher rents. The upland pastures of Derbyshire do seem to have prospered in the years before the Reformation, and monastic lands had tended to be undervalued.[39] But the sheer scale of the rises and the attack on money tithes are evidence that Shrewsbury had determined to resist the existing, conservative conventions of arbitration: the conventions that in the end a landlord should be prepared to accept a bargain which was tolerable to existing tenants, and to maintain practices sanctioned by custom.[40]

The most telling evidence of that rejection, however, lies in the closing words of Shrewsbury's reply: that he had many suitors for the land at the new prices rated, which the existing tenants had originally been willing to pay; and that he could do no more except give them the land.[41] Robert Crowley, or the author of the 1553 *Prayer for Landlords*, saw rackrenting in moral terms, as the result of the timeless avarice of 'covetous worldlings'. But Shrewsbury's bleak choice for the Glossopdale men, 'ether to pay an other exstreame rent ... or els to be quytt putt fro[m] ther lyvings', demonstrates a hard-headed awareness that population growth, the struggle between tenant and prospective tenant for land, was a new weapon for landlords. In doing so it chimes better with the comment of the Pembrokeshire observer of about 1600: 'in tymes past ... most commonly the landlord rather made suite for a good tenante to take his lande than the tenant to the landlord ... nowe ... the worlde ys so altered with ye poore tenants that he standeth ... in bodylie feare of his greedy neighbour'.[42]

Shrewsbury's intentions in this area were made clear early on. Scargill and Roberts, on that first visit to Glossop, reported to Shrewsbury that they had told one 'Black' Harry Botham, a notorious trouble-maker, that they had had no commandment to deal with him. Botham had replied that he had been assured that if he behaved like the others he could keep his tenement. But they said his past doings had already made him unworthy to have it, and ordered him to remove both himself and his cattle from his erstwhile home and grounds. Botham retorted that 'he wolde not leave yt but by lawe, and for his hawse, who wold or durst come with in yt for yt was his castle'. He added darkly that he had something prepared for anyone Shrewsbury should send thither, and that either he or the one who came thither would die. The officers inferred from this that Botham had weapons in his house. Since he was 'a Ringeleader to all that Towne', they thought it best to send him to the earl for punishment. If he were treated as he deserved, they were sure all else would be dealt with quietly. Meanwhile he was put in the stocks for half an hour, still insisting – with the same curious faith in Shrewsbury – that his lord neither would nor could without law evict him.[43]

Shrewsbury himself considered eviction to be the fundamental issue in the dispute. In April 1579 he told the Council that the tenants had been prepared to pay up until they discovered that three or four of their seditious ringleaders were to be replaced in their tenements by Talbot servants, in recompense of service. *This* 'was the cause of myslyke and not the raysinge of the rents'; *this* had led them to 'seke reformacon of things a farre of, which might and shuld quietly have bene determyned here uppon informacon geven of any imperfeccon or defalte'.[44] Throughout the dispute Shrewsbury claimed that eviction was to be the fate only of those, like Harry Botham, he considered to have been the source of enmity and hate among the Glossop men for the previous twenty years, and had long vowed to eject; and he clearly had well-laid plans for their replacement.[45] And indeed, Botham, with little to lose, was to be a severe thorn in Shrewsbury's and the Council's sides by his uncomfortable persistence and refusal to accept his fate. The earl no doubt nursed a simple desire for revenge against those who had crossed him, growing as the dispute dragged on.[46] Grants of land – in more peaceful circumstances – were a fairly common alternative in the period to paying decent wages. And the opportunity to replace dangerous and – as we shall see – popular local men with dutiful, grateful and no doubt watchful servants must have seemed an excellent way of killing two birds with one stone. But even these limited evictions may well have been intended to intimidate the rest of the tenants into accepting the new rentals. Certainly, the tenants believed that they were all at risk, claiming in 1579 that Shrewsbury 'did set downe this excessive rentes onelye to get [the land] into his owne hande':[47] was it not what his servants had told them?

Shrewsbury was propelled further down this path by an unfortunate and extraordinary error he had made. The Council found that in fact the Glossopdale leases did *not* expire at Michaelmas 1578, but in 1579. The 1578 entries and attempted evictions by his officers had therefore been quite illegal. Shrewsbury's claim that the tenants had not realised this either was hardly the point.[48] Of course, even if the leases *had* expired, the boundaries of custom and good lordship remained. M. E. James and Dr Richard Hoyle have charted how even the most apparently vulnerable of tenants at will developed in this period a legal personality, a protective shield of custom and rights.[49] To escape from his legal error, and, more fundamentally I think, to excuse his general emancipation from the past and its duties, Shrewsbury now sought to deny the very nature of the Glossopdale men's tenure as proud leaseholders and respectable tenants. Their leases, he announced, had been rendered void at a (conveniently) distant time in the early 1560s by their conduct in dividing tenements, letting without licence, and spoiling, stocking up and ploughing his woods and underwoods. Hence his men had *not* entered 'before thexpiration of a supposed term', since the tenants held only 'as tenaunts at will by my sufferance and not by lease as they surmyse'.[50] The implication was that he could therefore do with them entirely as he wished: it was this apparent readiness to contemplate the ultimate destruction of the symbiotic relationship between lord and tenant rather than settle for less which makes Shrewsbury a 'new man', and brought the Glossopdale men to London.

Shrewsbury's originality, then, lay in his methods – his stress on long-term revenue-raising through rents rather than fines – and, even more importantly, in his ruthlessness – his readiness to bully and evict, even to change the rules of the game, rather than bargain and compromise in the traditional manner. His view is perhaps summed up by his comment that 'every tenaunt is to conclude with his Lorde at the pleasure of the Lorde'.[51] Nor at first sight does there seem much reason why he should not have prevailed in these policies, and so have shown his slower colleagues the way ahead. The lowly, troublesome tenants, with or without leases, seem at his mercy. The fourth and fifth earls, Dr Bernard concluded, 'in their "country" ... ran things without much fuss or opposition'. The seventh earl was described in 1590 as 'a Prince, alone in effect, in two counties in the heart of England'. A very senior and ancient peerage indeed, vast landed, industrial and other financial resources, and many servants had given Shrewsbury local prestige and power. As lieutenant of Derbyshire, creditor, arbitrator, he was both officially and personally a close associate of local potentates such as the Cokaynes and the Leakes, and had grown up with and married into the Manners family, earls of Rutland. His many local offices held of the crown, such as the Stewardships of the Honours of Tutbury and of the High Peak, allowed him to dismiss many Duchy officers at will.[52] At a national level, Shrewsbury was Lord Steward, Earl Marshal and a member of the Privy Council to which the Glossopdale men came. His friendships with Lord Burghley and the earl of Leicester, fellow Councillors, seem to have been more than mere political convenience on either part. His position in the eyes of the queen as heir to one of the few noble names never to have brushed with treason, and, in his own right, as a substantial, able and trusted member of the Elizabethan governing class, could not have been better attested than by his choice for the crucial role as keeper of Mary Stuart. All this argues for an apparently impregnable position; yet the next four years were to see only abject failure for the sixth earl in Glossopdale. It is time to explain how and why.

III

The most disconcerting sign of failure for Shrewsbury must have been the readiness of the Privy Council, collectively and severally, to interest itself in what he considered a private matter. As he said, 'I must thynk my celf hardly delt with all that so many wylfull pepell hath bene suffered to exclame agenst me so longe ... & are nott Remytted to me to be used as shold seme best to my celfe'.[53] Barebone statistics will suffice here. Between 1579 and 1582 there are references to at least fourteen meetings between tenants and members of the Council; Gilbert Talbot or Thomas Baldwin, usually present at these, attended seven other meetings; the Council met in full private session once, and Councillors were lobbied on five other occasions. The whole Council wrote seven letters to Shrewsbury, Leicester five, Wilson and Walsingham one each; the Council also wrote once to the Cheshire local authorities and twice to those in Derbyshire. The queen spoke to Lord Burghley and others about Glossopdale four times, and wrote to Shrewsbury once. In reply, the earl was forced to write two letters to the queen, ten to the whole Council, five to Burghley and four to Leicester, and one each to Lord Hunsdon and the two secretaries. All these, of course, are minimum figures. The *Acts of the Privy Council* alone contain fourteen references to the dispute. Undeniably, Shrewsbury found himself playing on a grander stage than he had bargained for.

Shrewsbury's robust defence of his rent rises did not last long either. His initial vague talk of local mediation soon became a promise to deal reasonably with the tenants 'if they wolde deliver upp possessession [sic] of theyr houses for one night only':[54] a rather feeble face-saving exercise, in its attempt to persuade the tenants to acknowledge their alleged forfeiture in return for (non-profitable) sweetness and light? A few days later, his original belief in the tenants' ability to pay up was jettisoned in favour of the claim that the vast rent rises were merely a ruse to force out trouble-makers and replace them with servants; as for the other tenants, 'it was never ment they should pay eny suche rent'. The survey was solely 'to the ende that I might know the valew of the things which I departed with all and that my servants might know the valew of the things and what every man did offer not mynding that the same rent shold be paid'.[55] It all seems rather elaborate; strange, too, that neither the officers involved in the extensive – and expensive – new survey of Glossopdale, nor Gilbert Talbot, seem to have been aware of all this until Shrewsbury revealed it to Burghley and Leicester. In December 1579 Baldwin, whilst still bravely maintaining that the lands were worth 'the first demaundes', told the Council that his master was content to take the third penny. Early 1581 saw the earl declaring to the Council that all the tenants except four might occupy their tenements without any fine, paying the same yearly rents they had done for the previous sixteen years.[56] Self-righteous hope of large profits from increased rents has become a sad complaint at an apparent rent strike: 'if any have cause it is I, for now cum mydsomar [the tenants] arr ii yeres Rentes behynd with me & nethar a tenant wyll that wyll paye me Rent but okupye agenste his lordes wyll'.[57] If they will only pay their old rents, Shrewsbury seems prepared – even relieved – to let the matter drop.

This climb-down from his original threat, to evict tenants who did not pay the new rentals as being 'in so deepe a dreme of tenaunte right or rather drowned in this imaginacon that I was tenaunte or they lords',[58] did not end there. Certainly, his contention that the Glossopdale tenantry as a whole were merely tenants at will, who by their behaviour had lost any claim on his good lordship, was maintained in a stubborn refusal to renew their leases although he allowed them to continue as tenants; but in practice he now concentrated on a vendetta against the four tenants he considered 'chiefe and contynuall kindlers of theise coales of contencion' between him and the rest of his 'tenauntes of the simpler sort'.[59] Harry Botham, the first real trouble-maker in October 1578, had apparently been to London before. In January 1579 he, Nicholas Mellor and Thomas Jackson were spoken of as intending to lead the tenants to London. All three said they would die before they were forced out of their grounds. The latter two prevented an entry into their lands by Scargill, and refused to attend on Mr Eyre, a local JP, when he sent for them. Botham and Mellor were among the four tenants who attended the Council meeting on 18 April 1579 on behalf of the rest, along with one Thomas Booth; these three were to be present again at the meeting on 28 April.[60] In his letters to the Council, therefore, Shrewsbury sought constantly to exclude them from any settlement he might reach with the other tenants.[61] In April 1580 he was pursuing a suit against Mellor to make him 'fele the smarte for his wild speches of me'; by early February 1581 it appears that Shrewsbury had obtained judgement at common law, that Mellor and Jackson had gone and that Harry Botham and Thomas Booth were due to depart at the next Lady Day. He was still urging Leicester 'to procure sum sharpe ponesmente apon them wyche they have very well desarved'.[62] A victory then?

Yet in April of 1581 the Council noted that Shrewsbury 'promiseth to place [Jackson] in as good a thing within that lordship as the same from which he is removed', though he utterly refused to give him his old house back. Jackson rather graciously agreed to consider this and give Shrewsbury his decision in three weeks' time.[63] Botham was finally forced out of his house in May by the JPs and forty of Shrewsbury's servants, armed with guns and bows, and was back in London in September. But in June 1582 Shrewsbury is to be found telling John Manners that in 'what he thinks I shall do for young Botham he shall rule me'. Some years later Botham was still in Glossopdale – and still not paying his rent.[64] Also in 1582, Shrewsbury was considering giving Mellor and his family a house and grounds in the Dale to sustain them.[65] It was hardly unalloyed triumph.

One further cameo should be enough. In April 1579 Shrewsbury reported to the Council one Otwell Higginbotham of Marple in Cheshire, lately servant to Sir Thomas Stanley, for allegedly stirring up the Glossopdale tenants by openly professing that he had 200 good fellows to assist him against their lord. The Council had the sheriff of Chester send him up, and he 'was uppon his appearance committed to the Marshalsea'. Shrewsbury was predictably keen to have such an example made of him that, as the Council put it, he '& others should thereby have learned to take better heede what speaches they used of a noble man'; so keen that he ordered Thomas Baldwin to bolster the confidence of his servant Robert Booth, the star witness, since he was likely to be called before the Council. Yet on 29 May the Council wrote to Shrewsbury that Booth – despite the coaching – had admitted that Higginbotham had *not* said 'that he had the persons in a readiness, but simply that he said two hundred would assist the tenants'. Losing his head entirely, Booth had even called Higginbotham an honest poor man, living quietly in the country. Hence, pleading 'no sufficient proofe', the Council merely sent Higginbotham back to Shrewsbury to 'submit himself to his favour': if the earl 'should see more cause than their lordships do, [he should] bind him to the good behaviour'.[66] It is doubtful if Shrewsbury was satisfied with this.

Consequently, despite his apparent power and influence Shrewsbury seems to have been forced into humiliating retreat at every turn. Why?

IV

It is tempting to present Shrewsbury's failure in terms of court machinations: history as *Smiley's People*. Certainly, various local foes of Shrewsbury battened on to the Glossopdale dispute's apparent potential for embarrassment. Indeed, as early as 1577 Shrewsbury had even accused Sir John Zouche, an old enemy, of having 'bene by secrete meanes and instruments the anymater and setter on of clamoruse people [from the Peak Forest] to exclayme against' him, at a time when the queen was already furious at the clandestine marriage of the earl's step-daughter to the earl of Lennox. Zouche's London solicitor had allegedly advised them and had helped them openly when the case was heard in the Duchy.[67] In 1579 Bess of Hardwick's servants were accused of trying to persuade the Glossopdale men 'and as maynie more of theire frends as the[y] could get' to refuse to pay rents and to go to London: 'the[y] doo saye that hir Ladyship would not have bulden so manie howses in the peak forest but to have relived those which your Lordship put forth'. The servants of Edward Talbot, Shrewsbury's estranged third son, were also suspected of preparing the ground for the tenants in London. Leicester was to tell the tenants that 'he knew that they were sett on by others'.[68]

More importantly, senior but disaffected members of the government may have deliberately tried to damage Shrewsbury's reputation in order to encourage the queen to remove Mary Stuart – whether because they thought her custody not safe enough or too safe is unclear. Leicester was to warn that Shrewsbury 'must stoppe the mouthes of such knaves [as the tenants] ... [since they] gyve ... matter for [Shrewsbury's] enemyes to work uppon, to [his] great harme & disadvantage'. All this, Gilbert Talbot said, was above his reach, though he spoke of a confederacy of at least three or four 'of whom your Lordship may gesse'.[69] Some Councillors had apparently been expecting the Glossopdale men's arrival. Rumours 'that there was no good agreement betwyxte my Lord and my Lady', which, if credited by the queen, 'wolde sooner be the cause of the removynge of my Lord's charge then any other thynge'; the queen's awareness of the Glossopdale dispute itself, and belief that Shrewsbury was making vast sums from the Peak already, despite his stout denials; and the move to reduce his allowance for Mary, may all have been part of the same whispering campaign. Shrewsbury himself believed so.[70] And certainly, Elizabeth would not have welcomed a large group of armed and mutinous men near Mary. George Scargill's encounter and exchange of threats with two Glossop men in Sheffield town itself was hardly desirable.[71] When Walsingham wrote that a settlement with the tenants was more important to Shrewsbury than he realised,[72] he was no doubt well aware of these intrigues.

In a sense, of course, to be rid of Mary would have suited her captor very well. Facing the halving of his allowance, Shrewsbury had declared that 'rather than ... abyde this deskredett I wylbe anumbell sutar to hur Majestie to be dysburdenyd of this weyghty penefull charge'. But in the same letter he admitted that 'lothe wold I be in this trobelsum tyme to be ridd of hur to my deshonore, thow in aquyett tyme I shuld make less acomte'.[73] Interestingly, Bess of Hardwick made a surprisingly generous settlement in a contemporary dispute with her Ashford tenants: Gilbert Talbot concluded that she had considered the possible 'inconvenyence' if complaints should reach the queen or council.[74] Mary's removal because the Talbots could not control their tenants would have been a shattering blow to their national and local prestige. Fear of such humiliation may have induced Shrewsbury to retreat in Glossopdale at the urging of queen and Council.

But those who have not done too well in finals are always the first to conclude that it is a conspiracy. In practice it is hard to believe that Shrewsbury's enemies at court, real or imagined, were the sole cause of his difficulties. After all, Shrewsbury himself knew that his position was strong: Secretary Wilson had admitted to him that no man 'that hath iudgement' would be willing to replace him as Mary's keeper.[75] And if Mary's security was the sole issue, one might have expected the government to *bolster* both his finances and his local control, rather than alienate the holder of such a sensitive post by protecting his tenants against him. A pact between Shrewsbury and Mary would have been infinitely more dangerous than one between Mary and even 100 unruly tenants. Yet the earl was left to complain bitterly that the dispute 'co[uld] nott have hadd this contynuans if all men were my frendes', and that he and his service were so summarily regarded that he 'must lyke a novar reden horse synke under [his] burden when he may no more'. To make Shrewsbury think, with Sir John Holles, that 'Court friendship is a cable that in storms is ever cut', seems neither good nor credible politics.[76] Logically, conciliar sympathy for the tenants was despite rather than because of Mary Stuart. Let us dig deeper.

That sympathy was partly the result of the determination and skill with which the Glossopdale tenants themselves sought to drag their grievances into the public domain, to 'tel their own tale'. The Peak men had a tradition of sturdy independence. Despite A. B. Macfarlane's talk of 'rampant individualists ... ego-centred in kinship and social life', an impressive solidarity seems to have been these villagers' watchword.[77] They all, of course, feared Shrewsbury's rent rises. But the dispute was really a collective protest at the eviction of the four ringleaders, able, popular and well-established in the community[78] – which was why Shrewsbury hated them. On various occasions the tenants go to London 'devided in several companies', in Shrewsbury's words 'hopinge by the name of a multitude to prevaile', forty, forty-two or fifty-two of them, once even contemplating taking their wives and children with them to emphasise their case.[79] Those who do not go up to London give money to those who do. In January 1580 some tenants declare that unless the four might enjoy their farms like the rest they will refuse any offer by Shrewsbury; there is talk of bonds and oaths to this end. In the very act of submitting to Shrewsbury, tenants beseech the Council 'to sett our poore neighbours at libertie' – which was unlikely to endear them to him.[80] The tenants clearly laid great stress on community of action: on one occasion, with shouts and cries and hats thrown up, they openly condemned as turncoats those who disclaimed their doings. One such faintheart had his ancient enclosed waste pulled down. Shrewsbury claimed to the Council that some tenants might have settled, but feared murder in their beds if they were the first to do so. The Council even ordered the tenants 'to sever themselves and that everyone should seeke onely for himself'.[81]

The expeditions to London undoubtedly brought home to worldly courtiers the harshness of the Peak. But meetings of the Council must have been intimidating occasions for such men as these – some could not even write.[82] Even Gilbert Talbot and Thomas Baldwin found them an ordeal, despite their contacts and status;[83] and the Council frequently presented a reproving face to the tenants. In April 1579 Leicester called them wicked and unworthy, and Lincoln and others demanded prison for those who would not go home and submit; the lord chancellor told Botham he was a ringleader, Hunsdon threatened him with the pillory, and Bedford said that 'suche tenantes wolde anger any landelorde in Ingland'. Some tenants did suffer brief spells in prison for their obstinacy.[84] Yet they were clearly persuasive enough to evoke a series of letters to Shrewsbury from the Council seeking to mediate (which led eventually to his full retreat), and the Councillors, despite their irritation at the tenants' uncomfortable persistence, seem unable or unwilling to wash their hands of the matter. A door is always left open for the tenants to come up again if unsatisfied.[85] I return to this below.

The mirror image of the tenants' eloquence was Shrewsbury's inability to present his case as he would have wished. Tied to Sheffield, he was forced to use intermediaries. Gilbert Talbot was to prove no great diplomat as seventh earl, and Thomas Baldwin frequently bewailed the unreliability of promises, which meant he could 'not bringe hit to that perfection' Shrewsbury desired.[86] Even the intensive lobbying of individual Councillors, carefully-placed presents and thanks, and the despatch of a tame chaplain to plead his case did not help.[87] Letters were slow and inflexible, and even less personal. As a result, Shrewsbury always seemed to be on the defensive, excusing, explaining away the tenants' accusations,[88] rather than exploiting his rank and friends behind the scenes at court. Leicester was to fear even *his* temporary absences from court: Shrewsbury's absence was to last for fifteen years.[89]

Yet one might have expected none of this to matter. How could poor villagers expect to triumph over the sixth earl of Shrewsbury? To answer this properly we must look beyond the specific circumstances of the Glossopdale dispute. The 'basic ideological unity and . . . common political outlook'[90] of Elizabethan central government and the aristocracy has become a cliché. But I believe that this is both glib and wholly inadequate as an analysis of their relations. In fact, Glossopdale provides hints of a very real divergence of opinion over concern for the social fabric and the structure of Elizabethan authority between those peers who operated chiefly at court and those like Shrewsbury who, through choice or necessity, sought instead to maintain a role as great landowners and administrators at the head of local society: hints of an increasing *lack* of accord, even of understanding, between those who in the seventeenth century have sometimes been categorised as 'court' or 'country',[91] which developed as the very *result* of an attempt by the government to diminish the perceived gulf between rulers and ruled.

The Council's words reveal a strong vein of social concern in Elizabethan government. Perhaps they were stirred by the tenants' claim that Shrewsbury 'had kylled theyre hartes, & made them all halfe & more desperate, so that they nether cared nor scarce knewe what they did'. Shrewsbury's actions were seen not merely as 'hard dealing' but as positively harmful to social cohesion. Leicester hoped that he did not mean to 'make ... beggars of his tenants ... for lack of reasonable food to kepe them and ther wreched children'. The Council feared depopulation: the tenants could not pay these unprecedented rents, yet such a multitude could not be sent begging. 'It may be that so muche hathe ben offered and wil be given but at ii yeres ende the tenantes wyll depart.' Hatton said 'if all men sholde do soe it were to depopulate the lande which maye not be suffered'. 'God defend', said Lincoln.[92] Hence the many appeals by the Council to Shrewsbury 'of meere compassion' to settle with the tenants, and to restore even ringleaders like Jackson to their houses.[93] The Council's advice to Shrewsbury to deal favourably to the poor men's contentment as a matter greatly importing to him in honour and security, on which the queen's favour or displeasure hung,[94] was a clear warning.

Indeed, Shrewsbury suffered strong moral as well as practical criticism. With some relief Lancaster had originally blamed the luckless Dickenson and Scargill rather than their master: 'for truly my lord yf hit be trew that your officers have so exstremely grated uppon your tenaunts ... hit is pittye [they] respect so lyttle your honor['s] good name in the world to seek to make so hard Improvements'. Burghley, too, told the queen that they had acted 'two much for theyr lords profytt'. Even this, of course, was implicit criticism of Shrewsbury – a lord was responsible for his servants' actions. But when the earl defended the rent rises, Burghley told him forthrightly that he was sorry he, Shrewsbury, had known of and agreed to them.[95] It was made clear that he had departed from the perceived behavioural norms of a noble landlord, restraint and mercy. The crown itself was slower than most to press its tenants – rents rose very slowly on the Duchy lands it farmed directly,[96] no doubt an extra spur to the nearby Glossopdale men. The seventh earl of Northumberland restored an evicted tenant, 'being moved in his conscience'. The Stanleys were to be praised for 'making even at the yeeres end, never trubling themselves with the art of Arithmetique', the ruined earl of Huntingdon hymned because his tenants'

rents were not raised, their fines were but small,
And many poor tenants paid nothing at all.[97]

Leicester's exhortations to Shrewsbury reinforced these notions of traditional good lordship – perhaps best represented by the earl of Arundel's genial dispensing of even-handed justice and mercy to Ket's men in 1549 – with newer concepts, those of Christian responsibility, 'conscience'. 'God almighty hath blest you with a goodly patrymony & made you a lord of many tenaunts, for gods love' Shrewsbury should not 'for any gayn in this world deall hardly with them'. The poor oppressed were with God. God only allowed the getting of riches 'which both in honor and conscyence' might be enjoyed. The queen told Shrewsbury cuttingly that she 'wolde be lothe to have you lose honor to gayne a lyttell mony'.[98]

It might be contended that these were conventional pieties; that, as ever, words and actions differed somewhat. Certainly, Leicester himself was not exactly a spotless landlord. Yet in that case it is difficult to see why his and Burghley's private letters to Shrewsbury should have been so trenchant. In fact, their positions *were* different. *Leycester's Commonwealth* suggests that he was something of a sixteenth-century asset-stripper, obtaining neglected lands from the crown, grabbing quick and easy profits from them, and then hastily redisposing of them. Like Lords Lincoln and Morley, he was primarily a court figure whose land revenues accrued from tough measures originated and carried out by servants on tenants never seen by their lord. Court gentry like Hatton and Walsingham, even Lord Burghley, lived off the fruits of office rather than their estates. Shrewsbury, on the other hand, was directly involved in Glossopdale, and made no secret of it. Three earls of Shrewsbury had held the lands – note Leicester's stress on patrimony. Shrewsbury seems to have suffered from a loss of empathy with his erstwhile colleagues on the Council. Long exile had made him a 'country cousin': while Leicester and the rest played at court intrigue, and lived off royal favour, their landed sources of finance conveniently off-stage, Shrewsbury stayed at home brawling with tenants and tussling with leases to keep the Talbots afloat. Cushioned from the cold wind outside, the conservative Councillors may have simply found it hard to understand and sympathise with Shrewsbury's new, desperate remedies. They could afford to pontificate about the old, simple ideals of *noblesse oblige*, to preach and work for social cohesion and noblemen's 'obligations to the commonweal and one another', in a way that Shrewsbury no longer could. No wonder Gilbert Talbot regretted the Councillors' impartiality.[99]

The Council's compassion cannot, of course, be separated from its desire for social order,[100] and it is here that the division between Shrewsbury's and the government's view of society becomes most apparent. Here Shrewsbury was the reactionary. With the local JPs, he saw the Glossopdale tenants' action simply as a dangerous challenge to the social order, frequently claiming that they wished to be both lords and tenants. If the Council were to be involved at all, it should be only to reinforce his own authority over the Glossopdale men, for example by punishing Higginbotham.[101] Any favour shown to them by the Council would not only reflect badly on him but perilously undermine the established order. Shrewsbury was quick to claim that Sir Humphrey Bradborne's tenants, and those of Bess of Hardwick in Ashford, had made for London to exclaim because they had been 'boldened with the favore my tenants of Gloss[opdale] hadd lately at the Courte', and to urge punishment for their presumption. Certainly, the tenants exploited their ability to 'there returne with outte ponesmente' to encourage local support, and grew in confidence as the dispute wore on. Botham was to boast that when Shrewsbury sent for him 'he came not at the charge there for'. By 1581 the tenants even refused to accept those 'who belatedly offered cow or corn to be accounted of their crew' to 'be partakers of their assured success', and threatened to kill 'a poore sillie servant' whom Shrewsbury had 'placed amongest them' – perhaps in the house of one of the evicted ringleaders. Shrewsbury was deeply mortified when they openly defied him in the presence of Lord Darcy. Some tenants even wished that 'they had nether coate nor shirte so the[y] mighte but retorne to the Courte ... with complainte', and threatened their lord that unless he settled they would be 'speedilie upp againe'.[102] Hence Shrewsbury's warnings to the Council that 'if it will be suffered yt wylbe othar menes cases as well as myne', and demands that the tenants might be 'openly poneshed to the insampell of others to bely me' at the local assizes.[103]

The Council, however, took a very different view. Disorder, they felt, was the product not of their lenience, but of landlords' harshness. The *Mirror for Magistrates*, whilst never condoning rebellion, saw it as the prince's responsibility, since its true cause was misgovernment. The Elizabethans constantly argued by correspondence: the question 'is not every mannor a little commonwealth, whereof the tenants are the members, the land the body and the lord the head?', hence implied that the landlord had as much duty to treat his tenants with restraint in the interests of social cohesion and order as any prince his subjects.[104] In April 1579 Shrewsbury hoped, in pained tones, that the Council did not think him so careless of the estate of his country that he would give occasion for uproar and tumults by any of his dealings. That was indeed their fear. Whilst the Council respected Shrewsbury's honour, the Lord Chancellor told Gilbert Talbot, they respected 'the common quyett of her majesties people, and her Realme, above all'. Gilbert told his father that the queen and Council secretly understood that in most of England there were discontented tenants, whom they rather sought to satisfy than punish as they deserved, 'doubting further inconvenyence'. He added comfortingly that if this were not so he thought the fellows would not 'pass ... away so easily'. In 1580 Walsingham said the Council was lenient because the queen was 'disposed at this time in respect of some practises discovered, tendinge to the disquiett of this estate, to have all cawses of greifes of her subiectes removed, and therfore thoughte good to procede the more mildelie at this presente then otherwise they wolde have doone'.[105] We should never underestimate the Council's fear of disorder in a nation Conrad Russell repeatedly tells us was a police state without police. Early in her reign Elizabeth had said that her 'antient nobility' should have 'the more naturall care for maintaining of my Estate, and this commonwealth': Shrewsbury had let her down. Significantly, his anxious assurances that except in Glossopdale his 'country' was loyal and tranquil were ignored. Instead, Secretary Wilson urged him to 'make an end with them, and rather be a loser, than abyde their clamor'.[106] The Council's priorities were clearly not Shrewsbury's.

And indeed, Shrewsbury's failure to recognise this potential clash raises the wider issue of the relationship between crown and noble landlord, centre and locality. Lawrence Stone and others have carefully described how the Tudors whittled down the powers and privileges of the nobility. By Elizabeth's reign many peers had begun to make a conscious choice between a courtly and a local role. For those who chose the latter, often their chief remaining contribution to the Tudor regime was to keep the peace, by their example to and contact with their own tenants on their own estates. If attitudes like Shrewsbury's towards his tenants were to become widespread and, in the Council's view, positively endanger that peace rather than maintain it, then perhaps even that residual role would have to be reassessed.

Glossopdale highlights the nature of that reassessment. Wallace MacCaffrey has provided a vivid account of how a violent struggle for local dominance between Talbots and Stanhopes in the 1590s was overlain by court intrigie, and evoked a heavy but slow governmental response.[107] Dr James talks of a move from an 'autonomous, self-authenticating honour community of nobles' to a system in which honour found its source and sanction in the crown: civil order, dependent on 'the effective internalisation of obedience'. For example, peers became lieutenants, unpaid crown functionaries presiding over a 'national' military apparatus.[108] But Glossopdale suggests that under Elizabeth this process of 'internalisation of obedience' went beyond the nobility: that men who, unlike Talbot or Stanhope, had no claim by rank on the attention of the court were also beginning to turn to the centre for relief. Of course, Tudor disorder had often had, in Peter Clark's words, a 'customary, deferential character, exemplified by the citation of authorities, the claim to be acting in the Prince's name, and the absence of personal violence'.[109] But even Ket's rebellion, the best example of this model, was still seen as being outside the governing structure, and put down with bloodshed. Rebellion may well have asserted self-respect and worked off frustration:[110] but the Glossopdale men pursued a safer – and in practice more effective – strategy for maintaining their customs, living standards and sense of worth. An orderly and direct appeal to the Privy Council, without much aid from social betters, seeking a limited, practical remedy in a competent manner, reveals a very different set of attitudes and expectations to the traditional bitter hopelessness, interspersed with brief crises of passion, of similar men in 1549 or 1536. If the aristocracy had become 'peaceful demonstrators',[111] so *a fortiori* had the Glossopdale men. Nor were they alone. Shrewsbury himself referred to others coming up to complain to the Council; in the early 1590s the desperate Cranbrook clothiers in Kent intended to do the same; and in 1589 the Council noted that it was 'so troubled and pestred' with private suitors that it could scarce attend to the business of the state.[112]

Yet it was unwilling to spurn them, even, often, to transfer them to Star Chamber or the Court of Requests. Rather, its brand of 'popular equity' based on prerogative justice suggests a new confidence and commitment in Tudor rule. Glossopdale even indicates that the readiness of the aggrieved to 'internalise' their problems in this way was rewarded by access and a sympathetic hearing. The queen feared that if the Council merely sent the Glossopdale men home again, 'peryll ... myght insue thereby'. In 1579 the Council specifically asked Shrewsbury not to single out the four tenants whom they had chosen to represent the rest 'for the following of their causes here before their lordships' for harder dealing than their fellows.[113] Perhaps this new receptiveness, part of what Dr Wrightson calls 'a process of slow incorporation', helps to explain the reduced level of rioting in Elizabethan England.[114]

At any rate, to allow tenants to appeal over their lord's head further undermined an aristocracy with claims to autonomous local power. Initially, Shrewsbury was eager to keep the dispute within the county, because of his influence there. The tenants told the Council that 'they knew not where to have redresse but here'. So pleased was Shrewsbury with the Derbyshire JPs' original condemnation of the tenants that he sent it straight on to Walsingham. He regretted that the tenants were troubling the Council, and noted rather ingenuously that it was too much for him to send men up to be charged when it might have been best proven by a commission of JPs in the country. This selfless commitment to practical justice is impaired somewhat by his immediate attempt to have friendly JPs included, and Sir John Zouche and others excluded because they will 'forbear to do what they ought'.[115] But the JPs, having been ordered by the Council to reach a settlement 'meet and agreeable with justice and equity', for which they would be answerable, seem to have accepted this higher allegiance, and subsequently acted as impartial agents of the Council.[116] Even local action thus became slow, costly, public and humiliating for Shrewsbury.[117]

There was direct action too. The Council sent a pursuivant to observe Shrewsbury's negotiations with his tenants. Worse still, they closely questioned his officers about his leases and rentals, and even sought to lay down a rate of rentals as a guide for him in Glossopdale. Shrewsbury told them that land could not be rightly valued by those to whom it was unknown, and that their requests that tenants should pay as they were able would punish hard workers and 'continewe [the lewd] alwayes in Idlenes, dronckennes & disorder'. The case was 'hard a man shuld be enforced to declare the value of his owne'; to 'despose [his] owne' was a 'benyfete ... nott withholden from the menest in England'; such actions were to his infamy, he being neither idiot nor lunatic. But only Lord Hunsdon seems to have had misgivings, saying 'that it was not for theire honore to move [Shrewsbury] to do that wiche heretofore [he] had tolde them that [he] cold not in honore doe'.[118] Otherwise, Shrewsbury's defence of local knowledge and authority seems to have fallen on increasingly deaf ears, as it threatened to impair the needs of government.

This is not to suggest open, full-scale conflict between central government and the aristocracy. In fact, any great landowner would have been pulled into line, and peers themselves (apart from Shrewsbury) were fairly restrained until the 1590s, as we have seen. In the north, traditionally sensitive, the mid-Elizabethan Council protected Durham cathedral tenants against the dean and chapter, and Weardale tenants against Bishop

Barnes, by declaring their tenures customary.[119] And Councillors were embarrassed at having to call a friend and equal to account. Lord Burghley was glad that Shrewsbury took his 'plain dealing' with him so well, and wished 'this tragedy' at an end. The Council was eager to blame his servants instead; in public they often reproved the tenants and defended Shrewsbury; and assured him that the tenants were 'gonne from us with out any comfort or Incouragement at all'. The bitter pill of Shrewsbury's climb-down was sugared by representing it as a voluntary act of good lordship and Christian fellowship, 'requiting good for evil & preferring pity & charity before revenge'. Their appeals for mercy were meant 'not to preiudice or abridge the state of his lordship's inheritance, [but] of meere compassion'.[120] Considerable tact, then. But Shrewsbury's retreat suggests that such 'appeals' by the Council were of the kind best not ignored. In this case even delay, often seen as a valuable weapon against central directives, benefited only the Glossopdale tenants: for two years most of them kept their houses while paying Shrewsbury no rent at all.[121] Stone's comment that the Elizabethan crown 'remained friendly and protective' to the aristocracy[122] is thus not the whole story.

In short, then, Dr Wrightson's inverted snobbery ('there have long been students of the past who have preferred peasants to courtiers, a "disorderly company" in an ale-house to the Privy Council')[123] paradoxically sets up an historiographical dichotomy just when, in reality, that divide was for a brief moment breaking down. In 1592 Lord Buckhurst was to tell Gilbert Talbot, as seventh earl of Shrewsbury,

> that in the policy of this Common Wealth, we are not over ready to add encrease of power & countenance to such great personages as you are. And when in the country you dwell in you will needes enter in a Warr with the inferiors therein, we thinke it both justice, equity and wisdom to take care that the weaker part be not put down by the mightier.

The crown still needed noblemen; but it no longer feared and depended on them. Glossopdale suggests that, for a time under Elizabeth, central government was both willing and reasonably able to thwart their endeavours if they seemed incompatible with its own priorities.[124] The slow but steady integration of the aristocracy into the national community was accompanied, hastened even, by the partial integration of solid but relatively lowly men like the Glossopdale villagers, using the system to win protection by persuading the Council or the lesser courts that it was in the interests of order and social cohesion within that community so to respond. Peers, the greatest landlords, had heavy responsibilities and high profiles, and when they strayed they would have been the first to be noticed and pulled up short. Perhaps this was why they did not lead the sixteenth-century assault on tenants; Shrewsbury was the exception, and we have seen the consequences. The great still struggled in a web of custom and noble tradition, with conciliar incomprehension, even disapproval and obstruction, the likely rewards for those who broke free. Meanwhile the smaller fry, the new parish and middling gentry, had fewer qualms and were better able to keep their exactions out of the public eye.[125] Only in the 1590s and early seventeenth century, as the grip of central government slackened, and real economic crisis spurred the aristocracy, did the latter begin to catch up, even forge ahead in this field. In the 1570s and 1580s, however, the Glossopdale dispute helps to explain the time-lag between problem and solution; why there was a real but temporary crisis of an aristocracy which had not yet finally decided whether it had a glorious future behind it – or not.

NOTES

1   Earlier versions of this chapter were read to seminars in Oxford and London in 1983. I am more grateful than I can say to Cliff Davies for his interest and advice in this and other matters. I also owe warm thanks to all those who granted me access to the archives cited below (and much hospitality besides); to Dr Richard Hoyle and Dr George Bernard; to Martin Parker and Jonathan Kiek; and, above all, to my parents, who made everything possible.

2   I write this whilst fully acknowledging Dr R. W. Hoyle's magisterial contention that 'we cannot expect to produce answers of national applicability by investigating individual, well documented instances of conflict or litigation, enlightening though they may be about local circumstances': 'Tenure and the land market in early modern England: or a late contribution to the Brenner debate', *Economic History Review*, Second Series, xliii, 1990, p. 19.

3   Arundel Castle MSS in Sheffield City Libraries, (hereinafter A/S), DD 100. These papers are briefly calendared in R. Meredith, (ed.), *Catalogue of the Arundel Castle Manuscripts [in Sheffield City Libraries] with an appendix consisting of a Calendar of Talbot Papers part of the Bacon–Frank Collection*, Sheffield, 1965.

4   G. W. Bernard, 'The fourth and fifth Earls of Shrewsbury: a study in the power of the early Tudor nobility', unpub. Oxford D.Phil. thesis, 1978, p. 266. Some, but by no means all, of this thesis has been published subsequently in *idem*, *The Power of the Early Tudor Nobility: A Study of the Fourth and Fifth Earls of Shrewsbury*, Sussex, 1985. M. E. James, *Change and Continuity in the Tudor North: The Rise of Thomas, first Lord Wharton*, Borthwick Papers, xxvii, York, 1965; D. Willen, *John Russell, First Earl of Bedford: One of the King's Men*, London, 1981.

5   J. R. Dias, 'Politics and administration in Nottinghamshire and Derbyshire 1590–1640', unpub. Oxford D.Phil. thesis, 1973, p. 30. E. Kerridge, *The Agricultural Revolution*, London, 1967, pp. 165–9.

6   Bernard, thesis cit., pp. 268, 366–7, 371. See also *idem*, *Power of the Early Tudor Nobility*, Chapter 5, especially pp. 143–4, 175.

7   Shrewsbury MSS in Lambeth Palace Library (hereinafter in this chapter LP),

697/111, 697/121, 697/113. These MSS are briefly described in C. Jamison and E. G. W. Bill, (eds.), *A Calendar of the Shrewsbury and Talbot Papers, i. Shrewsbury MSS in Lambeth Palace Library* (MSS 694–710), Historical Manuscripts Commission Joint Publication 6, London, 1966.

8 Talbot MSS formerly in the College of Arms (hereinafter CA), P/981, P/985. In 1983 these MSS were transferred to Lambeth Palace Library. They are briefly described in G. R. Batho, (ed.), *A Calendar of the Shrewsbury and Talbot Papers, ii. Talbot Papers in the College of Arms,* Historical Manuscripts Commission Joint Publication 7, London, 1971. Some items are printed (not always accurately) in E. Lodge, (ed.), *Illustrations of British History, Biography and Manners . . . ,* 3 vols., London, second (revised) edn. 1838. LP 699/59.

9 C. Cross, *The Puritan Earl: The Life of Henry Hastings, Third Earl of Huntingdon 1536–1595,* London, 1966, pp. 99–103, 105. S. Doran, 'The finances of an Elizabethan nobleman and royal servant: a case study of Thomas Radcliffe, 3rd Earl of Sussex', *Historical Research,* lxi, 1988, pp. 292–4, 299–300.

10 LP 699/55, 697/123.

11 Talbot MSS at Arundel Castle (hereinafter AC), no. 87. These papers are to be found in Autograph Letters volumes 1513–1585 and 1585–1617, calendared in F. W. Steer, (ed.), *Arundel Castle Archives,* i, pp. 200–3, Interim Handlist no. 11: Correspondence, Chichester, 1965. CA G/122.

12 CA G/63, AC no. 97.

13 L. Stone, *The Crisis of the Aristocracy 1558–1641,* Oxford, 1965, *passim,* but especially Chapters I, IV, VI and XIV, and usefully summed up on pp. 163–4; AND *cf. idem,* 'The anatomy of the Elizabethan aristocracy', *Economic History Review,* xviii, 1948. Doran provides her own noble case study, and a rapid overview of others, in 'Earl of Sussex', especially pp. 286–7, 299.

14 J. T. Rosenthal, 'The estates and finances of Richard, Duke of York (1411–1460)', *Studies in Mediaeval and Renaissance History,* II, 1965, pp. 160, 192–3; A. J. Pollard, 'Estate management in the later middle ages: the Talbots and Whitchurch, 1383–1525', *Economic History Review,* Second Series, xxv, 1972, p. 566.

15 A. Hassell Smith, *County and Court: Government and Politics in Norfolk 1558–1603,* Oxford, 1974, p. 24; W. R. Emerson, 'The economic development of the estates of the Petre family in Essex in the sixteenth and seventeenth centuries', unpub. Oxford D.Phil. thesis, 1951, p. 12; W. R. B. Robinson, 'The Earls of Worcester and their estates 1526–1642', unpub. Oxford B. Litt. thesis, 1958, p. 189.

16 Quoted, Stone, 'Anatomy', p. 19; M. E. James, *Family, Lineage and Civil Society: A Study of Society, Politics and Mentality in the Durham Region 1500–1640,* Oxford, 1974, p. 39.

17 C. Cross, 'Supervising the finances of the third Earl of Huntingdon 1580–1595', *Bulletin of the Institute of Historical Research,* xl, 1967, especially p. 39; G. R. Batho, 'The finances of an Elizabethan nobleman: Henry Percy, ninth Earl of Northumberland (1564–1632)', *Economic History Review,* Second Series, ix, 1956–7, pp. 436–7; E. Kerridge, 'The movement of rent 1540–1640', *Economic History Review,* Second Series, vi, 1953–4, p. 17.

18 Stone, *Crisis,* pp. 303–22, especially pp. 314–15. Batho, 'Finances of an Elizabethan nobleman', p. 439.

19 R. H. Tawney, *The Agrarian Problem in the Sixteenth Century,* New York, new edn. 1967, and see also the Introduction to that edition by L. Stone, especially p. xii; Doran, 'Earl of Sussex', p. 291; M. E. James, 'The first Earl of Cumberland (1493–1542) and the decline of northern feudalism', *Northern History,* i, 1966, pp. 47, 53–4. Dr Hoyle even has doubts about Cumberland: 'The first Earl of Cumberland: a reputation reassessed', *Northern History,* xxii, 1986, especially pp. 75–8, 94. Bernard, thesis cit., pp. 311, 357, and see also *idem, Power of the Early Tudor Nobility,* pp. 144–5, 163.

20 Dr Hoyle has now published a substantial corpus of work on landlord/tenant relationships, suggesting that landlords could not expect the law routinely to be manipulated in their favour, and that, in any case, informal, personal bargaining was more likely to determine outcomes. See his 'Lords, tenants, and tenant right in the sixteenth century: four studies', *Northern History*, xx, 1984 (the quotation in the text is from p. 41); 'An ancient and laudable custom: the definition and development of tenant right in north-western England in the sixteenth century', *Past and Present*, 116, 1987; and 'Tenure and the land market'.

21 LP 699/55. For Shrewsbury's industrial activities see D. Kiernan, *The Derbyshire Lead Industry in the Sixteenth Century*, Derbyshire Record Society, 1989, especially pp. 195–8, 214–16, 249–50, 252, 255.

22 LP 698/11. Stone, *Crisis*, p. 299; and cf. M. E. Finch, 'The wealth of five Northamptonshire families 1540–1640', *Northamptonshire Record Society*, xix, 1954–5, p. 170.

23 L. Stone suggested otherwise in *Crisis*, pp. 382–3. Cf. M. E. James, 'The concept of order and the Northern Rising 1569', *Past and Present*, lx, 1973, pp. 75–6.

24 CA P/421, P/422.

25 CA F/217; CA F/133.

26 CA P/907.

27 CA P/955.

28 CA P/935.

29 CA P/951; P/937.

30 Public Record Office (hereinafter PRO), SP/12/149 ff. 109–10 (summarised in R. Lemon and M. A. Everett Green, (eds.), *Calendars of State Papers Domestic* (hereinafter *CSP (Dom.)*), 8 vols., London, 1856–72, *1581–90*, p. 6 nos. 58–9).

31 CA P/907; CA P/955, F/315, P/961, LP 698/111, etc.

32 CA M/368.

33 LP 698/11.

34 PRO SP/15/26 f. 166 (summarised in *CSP (Dom.) Additional 2, 1566–79*, p. 573 no. 36), PRO SP/12/149 ff. 109–10.

35 Talbot Appendix to Arundel MSS in Sheffield City Libraries (hereinafter A/S(T)), 2/47. These MSS are summarised in Meredith's *Catalogue*. J. R. Dasent and others (eds.), *Acts of the Privy Council of England* (hereinafter *APC)*, 46 vols., London, 1890–1964, *1581–2*, p. 22, and cf. CA G/66.

36 *Historical Manuscripts Commission* (hereinafter *HMC), Rutland*, I, London, 1988, p. 183: regrettably, I have been unable to gain access to the originals of these papers. Cf. Robinson, thesis cit., p. 205.

37 CA P/951; P/937.

38 CA P/941, F/315; LP 698/111.

39 I. S. W. Blanchard, 'Economic change in Derbyshire in the late Middle Ages, 1272–1540', unpub. London Ph.D. thesis, 1967, p. 468. H. J. Habbakuk, 'The market for monastic property 1539–1603', *Economic History Review*, Second Series, x, 1957–8, p. 364 n. 3.

40 Cf. James, *Family, Lineage and Civil Society*, p. 38, Robinson, thesis cit., pp. 221–9, and Hoyle, 'An ancient and laudable custom', pp. 43, 47, 54–5.

41 CA F/315.

42 R. H. Tawney and E. Power (eds.), *Tudor Economic Documents*, 3, London, 1924, no. 13 p. 63. Pembrokeshire quotation from F. J. Fisher, (ed.), *Essays in the Economic and Social History of Tudor and Stuart England: in honour of R. H. Tawney*, Cambridge, 1961, p. 9.

43 CA P/907.

44 CA F/315; PRO SP/15/26 f. 166.

45 CA P/985, and cf. P/907, F/319, P/961, P/965, A/S(T) 2/108, etc., PRO SP/12/147 ff. 109–10.

46 *APC 1578–80*, p. 411, *APC 1581–2*, p. 22. PRO SP/53/11 no. 12 (summarised in W. K. Boyd, (ed.), *Calendar of the State Papers relating to Scotland and Mary, Queen of Scots 1547–1603*, vol. v, Edinburgh, 1907, *1574–81*, p. 656 no. 746).

47 Cross, *Earl of Huntingdon*, p. 97; CA F/349.

48   CA P/951, P/935, P/955.
49   James, 'Concept of order', pp. 63–4; Hoyle, articles cited in note 20 above.
50   CA F/315.
51   PRO SP/12/147 ff. 109–10.
52   Bernard, thesis cit., pp. 343, 349, 363; CA H/215. Kiernan, *Derbyshire Lead Industry; HMC Rutland*, IV, London, 1905, pp. 288–9, 295, 302–4, 306, 310, 312–18, etc. Dias, thesis cit., pp. 114–15; CA H/143.
53   PRO SP/53/11 no. 12, and cf. CA F/315.
54   CA F/315; CA P/941.
55   CA F/319; and cf. CA F/349, P/941, P/961.
56   CA F/349; PRO SP/15/26 f. 166.
57   AC no. 93, and cf. no. 94.
58   CA F/315.
59   CA F/275, and cf. P/985, A/S(T) 2/108.
60   CA P/907; CA P/957; CA P/935; CA P/951; CA P/941.
61   E.g. CA P/941, F/331, LP 697/123, AC nos. 93, 94, PRO SP/15/26 f. 166, etc.
62   LP 699/33; PRO SP/12/147 ff. 109–10; PRO SP/53/11 no. 12.
63   *APC 1581–2*, p. 22, and cf. CA G/66; CA G/76.
64   CA G/76, *APC 1581–2*, p. 204, CA G/162(B), A/S D/13, D/15.
65   LP 707/163.
66   CA F/315, *APC 1578–80*, p. 135, CA F/303, LP 697/121.
67   CA F/217, and cf. James, 'Earl of Cumberland', p. 61.
68   CA P/957; LP 697/113; CA P/951.
69   CA P/941.
70   CA F/331; CA P/945, AC no. 109; LP 697/121, AC no. 92; CA G/6.
71   CA P/973.
72   CA P/941.
73   AC no. 92.
74   CA F/331, and cf. CA P/967.
75   A/S(T) 2/47.
76   PRO SP/53/11 no. 12; AC no. 93. Holles quotation from P. Zagorin, *The Court and the Country: The Beginning of the English Revolution,* London, 1969, p. 45. P. Collinson leans towards a different view (ironically, partly on the grounds that Shrewsbury's colleagues may simply have been envious of his 'notorious wealth'), in *The English Captivity of Mary Queen of Scots,* Sheffield History Pamphlet 1, 1987, pp. 15–16.
77   A/S(T) 2/47; CA H/571, M/44, and cf. Hoyle, 'An ancient and laudable custom', p. 50; P. Clark, 'Popular protest and disturbance in Kent 1558–1640', *Economic History Review,* Second Series, xxix, 1976, p. 378; A. B. Macfarlane, *The Origins of English Individualism,* Oxford, 1978, p. 163.
78   CA F/315, A/S(T) 2/108, etc.; CA P/907, *APC 1580–1*, pp. 363–5.
79   CA G/12; PRO SP/12/147 ff. 109–10; LP 709/12; *APC 1581–2*, p. 204; LP 699/33.
80   LP 709/12, and cf. PRO SP/12/147 f. 111 (summarised in *CSP (Dom.) 1581–90*, p. 6 no. 60); LP 697/123; PRO SP/15/26 f. 166, SP/12/147 ff. 109–10.
81   LP 698/11; LP 709/12; PRO SP/12/147 ff. 109–10.
82   PRO SP/12/147 f. 111.
83   CA P/951.
84   CA P/941; *APC 1578–80*, p. 411, etc.
85   CA G/12, F/331; *APC 1581–2*, pp. 208–11.
86   W. T. MacCaffrey, 'Talbot and Stanhope: an episode in Elizabethan politics', *Bulletin of the Institute of Historical Research,* xxxiii, 1960; CA F/349.
87   See, for example, CA P/941, F/349; CA F/331, LP 697/113; CA F/319, P/965, LP 699/55.
88   See, for example, LP 698/11, PRO SP/12/147 ff. 109–10.

89 J. E. Neale, 'The Elizabethan political scene', *Proceedings of the British Academy*, xxxiv, 1948, p. 108; and cf. Dias, thesis cit., especially pp. 168–89, 461.

90 W. T. MacCaffrey, 'England: the crown and the new aristocracy, 1540–1640', *Past and Present*, xxx, 1965, p. 61.

91 The classic discussion of these (highly controversial) terms is to be found in Zagorin, *The Court and the Country*.

92 CA P/941, P/951, P/937, F/349.

93 See, for example, A/S(T) 2/47; *APC 1580–1*, pp. 363–5.

94 LP 698/11.

95 CA P/937, P/941.

96 Kerridge, 'Movement of rent', p. 33, and Dias, thesis cit., p. 32. Hoyle notes 'the Crown's own … innate conservatism' in this respect elsewhere, in 'Lords, tenants, and tenant right', p. 83.

97 Quoted, James, 'Concept of order', p. 81; B. Coward, 'A "crisis of the aristocracy" in the sixteenth and early seventeenth centuries? The case of the Stanleys, Earls of Derby 1504–1642', *Northern History*, xviii, 1982, p. 58; Cross, *Earl of Huntingdon*, p. 105.

98 L. Stone, 'Patriarchy and paternalism in Tudor England: the Earl of Arundel and the peasants' revolt of 1549', *Journal of British Studies*, xiii, 2, 1974, especially p. 23. James, 'Concept of order', pp. 64–6; CA P/937; AC no. 97, CA P/941.

99 Stone, *Crisis*, p. 405; P. Williams, *The Tudor Regime*, Oxford, 1979, p. 435; Zagorin, *The Court and the Country*, p. 30; CA P/941.

100 Cf. Williams, *Tudor Regime*, pp. 348–9.

101 CA P/955; CA P/935; A/S(T) 2/108, AC nos. 91, 92, 94, etc.; and cf. Tawney and Power, *Tudor Economic Documents*, 3, p. 58, and A. Fletcher, *Tudor Rebellions*, London, 1968, p. 111, *APC 1578–80*, p. 135, and cf. CA P/955–6.

102 CA P/967; CA P/1,027, and PRO SP/12/149 ff. 109–10; LP 709/12; LP 698/11.

103 AC nos. 92, 93, 94.

104 M. E. James, 'Obedience and dissent in Henrician England: the Lincolnshire Rebellion 1536', *Past and Present*, xlviii, 1970, p. 8; Williams, *Tudor Regime*, p. 354. Commonwealth quotation from E. Kerridge, *Agrarian Problems in the Sixteenth Century and After*, London, 1969, p. 31; and cf. Bernard, thesis cit., pp. 372–3, 401, 409.

105 CA P/955–6; CA P/941; CA G/12.

106 Quoted, James, 'Concept of order', p. 82; CA P/961, P/967; A/S(T) 2/47, and cf. *APC 1581–2*, p. 22, CA G/66.

107 MacCaffrey, 'Talbot and Stanhope'.

108 M. E. James, 'English politics and the concept of honour 1485–1642', *Past and Present, Supplement*, iii, 1978, p. 44; and cf. James, 'Concept of order', pp. 78–80. J. GORING, 'SOCIAL CHANGE AND MILITARY DECLINE IN MID-TUDOR ENGLAND', *History*, lx, 1975, p. 188; and cf. J. Hexter, 'Storm over the gentry', (in) *idem, Reappraisals in History*, London, 1961, pp. 145–6, and Williams, *Tudor Regime*, p. 436.

109 Clark, 'Popular protest', p. 380; and cf. J. Walter and K. Wrightson, 'Dearth and the social order in early modern England', *Past and Present*, lxxi, 1976; C. S. L. Davies, 'Les revoltes populaires en Angleterre (1500–1700)', *Annales, ESC*, xxiv(i), 1969; R. B. Manning, 'Violence and social conflict in mid-Tudor rebellions', *Journal of British Studies*, xvi, 2, Spring 1977; C. S. L. Davies, 'Peasant revolt in France and England: a comparison', *Agricultural History Review*, xxi, 1973, p. 130; R. B. Manning, *Village Revolts: social protest and popular disturbance in England 1509–1640*, Oxford, 1988, especially Chapters 2, 6 and 12.

110 S. T. Bindoff, *Ket's Rebellion*, Historical Association Pamphlet, London, 1949; Davies, 'Peasant revolt', p. 133.

111 Cf. J. R. Ravensdale, 'Landbeach in 1549', (in) L. M. Munby (ed.), *East Anglian Studies*, Cambridge, 1968; James, 'Concept of honour', p. 57.

112 Clark, 'Popular protest', pp. 372–3; J. P. Dawson, 'The Privy Council and private law in the Tudor and early Stuart periods: I', *Michigan Law Review*, xlviii, 4, 1950, p. 629.

113 Dawson, *ibid.*; CA P/941; CA F/275, *APC 1578–80*, pp. 309–10, and cf. A/S(T) 2/108 and PRO SP/12/147 ff. 109–10.

114 K. Wrightson, 'Aspects of social differentiation in rural England *c.* 1580–1660', *Journal of Peasant Studies*, v, 1977, p. 40; P. Clark, *English Provincial Society from the Reformation to the Revolution: Religion, Politics and Society in Kent 1500–1640*, Hassocks, 1977, p. 138.

115 CA P/951, and cf. A/S(T) 2/47; CA P/955; CA P/955–6; CA F/315, P/967; LP 699/33, and cf. AC no. 94.

116 *APC 1581–2*, pp. 208–11; LP 707/183, 699/25, CA G/162(B).

117 CA G/68, AC no. 94.

118 CA F/331; CA P/951, F/349; LP 698/11; CA F/315; PRO SP/53/11 no. 12, A/S(T) 2/48.

119 James, *Family, Lineage and Civil Society*, pp. 82–4; and cf. M. B. Pulman, 'An interjection of the royal prerogative into the legal and ecclesiastical affairs of Cheshire in the 1570s', *Albion*, v, 3, 1974.

120 CA F/331, and cf. P/937; CA P/941; CA P/951, G/12, *APC 1581–2*, pp. 208–11, AC no. 97, and cf. CA F/275. *APC 1581–2*, p. 22; *APC 1580–1*, pp. 363–5.

121 LP 698/11.

122 Stone, 'Anatomy', p. 25.

123 K. Wrightson, 'Villages, villagers and village studies', *Historical Journal*, xviii, 3, 1975, p. 639.

124 Buckhurst quotation from Stone, *Crisis*, p. 237. Cf. Williams, *Tudor Regime*, Chapter XIV, especially pp. 456–67; and also G. R. Elton, review of *The Causes of the English Revolution* by L. Stone, *Historical Journal*, xvi, I, 1973, p. 207.

125 Williams, *Tudor Regime*, p. 185. Hoyle sets Shrewsbury's untypical behaviour in context with his conclusion: 'There are ... good reasons to believe that the costs, risks, and high chance of failure, together with the moral constraints of the time acted together to make oppression an unappealing course for the average lord' in 'Lords, tenants and tenant right', p. 87; J. Thirsk, (ed.), *The Agrarian History of England and Wales, IV, 1500–1640*, Cambridge, 1967, pp. 293–4.

Index